King Orry

1913-1940

Ferry Publications
PO Box 33,
Ramsey,   Tel: +44 (0) 1624 898445
Isle of Man IM99 4LP   Fax: +44 (0) 1624 898449

E-mail: ferrypubs@manx.net   Website: www.ferrypubs.co.uk

David Handscombe

Contents

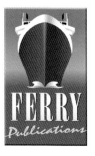

Published by Ferry Publications Ltd
PO Box 33, Ramsey, Isle of Man,
British Isles, IM99 4LP
Tel: +44 (0) 1624 898445 Fax: +44 (0) 1624 898449
E Mail: ferrypubs@manx.net

Published: February 2006
Copyright: David Handscombe

Contents

Introduction

The Isle of Man Steam Packet Company is well known to those who live on the coast of the Irish Sea. The Company has proudly served the Manx people since 1830 when its first vessel, a 200 ton paddle steamer named the *Mona's Isle*, entered service. Since that time the Steam Packet vessels have endured some of the worst weather conditions encountered around the British coastline and survived the wrath of the German nation in two world wars.

This book concerns one particular vessel, the *King Orry* (3) of 1913. A total of five ships have been named *King Orry*, the last one being a 4,648 ton car ferry that served as the Steam Packet's flagship from 1990 until she was withdrawn from service in September 1998.

The *King Orry* (3) was ordered during the heyday of the pre-First World War holiday boom when the traffic to the Isle of Man achieved some of its highest-ever records. However, it was not for passenger traffic that this vessel succeeded in establishing her place in history. Shortly after entering service in the summer of 1913, the war clouds drifted across Europe and in September 1914 the *King Orry* was called up to serve her country. Commissioned into the Royal Navy as an armed boarding vessel, she patrolled our fragile but vital sea lanes for four tragic years.

Her proudest moment came in November 1918 when she was given the honour of being the sole representative of the Mercantile Marine at the surrender of the German High Seas Fleet.

Returning to the Steam Packet in 1919, she was quickly inserted into the Company's peacetime trade, serving on every route over the next 20 years.

In 1939, when a new German threat again rattled its sabre, the *King Orry* once more answered the call to arms. Commissioned yet again as an armed boarding vessel with the Royal Navy, she patrolled the battle-strewn inshore waters of the English Channel.

The *King Orry* continued these patrols until the dark days of May 1940 when a British victory looked impossible and a tired and defeated British Expeditionary Force was fighting for survival on the beaches of Dunkirk in France.

An armada of ships, which included the *King Orry*, was hastily put together and dispatched to Dunkirk with orders to rescue as much of the British army as possible.

The **King Orry** *approaching Douglas with her stokers hard at work below. (Richard Danielson collection)*

In the early hours of 30th May, having already made one trip back to England with 1,139 soldiers aboard, the carnage of war eventually caught up with the *King Orry*.

Extensively damaged and slowly taking in water as a result of repeated attacks from German aircraft and bombardment from shore batteries, the proud *King Orry* finally succumbed to her wounds. As she manoeuvred to clear the harbour entrance, the ingress of water into her Engine Room suddenly increased and overwhelmed her pumps. Within minutes, the *King Orry* had rolled over onto her side and slowly sank from sight below the dark waters.

INSPIRATION

The inspiration to write this account of the *King Orry* began in May 1990 from a gentleman called Crispen Redshaw.

While browsing through a second-hand bookshop in Weymouth, I chanced upon an old photograph album which had been compiled by Crispen while he was serving aboard the *King Orry* as a Royal Navy Reserve Wireless Telegraphy Operator during the First World War. His album portrayed life aboard the ship and gave an insight into the type of duties she performed, most of which had long been forgotten. Unfortunately, investigations revealed that Crispen had died in 1974 but I managed to trace both his wife Marjorie and son Paul who supplied me with considerable information about Crispen, and access to his memoirs later provided vital information about the exploits of the *King Orry* during this period.

Since then I have met many people who were connected with the *King Orry* in some form or another and have spent many enjoyable hours listening to their recollections. Some periods of her service are well documented while others are only briefly covered.

At one point I began to consider that there was insufficient information available about the *King Orry* to make it worthwhile to write a detailed account of her service. Then purely by chance, I was informed that the National Maritime Archive at the University of Newfoundland held many records belonging to former British-registered ships. Apparently, in the early days of the Second World War when the survival of Britain was in the balance, the Board of Trade sent many of their records to Canada for safe keeping. Presumably when the war was over, the only records that were returned to the United Kingdom were those for the merchant ships that had survived the war. Correspondence with the university confirmed that they held the Half Yearly Agreement and Account of Voyages and Crew belonging to the *King Orry* for 1914 and from 1919 until 1938.

I had already established that the Manx Museum held the 1913 copy and the Register of Shipping and Seamen (now the Maritime and Coastguard Agency) held the 1939 copy. Likewise, consultation with the Public Record Office at Kew (now the National Archives) confirmed that they held the *King Orry's* original registration documents, all of her Royal Navy ship's log books for the First World War and most of them from the Second World War, plus various Admiralty orders and signals relating to her war service. Having discovered all of these documents, it became apparent that many of the books that had previously been written about the Isle of Man Steam Packet appeared to have only updated what had been written in previous books. Some of the facts I discovered relating to the *King Orry's* service with both the Steam Packet and the Royal Navy confirmed that very little serious research had ever been carried out on her.

In compiling this account I have attempted to cover as much as possible, in particular her service with the Royal Navy in both wars. I have included the recollections of some of the former members of her crew and have used many previously unpublished photographs. Additionally, it has been necessary to include details of a few other vessels owned by the Steam Packet as without them some aspects of the *King Orry's* story would appear disjointed. Where mentioned, I have only given brief details of their service, as I did not want this book to become just another detailed account of the ships of Isle of Man Steam Packet.

Additionally, a short summary of the major events in history has been included such as the gradual build up to both wars. This will allow the reader to get some feeling as to the mood of the time and its effect on the *King Orry* and her crew.

I hope that you will find the story of the *King Orry*, both interesting and useful as a source of reference, whether or not you follow the life and times of the Isle of Man Steam Packet Company or just enjoy reading about ships and the sea.

David Handscombe
Castletown
Isle of Man
January 2006

Foreword

Air Marshall Ian Macfadyen CB OBE

King Orry was the first Norse King of Mann, of whom the Manx are justly proud. It was King Orry who in 979 AD instituted, in Tynwald, the longest continuously representative Parliament the world has ever seen. His reign, achievements and character afford a historical parallel to that of Alfred the Great of England.

The vessels bearing the name SS King Orry have formed an important part of the history of the Isle of Man Steam Packet Company. This study is of the third such ship named after the Viking King, and it must be one of the most detailed ever undertaken on a single vessel. It marks the completion of fourteen years of painstaking research which has taken the author as far afield as Canada, where Board of Trade records of such ships exist even to this day.

This is the story of the whole life of a ship; it is a tale of both peace and war, full of adventure and service to the Isle of Man Steam Packet Company, and to the Royal Navy in both World Wars. It traces Manx and Naval history alike. The *King Orry* sailed in the Irish Sea in an age when thousands flocked to the Isle of Man ever summer to enjoy a relaxing holiday, and to experience the beauty of the island. Sir John Betjeman once described it as ia jewel in the midst of the Irish Sea. She also sailed in far more hostile waters, sadly ending her days on the beaches of Dunkirk in the dark days of 1940.

His Excellency Air Marshall Ian Macfadyen, CB, OBE, the Lieutenant Governor of the Isle of Man (2000-2005).

This book is a valuable addition to Britain's rich maritime history, in the 175th year of the Isle of Man Steam Packet Company, the world's oldest passenger shipping line.

I D Macfadyen
Government House

CHAPTER ONE

The Edwardian Holiday boom brings prosperity to the Steam Packet

The early 1900's were boom years for the Isle of Man Steam Packet Company. The Edwardian era had introduced the holiday package for the ordinary man in the street. For those not affluent enough to be able to venture to the continent, the chance of a holiday overseas on the Isle of Man, was definitely the next best prospect. The holidaymakers flocked to the Island in their thousands and Douglas soon became one of the key resorts within the British Isles. As this was long before the days of air travel, the main way of reaching the Island was by passage on one of the steamers belonging to the Isle of Man Steam Packet Company.

A couple of railway companies had introduced rival steamship services to the Island but they were in no way large enough to challenge the dominance of the Manx fleet. The Steam Packet maintained a daily, year-round passenger service between Douglas and Liverpool and in the winter months operated the service with only two or three ships, the remainder of the fleet being laid up, often in the inner harbour at Douglas. However, during the summer months it was a very different story, tourists were brought to the Island via many additional routes, which included sailings to and from Belfast, Dublin, Ardrossan, Glasgow, Workington, Whitehaven, Blackpool, Fleetwood and Llandudno. During 1899, the Steam Packet carried 400,000 passengers to the Island; by 1913 this had increased to 1,152,000 per year, a visible indication of the prosperity that had come to both the Island's holiday trade and the Steam Packet Company. At the turn of the century the Steam Packet had possessed a fleet of eleven ships, however, many of the large passenger carriers were ageing paddle steamers, and some of the newer additions to the fleet had been bought second hand. The increase in trade dictated the necessity to modernise the fleet in order that the Company could still provide its passengers with a comfortable and fast service, the provision of which

had for years given the Steam Packet great pride, and they staked their reputation on it.

NEW SHIPS

The first of these new vessels was the 1.957 ton *Viking*, which was built by Messrs Armstrong Whitworth at Newcastle on Tyne and had an overall length of 361 ft. Entering service in 1905, she was the first Steam Packet ship to be fitted with steam turbines and had a certified speed of 22.5 knots. However, on 5th May 1907, she achieved the honour of being the fastest vessel in the fleet, steaming from Fleetwood to Douglas in 2 hours 22 minutes at an average speed of 23.2 knots.

At this period in time, the only ships flying the Red Ensign that were faster than the *Viking* were the mighty liners of the Cunard company. This was indeed a feather in the cap for the Steam Packet and earned the *Viking* the honour of being the first Manx ship to be called a mini-liner. During the First World War, she was requisitioned by the Royal Navy, renamed *Vindex* and converted into a seaplane carrier. At the end of the war, she returned to her peacetime trade with the Steam Packet only to be called up again in 1939. This time she retained her name and saw service mainly as a transport, returning to the Steam Packet in 1945.

The *Viking w*as finally retired in August 1954, having clocked up an incredible 49 years service. Towards the end of her career, as the last coal burning passenger ship in the fleet, she always announced herself with clouds of black smoke billowing from her two funnels.

Following the success of the *Viking*, the Steam Packet was quick to realise the potential of this class of ship and soon ordered a running partner for her. Built in 1908 by Vickers Sons and Maxim at Barrow, the *Ben-my-Chree* with a length of 389 ft and displacement of 2.651 tons was slightly larger than the earlier ship, although externally she was very similar in design. The

The Isle of Man Steam Packet Co. Ltd. Board of Directors 1910

R. T. Curphey, W. A. Waid, C.T.W. Hughes-Games, W. H. Kitto, D. Maitland (Chairman), E. J. Baldwin, J. G. Elliott

"Ben", as she was soon called, was also fitted with steam turbines, but these were far more powerful than those fitted in the *Viking* and developed 14,000 shaft horse power, giving her a service speed of 24.5 knots. However, she is known to have achieved 26.64 knots and it is claimed that she reached 26.9 knots on one occasion which made her the fastest and most-powerful vessel that the Steam Packet was to own for the next 90 years.

On 6th July 1909 she earned herself an accolade that remains unbeaten to this day; the fastest trip by a steam ship between Liverpool Landing Stage and Douglas, completing the journey in 2 hours 57 minutes. The shade of red paint used on the funnels of the Steam Packet ships was vermillion which is only marginally lighter than the shade of red used by Cunard and it was said that the "Ben" looked more like a Cunard liner than an Irish Sea packet vessel. On a calm sunny day, at full speed, with her turbines producing a high-pitched whine and her stem throwing out a foaming bow wave, the *Ben-my-Chree* created a spectacular sight as she raced through the Irish Sea.

Sadly, the pride of the Manx fleet was only to have a short career. In January 1915, she was called up for war service with the Royal Navy and like the *Viking* was converted into a seaplane carrier. Most of her war service was spent in the Mediterranean theatre, although there is a popular story that shortly after she was requisitioned, she made a high speed excursion to East Africa and carried urgently needed ammunition and explosives that were required as part of the impending attack on the German light cruiser *Konigsberg*. Examination of the few records that remain about the *Ben-my-Chree* put doubt on this story as there would appear to be insufficient time between her being requisitioned and deploying to the Mediterranean for this voyage to have taken place.

Following the disastrous Gallipoli campaign, the *Ben-my-Chree* assisted with the evacuation of the British and ANZAC troops, her aircraft being used as target spotters for the battleships and monitors that were covering the withdrawal. On 12th August 1915 she launched the aircraft that made naval aviation history. A Short 184 seaplane, piloted by Flight Commander C.H.Edmonds attacked and torpedoed a Turkish supply ship. The sinking of this vessel was the first recorded successful use of an air-launched torpedo.

The "Ben" continued to support the Mediterranean fleet until the morning of the 17th January 1917. While at anchor off the island of Castellorizo, which is some two miles from the Turkish mainland, suddenly and without warning she became the target for concentrated shellfire and almost immediately began to take direct hits. The French army, who occupied the island, had neglected to inform the *Ben-my-Chree* about the presence of a Turkish gun battery on the mainland. The "Ben" was soon set ablaze as burning aviation fuel ran along her decks and within half an hour it became obvious that she would have to be abandoned. Incredibly, three of her motorboats remained undamaged and her crew of 250 managed to escape, but the *Ben-my-Chree* became a constructive total loss. A sad end for the Isle of Man Steam Packet's, mini - Cunarder.

THE WINTER SERVICE

In 1909, with the addition of the *Viking* and the *Ben-my-Chree* to their fleet, the Isle of Man Steam Packet were able to boast that it had two of the best cross-Channel packet steamers in the United Kingdom. However, they were both large vessels and the Company soon realised that it was not economical to use them during the quiet winter period when only the Douglas to Liverpool service was maintained and their passengers normally consisted of either Manx residents or businessmen.

The Directors of the Company decided that two smaller vessels were required. Both would be new builds, and although on a smaller scale than the previous ships, were to have all of the improvements and comfort of the two mini-liners.

Messrs Cammell Laird and Company of Birkenhead won the order for the first vessel with the promise of the order for the second if the first met the Steam Packet's approval. Delivered to the Steam Packet in 1910, the *Snaefell* had a displacement of 1,368 tons and a length of 282 ft, making her 100 feet shorter than the *Ben-my- Chree*. Her propulsion machinery consisted of two triple- expansion engines developing 5.300 shaft horsepower, with a speed of 19 knots. Although she was slower than her two big sisters, adopting this type of engine made the *Snaefell* a very economical vessel for year-round service.

She soon became a popular ship with passengers, being particularly comfortable during the winter storms and it was not long before the Steam Packet's Directors decided that their new ship had achieved everything that was expected of her. As the *Snaefell* was smaller than either the *Viking* or the *Ben-my-Chree*, during the summer season she was usually employed on the Company's secondary routes, often using Ramsey as her port of call on the Island.

However, as with the *Ben-my-Chree*, the *Snaefell's* career was to be cut short by the First World War. Along with the majority of the Steam Packet's modern vessels, she was called up for service with the Royal Navy on 23rd November 1914 and converted into an armed patrol vessel by Cammell Laird. She left the Mersey for the last time in December 1914 and sailed to Plymouth where she was employed patrolling the English Channel from Start Point to Land's End.

In June 1915, she was ordered to escort the monitor HMS *Raglin* from Milford Haven to the Dardanelles, where the Gallipoli campaign was at its height. She remained in the Mediterranean theatre of operations until her tragic loss on 5th June 1918. While sailing in convoy from Alexandria to Malta, she was torpedoed by a German submarine and sustained extensive damage to her Boiler Room. Although this compartment quickly flooded, killing three of the stokers, the *Snaefell* took nearly an hour to sink, which allowed the remainder of her crew to be rescued.

In summer 1911, with the holiday season at its height, few of the happy laughing holiday makers would have thought it possible that a world war was only just around the corner and such fine ships as the *Ben-my- Chree* and *Snaefell* would be lost. Business was booming for the Steam Packet and it soon became obvious that the expansion in trade had overtaken their replacement programme for the older vessels in the fleet.

As a result of this, it was decided to purchase two second-hand but relatively new ships from the Lancashire & Yorkshire Railway who in conjunction with the London & North Western Railway had operated them on their Fleetwood to Belfast service. Therefore, in 1912, the *Peel Castle* (built in 1894 as the *Duke of York*) and *The Ramsey* (built in 1895 as the *Duke of Lancaster*) both entered service with the Steam Packet.

Now with a fleet of some 14 ships, the Chairman of the company, Mr D Maitland and the Deputy Chairman, Mr W A Waid decided that it was time to order the second of the new smaller vessels which as already mentioned, was planned to be the running mate of the *Snaefell*.

CHAPTER TWO

The birth of the King Orry

As 1911 drew to a close, a group of directors from the Steam Packet made a trip to Liverpool and then crossed the Mersey for a meeting with the management of Cammell Laird the shipbuilders. The purpose of the visit was to discuss and order their next new steamer, which they required to be ready to enter service in time for the holiday traffic in 1913. The new ship was to be slightly larger than the *Snaefell*, although of a similar layout and appearance. Although the *Snaefell* was proving to be a successful ship, her slightly reduced speed meant that she took longer to complete the scheduled services, compared with the *Viking* and the *Ben-my-Chree* or some of the older vessels. During the busy summer season, the delay of even a few minutes in the passage time from the Island, could often mean the

difference between catching or missing your train connection when you arrived on the mainland. This resulted in the *Snaefell* not being the best ship for the Liverpool service during this period, especially as a high proportion of the visitors who commenced and finished their voyage to the Isle of Man from this port, relied on rail travel for the remainder of their journey. It had therefore already been decided that the new ship would be given a higher top speed, which would enable her to be employed on any route during the holiday season, including the prestigious Liverpool service.

Within a matter of days the Steam Packet Directors had approved the design offered by Cammell Laird. The Chairman of the Steam Packet, Mr Dalrymple Maitland duly signed the contract on behalf of the Company and

*The **Snaefell**, the **King Orry**'s older half sister. Note the similarity in design. (Wirral Museum Service/Cammel Laird Archive)*

The **King Orry** *heads toward the open sea for the first time during her preliminary sea trials on 7th June 1913. (Wirral Museum Service/Cammel Laird Archive)*

their new ship, which had already been given the Yard No 789, finally became a reality.

Work commenced almost immediately, for the ship builders knew that any future order from the Steam Packet for another vessel might depend on the delivery of this ship on time.

As the plans and construction of the new ship went ahead, at the other end of the scale, one of the Steam Packet's stalwart ships was bowing out of service. The 41 year old, 806 ton paddle steamer, the *King Orry* (2) had been withdrawn from service at the end of the 1912 summer season. Being too old to be a viable proposition for resale, her Master, Captain Quine had delivered her to the ship breakers at Llanerch-y-mor, near Mostyn on the River Dee. While she was waiting to be broken up, she had been opened to the public for a modest admission fee, the proceeds from which went to the Holywell Cottage Hospital. With the paying off of the *King Orry*, her proud Manx name became available for reissue. At one of their many board meetings, the Steam Packet directors decided to reuse the name on their new steamer. Therefore, yard order number 789 ceased to be just an entry on Cammell Laird's register and finally gained her own identity as the future turbine steam ship *King Orry*(3)

The name was not made public at this stage, as it was still traditional to reveal a new ship's name at the launching ceremony. The Steam Packet had appointed Captain Keig, their Marine Superintendent and Mr Blackburn, the Superintendent Engineer to oversee the construction of the *King Orry*. These two men subsequently made numerous trips to Cammell Laird and studied every aspect of the ship as the work progressed. By February 1913, it became obvious that the builders were going to meet the target date for the ship's launch and subsequent delivery. Detailed arrangements for the launching ceremony, which was planned for early March, now began to be put together.

The *King Orry* was to be fitted with a revolutionary new engine design, the geared steam turbine. This system, which was still in its infancy, would make the *King Orry* one of the pioneer vessels in marine engine development and would continue to be fitted into many of the world's great liners and warships for the next fifty years. (Rather than dwell on the details and advantages of the geared steam turbine at this point in the *King Orry's* story, they have been included in the later general description of the vessel).

Work on the *King Orry* progressed at a rapid pace and as the cold February days slipped by, the date for the launch was finalised. Providing that there were no unforeseen set backs, she would take to the water for the

first time on the midday tide on 11th March 1913. The hull was given a thorough inspection to ensure that it was watertight and was then painted a gleaming black above the water line, and oxide red below it. Finally the scaffolding that had been erected around the hull was dismantled and for the first time the graceful lines of her hull were displayed. In order to stop her careering into the mid-stream of the River Mersey after she had been launched, it was necessary to attach a temporary braking system to her hull. This was achieved by laying heavy chain cable, known as drag chains, on the slipway alongside her. This cable was then secured to the wooden cradles that supported the hull and would be dragged along as she slid down the slipway, hopefully keeping her speed of descent under control and stopping her once she had entered the water.

PREPARATIONS

As well as the preparations that were being made at Cammell Laird's yard, the Steam Packet were busy making their own arrangements in Douglas. The guest list had been compiled and included many prominent figures from both the company and its associates, as well as representatives from the Manx press. The wife of the Deputy Chairman, Mrs W A Waid had been invited to officially name the ship at the launching ceremony and, realising that this was a great honour, she had graciously accepted.

Monday 10th March 1913 was cold and blustery, with a moderate sea swell. The Head Office of the Steam Packet, which was located in the former Imperial Hotel in Douglas, was bustling with people. Since early morning the dignitaries of the Company and their guests had been congregating in preparation for their passage to Liverpool to attend the launch of the *King Orry* on the following day. Among those present, together with their wives were: Mr D Maitland (Chairman), Mr W A Waid (Deputy Chairman), Mr R Curphey, Mr J Elliott and Mr W Fletcher (Directors), Mr W Corkill (Secretary and Manager), Captain T Keig (Marine Superintendent) Mr C Blackburn (Superintendent Engineer), Mr J Halsall (Foreman Carpenter) and Mr W Kelly (Foreman Boilermaker).

Berthed alongside the Victoria Pier, waiting to commence the morning sailing to Liverpool was the steamer *Snaefell*. It was appropriate that she should be taking the dignitaries to Liverpool, as she herself had been built by Cammell Laird only three years earlier, and it was as a result of her success as a year-round steamer that Cammell Laird had once again been commissioned to build a ship for the Manx Company. The *Snaefell* backed out of Douglas Harbour shortly after 09.00, the dignitaries having boarded as the last passengers. For those who wished to partake, breakfast was served in the First Class Dining Saloon, although many of the dignitaries chose to catch up on lost sleep, having left their homes at the crack of dawn in order to catch the sailing. The passage to Liverpool was uneventful and surprisingly comfortable, despite the blustery weather and sea swell. Having been able to maintain a good speed, the *Snaefell* sped up the busy River Mersey and berthed alongside Princes Landing Stage as the hands of the clock on the Liver Building showed 1.15 pm.The head of the official party, Mr D Maitland thanked the Master of the *Snaefell* for getting the party to Liverpool in such a good time and then made a point of personally thanking Mr Ritchie, the Steam Packet's Catering Manager, for looking after them during the voyage. Mr Ritchie had been on board to ensure that all of the catering arrangements for the official party were to the highest standard. The dignitaries quickly disembarked and were then taken to the North Western Hotel, where they were going to be accommodated overnight.

The following morning, 11th March 1913, started off cloudy and damp, although the blustery wind from the previous day had dropped. By the time that the Steam Packet dignitaries and their quests arrived at Cammell Laird, the ship yard's Managing Director, Mr G J Carter and the Chairman, Mr W L Hichen had already inspected the arrangements for the launch and were satisfied that all was in order. The main aspect that they had checked was the mechanism that would release the *King Orry* and allow her to slide down the slipway. During her construction, wooden cradles had been positioned between the hull and the slipway to prevent her from toppling over. As the slipway sloped towards the river, heavy wooden wedges were inserted into the cradles to stop the *King Orry* taking to the water prematurely. These wedges were now being removed and grease was being applied to the slipway to assist the movement of the ship. All that kept the *King Orry* on the slipway was a heavy wire hawser, fastened to the cradle under her bow and connected to the release mechanism at the top of the slipway. The release mechanism was fitted with a quick release shackle, which was known as a "slip" to which the wire hawser was attached.

At the appropriate moment during the launching ceremony, a workman with a large hammer would knock the retaining lever off the "slip", freeing the wire hawser and allowing the *King Orry* to slide down into the river. If gravity failed to move the *King Orry*, a set of hydraulic rams would give the ship a push in the right direction.

Apart from the work that was being carried out on the *King Orry*, the remainder of Cammell Laird's shipyard was a hive of activity. To the eye of a layman, the numerous cranes and gantries that surrounded the ships must have created an impressive spectacle. It was plain to see that these were very prosperous times for the shipbuilding industry.

IN THE YARD

Two large vessels were under construction for the Norske - America Line and once completed they would ply between Norway and America, mostly on the immigrant trade. The first of these two vessels, the *Kristianfjord* (Yard No 784) was nearing completion, while the second, the *Bergensfjord* (Yard No 787) was ready to be launched. At the southern end of the yard, two large steamers for the P & O Company were beginning to take shape. With the Yard Numbers 793 and 794, the *Khiva* and *Kyber* were to be 8947 ton passenger and cargo liners, destined for the Far East trade.

Alongside the *King Orry*, also nearing the time when she would be launched was the torpedo boat destroyer *Garland* (Yard No 786), which was being built for the Royal Navy, her low sleek hull giving her a menacing profile.

Not far from the slipway on which the *King Orry* sat was the graving dock where a large amount of repair work was being carried out. Here could be seen the Canadian Northern Railway's *Royal George* which was undergoing extensive repairs after running aground in the St Lawrence River a few months earlier.

In the fitting-out basin, beside the first of the Norske - American liners, sat the new Super-Dreadnought *Audacious*. As she neared completion, the last of her huge gun turrets, each containing two 13.5 inch guns was being installed. Sadly this fine battleship was to become the first major casualty for the Royal Navy during the Great War.

On 27th October 1914, having only been in service for 12 months, she ran into a German minefield and detonated a mine, which blew a massive hole in her stern.Despite repeated attempts to stop the rapid ingress of water and put the fires out that had been started by the explosion, all efforts to save her failed. At 21.00, less than 12 hours after hitting the mine, there was a large internal explosion and she rolled over and sank. Fortunately nearly all of her crew were saved, being picked up by an attendant destroyer.

One of the other interesting vessels that could be seen in the shipyard was the *Doon* (Yard No 790) which was being specially constructed for the carriage of frozen meat from the upper reaches of the River Plate to Buenos Aires in Argentina where her cargo would be transferred to ocean-going refrigerated vessels for the long sea passage to Britain and Europe.

As well as the many slipways, docks and basins, there were also numerous large workshops located around the yard. Two of the largest were the boiler and engine shops, in which the *King Orry's* completed boilers and geared turbines already sat, waiting to be placed in position on board. However, the *King Orry's* turbines were dwarfed by a completed set of turbines for the new battleship *Iron Duke*, which was being built in Portsmouth Naval Dockyard.

The *King Orry* had been built on No 6 slipway. The scene around this area had changed considerably over the previous few days with the piles of surplus steel plates and rivets having been removed and the towering scaffolding dismantled around the hull. The paintwork was now complete and colourful bunting had been draped over both sides of her bow and around the stern, carefully covering the brass letters that spelt out her name. A large wooden platform and grandstand, which were both decorated with red bunting, had been constructed at the bow, it would be from here that the dignitaries of both the Steam Packet and Cammell Laird would watch the ceremony.

On arrival at the shipyard, the guests had been ushered into the Reception Hall in the main administration building and had been offered refreshments while the final arrangements for the launch of the *King Orry* were made ready. Just before midday, they were invited to proceed down to No 6 slipway, where on arrival they were shown to their seats and given a copy of the official programme to commemorate the event. Already congregated down both sides of the slipway were dozens of the shipyard workers and their families who had been allowed to attend the ceremony in order that they could watch with pride and cheer the ship as she took to the water for the first time.

Mrs Waid and her husband were shown to the raised platform in the centre of the grandstand, which was located some five feet in front of the bow. Mr G Carter (Managing Director of Cammell Laird) accompanied them and explained the operation of the release mechanism to Mrs Waid, showing her the coloured cord that she would cut after she had named the vessel. Mrs J W Laird, the wife of one of the directors of the shipbuilders, then stepped forward and presented her with a beautiful bouquet of flowers. As if specially ordered for the ceremony, the sun suddenly broke through the clouds and bathed the slipway in sunshine.

*Mrs W A Waid names the **King Orry** and smashes the bottle of champagne against her bow. (Isle of Man Examiner-Manx Museum)*

This unexpected change in the weather put the final stamp of approval on the occasion.

At 12.25, as the high tide reached its peak, rockets were fired to warn any shipping on the Mersey that the launching was about to take place and that they should stand clear of the slipway. Once the echo of the rockets had died away, Mr Carter invited Mrs Waid to officially name the new ship and handed her a pair of ornate scissors, indicating that she should now cut the brightly coloured cord, on which a bottle of Champagne was suspended. With a slightly nervous voice, Mrs Waid announced, "I name this ship *King Orry* and may God bless all who sail in her."

As the liquid from the smashed bottle of Champagne ran down the *King Orry's* paintwork, Mr Carter pressed a small bell push, which rang below the platform indicating to the workmen waiting there that they should knock off the retaining slip on the release mechanism. With a loud crack, that made Mrs Waid jump with surprise, the release mechanism operated and the retaining hawser was freed. Almost immediately, although very slowly at first, the *King Orry* began to slide down the slipway. At the same time, workers on board the ship quickly pulled up the bunting from around the bow and stern to reveal her brass name letters to the general public for the first time. Three cheers were called for the ship and the crowd roared in reply as clouds of rust blew out from beneath the hull as the drag chains began to be pulled along. The *King Orry* gathered speed and slid gracefully down the slipway, entering the River Mersey in a plume of spray before being pulled to a halt some fifty yards after leaving the slipway, the drag chains having down their job. From the time that the *King Orry* begun to move, to her being stopped in the water, less than a minute had elapsed.

As the flood tide slowly drifted her to port, two tugs quickly closed in and brought her under control. After the remains of the wooden cradles that had held her upright on the slipway had been cleared away, she was slowly nudged into the fitting out basin and berthed opposite the near complete battleship *Audacious*.

While the ship was being moved into the fitting-out basin, the dignitaries and guests of both companies adjourned to Cammell Laird's spacious Model Room, which had transformed into a banquet hall for the occasion. The room had been decorated with bunting and flags, which set against the starched white linen tablecloths, created an attractive setting for the meal that would shortly be served. Taking pride of place in the centre of the room was a large-scale model of the *King Orry*, which in itself was a work of art. This model is believed to be the same one that is now on display at the House of Mannanan (Manx National Heritage), at Peel on the Isle of Man. Prior to its acquisition by Manx National Heritage, the model had spent many years on display at both Lancaster and Preston railway stations.

The luncheon, which had been prepared by the prestigious firm of Bolland and Company of Chester, whose customers included members of the Royal Family, consisted of:

Salmon Mayonnaise
French Raised Pie
York Ham
Glazed Ox Tongue
Welsh Haunch Of Ham
Sirloin of Beef
Salads Season
Apple Tart
Jellies and Cream
Coffee

SPEECHES

The luncheon was attended by over 150 people and lasted for about an hour. As the last course was finishing and coffee was being served, the Chairman of Cammell Laird, Mr W L Hichen, stood up and asked for everybody's attention as he proposed a toast to, " The success of the *King Orry*" which received a rapturous round of applause.

Continuing, he explained that Cammell Laird had a long connection with the Steam Packet, as far back as 1878 they had built the *Mona* and only a couple of years ago they had completed the *Snaefell*. He hoped that once the *King Orry* had been delivered, that she would meet all of the predictions of his Company and every expectation of the Isle of Man Steam Packet. He then went on to thank Mrs Waid for performing the naming ceremony so successfully. As a reminder of the occasion, he gave her the ribbon that had encased the bottle of

Champagne which had been smashed on the *King Orry's* bow and then asked her to accept a small gold and pearl necklace as a token of appreciation from his company. As Mrs Waid accepted this gift, loud applause was given. Replying on the behalf of the Steam Packet, Mr D Maitland thanked Cammell Laird for launching the ship on time, saying that he was also confident that she would be ready for the Whitsuntide services. If the *King Orry* was as successful as the *Snaefell*, Cammell Laird and Company could rest assured that they would receive further orders from the Isle of Man. Like Cammell Laird's Chairman, he also thanked Mrs Waid for naming the Steam Packet's new ship before asking her to accept a diamond pendant gift from a grateful Steam Packet Board of Directors.

As yet another round of applause died down, he informed those present that this was the third ship owned by the Company that had borne the name *King Orry*. The first was built in 1842 and had cost £10.000. The cost of the present vessel was considerably more than was paid 71 years ago, although he was not going to tell them how much they would be paying on this occasion (scrutiny of Company records reveal that the *King Orry (3)* cost the Steam Packet £96.000). The second vessel to bear the name was completed in 1871 and had given many years service to the Island's community, she had only recently been sold out of service and was presently being broken up on the River Dee in North Wales. The Steam Packet Directors felt

*The **King Orry** pictured at her launch. (Peter Stewart collection)*

that it was appropriate that their new vessel should continue the proud name within the Manx fleet. The Isle of Man Steam Packet looked upon the River Mersey as its second home and it was therefore logical that they should give an order to the Birkenhead firm, as it was after all a home industry. He concluded his speech with a toast "Prosperity to the eminent firm a Cammell Laird and Company"; a rapturous round of applause was given.

As Mr Maitland sat down, Mr Waid took the opportunity to thank both Cammell Laird and the Steam Packet for the generous gifts that they had both given to his wife, he was sure that they would remain treasured items and provide a constant reminder to this memorable occasion. Mr Carter responding for Cammell Laird thanked Mr Maitland for his kind remarks. Cammell Laird and Company were very proud of their connections with the Steam Packet and were pleased that their workmanship was considered to be of such a high standard that the Manx Company sought their expertise once again. He said that credit must be given to everyone who worked within the shipyard, and that the close liaison between the management and the men who actually built their ships paid dividends, as was evident by the amount of work that was being carried out within the yard. They had several important contracts, not only with other shipping companies, but also with the British Government, and they were doing their utmost to fulfil every requirement of each individual order. Finally, in proposing a toast to the owner's representatives, he thanked the Steam Packet Company for providing such a good liaison in the form of Captain Keig and Mr Blackburn. Although these two men obviously had the interests of their own company at heart, they provided tremendous assistance to his own company and he wished them good health and prosperity.

Captain Keig acknowledged the tribute, saying that he had served on the first *King Orry* during the 1850's, he hoped that the new *King Orry* would be as successful as her predecessors and wished Cammell Laird and Company many years of profitable business.

Mr Blackburn added that he was glad to be able to endorse what Captain Keig had said and thought that the Steam Packet should have no doubts about adopting the geared steam turbine. The *Viking* had been running for seven years with conventional turbines and had only suffered from minor defects. If the engines which were about to be fitted into the *King Orry* only suffered from similar minor teething problems, then his Company would have no regrets about pioneering this type of propulsion system. The Isle of Man Steam Packet Company and Cammell Laird should be proud that the

King Orry would be the first vessel fitted with geared turbines that will operate from the River Mersey. As the applause from this speech drained away, Mr Hichen offered to conduct a short tour of the engine and boiler shops in order that the machinery which was to be fitted into the *King Orry* could be inspected. As this gesture signalled the end of the luncheon, those guests who did not wish to inspect the new engines began to say goodbye to each other and started to leave the banquet hall. The time was now nearly 16.00 and a very successful and memorable event had drawn to a close. The next occasion when they would all meet again would be for the official sea trials which were scheduled for mid-June.

Once the official parties had left the shipyard, work immediately commenced to complete the *King Orry*. Over the next few weeks, the boilers and turbines were installed within her hull and the superstructure was built up. Additional teams of workman now descended upon the ship, these included carpenters, plumbers, electricians and marine engineers, whose task was now to install the thousands of internal fittings that would be required for the ship to put to sea as a passenger vessel. Hand basins and W.C's, ovens for the galley, ancillary machinery for the engine room, wooden panels and carpets for the saloons and numerous other items, all began to arrive at the shipyard. Towards the end of May, the boilers were fired for the first time and steam was put into the turbines, although the propeller shafts were only turned a few times, Mr G Wright, the Cammell Laird Engineering Manager was happy that all was in order.

SEA TRIALS

The ship was ready to start her initial sea trials by early June as all the major work was now complete, leaving only a few areas such as a final coat of paint to her exterior and the installation of the furniture in the saloons and cabins.

Preliminary sea trials commenced on Sunday 7th June 1913, when the *King Orry* proceeded out into a stormy Liverpool Bay to undergo engine and machinery drills, to ensure that everything worked correctly. After a slow run up the River Mersey to check that all was in order, she made her first power trial. Starting at the North West Lightship, she steamed up to the Bar Lightship and then returned along the same route.On the first run, she achieved 18.21 knots, but on the return journey this was increased to 19.53 knots, with a mean speed of 18.87 knots overall. The trial identified a few malfunctions, the main one being an air leak through the stoke hold doors, which meant that it was difficult to maintain a positive air pressure within the stoke hold. She returned to the shipyard towards the end of the afternoon, where on arrival the defect was examined and work commenced to rectify the problem.

By 10th June, the repairs were complete and a successful air pressure test was carried out. At 17.30 on Thursday 12th June, the *King Orry* left Cammell Laird's fitting-out basin and proceeded down the Mersey to commence her second preliminary sea trial.

The route was exactly the same as on the previous occasion, but this time she achieved 19.5 knots on the first run and 21.32 knots on the return which was to remain her highest-ever recorded speed. The next ten days were spent adjusting various components and carrying out additional tests on every aspect of her equipment.

Just after midday on Sunday 22nd June, she left the Mersey for a slow overnight passage up to the River Clyde, where she was to undergo her full power trials on the following day. All new vessels are required to conduct a full power trial over a measured distance as part of their acceptance trial. In the Firth of Clyde, just off the coast at Skelmorlie, the Admiralty measured mile is located and it was over this course that the *King Orry* would conduct the required run. Monday morning dawned as a bright day, with a fresh breeze and smooth sea state, ideal conditions for a full power trial. The *King Orry* would have to complete five runs over the measured mile, although this was in fact ten runs up and down the course as each run had to start and finish at the same point, therefore five runs were made from north to south and five vice versa. She attained her best overall speed on the third run, when she averaged 20.96 knots which pleased the Cammell Laird engineers as they had guaranteed the Steam Packet that she would achieve 20.75 knots under normal sailing conditions. The trial was complete by early evening at which time she made a fast passage back to Birkenhead, arriving just after midnight, having averaged nearly 17 knots throughout the journey.

The next set of trials were organised for Wednesday 25th June. These were to be classed as her official sea trials and the dignitaries of both companies had been invited to witness the event. Much interest was being shown in the geared steam turbine and as a result quite a few representatives from other shipping companies had also been invited to attend. One of these, Signor Don Nicholas Mihanovich, a director of the Mihanovith Navigation Company was particularly interested as his company had just ordered two new ships from the Birkenhead yard, both to be fitted with geared turbines. As Wednesday 25th dawned, it became obvious that the blustery weather conditions were not suitable to conduct a satisfactory sea trial and regrettably the decision to postpone it to the following day had to be made. This caused a problem with some of the guests, as not all of them could afford to remain on Merseyside for the extra day.

It was therefore decided to put the *King Orry* to sea for a couple of hours, which would give those people who could not remain until the following day a chance to see the new ship and her engines function under running conditions. The *King Orry* was laying at a buoy in mid-river and after the guests had been conveyed out to her she slipped her mooring at just after 09.30 Even though the weather conditions were not ideal, she achieved her contract speed of 20.75 knots and returned to the river by 13.00 to disembark her passengers. While at sea, lunch was served on board, the catering once again being carried out by Bolland and Co of Chester.

THE OFFICIAL TRIAL - THURSDAY 26th JUNE 1913

Much to everyone's relief, the weather was much improved and more congenial to performing a sea trial than on the previous day. The sky was overcast with a slight breeze from the south west, but the sea state was smooth. At just after 09.00, with the *King Orry* once again laying in mid-river, the tender left Princes Landing Stage with the dignitaries and official guests. As the tender approached the *King Orry*, more then one person commented that there was marked resemblance between the new ship and the *Snaefell*. This was however to be expected, as Cammell Laird had merely modified the *Snaefell's* successful design. The *King Orry* slipped her buoy at exactly 09.30, after which she slowly turned up river and moved away from her overnight position, opposite the Cunard Building. The trial would involve a return trip to the Isle of Man, with the Bell Buoy (Bar Lightship) at the mouth of the Mersey and a point off Douglas Head acting as the official markers for the timed run. The bar at the mouth of the Mersey was crossed at 10.28 and after cruising around in a large circle for a few minutes to allow a full head of steam to be raised, she passed the Bell Buoy at 10.41 and commenced the run to Douglas. Although the wind was against her, it would be in her favour on the return trip. As she ploughed out through Liverpool Bay into the Irish Sea, her turbines were brought up to full power under the watchful eye of Mr G Wright and his team of engineers from Cammell Laird.

Standing on her bridge, as he had done on every trial so far, was Captain Andrew. In his capacity of master pilot for the shipbuilders, it was his duty to command the *King Orry* while she was at sea, until she was handed over to the Steam Packet. He now had a good feel for the new ship and was convinced that she would achieve all that was expected of her.

As the passage to the Island progressed, two of the Steam Packet's ships, the *Fenella* and *Mona's Queen*, both outward bound from Douglas were passed. The latter of the two ships, which was passed at 11.28 was on the 09.00 passenger service to Liverpool, dipped her ensign and sounded her siren as she greeted the new ship for the first time. At about the same time, a distant trail of smoke was noted astern, this was soon identified as belonging to the Company's "flyer", the *Ben-my-Chree*. The *King Orry* was now steaming at nearly 21 knots and speculation went around as to whether the "Ben" would manage to close the distance between the two vessels and eventually overtake her. However, as the Island began to loom over the horizon, it became evident that the new steamer would hold her own and be the first to reach Douglas. To onlookers, watching the impromptu race from Douglas Head, the sight of the *King Orry* racing towards the Island with smoke billowing from her funnel, with the *Ben-my- Chree* charging up behind, must have been an impressive spectacle.

To help pass the time during the passage to the Island, luncheon had been served. An excellent menu was once again provided by Bolland and Co, the provision of which had given the caterers a slight headache, as they had only planned to provide a meal for the previous day's trial. However, in line with their reputation, a superb meal was provided, consisting of the following:

> *Salmon Mayonnaise and Cucumber*
> *Cold Roast Lamb and Mint sauce*
> *Cold Roast Beef and Horseradish sauce*
> *Roast York Ham and Roast Chicken*
> *Salads*
> *Liqueur Jellies*
> *Bohemian Creams*
> *Strawberries*
> *Cheese, Biscuits and Cress*
> *Coffee*

It was no mean feat to provide this range of fare, especially as it had to be boxed up and transferred to the *King Orry* on board the tender as her own galley was not operational during the trials. By the time that luncheon was reaching its conclusion, the *King Orry* was drawing close to Douglas Head and turning in towards the bay. A signal was hoisted on her foremast, spelling out "all's well" and was simultaneously accompanied by firing of rockets and blowing of her siren and whistle. A

deafening reply to the *King Orry's* announcement of her arrival was given by the *Manxman* which was berthed at the Victoria Pier and *The Ramsey* which was at anchor in the bay. Their combined reply drowned the sound of the new vessel's siren and caused hundreds of seagulls to take flight from their nests on Douglas Head.

The *King Orry* swept across Douglas Bay towards Onchan Head, continually sounding her siren. As she turned around for a sweep back towards the harbour, the *Viking* steamed into the bay, inward bound from Fleetwood and added her siren to the rapturous welcome. The signal flags on the *King Orry's* foremast dropped, only to be quickly replaced with a second message "glad to see you". By this time, the Douglas promenade and piers had become crowded with spectators, all eager to see the new ship or find out what all of the noise was about.

The *King Orry* completed the return run across the bay and steamed past the Tower of Refuge and harbour entrance, before turning out towards Douglas Head and the open sea again. The return trip to Liverpool commenced at 13.32, but not before she passed the *Ben-my-Chree* which was now approaching the harbour having failed to overhaul the new steamer on her outward voyage. The "Ben" dipped her ensign in salute to a worthy addition to the fleet, followed by a short blast of her whistle. As Douglas Head began to disappear in the *King Orry's* wake, excitement ran high on board as Mr Blackburn; the Steam Packet's Superintending Engineer announced the official times for the first part of the trial:

Depart Bell Buoy in the Mersey	10.41
Arrive Douglas Head	13.22
Passage Time	2 hours 41 minutes
Speed Overall	21.71 knots

Cheering could be heard throughout the vessel as the good news was passed around. The weather conditions remained unchanged, which enabled the *King Orry* to proceed at a fast rate. As she reached the halfway point on the return journey, both the *Queen Victoria* and the *Mona's Queen* were passed; the former was on the 14.15 sailing from Liverpool, while the *Mona's Queen* was returning to the Island unladen. The Bell Buoy was passed at 16.07, signalling the end of the final part of the trial. The official readings for this run were:

Depart Douglas Head	13.32
Arrive Bell Buoy	16.07
Passage Time	2 hours 36 minutes
Speed Overall	21.35 knots.

Although her overall speed on the return trip was marginally slower, with the wind in her favour, she managed to knock five minutes off the 55mile run.

Having made a slow sweep out to the N.W buoy, she passed the Bar Lightship and headed up river, during which time tea was served in the Dining Saloon. The trial had been a complete success and during the short speeches, which accompanied the serving of tea, Mr Carter said that he was very proud of what Cammell Laird had achieved. The final readings for the six hour trial had now been calculated and he could confirm that the overall mean speed for the voyage was 21.03 knots. If these results could be achieved with a scratch crew, then the *King Orry* should be able to achieve much more when she was manned by her full-time Manx crew.

Mr Maitland replied for the Steam Packet, congratulating the shipbuilders for giving them such a fine ship. He continued by saying that the eyes of many shipping companies had been watching the *King Orry's* progress, and now that her turbines had proved their worth, he expected that Cammell Laird would receive many orders for similar vessels and was confident that this would again include the Steam Packet.

At a few minutes before 18.00, the *King Orry* tied up alongside Princes Landing Stage in Liverpool for the first time. As the dignitaries and guests filed ashore, Mr Maitland commented that this berth would soon become her second home.

Once she had unloaded her passengers, the *King Orry* proceeded across the river to Birkenhead and berthed alongside in Cammell Laird's fitting out basin. Over the next couple of days, as the engineers gave her machinery a final check, various contractors installed the last few items of furniture and various fittings.

ON BOARD

By modern standards, the *King Orry* was a small Irish Sea packet vessel, but in 1913 she was quite a large ship. With an overall length of 313 ft, beam of 43 ft and a gross tonnage of 1,877 tons, she was the fourth largest ship in the Manx fleet, although the second largest ship was the paddle steamer *Empress Queen*.

The *King Orry* had a straight stem, counter stern and was flush decked, which meant that her Upper Deck extended from the forecastle, through the superstructure (Shelter Deck) to her Poop Deck on the same level. Around the outside of her hull, extending for most of her length, longitudinal wooden fenders were fitted, referred to as the belting which allowed her to berth along the pier without the fear of damaging her hull plating.

Her elegant lines were enhanced by a tall, single funnel, which rose for 36 ft above the Boat Deck, and two raked masts, the foremast being sited on the forecastle in front of her bridge. The bridge was located on the forward end of the Boat Deck, being a wooden structure with windows on three sides, which gave a good view to her watch-keeping officers and helmsman. Leading off from the after part of the bridge was a small chart house and wireless office. On top of the bridge was her auxiliary magnetic compass, which was housed inside a large brass topped binnacle. Although she was usually steered from the bridge, she had an emergency conning position, located aft on her Poop Deck. The emergency conning position comprised of two large wooden steering wheels and a rudder indicator, as the wheels were connected directly to her steering gear via a chain linkage, they were very heavy to operate and required two men on each wheel. Her spacious Promenade Deck ran for a length of 200 ft and was the only deck that gave access for passengers to walk all of the way around and complete a circuit of the ship, although this was not usually possible as it was sectioned off to segregate First and Second Class passengers. Immediately above the Promenade Deck was the Boat Deck, which was 152 ft long. All of her exposed decks were planked with teak, while those under cover were of yellow pine. The Shelter Deck was constructed of steel plating, which in turn was covered in Columbian Pine planking.

As previously mentioned, the external appearance of the *King Orry* was very similar to her older half sister, the *Snaefell*. However to the trained eye, they could easily be told apart. The *King Orry* a single foremast, whereas the *Snaefell* had two cargo derricks mounted at the after end of her foremast. These were usually stowed in the upright position and were always noticeable. The *Snaefell* only had three lifeboats on each side, whereas the *King Orry* had four. The major difference between the two steamers was in their superstructure. The *Snaefell* had been built as a dual passenger and cargo vessel (albeit small amounts) and therefore had cargo facilities both forward and aft. Her superstructure was split into two sections by her mainmast (aft mast), on which was mounted another small derrick. This mast was located in a small well deck, behind which was a deckhouse that formed the after part of the superstructure. This distinctive break in the superstructure made her instantly recognisable from the new steamer.

Chapter Two

ACCOMMODATION

The accommodation on board the *King Orry* was of a very high standard for this period of time and both classes of passengers were well catered for. She had a large Dining Saloon on her Shelter Deck, which was divided into both First and Second Class and capable of providing a silver service a la carte menu for 88 persons in one sitting. A well-equipped galley was located on the deck below; this was connected to the Dining Saloon's pantry by a lift. The Dining Saloon had a magnificent oak parquet deck with oak paneling on the bulkheads. These panels were embellished with electro-plated chrome light fittings.

Sleeping cabins for both classes were also located on the same deck as the galley. The First Class Saloon, which could accommodate 86 people, was in the forward end of the ship, while the Second Class Saloon could accommodate 92 people and was at the after end. Both saloons were panelled in light mahogany, although the First Class was upholstered in light green moquette and the Second Class in old-gold moquette. Washbasins and lavatories for both classes were located in adjacent compartments.

As well as the Dining Saloon, the First Class General Saloon was also located on the Shelter Deck. This was indeed a grand compartment; the bulkheads were panelled in both light and dark mahogany with elaborately carved pilasters. The upholstery was light blue moquette, while the deck was covered in a thick Axminster carpet. French grey velvet plush drapes and curtains added to the saloon's luxurious appearance. Writing desks were provided, while numerous settees were placed around the saloon, each one being fitted with a specially designed spring mattress. These allowed the First Class General Saloon to be quickly converted into an additional sleeping cabin for 59 passengers.

A barber's shop was provided for both classes, which would prove to be very popular with male passengers when they wished to look refreshed after a long overnight passage. Above the Shelter Deck was the Promenade Deck and again superb facilities for passengers were provided.

One of the main compartments on this deck was the First Class Ladies Saloon. Once again it was elaborately panelled in birch and dark mahogany with moquette upholstery and velvet plush drapes and curtains. To add to the degree of comfort, adequate amounts of divan chairs and settees were provided as this saloon could also be converted into a sleeping cabin.

The entrance hall to the saloon was panelled in a similar design to that in the main compartment but instead of an Axminster carpet, the deck was covered with black and white india rubber tiles. A staircase ran down from the entrance hall into the Dining Saloon below.

Six private State Rooms were located on the Promenade Deck. Not to be out done by the First Class accommodation, the Second Class was also of a high standard and was probably the best available on any Steam Packet vessel so far. The Second Class General Saloon was located in the after end of the ship and had its own entrance hall which no previous vessel in the Manx fleet had. The entrance, which was on the Shelter Deck, was similar in design to its First Class equivalent, being panelled in mahogany, with a walnut dado and door mouldings, while walnut bench seating was fitted to the bulkheads which allowed passengers to be seated but still look out onto the Upper Deck. A few steps led down from the entrance into the saloon itself. The noticeable difference between this saloon and the First Class Saloon was the lack of the thick Axminster carpet. In its place was an oak parquet floor which was covered with numerous Brussels carpet runners. The bulkheads were panelled with painted birds eye maple with mahogany moulding. The furniture was upholstered in dark and light brown moquette, with matching curtains and drapes.

Leading off from the Second Class Saloon was the Second Class Ladies Saloon, which was upholstered in green moquette. The bulkheads were once again panelled, although this time in ash with mahogany moulding. Both Second Class saloons had similar style settees to those in the First Class areas and could also be converted into sleeping cabins for night sailings.

A total of 345 sleeping berths were available on the *King Orry* which made her a very popular ship to travel on during a night passage. In total, an area equal to 58,880 cubic feet was available on the *King Orry* for passenger accommodation, while an additional 11.390 cubic feet was allocated for storerooms.

All of the furnishings and upholstery on board the *King Orry* were designed and fitted by the Liverpool firm of A.Blain and Sons. She was illuminated throughout with electric lighting but traditional bulkhead-mounted oil lamps were positioned in all of the saloons, just in case the electric lighting failed.

As well as a high standard of passenger accommodation, the crew of the *King Orry* was also well catered for. The stewards and cooks had quarters adjacent to the Dining Saloon and pantry, while the seamen and Engine Room personnel had their accommodation on the same deck as the galley and sleeping cabins. Although the accommodation was of a high standard for this period of time, compared with ships of today it was very basic. The Steam Packet did not provide any form of bedding or victualling and an entry on the front cover of her 1913 ship's log and crew list, clearly states that "the crew are to provide their own provisions". Crew members brought their own food on board and usually slept on a straw palliasse, the straw being purchased ashore each time they signed on to a new vessel.

Although it was an unofficial practice, the stewards often used bedding and linen that was provided for passengers and obtained meals from the galley and being a steward obviously had its advantages. The officers fared better as they had cabins on the Promenade Deck and were provided with both bedding and food. It was common practice, even until quite recently, for officers' cabins to be loaned to passengers during a voyage if they were not being used by their normal occupant.

LIFE SAVING

As well as the comfort of the passengers being paramount, so was their safety. With the *Titanic* disaster and its appalling loss of life only occurring in the previous year, great attention was given to ensure that every possible form of life-saving aid was fitted to the new steamer. The hull was divided into nine watertight compartments rising to the level of the Shelter Deck, which meant that they rose to well above the water line. Some of these compartments required to be accessed from those adjacent to them, for example, the Engine Room and stoke holds. The watertight bulkheads of such compartments were fitted Stone Lloyd automatic watertight doors, these could be either closed or opened by operating a switch adjacent to the door, or in an emergency, by operating an master switch on the bridge. The *King Orry's* eight life boats, each one being capable of carrying between 49 and 51 survivors. Four boats were carried on each side of the Boat Deck, they were numbered 1 to 8, with the odd numbers being on the starboard side and the even on the port side. Examination of her engineering details establishes that no two boats were the same size, with No 3 and No 5 boats being the largest. Their davits were arranged at a slight angle (or herring boned) to the ship's side. This was a common feature, but sometimes meant that extra boats had been installed onto the ship. It is possible that an additional two lifeboats were added to the *King Orry's* Boat Deck after the initial design had been drawn up.

Additionally, 88 buoyant life rafts, capable of supporting 1,296 people, were stowed on the upper decks; some of these were designed to be used as seats during normal sea passages to and from the Island. Lifejacket lockers, which held a total of 1,672 life jackets, were located throughout the accommodation areas as well as occupying prominent positions on the upper decks. Twelve lifebuoys were also positioned around the weather decks which could easily be removed from their stowage should there be a need to throw them to a survivor in the water.

One of the other factors that came out of the *Titanic* disaster enquiry, was that ships were not required maintain a 24 hour radio watch. Had this been a requirement (even when a ship was stopped), then perhaps the controversy about the *Californian* and the accusation that her Master, Captain Lord was negligent in not coming to the *Titanic's* assistance, would never have occurred and many lives might have been saved. A regulation stating a requirement to maintain a listening watch on the distress channel at regular intervals throughout the day was soon introduced and closed this loophole.

However, returning to the *King Orry*, exact details of the wireless initially installed are not known, but it was undoubtedly of the latest type. A photograph taken in 1914 shows a Marconi nameplate on what appears to be part of a wireless transmitter. Copies of the Marconi ships' radio manual dated between 1913 and 1921, record her as having a 600 metre wave band wireless set with a range of 100 nautical miles.

These manuals also record her radio call sign as being MPE. This has caused some confusion, especially as "Lloyd's Register" records that the *King Orry's* call sign was JFPC. However, there is a simple explanation to this confusing duplication of call signs. In 1913, and indeed up until the early 1930s, ships that were fitted with a wireless had two call signs. The first call sign which consisted of four letters was used when communicating by signal flag and the latter which consisted of three letters was used when communicating by wireless. It must be remembered that in 1913 it was not compulsory for a ship to be fitted with a wireless, so it was still a necessity to be able to communicate by using signal flags. Therefore, a vessel's International Call Sign, as recorded in the "Lloyd's Register" was still the four letter signal hoist version. It was common practice in 1913 for the Marconi company to supply wireless officers to ships fitted with their own equipment and it is possible that the "M" prefix to all British three letter wireless call signs relates to the Marconi name.

During the early 1930s, when the majority of vessels were fitted with a wireless, or radio as they were now called, the Board of Trade decided to end the confusion and combined the two call signs into a single four letter version. As a result of this directive, during 1934 the *King Orry's* 1913 signal flag call sign JFPC and the wireless call sign MPE were changed to a single GRMF, "G" being the prefix that was adopted by all British

King Orry

One of the **King Orry's** single-reduction geared turbines with the casing removed to expose the ahead and astern turbine rotors in the engine shop at Cammell Laird's, prior to being installed onboard during March 1913. (Wirral Museum Service/Cammel Laird Archive)

vessels. In addition to her wireless equipment and signal flags, the *King Orry* could communicate with other ships by using a Morse signal lamp or semaphore flags.

The *King Orry* could also summon assistance, or warn of her presence in poor visibility by using her whistle or siren. She was fitted with a single-chime steam whistle and a naval-type steam siren, both of which were attached to the forward side of her funnel.

THE GEARED STEAM TURBINE

As already mentioned, the significant feature of the *King Orry* was her geared steam turbines, or more correctly the single reduction geared turbine.

The steam turbine had been designed as early as 1884 by Charles Parsons. Parsons experimented with turbines in the laboratory of his country home, Holeyn Hall at Wylam on Tyne and by 1890 he had installed a prototype in the Clyde paddle steamer, *Duchess of Hamilton*. However, it was his powerful steam yacht, appropriately named the *Turbinia*, which put the steam turbine into the limelight.

During Queen Victoria's Diamond Jubilee Naval Review in 1897, Parsons raced the 100ft yacht along the lines of anchored warships at nearly 35 knots, the fastest recorded speed at which a vessel had then travelled.

The Royal Navy soon capitalised on the invention and ordered two torpedo boat destroyers, *Viper* and *Cobra*. Unfortunately, both of these vessels were soon

lost due to a design fault in their hulls, albeit not related to the installation of the steam turbine.

Parsons, who by now had opened a factory at Wallsend on the River Tyne, was keen to break into the lucrative merchant shipping market and turned his attention back to the Clyde steamers. This time he fitted his turbines into the new 550 ton screw-driven steamer, *King Edward* which was built at Denny's Dumbarton yard in 1901 and achieved a speed of 20.5 knots.

The same year as the *King Edward* entered service, the Allan Line adopted this revolutionary new propulsion system for their two new liners, the *Victorian* and *Virginian* which was the break that Parsons had hoped for and it was soon followed by the Cunard Line fitting similar engines into their *Carmania*. The Isle of Man Steam Packet did not drag its heels with regard to advances in technology and decided to fit steam turbines into their new ships the *Viking* and *Ben-my-Chree* when they were built a couple of years later.

However, there was a problem with the steam turbine which only became apparent as shipping companies tried to out-race each other and own the fastest ship afloat. The propeller shaft was connected direct to the turbine, which meant that both the turbine and propeller rotated at the same speed.

As technology advanced and the power of the turbines increased, it was noted that increasing the power of the turbines did not necessarily increase the speed of the ship. Investigations revealed that once a

*The engineer's control position in the **King Orry's** engine room: April 1913. (Wirral Museum Service/Cammel Laird Archive)*

*The **King Orry's** engine room: the wooden casing covers one of her steam turbines. (Wirral Museum Service/Cammel Laird Archive)*

propeller reached a certain number of revolutions it began to cavitate (or create a vacuum around itself) and no longer had any thrust in the water.

Using a modified propeller which provided more thrust, Parsons tried to lower the speed of the propeller shaft by installing three turbines in series, exhaust steam from the first turbine (or high pressure) would drive a further two turbines (low pressure purbine), the propeller shaft being connected to the last turbine in the series. Although this eased the problem, it did not completely overcome it, so Parsons decided to introduce a gearbox to reduce the shaft speed even more. The addition of a gear box solved the problem and the new turbine was given the name geared steam turbine, while the original system adopted the name direct drive steam turbine. The principle behind the new system was that

as a turbine was most efficient when running under maximum load, a slower rotating propeller shaft fitted with an improved design of propeller might achieve the same high speeds through the water, but without the risk of the propeller cavitating.

The *King Orry's* engine consisted of six turbines built by Cammell Laird to a design supplied by Parsons' Marine Steam Turbine Company - the engine's serial number being 1573. She had four ahead turbines, two high pressure, which were mounted in the centre of the Engine Room, and two low pressure, which were, mounted one on either side of the former. The remaining two turbines were known as the astern turbines, both being low pressure, they could be coupled to the propeller shaft to allow it to rotate astern, as well as ahead. The two high pressure turbines weighed 19

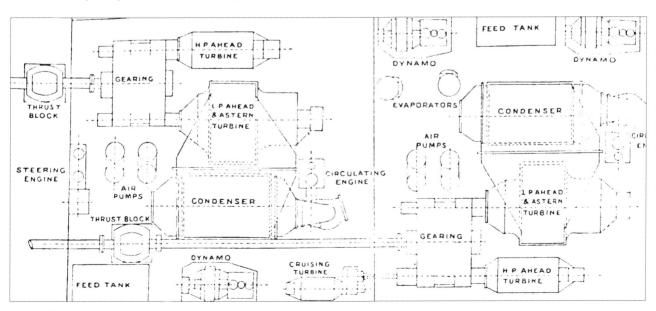

*A plan of the **King Orry** Engine Room*

*The **King Orry** in the River Mersey as she undergoes her preliminary sea trails on 7th June 1913. (Wirral Museum Service/Cammel Laird Archive)*

King Orry

tons, while the four low pressure weighed in at impressive 31 tons.

The turbines were designed to produce 9.400 shaft horsepower under normal conditions, which would rotate the propellers at 300 revolutions per minute and give the *King Orry* a cruising speed of nearly 20,5 knots. As already recorded, she achieved her best speed during the sea trial, which took place on 12th June 1913. On this occasion, her turbines were recorded as producing just under 10.000 SHP, which rotated the propellers at 304 revolutions and attained a speed of 21.32 knots.

The two gear boxes (one for each shaft) were built by Parsons Marine Steam Turbine Company at Wallsend on Tyne; they were then disassembled and shipped down to Birkenhead, where they were rebuilt for eventual installation into the *King Orry*. The combined weight of the gearboxes was 28 ton 10 cwt. The gearing, which was known as single reduction, consisted of two sets of helical gearing. Each set had two pinions; one end was coupled to the high pressure turbine, with the other end being connected to the low pressure turbine. A wheel, which was common to both pinions, then coupled the gearing direct to the propeller shafts. The gearboxes were only designed to reduce the speed of the propeller shaft, but unlike the modern car gearbox, the gear ratio could not be altered.

The only way of reducing or increasing the shaft speed was by altering the speed of the turbine. Attached to the seaward end of the two 19ft 2$^{3/4}$ in long propeller shafts were the huge phosphor bronze three-bladed propellers, each having a diameter of 8ft 9ins and weighing nearly 2.5 tons.

Steam to drive the turbines was provided by two double-ended and one single-ended boiler, built by Cammell Laird to the closed stoke hold design. These had a normal working pressure of 170 lbs per square inch, but achieved 240 lbs per square inch during boiler trails which were carried out prior to her putting to sea for he first time. The two-doubled ended boilers each had six furnaces, three in either end, while the single-ended boiler had three at one end only, making a total of fifteen furnaces.

The boilers onboard the *King Orry* were heated by coal, although later designs of furnace had a mechanical-feeding device, the coal on the *King Orry* was fed into the furnace by a team of sweating stokers using shovels, this must have been one of the worst jobs encountered at sea.

The *King Orry* had four coal bunkers, which held a total of 210 tons. Two were positioned on the port side and two on the starboard; the two forward bunkers each held 51 tons of coal, while the two after ones held 54 tons. To maintain a speed of 20 knots at 288 revolutions,

she would use 4.8 tons of coal per hour and at 10 knots, would use about 1.50 tons. A return trip to Liverpool would use 28 tons of coal, so she was required to take on coal or rebunker at least once a week. Although this was not a problem for normal peacetime trading, during her service with the Royal Navy in the First World War, the constant need to re bunker would limit her endurance when out on patrol.

Although she never gained the titles "The Flyer" or "mini-Cunarder" like the *Ben-my-Chree*, the *King Orry* could maintain a good speed in most sea states. Combined with the added bonus of decreased wear and tear to her turbines due to the single reduction gearing, she proved to be very economical to run.

The *King Orry* was the first ship built by Cammell Laird to be fitted with geared turbines and the first to sail out of the River Mersey and operate a regular service on the west coast of the United Kingdom.

Official records show her as being the eighth vessel to be fitted with the new geared turbine. With the exception of the *Normannia* and *Hantonia*, which belonged to the London & South Western Railway, most of her predecessors appear to have been converted from the direct drive system. The first ship to have geared turbines installed was the Cairn Line's *Vespasian*, which entered service some three years before the *King Orry*.

The Steam Packet's proposed ship building programme was curtailed by the First World War. Although a few relatively new ships were purchased second hand immediately after hostilities, the company did not invest in another new vessel until 1927. This vessel, the *Ben-my-Chree (4)* was very similar in design to the *King Orry* although she was built to a larger specification.

The *King Orry* can claim to be the forerunner of the design used by the Steam Packet for its new passenger vessels for the following fifty years. Apart from minor improvements, the basic design remained little changed until the car ferry *Manx Maid* entered service in 1962.

Right: *The **King Orry's** orginal registration document*

Form No. 19.

Signal Letters (if any) ~~JFPG~~

G.P.M.F.

Transcript of Register for Transmission to Registrar-General of Shipping and Seamen.

Official Number	Name of Ship	No., Date, and Port of Registry
118.608	King Orry	2 – 1913. Douglas Isle of man

No., Date, and Port of previous Registry (if any) —

Whether British or Foreign Built	Whether a Sailing or Steam Ship; and if a Steam Ship, how propelled	Where Built	When Built	Name and Address of Builders
British	Steamship Twin-Screw	Birkenhead	1913	Messrs Cammell Laird & Co Ltd Birkenhead

		Feet	Tenths
Number of Decks ... ... Two	Length from fore part of stem, under the bowsprit, to the aft side of the head of the stern post	300	00
Number of Masts ... ... Two	Length at quarter of depth from top of weather deck at side amidships to bottom of keel	300	00
Rigged ... Fore & aft Schooner	Main breadth to outside of plank	43	15
Stern ... Elliptical	Depth in hold from tonnage deck to ceiling at midships	15	95
Build ... Clincher	Depth in hold from upper deck to ceiling at midships, in the case of three decks and upwards	~	~
Galleries ... None	Depth from top of beam amidships to top of keel	16	96
Head ... None Straight Stem	Depth from top of deck at side amidships to bottom of keel	17	15
Framework and description of vessel Steel Passenger	Round of beam		85
Number of Bulkheads ... Nine	Length of engine room, if any		
Number of water ballast tanks, and their capacity in tons Nine 278 tons			

PARTICULARS OF DISPLACEMENT.

PARTICULARS OF PROPELLING ENGINES &c (if any)

No. of sets of Engines	Description	Whether British	Reg No	Where made	When made	No. of Cylinders each set	Diam. of Cylinders each set	N.H.P. I.H.P. Estimated Speed of Ship
Two	Geared Turbines	B.	Regn 1913	Cammell Laird & Co Ltd Birkenhead	any	1941	Two	96 ...
No. of Shafts Two	Particulars of Boilers		1913	Cammell Laird & Co Ltd Birkenhead.				

PARTICULARS OF TONNAGE.

GROSS TONNAGE.	No. of Tons	DEDUCTIONS ALLOWED.	No. of Tons
Under Tonnage Deck	118.87	On account of space required for propelling power ...	931.61
Space or spaces between Decks ...		On account of spaces occupied by Seamen or Apprentices, and appropriated to their use, and kept free from Goods or Stores of every kind, not being the personal property of the Crew ...	139.16
Turret or Trunk			
Forecastle	206.17		
Bridge space	134.63		
Poop	128.04		
Side Houses	45.47		
Deck Houses	175.54		
Chart House			
Spaces for machinery, and light, and air, under Section 78 (2) of the Merchant Shipping Act, 1894			
Excess of Hatchways			
Gross Tonnage	5311.12		
Deductions, as per Contra	3154.04		
Register Tonnage ...	762.22 2157.08	Total	1114.50

NOTE.—1. The tonnage of the engine room spaces below the upper deck is **652.63** tons, and the tonnage of the total spaces framed in above the upper deck for propelling machinery and for light and air is **175.65** tons.

NOTE.—2. The undermentioned spaces above the upper deck are not included in the cubical contents forming the ship's register tonnage: Under shelter deck amidships:- length 128.0' less side houses, engine & boiler casing galley fan room & companions = 180.45 Tons; Open recess abaft engine casing on shelter deck 10.5 × 16.0 × 7.5 = 11.74 tons.

Name of Master	John Bridson	Certificate of Service (Competency) No. 102727

Names, Residence, and Description of the Owners, and Number of Sixty-fourth Shares held by each ... viz.,

The Isle of Man Steam Packet Company Limited having its principal place of business at Douglas Isle of Man

Sixty four

64.

Dated	3rd July 1913.	Porter	Registrar.

NOTE.—Registrars in the Colonies are requested to distinguish the Managing Owner by placing the letters " M.O." against his name.

N.B.—To be sent in an envelope addressed to the Registrar-General of Shipping and Seamen, Tower Hill, London, E.

20992 10,000 10–10 HWV 9 28 9
6247 10,000 5–11

No. 345. Instructions to Registrars of British Ships, para. 26.—Sec. 2345 1910.

King Orry

Entering Service

Records show that the *King Orry* was awarded her passenger certificate on 2nd July 1913 while at the same time she was given the official number 118608 on the Lloyd's Register.

She was certified to carry the following personnel:

First Class Passengers	884
Third Class Passengers	716
Total	1,600
Crew	72

At this period of time, the term Third Class was often used in lieu of Second Class although the *King Orry* only had two classes of passenger throughout the whole of her service with the Steam Packet. Due to her conversion to oil fuel and the subsequent reduction in firemen, her crew was reduced from 72 to 59 in 1939.

MASTER

The Steam Packet appointed Captain John Bridson to be her Master. Born in Peel in 1860, Captain Bridson had been connected with the Company since 1883, but joined on a permanent basis in 1887. By coincidence, his first ship was the old *King Orry*, although he was soon appointed to the *Douglas*.

In 1891 he became the Chief Officer of the *Tynwald* and then went on to serve on practically all of the Steam Packet's larger vessels. His first command came in 1902, when he was appointed as the Master of the *Ellan Vannin*, a position he held until just three weeks before her tragic loss in a violent storm on 3rd December 1909.

Before being appointed to the new *King Orry*, Captain Bridson had been the first Master of the *Snaefell* but was later transferred to the *Tynwald*; he was therefore the obvious choice when the time came to find a Captain for the *Snaefell's* new half sister.

Captain Bridson had married a Miss Cain from Kirk Michael in 1883 and at the time he was appointed to the *King Orry* they resided with their five children at 22 Kensington Road in Douglas.

He was a respected officer within the Company and rightly deserved much credit for the successful introduction of both the *Snaefell* and the *King Orry* into the Manx fleet.

The crew are shown as having signed on at Birkenhead on 8th July 1913 and consisted of 8 officers and 72 men. Apart from Captain Bridson, her officers consisted of the following personnel:

Chief or First Officer	John Quirk
Second Officer	William Sanderson
Purser	Charles Matthews
Chief Engineer	Thomas Kelly
Second Engineer	Robert Faragher
Third Engineer	Samuel Nelson
Fourth Engineer	Thomas Lightburn

Not all of her crew were former Steam Packet employees, for example, Pantry Boy Thomas Sharp joined the *King Orry* from the giant Cunard liner *Lusitania* and Fireman Alfred Holland joined from her sister the *Mauritania*. Both of these men must have found the *King Orry* very small after serving on two of the mightiest liners in the world. The newspapers, "The Isle of Man Weekly Times" and the "Birkenhead and Cheshire Advertiser" both record that her maiden voyage for the Steam Packet was due to take place on 3rd July 1913, when she would replace the *Ben-my-Chree* on the 10.30 sailing from Liverpool to Douglas.

However, examination of the ship's log records her first sailing as being on 8th July 1913 when she sailed from Liverpool to Douglas. It is probable that the planned sailing on 3rd July 1913 was cancelled for one reason or another and wrongly reported by both newspapers. This theory is supported by the fact that her crew did not sign on until the morning of 8th July 1913.

As predicted, the *King Orry* soon proved to be popular with passengers, especially on the overnight sailings to and from Ardrossan when the comfort of her sleeping saloons was tested to capacity.

The ship served on all of the Steam Packet's regular services during her first summer season. Her log records that the crew were exercised at life boat stations and fire drill on three occasions, 22nd July, 28th August and 22nd September 1913. The fact that they did not appear to exercise these drills prior to her first-recorded sailing, seems odd. Her successful entry into service was marred by an incident on 30th September 1913 when her log recorded the following:

30th September 1913 - Liverpool to Douglas.

Sailed at 10.39 with passengers - wind E.N.E - fresh breeze. Arrived at Douglas Head at 14.05. The ship was slowed and then engines stopped inside the Battery Pier. The helm was put hard a starboard to go to the south side of the Victoria Pier. When the ship failed to answer the helm, the port engine was put full speed astern and seeing no effect, both engines were put full speed astern but struck the end of the pier damaging the stem.

Signed   J Bridson. Master
*   J Quirk. First Officer*

The stem-post was buckled, but the damage was not extensive, however she was taken off service and replaced by the *Peel Castle* for the afternoon sailing back to Liverpool. This incident must have been embarrassing for Captain Bridson, as no obvious defects were found with her engines and a ship-handling error was recorded as the probable cause of the accident. Luckily, this incident occurred on the last day that the *King Orry* was required on service during 1913. On the following morning, 1st October 1913, she sailed for Birkenhead where she would be laid-up for the winter.

On arrival at Birkenhead, arrangements were made for her to be taken into one of Cammell Laird's dry docks in order that a close examination of her damaged bow could be carried out. It was necessary to replace part of the stem-post and at the same time a modification was made. The original stem-post was made of two sections but the collision with Victoria Pier had identified an area of weakness where the two sections were riveted together.

When the replacement stem-post was fitted it was made in one piece thus removing this potentially weak area.

Captain John Bridson the King Orry's first master

The ship's log records that most of her catering department were paid off in Douglas, before she sailed for winter lay up in Birkenhead. The remainder of her crew, including Captain Bridson, the deck and engineer officers were paid off at Birkenhead on 3rd October.

Thus the *King Orry's* first season with the Steam Packet came to a close. She would remain at Birkenhead until required for the Easter holiday traffic the following year, with only a small care and maintenance party left on board to look after her.

The *King Orry* was available for service for a total of 86 days during the 1913 summer season, of which 78 days were spent at sea. She made a total of 126 separate sailings, with passengers being carried on 125 of them. The breakdown of sailings is as follows:

Douglas - Liverpool	36
Liverpool- Douglas	36
Douglas - Ardrossan	5
Ardrossan- Douglas	6
Liverpool- Ardrossan	1
Douglas - Dublin	15
Dublin- Douglas	15
Douglas - Fleetwood	4
Fleetwood- Douglas	4
Fleetwood- Liverpool	1
Douglas - Douglas	3 around the Island day trips.

The Steam Packet's new steamer had been a complete success, she had proved that she was economical to run and had maintained her design speed on nearly every sailing. Passengers gave good reports on her accommodation and comfort, especially those who had travelled Second Class. During the winter months, she would be overhauled and repainted, ready for the anticipated busy 1914 season.

1914

Apart from the period of docking at Cammell Laird's yard to repair the damaged stem-post, the *King Orry* spent the winter lay up period in Morpeth Dock at Birkenhead, along with other Steam Packet vessels. Throughout this period, Mr Blackburn (Superintendent Engineer) and members of his staff regularly visited the ships to ensure that they were kept in good order and to organise for the rectification of defects, or refurbishment, if required. The *King Orry* was given a Board of Trade inspection on 29th April when all of her life-saving equipment and lifeboats were passed as serviceable for the forthcoming season.

The crew rejoined the vessel on 15th May 1914 at Birkenhead. Once again the Steam Packet had appointed Captain John Bridson to be her Master, although he had spent the winter season back in command of the *Snaefell*. The *King Orry* was immediately made ready for sea and as soon as the engineers obtained a head of steam, she slipped out of Morpeth Dock into the Mersey and proceeded down river towards the bar in order to carry out short sea trial in Liverpool Bay. The majority of her crew were familiar with the ship as they had sailed in her during the previous summer season.

Amongst her officers only the Third Engineer had changed and been replaced by William Lightburn who had recently joined the Company after serving on board the Cardiff-registered steamer *Cambro*. During the sea trial, a lifeboat drill was carried out, thus ensuring that the crew knew their allotted emergency stations should there be an emergency once she was on passenger service.

Having satisfied himself that all was well, Captain Bridson returned the *King Orry* to the river and berthed alongside Princes Landing Stage in preparation for her first passenger sailing the following morning.

Friday 15th May 1914 is recorded as a bright sunny day with a slight sea swell. The *King Orry* was due to re enter service with the morning sailing to Douglas. Her crew had been up since the crack of dawn, preparing the ship for sea. The First Steward, Donald McNicoll would have walked around the passenger saloons to ensure that nothing had been overlooked, while the First Cook; George Lace supervised the last minute loading of fresh provisions. Likewise, the First Officer

John Quirk would inspect the upper decks and as the time of departure drew near he would have reported to Captain Bridson that the ship was ready for sea, Chief Engineer Kelly having already made a similar report about the Engine Room.

As the hands of the clock on the Liver Building approached 10.25, the *King Orry's* whistle blew a long single blast, this was to warn any visitors on board who were not sailing, that they had to proceed ashore immediately, and likewise inform any passengers who were still on the Landing Stage, that they had to board quickly as the gangways were about to be pulled ashore.

The last gangway would have been pulled away from the ship's side as the Liver Building clock showed 10.30 while at the same time the crew would be closing the passenger and cargo doors and the seamen on the forecastle and Poop Deck would be hauling in the heavy berthing ropes.

Now that the *King Orry* was free to proceed down river, Captain Bridson would order "slow ahead" on the engines and sound two short blasts on the whistle to warn any shipping already under way in the river, that the *King Orry* was about to turn to port and move out into the channel.

While this was taking place, the happy laughing passengers would be milling around the saloons and decks, all eager to secure a comfortable seat for the voyage to the Island. Thus the 1914 season had begun for the *King Orry*. As she proceeded down river, resplendent in her fresh coat of paint, few people would have dreamed that within three months, many of the male passengers on board would be fighting for their lives in France and Belgium.

For the remainder of May, the *King Orry* was employed on the daily Liverpool to Douglas service, although she did a round trip to Dublin on 31st May 1914.

As the *King Orry* plied to and fro across the Irish Sea, the situation in Europe was beginning to give cause for concern. There was a struggle for power by Germany, the Austro-Hungarian Empire, Russia and France. Great Britain, already a powerful voice in Europe, was being pulled into conflict with her former ally Germany, as a great arms race developed between the two countries.

However, to the crew of the *King Orry* little of this mattered, their day to day routine consisted of conveying the thousands of holiday makers between the Isle of Man and the English mainland. Replacing the smashed crockery from a rough passage was more of a priority, than worrying about European warlords rattling their sabres. The only change to the daily routine was a lifeboat drill in the River Mersey on 3rd June 1914.

The ship's log records that she was stood down for 20 days between 6th and 26th June 1914 and remained at Liverpool although the reason for this is not clear. It is possible that she required some form of maintenance at Cammell Laird's yard as examination of her engineering details indicate that she had problems with her turbines, although the more probable reason is that there was a decline in passenger trade after Whitsun and the Company did not require to use all of its vessels.

On returning to service, she was employed once again on the Liverpool run but also made excursions to Llandudno, Fleetwood, Ardrossan and Dublin.

SARAJEVO

On Sunday 28th June 1914, the seriousness of the situation in Europe took a sudden upsurge as the result of an incident in a place that most people in the United Kingdom had never heard of.

Archduke Franz Ferdinand, the nephew of the Emperor of Austria-Hungary and heir to the Imperial throne was visiting the city of Sarajevo in the province of Bosnia which had been recently annexed by Austria. As he and his wife drove through Sarajevo in their open-topped car, a young Serb named Gavrilo Princip stepped out from the crowd and emptied a revolver into the Archduke and his wife. Although Princip was immediately arrested, his gun-shot wounds proved fatal to the occupants of the car.

UNSEASONAL INCIDENTS

Meanwhile, back on board the *King Orry* it was not all plain sailing. While on service to Dublin on 14th July 1914, she suffered the first of two incidents that occurred during this hot summer month. At 13.15, as she approached her berth at Dublin's Sir John Rogerson Quay, she was involved in a collision with the Dublin-registered coaster, the *Saint Margaret* which was owned by the shipping company Heiton's.

As she attempted to manoeuvre past the Steam Packet vessel, the coaster which was also inward bound, struck the *King Orry* on the stern. The *King Orry's* log records that two steel plates were badly dented in her counter and considerable damage was done to the stern belting. As the *King Orry's* engines were stopped when the collision occurred, the blame for the collision went to the *Saint Margaret*. As none of the damage appeared to affect the sea-worthiness of the *King Orry*, a thorough examination of her stern was delayed until

she returned to Douglas that evening. Her log records that she remained in Douglas on 15th July 1914, presumably to carry out essential repairs. The next incident, which was far more serious, occurred in the early hours of 18th July 1914.

The *King Orry* had left Liverpool at 23.00 the previous night in an unladen condition to make an overnight passage to Ardrossan. The weather was recorded as a light N W wind, with fine clear visibility until 03.00.

At this time it became a little hazy, so Captain Bridson reduced the *King Orry's* speed and warned the Engine Room to stand by to stop, should the weather deteriorate any further. Twelve minutes later, the haze had developed into thick fog, making it impossible to see for more than a few hundred yards ahead. Being a cautious man, Captain Bridson ordered the ship's engines to be stopped with the intention of allowing her to drift until the visibility improved.

Suddenly, within a few seconds of Captain Bridson uttering this order, and with the *King Orry* still making headway, land loomed up ahead. Captain Bridson immediately passed the order for the engines to be put full astern but it was too late. As the propellers raced astern and the headway began to drop off, the *King Orry* crashed over rocks at the base of a low cliff and with a grating and screeching of tortured steel, the vessel came to a halt.

The watertight doors were quickly closed by operating the master control switch on the bridge. The startled crew began to pour out onto the upper decks, many of them having been thrown out of their bunks. As the noise of grounding died away and the *King Orry* came to a rest, it became obvious that the vessel was not in any immediate danger of sinking but as a precaution the crew were ordered to swing out all of the lifeboats and make them ready to lower.

At this moment of time, the exact position of the ship was still unknown as the fog precluded any visual surveillance of the surrounding area. Distress flares were fired in an attempt to summon assistance and alert any other vessel which happened to be nearby of the danger.

The First Officer and Chief Engineer were called to the bridge, to discuss the predicament with Captain Bridson and await his instructions. The Carpenter, Robert Sweeny was ordered to inspect all of the forward compartments and attempt to confirm the extent of damage. After a short while, he returned and confirmed that both the fore peak and cable locker were flooded and that No 1 ballast water tank (located below the forward hold) had salt water contamination

King Orry

*The **King Orry** docked down at Cammell Laird as she undergoes repair to her damaged bow plating. (Wirral Museum Service/Cammel Laird Archive)*

*The extent of the damage to the **King Orry's** bow following her grounding on Cornaa Head. (Wirral Museum Service/Cammel Laird Archive)*

which probably meant that it was also open to the sea.

The Chief Engineer had started the pumps as soon as the watertight doors had been closed and everybody on board must have been relieved when it was reported that they were controlling the inrush of water. The *King Orry* was stuck fast by the bow but her stern floated freely in the light swell.

Captain Bridson decided to attempt to lighten the bow in the hope that they may be able to pull the ship from her precarious position by putting the engines slow astern. The after peak, which was normally a dry compartment, was flooded to compensate for the extra weight in the bow caused by the water in the flooded forward compartments. This had the desired effect and raised the damaged bow slightly and levelled off the bow-down effect on her trim.

It was 05.40, some two and a half hours after the *King Orry* had run aground, before Captain Bridson decided to attempt to pull her off the rocks. The visibility had also cleared sufficiently for him to confirm the ship's position. The *King Orry* run onto the rocks at the base of Cornaa Head (sometimes spelt Cornah), which is some two miles south of Maughold Head on the Isle of Man.

A glance at a map would have quickly confirmed that the *King Orry* was some considerable distance off

course. Presumably, as she had cruised at slow speed through the fog, which made it impossible for her navigator to confirm her position by taking star sightings or navigational fixes from any headland or lighthouse, the *King Orry* had slowly drifted away from her correct heading. Captain Bridson ordered all spare members of crew to go to the stern of the vessel in an effort to lighten the bow even further and then ordered the engines to be put slow astern. After a few moments the *King Orry* began to move and accompanied by the noise of steel grating on the rocks, she floated clear.

The Carpenter was sent to check the damaged compartments again and confirmed that the pumps were still controlling the level of water. Captain Bridson decided to head for Douglas where he knew the damage could be inspected and the vessel made more seaworthy before the journey to a ship repair facility was attempted.

Although her log records that distress flares were sent up, there is no mention of any ship coming to her assistance and so it is assumed that all the efforts to remove her from the rocks were made by her own crew.

At slow speed, it took the *King Orry* a couple of hours to reach Douglas, where on arrival she was instructed to berth adjacent to the Steam Packet's Head

Office in the Imperial Building as this berth dried out at low tide and would therefore allow the Steam Packet engineers to carry out any emergency repairs that may be necessary to make the *King Orry* sea worthy.

At low tide, with the *King Orry* sitting high and dry on the harbour bottom, Mr Blackburn, the Steam Packet's Superintendent Engineer conducted an inspection of the foreward part of the vessel confirmed that the damage was not serious, although the *King Orry* would need to go into a dry dock to have her bottom plates repaired.

As an interim safety measure, the bulkheads in the fore peak and chain locker were shored up with heavy timber.Captain Bridson was instructed to take the *King Orry* to Cammell Laird's yard at Birkenhead, where Mr Blackburn had already made arrangements for her to be put into dock. She left Douglas at 11.30 and made a slow passage to the Mersey, arriving off the Cammell Laird Graving Dock at 18.00. She was taken into the dock that evening as Cammell Laird wished to commence work on her repairs the following morning by which time the dock would have been drained to expose the damaged bow section.

Examination of the her bottom plates revealed that some fifteen feet of her bow had been damaged, the plates covering the bottom of her fore peak and chain locker were badly dented and their riveted seams had split open.

The plates beneath No 1 ballast water tank were sound, but there was a split in the bulkhead that divided it from the chain locker.

Pictures taken by Cammell Laird's official photographer show that a large number of her bow plates were removed to effect the repair and presumably to be replaced or straightened out. The repairs took some six days to complete and also included replacement of the stern belting that was damaged in the Dublin incident.

It is a great credit to the work force of Cammell Laird that they were able to strip down the *King Orry's* damaged bow section and repair it in such a short time which no doubt pleased the management of the Isle of Man Steam Packet. On the evening of 24th July 1914, following water tightness checks in the reflooded graving dock, the *King Orry* was towed over to Princes Landing Stage by the Cammell Laird tug, where she would remain overnight in preparation for her return to service on the 10.30 sailing to Douglas the following morning.

THE STORM CLOUDS GATHER

As the *King Orry* had lain in Cammell Laird's yard, the situation in Europe had taken yet another very serious escalation towards conflict.On 23rd July 1914, Austria supported by Germany, seized the opportunity to humiliate Serbia and issued what was to become known as the Austro-Hungarian ten point ultimatum. Serbia accepted most of the points, but they refused to agree to the demand for Austrian officials to be allowed to take part in the investigation into the assassination plot. As a result of Serbia's resistance, the Austro-Hungarian Empire declared war on Serbia on 29th July 1914. Two days later on 31st July 1914, Czar Nicholas ordered Russia to mobilise in support of Serbia.

The British Government was now monitoring the situation very closely and took the precaution of ordering the Royal Navy to its war bases on 28th July 1914.

On 1st August, after Russia had failed to respond to the German ultimatum to stop mobilising, Germany declared war on Russia. It was now obvious to the man in the street, that war was about to engulf the European continent. In response to Germany's declaration of war against Russia, France mobilised its armed forces the same day, while the British Admiralty ordered the Royal Navy to call up its reservists.

The events over the next few days deteriorated rapidly, on 2nd August, Germany demanded the right to have passage through Belgium, which was firmly refused. The next day, Germany declared war on France, followed by the invasion of Belgium on the 4th August 1914. At 23.00 on 4th August, the Government of King George V rallied in support of its European allies and announced that a state of war existed between Great Britain and the combined forces of Germany and the Austro - Hungarian Empire.

On the day that war was declared, the *King Orry* was engaged on a return trip from Douglas to Dublin. As the news was spread around the ship, some of the passengers were probably very worried, as they expected the German High Seas Fleet to loom over the horizon at any moment and blast them into eternity. The six monthly crew agreements for the *King Orry* that cover the period July - December 1914, show that amongst her crew there were eleven Naval reservists. As these men were all paid off on either 27th July or 3rd August, it is probable that they had already received their call-up papers for service with the Royal Navy.

The next few days left the Steam Packet Company somewhat in limbo. There had been a noticeable drop in the amount of tourists visiting the Isle of Man since

*The pier head at Douglas during summer 1913 showing the **King Orry** approaching the harbour entrance. (David Handscombe collection)*

the previous weekend as the navy and army began to mobilise their reservists, although some holiday makers had just cancelled their holiday for fear of being attacked during the sea passage.

The Steam Packet Board of Directors convened a special meeting on 10th August 1914 to discuss what action they should take. They decided to immediately withdraw the *Ben-my-Chree*, *Viking* and *Empress Queen* from service as these three ships had large passenger carrying capacities and with the marked reduction in tourists, they were no longer economical to run.

As traffic on many of the summer season routes had declined to almost nothing, they decided to maintain the daily Liverpool service, but suspended many of the other routes. The service to Whitehaven ceased within a week while those to Dublin, Ardrossan, Belfast and Fleetwood followed shortly afterwards. The *King Orry's* log records that she completed her last excursion to Dublin on 11th August and from then on she maintained the daily Liverpool service. Although passage to the Island was still unrestricted, certain precautions such as vessels not displaying any unnecessary upper deck lighting at night and all lifeboats to be uncovered, came into immediate force.

ROUGH WEATHER

Mr Raymond Pugh, a six-year old school boy in August 1914, recalled a very unpleasant voyage on board the *King Orry*, which took place within a couple of weeks of war being declared. Along with his mother and father, he had spent his summer holiday at Bradda House in Douglas. The family who owned the hotel were called Sweeney, and Mr Sweeney was a Quartermaster with the Steam Packet. The effect of the sudden decline in holidaymakers was already apparent in Douglas, this was particularly noticeable in the Palace Arcade where many shops had prematurely closed and boarded up their windows for the winter. As the Pugh family boarded the *King Orry* for the 16.00 sailing to Liverpool, a strong gale was blowing from the south west.

Like many other passengers, Mr and Mrs Pugh decided to remain on the Upper Deck rather than go below into one of the crowded saloons, where the effect of rough weather was bound to be more noticeable. Seating space on the Upper Deck was at a premium, but they found a space in a cross passage on the Promenade Deck. Owing to the narrowness of the cross passage, they left their suitcases on the starboard side of the Promenade Deck.

As the *King Orry* went astern from the Victoria Pier, a heavy rumbling noise that sounded like gunfire could be heard along the cliffs from the direction of Laxey. As the country was now at war, young Ray assumed that an army artillery unit was exercising with its guns.

Almost as soon as the vessel cleared the Battery Pier, she began to roll heavily in the swell and as she turned towards Liverpool and waves came crashing down over her forecastle. As Ray had never been on a ship in rough weather before, he was very scared, although he did not recall feeling sick.

Due to the bad weather, the *King Orry* made very slow progress to Liverpool, she rolled and pitched constantly and all of the decks were awash with water and vomit. By the time she crossed the bar at the mouth of the Mersey, it was already dark and as she headed up river many people must have been relieved that the violent motion had ceased. As the *King Orry* passed the New Brighton Battery, a searchlight beam suddenly stabbed out into the dark and illuminated the ship's starboard side while, allowing her identity to be confirmed by the soldiers manning the battery ashore.

Now that she was riding on an even keel, Ray decided that it was time to explore the *King Orry*. Having asked his parents' permission, he set off to along the deck in anticipation of a great adventure. As he walked down the stairs into one of the saloons he was amazed, and at the same time appalled, at the number of horizontal people around on the seats and carpets, many of them still lying in their own vomit, feeling too unwell to worry about how they looked.

The smell made him retch and he rushed out onto the Upper Deck into the fresh air again. The *King Orry* finally berthed alongside Princes Landing Stage at just after 23.00 and as the passengers began to surge ashore, many of them were grateful to set foot on dry land again. When Mr and Mrs Pugh recovered their suitcases, they found that they were sodden from their exposure to the water that had swilled around the deck. Although they eventually dried out, the staining caused by the salt water never disappeared.

Ray Pugh's account of this voyage on the *King Orry* highlights her one weak area: throughout the whole of her career, even though the Steam Packet disclaimed it, she was known to be a bad sea boat in rough weather.

END OF SEASON

The *King Orry* continued on the Douglas to Liverpool service for the remainder of August and into early September. The only significant change during this period was that Captain Bridson relinquished Command of the vessel on 30th August and was relieved by Captain Corkill, who had previously been in command of the *Viking*.

It must have been a sad day for Captain Bridson as it was common knowledge within the Steam Packet, that he was very proud of having commanded the Company's two newest vessels.

On the afternoon of 14th September 1914, the *King Orry* made her final passenger voyage for the 1914 season.

After unloading at Princes Landing Stage in Liverpool, she crossed the river and went into the Vittoria Dock in Birkenhead to commence her winter lay-up. Her log shows that her crew, including Captain Corkill, was paid off on 15th September although Wilfred Qualtrough, who had relieved William Sanderson as 2nd Mate on 14th August, remained on board until 24th September.

So ended the first two years of service for the *King Orry*. As she lay at Birkenhead being prepared for months of idleness during winter lay-up, few people would have predicted that within a matter of weeks she would enter service again, this time in a role for which she had never been designed.

The **King Orry** *arriving with a contingent of soldiers onboard. (David Handscombe collection)*

*The **King Orry** enters the dry dock at Cammell Laird shipyard following her grounding at Cornaa Head on 18th July 1914. (Wirral Museum Service/Cammel Laird Archive)*

King Orry

For King and Country

The *King Orry* lay at Birkenhead throughout the end of September and early October 1914. During late August, the British Expeditionary Force had been sent across the English Channel and was now engaged in a bloody conflict near the town of Mons in Belgium. This first engagement with the armies of Imperial Germany was expected to result in victory for Britain and her allies by Christmas. Sadly, this was not to be the case. The small, but highly trained and professional BEF was severely mauled by the Germans and within a matter of weeks the armies were already dug into massive defensive trench systems. This was to be the prelude to four years of death and destruction in the fields of France and Belgium, which would result in the loss of a generation of young men on both sides of the conflict.

Meanwhile at sea, the first engagements with the German navy had been just as quick. On the second day of the war, 5th August, the destroyers *Lance* and *Landrail* attacked and sank the converted Heligoland excursion steamer/ minelayer *Konigin Luise*, thus scoring the first naval victory of the conflict. However, on the following day, the light cruiser *Amphion* was sunk by a mine that had been laid by the *Konigin Luise* which somewhat dampened the euphoria created by the previous day's action. The first German U boat to be sunk was rammed by the cruiser *Birmingham* off the coast of the Orkney Islands on 9th August 1914.

HELIGOLAND BIGHT

The first real fleet action of the war took place on 28th August 1914. At just after 07.00 on a dull foggy morning, a flotilla of German destroyers was on patrol off the coast of Denmark in a region known as the Heligoland Bight. To their surprise, as the mist cleared they found themselves in the middle of a British raiding squadron consisting of 8 light cruisers, 31 destroyers and 8 submarines. At a discreet distance behind this raiding squadron were five powerful battle cruisers, which were under the command of Vice Admiral Sir David Beatty. The British raiding force had dashed across the English Channel during the night with the dual intention of destroying the methodical German destroyer patrol and drawing the German's attention away from the British troop landings at Ostend in Belgium.

However, things soon went badly wrong for both sides. The Germans quickly rushed up six cruisers, but four heavy battle cruisers were delayed, even though they had steam up and were ready to sail. Over the next few hours, the fighting was confused and further muddled by the fog. British communications failed and some British units lost contact with the remainder of the force. At just after noon, as the battle reached a critical point, the fog suddenly lifted to reveal the five battle cruisers of Vice Admiral Beatty's Squadron. The arrival of the Beatty's battle cruisers quickly gave the British the upper hand and over the next forty minutes their 12 inch and 13.5 inch guns pounded the German fleet, quickly sinking three enemy cruisers and a destroyer, with a total loss of 712 German seamen. As the remnants of the German fleet fled, the British rejoiced at their overwhelming victory. They had not lost a single ship. Amazingly, only 35 British sailors had been killed, all on board the cruiser *Arethusa*, which had taken a battering in the early stages of the battle.

CORONEL

Having won the first major naval action of the war, the Royal Navy now settled down to look at its overall strategy. Like Britain, Germany was a colonial power and therefore had naval units spread throughout the world to protect its interests, mainly in the Far East and Africa. To keep the German navy at bay, it would be necessary for the Royal Navy to deploy fairly large forces overseas. An early example of the threat from the German navy occurred on 1st November 1914, when the ageing armoured cruisers *Good Hope* and *Monmouth* were destroyed off the coast of Coronel in South America by superior German forces under the command of Vice Admiral Graf Von Spee. Likewise, on 9th November 1914 the German light cruiser *Emden* was destroyed by Australian units in the Indian Ocean after causing havoc in the Far East since the commencement of hostilities.

In order to release warships from minor duties such as contraband patrol and minesweeping, therefore making them available to be employed in their true role of tracking down the enemy fleet, selected merchant ships were requisitioned and put into naval service as auxiliary vessels. To this end, late in October 1914, the Isle of Man Steam Packet received notification that the *King Orry*, *Peel Castle* and *The Ramsey* were required for war service. Over the next few months, the *Ben-my-Chree*, *Snaefell*, *Queen Victoria*, *Prince of Wales*, *Viking*, *Empress Queen*, *Mona's Isle* and *Mona's Queen* would all be called up, leaving the Steam Packet with only four ships to continue its passenger and cargo service to and from the Island.

CONVERSION

The *King Orry* was taken into Cammell Laird's shipyard in Birkenhead for conversion into an armed boarding vessel. The first task was to remove much of the furniture and fittings from the passenger saloons, as these would be used by the Royal Navy as mess decks for the crew. However, unlike purpose-built naval ships, a luxury that she retained was her dining saloons which were partitioned off into sections to be used by both her officers, senior and junior ratings. Unfortunately for the

senior and junior ratings, the mahogany dining tables and chairs were removed and replaced with plain wooden trestle tables and bench seats.

A 12 pdr gun was installed on the forecastle, just forward of the mast. Unfortunately this gun mounting was to cause problems throughout the *King Orry's* naval service. Although she had a steel deck underneath the planking on the forecastle, it was not removed to allow the gun mounting to be bolted directly to it. The mounting sat on top of the planking, with the bolts passing through the wood into the steel deck. The deck had not been sufficiently reinforced to take the weight of the gun and the effects of the violent recoil when it was fired and, as a result, the deck tended to whiplash when the gun recoiled. After prolonged periods of firing, the bolts which secured the mounting began to work loose and the oakum that was used for caulking between the deck planking often fell out.

Immediately below the 12 pdr gun mounting, in what was originally a small hold, an ammunition magazine was installed to supply shells and cordite to the gun above. A second 12pdr gun was installed on the Promenade Deck, aft of the main mast. This gun appears to have been better installed, as there are no reports of any problem with it or the deck that it stood on, mentioned in the *King Orry's* log books for the First World War. Various photographs taken during the period show a ladder leading down from the *King Orry's* Promenade Deck to her Poop Deck and as this ladder does not appear on any

*The **King Orry** alongside Princes Landing Stage at Liverpool, circa 1930. (Ron Evans collection)*

pre-war photographs, it must be assumed that the Royal Navy installed it to allow quick access up to the after 12 pdr gun. However, whether the ladder was installed during the *King Orry's* initial conversion to an armed boarding vessel is not known. A couple of machine guns, some pistols, rifles and cutlass' completed the outfit of weapons installed on board the *King Orry*.

In order to bring the *King Orry's* communications equipment up to Royal Navy standards, additional wireless telegraphy sets were brought on board for installation in the ship's small wireless office behind the bridge. However, it soon became apparent that this compartment was far to small for all of the additional equipment and the navy wireless telegraphy operators that came with it, so a cabin on the after end of the Promenade Deck was converted into a new wireless office.

A bunk was then installed in the original wireless office to allow the Captain to use it as a sea cabin, although the Marconi wireless equipment was left in situ and the Chief Yeoman of Signals would use it as an office during the day. A small searchlight and a set of semaphore signal arms were installed on the bridge roof. Many other minor alterations and additions occurred during the conversion work, the last of which was to paint the whole vessel in Royal Navy dark warship grey.

COMMISSIONED

The *King Orry* was commissioned as one of His Majesty's Ships on 26th November 1914, under the Command of Lt Cdr Selwyn Day RNR, with a ship's company of 121, which included an eight man detachment of Royal Marines Light Infantry (RMLI). This increase in crew members, compared with her Merchant Navy crew of 72, was predominately due to the extra wireless telegraphy and communications personnel, gunnery crews, boarding party and prize crews for inspecting suspect shipping. Lt Cdr Selwyn Day was a notable seafarer who had spent many years at sea, especially off South America and in the Antarctic regions.

As the Royal Navy had little experience with the type of engines installed in the *King Orry*, or indeed many of the merchant vessels requisitioned during the war, it was common practice to recruit engineers from the original owners of the vessel. Many Steam Packet officers had volunteered for Royal Navy service and Chief Engineer John Keig was one of them. He was commissioned into the Royal Naval Reserve as an Engineer Lieutenant and became the *King Orry's* Engineer Officer. John Keig was well known and respected within the Steam Packet, while his father, Captain Thomas Keig was Commodore

of the Company between 1907 and 1915. The names of the officers who served on board the *King Orry* during the First World War are all recorded within an Admiralty publication called the "Navy List", the issue for January 1915 records that in addition to Lt Cdr Selwyn Day and Engineer Lt John Keig, the following officers were serving on board the *King Orry* when she commissioned in November 1914:

Probationary Sub Lt Robert Sharpley RNR
Probationary Sub Lt Walter Brothers RNR
Probationary Sub Lt Albert Tessier RNR
Probationary Sub Lt Norman Anderson RNR
Assistant Engineer Allan Garrett RNR
Assistant Engineer Albert Goodwin RNR
Assistant Pay Master Harold Reynolds RNR

Assistant Engineer Allan Garrett was another former Steam Packet engineer, the numbers of whom were to grow during December when Engineer Sub Lieutenants Joseph Weldon and George Keig joined the ship, although the latter was no relation to John Keig.

It is probable that other former Steam Packet personnel were included within her crew as there are many entries within the pages of her official Royal Navy log books that record seamen with Manx surnames. Apart from the Admiralty "Navy List", it was not naval policy during the First World War to produce lists of a particular vessel's crew, as was the practice within the Merchant Navy, so unfortunately no record exists of the names of the senior and junior ratings that served onboard the *King Orry*.

However, one member of her crew was Chief Petty Officer (Wireless Telegraphy Operator) Crispen Redshaw who joined the *King Orry* at Birkenhead on 21st November 1914. Born at Forest Gate in London in December 1895, Crispen had worked in the engineering department of the General Post Office in Croydon before volunteering for the Royal Naval Reserve in October 1914. Crispen Redshaw was an accomplished amateur photographer and many of the photographs in this book were taken by him while he was serving on board.

Having drilled at action stations, loaded with stores and ammunition and taken on 424 tons of coal, the *King Orry* proceeded from the basin at Cammell Laird's yard at 06.30 on the morning of 27th November 1914. She immediately went to anchor in the River Mersey to await the river pilot Captain Anderson who came onboard at 09.15.

Shortly afterwards, with the White Ensign billowing from her main mast, His Majesty's Ship *King Orry* proceeded down river to commence war service. She

The **King Orry** at anchor in Longhope, Scapa Flow during 1915. Note the absence of the wooden belting below her lifeboats. (David Handscombe collection)

passed the Bar Lightship at 11.00 and shortly afterwards again dropped anchor to carry out a compass swing and land the pilot. The Captain then took the opportunity to address all of the ship's company, after which life belts were issued to everybody. At 14.00, the King Orry weighed anchor and proceeded north towards her home for the next four years - Scapa Flow in the Orkney Islands.

Having remained at sea overnight, she anchored in Tobermory Bay on the island of Mull at 08.00 the following morning. At midday, after exercising her boarding party crews in boat drill, she weighed anchor again and continued her journey north.

Once out of sight of land, the Captain ordered the 12 pdr gun crews to close up for gunnery practice. This was the first time that the King Orry had fired her two 12 pdr guns since commissioning as a warship.

Now officially on war patrol, she was soon involved in what were to become her daily duties for the foreseeable future.

At 15.40, she stopped and boarded the Danish fishing vessel, the Carcidis, while at 18.20 she stopped another

Danish fishing vessel, the Paulus. Both vessels were inspected and found to be clear of contraband and in possession of the correct papers and were allowed to continue on their way.

The King Orry was making a slow passage to the Orkney Islands and did not pass Cape Wrath at the north-western tip of Scotland until 17.00 on 29th November.

At 22.55 she was met by an armed trawler at the southern-most entrance to Scapa Flow and duly escorted through the anti-submarine boom that stretched across Switha Sound after which she anchored off the island of Flotta and remained there over night.

SCAPA FLOW

Before continuing with the story of the King Orry's war service, it is necessary to describe Scapa Flow, and the Orkney Islands and explain their importance as a naval base during the First World War.

The Orkney Islands, which encompass Scapa Flow lie some 8 to 10 miles off the northern coast of Scotland, being separated by a notorious stretch of water known as

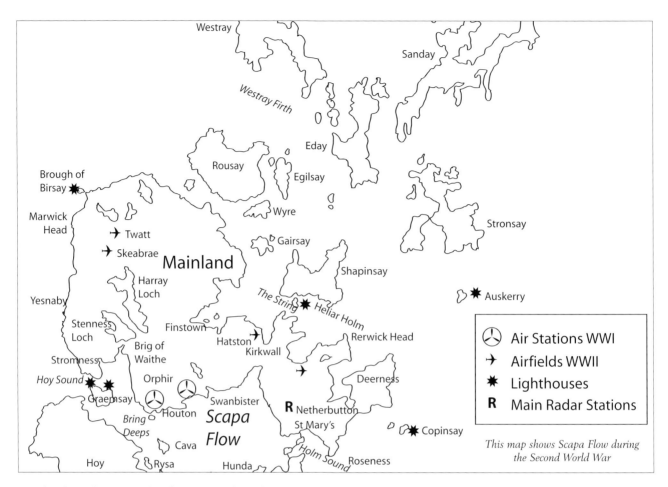

This map shows Scapa Flow during the Second World War

Pentland Firth. On a bright sunny day, the coast of Scotland can be clearly seen from the south of the Orkney group. However, when the wind blows in from the Atlantic and whips up the waters of Pentland Firth, the islands may as well be a thousand miles out to sea. Scapa Flow is a large inland sea approximately 120 square miles in area and almost totally surrounded by the southern islands of the Orkney group, the main islands being mainland Orkney, Hoy, Burray and South Ronaldsay. In the early part of the last century there were three main entrances, Hoy Sound to the west, Hoxa Sound to the South and Holm Sound to the east.

The importance of Scapa Flow as a protected anchorage had been known since the days of the Vikings, who had used its sheltered waters as a base for their longships, which raided Scotland and the Western Isles.

During the Napoleonic Wars and the 1812 war with the United States, the Royal Navy had anchored its warships in the Flow to protect the United Kingdom's northern trade routes from both French and American warships which roamed these waters looking for solitary British merchant ships to plunder and sink.

As the threat offered by the expanding German Empire at the turn of the 20th century began to grow, it became apparent that their mighty High Seas Fleet would be able to gain easy access to the Atlantic from both its Baltic and North Sea bases and then wreak havoc against British shipping.

As the Admiralty once against realised the importance of patrolling the northern waters around the United Kingdom, Scapa Flow came back into the limelight as a fleet anchorage. From this northern base, the Royal Navy could easily patrol the North Sea and the approaches to the Baltic Sea to intercept the Germans, if they dared to venture from their bases and approach the British coast or interfere with her trade routes. Elements of the fleet began to use Scapa Flow again on a regular basis, for example, in 1910 the Commander in Chief of the Atlantic Fleet, Admiral Lord Louis Battenburg anchored his huge fleet of over ninety warships in the sheltered waters of Scapa Flow for a few days during a period of fleet manoeuvres.

Over the next four years, the future of Scapa Flow as a naval base was discussed on many occasions and each time it was agreed that plans should be put into force to protect its entrances. Sadly after each round of discussion, little work to defend Scapa Flow actually took place apart from the provision of a few 4.7" and 6" guns as coastal defence.

When war was declared in August 1914, the entrances to Scapa Flow were still largely undefended, which gave grave concern to Admiral Sir George

Callaghan, the Commander in Chief of the recently renamed Grand Fleet.

However, by the time that the *King Orry* arrived in Scapa Flow at the end of November 1914, some action had been taken to protect the fleet anchorage from enemy intruders, especially German submarines. The eastern entrance to Scapa Flow, Holm Sound, had been blocked by sinking blockships (redundant merchant ships) across its entire width. This was in fact achieved by sinking the vessels in the narrow channels between mainland Orkney, the two small islands in the centre of Holm Sound (Lamb Holm and Glims Holm) and Burray. To complete the blocking of the eastern channel, further blockships had been sunk between Burray and South Ronaldsay. On the other side of Scapa Flow in Hoy Sound, Burra Sound, which is the narrow channel between Graemsay and Hoy, had also been closed with blockships.

With Holm Sound now completely blocked and Hoy Sound partially blocked, rudimentary anti-submarine boom defences had been laid across the remainder of Hoy Sound, Hoxa and Switha Sounds and these would be improved as the war progressed. The Royal Navy had established its headquarters at the Longhope Hotel, which sat on the shoreline of Longhope, a narrow sound at the southern end of Scapa Flow.

LONGHOPE

On the morning of their first day in Scapa Flow, 30th November 1914, the *King Orry's* crew were called from their sleep at 06.00 to be met with a bitterly cold wind and driving rain which was to become the familiar weather pattern for the next four years.

At 08.00 a signal was received from the Commander in Chief on board the battleship *Iron Duke* instructing the *King Orry* to proceed to anchor at Longhope which was to become her permanent base while operating from Scapa Flow.

The remainder of her first day at Scapa Flow was to be very busy. At midday, the Captain, Lt Cdr Selwyn Day proceeded to the fleet repair ship *Cyclops*, to meet Vice Admiral Sir George Warrender. The *Cyclops* was the headquarters ship for the armed boarding vessels operating out of Scapa Flow. During this meeting the *King Orry's* Captain was informed of the duties on which his ship was to be employed and given sealed orders detailing her forthcoming operations.

The Fleet Surgeon boarded the *King Orry* at 13.00 and inspected the ship's company, which resulted in Able Seaman Jackson being sent to the hospital ship *Plassey*, suffering from venereal disease.

At 15.00, having returned from the *Cyclops*, the Captain escorted the Commanding Officer of the fleet repair ship *Assistance* on an inspection tour around the *King Orry*. The *Assistance* provided all of the engineering support to keep vessels such as the *King Orry* in a seaworthy and fully-operational state. She passed this inspection with flying colours.

As the afternoon drew to a close, the collier *Mercedes* came alongside to commence delivering coal while the *Scandinavia* supplied 80 tons of fresh water. It was naval policy to darken ship at dusk which meant that all Upper Deck lighting was extinguished and all windows and portholes covered. "Darken ship" was ordered at 16.00 and this routine would continue each day throughout the *King Orry's* naval service although the time varied according to the actual time of dusk as the year progressed.

The following morning heralded another busy day and following divisions and morning prayers at 09.00, all hands were involved in helping to coal ship.

This particularly arduous and dirty task continued all day and was finally completed at 20.00, the work during the latter hours being carried out in virtual darkness. A total 196 tons of coal had been loaded during the day at approximately 10 tons per hour. Although coaling was now complete, the work was not over as it took the crew another two hours to wash down the decks and remove all of the residual coal dust and it was not until just after midnight that the exhausted men were allowed to go to their mess decks.

The *King Orry* lay at anchor in Longhope throughout 2nd December 1914, the only occurrence recorded in her log being the landing of Sub Lieutenant Robert Sharpley to the *Assistance* for medical treatment.

A severe gale greeted the crew as they awoke on the morning of 3rd December. They were immediately called to their own parts of ship to commence securing items of equipment that were in danger of being blown overboard.

Although the *King Orry* was secure inside Scapa Flow, the usually calm waters had been whipped up into a frenzy. As the morning progressed, a naval tender, the *Jessie* was blown onto the rocks and wrecked.

By 11.00, the *King Orry* had begun to drag her anchor and the crew were called to harbour stations and Engineer Lieutenant John Keig ordered to raise steam and put the engines slow ahead to relieve the pressure on the anchor cable. The gale reached its peak halfway through the afternoon and at one time the Captain considered weighing anchor and proceeding out of Longhope into Scapa Flow, where he would be able to steam the *King Orry* slowly up and down in relatively open water. The gale suddenly subsided and at about 18.00 and within an hour all evidence of the storm had gone.

The crew of the *King Orry* were allowed to fall out from their harbour stations and relax, although few of them went to their mess decks before 22.00 as the *King Orry* was putting to sea the next morning and final preparations had to be completed.

THE FIRST PATROL

Call the hands was at 06.00 on 4th December, with breakfast being completed and the ship's company closed up at harbour stations by 08.00 The anchor was weighed just before 09.00 and the *King Orry* slowly moved away from the anchorage. Having picked up an escort vessel to take her through the anti-submarine boom, she began to pick up speed.

It was necessary to pass through the boom at a fairly fast pace as it was feared that a submarine might be capable of creeping through the boom entrance below a slow moving ship. A ship moving quickly through the boom gate reduced the time that the gate was open, therefore reducing the likelihood of a submarine being able to slip through.

Having cleared the boom, the ship turned south and passed Swona Island before heading out into Pentland Firth. Her Captain, Lt Cdr Day, noted in the log that he was pleased that the *King Orry's* first exit from the anchorage had been trouble-free as he was certain that the Captain from the *Cyclops* would have been watching.

Once clear of Scapa Flow, the *King Orry* began to roll in the heavy swell of the Pentland Firth. It had been a calm trip up to the Orkney Islands from Birkenhead and many of the crew had not yet experienced any rough seas but within an hour they began to realise that they were not old sea dogs and began to feel unwell.

For those who wished to eat, lunch was served early, as the 12 pdr gun crews were to have their first shoot at a target just after midday. The target, which was a huge floating wooden structure, was being towed by the Admiralty tug *Stoic* which was waiting for the *King Orry* off Dunnett Head, some 12 miles west of the southern entrance to Scapa Flow. The forward 12 pdr gun was the first to fire, followed very quickly by the after gun.

Although both guns had fired a few rounds on the way up to the Orkneys, neither gun crew had actually shot at anything. Their gunnery was very erratic at first, but after about a dozen rounds per gun the accuracy improved and shells began to fall all around the target. The shoot was terminated at 15.00 after expending 20 rounds per gun. The Chief Gunner's Mate, Chief Petty Officer Jarvis informed the Captain that he was happy with the gunnery and that the gun crews could now be relied upon.

The *King Orry* was due to remain at sea overnight in order that her lookouts and boat crews could be

*Chief Petty Officer Wireless Telegraphy Operator Crispen Redshaw standing alongside the **King Orry's** after 12 Pdr gun: Scapa Flow 1915. (David Handscombe collection)*

exercised in the dark. As the night progressed, the *King Orry* exercised with an armed trawler. The trawler would crawl through the water so as not to make any wake, while the *King Orry's* lookouts would attempt to find her. Once she was found, she would be illuminated by searchlight and ordered to stop. The guns would be trained on her while the boarding party rowed across in one of the heavy lifeboats. As the *King Orry* wallowed in the heavy swell, an unforeseen hazard was identified, which had the potential to seriously damage one of the lifeboats as it manoeuvred back alongside the ship in order to be hoisted back onboard. The lifeboats were in danger of being damaged by the heavy wooden belting that protruded from the *King Orry's* side. If a wave lifted the boat up and smashed it against, or jammed it under the belting, the boat could be severely damaged with the possibility of injuring or throwing the crew into the sea. A solution to this danger would have to be found soon. The remainder of the night went without further incident.

The following morning, 6th December was overcast and a wind had whipped up from the north. After breakfast, the gun crews were exercised again and on this occasion demonstrated some very acceptable shooting at the target. The *King Orry* proceeded back to her

KING ORRY 1913-1940

anchorage in Longhope at just after 14.00, anchoring adjacent to another armed boarding vessel, the Great Eastern Railway's former North Sea ferry *Amsterdam*. The weather in Pentland Firth had become very unpleasant as the *King Orry* had made her way back home and by late afternoon a full-scale gale was forecast. At 18.00, as the crew of the *King Orry* settled down to a night in harbour, a signal was received from the *Cyclops* ordering her to proceed out of Scapa Flow and commence a patrol off Cape Wrath. The vessel that should have taken this patrol was the former Steam Packet vessel *Ramsey* but she had developed engine trouble and could not put to sea.

This was to be the *King Orry's* first actual war patrol and the ship was soon a hive of activity as the boilers were hastily brought back up to pressure while the Chief Gunner's Mate inspected the 12 pdr ammunition lockers to ensure that they were full.

At just after 19.00, the *King Orry* weighed anchor and slipped out of Longhope, passed through the anti-submarine boom and entered Pentland Firth. As soon as she was clear of the windbreak offered by the island of Hoy, she met the full force of the storm.

Turning westwards towards Cape Wrath, she buried her bows into mountainous waves and rolled heavily from side to side. Almost at once, the canvas awning on

*Lt Cdr Selwyn Day RNR, the **King Orry's** Commanding Officer between November 1914 and November 1916. (David Handscombe collection)*

the port bridge wing was torn away by a wave that crashed over the bridge, leaving the lookout exposed to the full force of the gale, soaking wet and cold. He made a hasty retreat to the safety of the bridge but was quickly reprimanded by the officer of the watch and sent back to his exposed position.

The *King Orry* pressed on towards Cape Wrath at a very slow pace and a large number of her crew were seasick. The continual downpour of waves onto the forecastle had caused some damage to the caulking between the deck planks and water was beginning to find its way into the decks below, the most worrying being the water that was now swirling around the low hatch leading to the forward magazine. Although this did not represent any immediate danger, should the ammunition get wet it would probably be rendered useless, which was not ideal on board an operational warship. Although Cape Wrath was only about 60 miles from the Orkney Islands, it took the *King Orry* until dawn the next day to reach the allocated patrol area.

It remained rough all day on 7th December and the *King Orry* sustained some damage to her forward superstructure, caused by the continual battering from the sea. Each time she reversed her course to back track her patrol line, she rolled so heavily that water crashed onto her Shelter Deck and poured down into the mess decks below, making life for the sailors who lived there wet and miserable.

No ships were sighted on this first complete day of the patrol and even if a suspect ship had been stopped, it would have been too dangerous to lower a boat to inspect her, which would have meant that the *King Orry* would have had to escort it into the nearest port. The crew may have found this prospect very appealing, but it would have meant that the patrol area would be left unobserved for many hours. As dusk was overtaken by night, the *King Orry* left her allotted patrol area and made her way south towards the shelter of Loch Ewe, on the west coast of Scotland.

With the sea now behind her she made fairly good time and anchored in the Loch at 07.00 on 8th December. The ship now looked a bit of a sorry state, the buffeting from the sea had removed some of the grey paint from her sides and the underlying black paint from her Steam Packet days showed through in many places. The decks below the forecastle were awash, although the magazine was still dry. After making a few emergency repairs and attempting to clear the lower decks of water, the *King Orry* weighed anchor at 10.30 and proceeded back to sea. Fortunately by the time she left Loch Ewe, the gale off Cape Wrath had subsided and the sea state was becoming smoother, although it was nowhere near being a beautiful calm day.

King Orry

*The **King Orry's** officers and senior ratings 1915 (David Handscombe collection)*

As she drew abeam of Handa Island (a few miles south west of Cape Wrath), a small trawler came into view. The vessel was immediately challenged, but failed to reply and continued on her way to the west. The log records that the *King Orry* took chase at just after 13.00 and quickly over hauled the small trawler. With her forward 12 pdr gun pointed at the offending vessel, the Captain of the *King Orry* ordered the trawler to stop utilising the ship's loud hailer. Not surprisingly, the trawler obeyed and, the *King Orry's* boarding party pulled away from the ship's side to carry out an inspection of their first catch.

The trawler turned out to be British, the *Andrew* from Hull. As her papers were in order and her holds contained only fish, she was given permission to continue with her fishing. After presenting the *King Orry's* Chief Cook with a basket of frozen fish and her skipper being advised not to ignore the signals from a British warship in the future, the trawler sailed off over the horizon

The remainder of the day was fruitless, as was 9th December. The *King Orry* steamed up and down a parallel from Cape Wrath to the Butt of Lewis, the northern point on the Island of Lewis in the Outer Hebrides for most of the day, but moved down towards

Loch Ewe again as dusk neared. During the afternoon, The Captain had sent a coded message back to Admiral Warrender at Scapa Flow informing him of the damage that the *King Orry* had sustained during the gale of 6th - 7th December.

Remaining at sea overnight, the *King Orry* cruised around between the entrance to Loch Ewe and the Shiant Islands, which lay off the Island of Lewis.

MERSEY BOUND

At 06.00 on 10th December, a signal was received from the *Cyclops* ordering the *King Orry* to proceed to Birkenhead for repairs. The message that the *King Orry* was to proceed to Birkenhead soon spread around the ship and the crew, now recovered from their storm battering and seasickness, began to look forward to a run ashore in Liverpool. The *King Orry* headed south at 18 knots with the intention of making the River Mersey before dawn the following day.

During the afternoon, the 12 pdr guns were exercised again, this time firing four rounds per gun. As dusk approached, she passed the Mull of Galloway and sped towards Morecambe Bay and Liverpool. Having made a very good time on the passage south, she approached the

*The **King Orry** alongside the dock wall in the Cammell Laird basin during December 1914. Note the bridge wing houses being constructed.*
(Wirral Museum Service/Cammel Laird Archive)

Bar at the mouth of the River Mersey at 23.30 and stopped to pick up the pilot, Captain John Sharp. After moving slowly up the river, she anchored off the Formby Light at 01.35 and remained there until 03.00 when she received orders to proceed to Birkenhead and Cammell Laird's yard.

At 04.10 she passed through the gate, which led into the shipyard basin. As she moved towards her berth, the steamship *Constantino* was manoeuvring to position herself to pass into the river. In the half-light of dawn, the distance between and the direction in which the *Constantino* was moving was misjudged by the *King Orry's* officer of the watch.

Before any evasive action could be taken, the *King Orry* was across the *Constantino's* bow and both ships collided, the *King Orry* being struck amidships on her port side.

Fortunately, as the *Constantino* had little headway, the damage to both ships was minimal and only minor damage was caused to the *King Orry's* port belting. Having extracted herself from under the other ship's bow, the *King Orry* was secured alongside the dock wall by 06.00.

Within minutes of the gangway being put ashore, officials from Cammell Laird's Shipyard and the Admiralty came on board and met with the Captain and

*The **King Orry's** Boat Deck showing the absence of her forward lifeboat davits: Scapa Flow 1915. (David Handscombe collection)*

Eng Lt Keig to discuss the repairs and modifications that would be carried out to the vessel. Although the *King Orry* was a sturdy ship, she had only been designed to remain at sea for limited periods within the Irish Sea. The Irish Sea could be a very rough, especially in the winter months, but the conditions that the *King Orry* would meet while operating from the Orkney Islands bore no reseblance to those encountered on the routes which the Isle of Man Steam Packet normally operated.

Dockyard workers began to stream on board shortly after the meeting between the ship's officers and Cammell Laird officials was over, as all of the repairs and intended modifications had to be completed within 10 days. The Fore Deck was sanded down and the missing caulking between the planking replaced.

How the water leaked into the compartments below the forecastle as a result of missing caulking between the planking is a mystery. The *King Orry* had a steel deck underneath the forecastle planking, which presumably was designed to be watertight. It is possible that the entry in her ship's log relating to the missing caulking and water leaking into the compartments below the forecastle are not related. It is not uncommon for water to enter a ship through ventilation trunking that had not been closed correctly or did not have any form of watertight cover.

However, even if the water leaking into the forward compartments was not related to the missing caulking between the planking, the fact that salt water was able to get underneath the planks would eventually cause corrosion problems to the steel deck. Remembering the incident when the canvas awning protecting the port bridge wing was ripped away by the wind, the exposed positions of the bridge wing lookouts was given a high priority. To this end, it was decided to construct wooden bridge wing houses on both bridge wings and install a crow's nest on the foremast. Work commenced to build these on that first morning in Birkenhead.

The small searchlight on the bridge roof had proved inadequate and was replaced by a larger model, which incorporated a Morse signal lamp.

The ship's heavy rolling and the potential danger to the other boats from the protruding belting has previously been discussed. This resulted in a decision to remove four of her lifeboats in an attempt to reduce top weight. On the starboard side of the boat deck, the most forward two boats and their davits were removed (boats 1 and 3), while on the port side the first lifeboat (boat 2) and its davit was removed. The second lifeboat (boat 4) was also removed, but the davit was retained. In place of the lifeboat, a 27ft whaler sea boat was installed as it had been agreed that the *King Orry's* heavy lifeboats were not ideal for boarding party use.

For a length of some 50 feet, the belting below life boats 5 and 7 on the starboard side and the 27ft whaler and number 6 lifeboat on the port side was removed, thus leaving a large gap through which the boats could now be safely lowed and hoisted.

All of the accommodation areas, including the officers' cabins, which were located on the Promenade Deck, had been affected by seawater ingress during the severe gales. Considerable work was carried out to ensure that in future these areas remained free from water, should the *King Orry* again encounter weather conditions like she had on 6th and 7th December.

In the crew's mess decks, the improvement work consisted of removing the peacetime wooden doors from the entrance foyers and replacing them with proper watertight doors.

By 14th December, the new searchlight was installed and the work on removing the lifeboats and their davits completed. While the dockyard employees were working 24 hours a day to get the *King Orry* completed and back to sea to resume her duties, her ship's company were enjoying the brief spell away the barren Orkney Islands.

Except when they were on duty, the crew were allowed ashore each evening and most behaved themselves. Unfortunately, two ratings were in trouble as a result of over drinking, Pte Williams of the RMLI was

*Looking down from the **King Orry's** funnel onto her bridge roof and signal deck: Scapa Flow 1915. (David Handscombe collection)*

involved in a fight and received 28 days detention while Able Seaman A Anderson was demoted to the rank of Ordinary Seaman for drunkenness.

The hard work and effort put in to the repairs and modifications to the *King Orry* paid dividends for by 18th December the majority of the work had been completed. The last two jobs that required to be undertaken were the installation of cutlass racks in the cross passage on the Promenade Deck and the repainting of the hull and superstructure. Although the cutlass was almost obsolete, the Royal Navy still considered it a formidable weapon for boarding parties, especially as hand-to-hand fighting was not uncommon if the crew of the boarded vessel decided to resist.

During the morning of 19th December, a collier came alongside and refilled the *King Orry's* stoke holds.

As dusk approached on 21st December, a shipyard foreman came on board and informed the Captain that all work on the *King Orry* was now finished, the repainting of the hull and superstructure being completed that morning. Having had this good news, no time was lost in making preparations for the ship to proceed back to sea.

The next high water was at 01.30 and the Captain decided to take advantage of this and move the *King Orry* out of the basin and back into the River Mersey. The boilers were lit and steam pressure was built up, by midnight the Chief Engineer informed the Captain that he had a full head of steam and that the *King Orry* was ready to move.

The pilot, Captain Anderson, came on board at 01.00 and by 02.15 the *King Orry* had passed through the dock gates and out into the river. Turning her bow towards the open sea, the *King Orry* proceeded down river towards the Bar Lightship, which was passed at 03.40. Once she was clear of the Lightship and the buoyed channel, the anchor was dropped to allow the mandatory compass swing to be carried out. Satisfied that all was well, the pilot was dropped at 07.10, after which the *King Orry* weighed anchor and proceeded out of Liverpool Bay, heading north towards her base at Scapa Flow now ready to resume her duties as an armed boarding vessel.

CHRISTMAS 1914

Throughout 22nd December, the ship raced up the coast of Scotland and rounded Cape Wrath by mid-morning the following day, eventually arriving back at Scapa Flow and anchoring in Longhope at 13.30.

As Christmas was only two days away, the Captain was pleased to inform the ship's company that the *King Orry* would not be required for duty until after the festivities and that they should take advantage of the break and enjoy themselves. The mess decks were

*Looking aft from the **King Orry's** forepeak showing the forward 12 pdr gun with its barrel trained to starboard: Scapa Flow February 1915. (David Handscombe collection)*

decorated and made to look as homely as possible, while the Chief Cook and his team made ready the Christmas turkeys and puddings, all of which had been obtained while the ship was in Birkenhead.

As Christmas Day dawned, the festive occasion was made complete when a blizzard covered the decks of the *King Orry* with a film of snow. The crew were not called from their bunks and hammocks until 08.00, as it was traditional for Christmas Day to be as relaxed as possible. While the crew rested in their mess decks, most of them probably thought of their loved ones far away at home, and no doubt wished that there had been some truth in the prediction that the war would be over by Christmas.

Christmas lunch was served at midday with the Captain and officers following the long-standing naval tradition of serving the meal to the crew. As the afternoon wore on, most people on board had retired to their bunks or hammocks as the effects of the large meal and the potency of the rum, which laced the Christmas pudding, took its toll.

Sadly, at 17.00, all of the enjoyment of Christmas Day was suddenly wiped away. In a flurry of signals and bugle calls, the fleet, which lay at anchor within Scapa Flow, was called to action stations.

A trawler patrolling near the island of Flotta, which was within Scapa Flow, had sighted a suspicious object which looked like a submarine's periscope. Suspecting that it belonged to a German U boat, destroyers and patrol boats began to race about dropping explosive charges.

The *King Orry's* crew toppled out of their bunks and hammocks and quickly closed up at their action stations, the guns were manned and preparations were made to weigh anchor.

After an hour and a half of activity and no trace of a U boat, it was decided that the 'periscope' was probably a seal or similar animal and the fleet was ordered to stand down. On board the *King Orry*, the crew returned to their mess decks to resume what remained of Christmas Day.

FALKLAND ISLANDS

However, not all of the news about the war was glum. Details were now being released of a great naval victory against units of the German navy operating in the South Atlantic. On 8th December 1914, Vice Admiral Sir Doveton Sturdee had wreaked revenge upon the Germans for the sinking of the cruisers *Good Hope* and *Monmouth* at the Battle of Coronel on 1st November.

Having been ordered to the South Atlantic to hunt the German squadron down, his ships which comprised of the powerful battle cruisers *Invincible* and *Inflexible*, plus five cruisers and the armed merchant cruiser *Macedonia*, finally caught up with the enemy off the Falkland Islands.

In a very one-sided action, the German heavy cruisers *Gneisenau* and *Scharnhorst* in addition to the light cruisers *Leipzig* and *Nurnberg* were quickly dispatched to the bottom of the South Atlantic.

The sole survivor of Admiral Graf von Spee's squadron, the *Dresden*, escaped only to be caught and scuttled at Juan Fernandez Island on 14th March 1915.

News such as this did much to boost the morale of the men in the Royal Navy.

THE YEAR ENDS

Boxing Day 1914 was cold and bleak. At 09.00 the *King Orry* was ordered to raise steam and proceed out of Scapa Flow and anchor in Kirkwall Bay where she was to remain at two hours notice to steam. This was achieved by 13.30 when she anchored adjacent to the armed boarding vessel *Royal Scot*.

Both ships remained at Kirkwall throughout remainder of the day and all of the following day, the only significant entry in the ship's log being the award of 12 days stoppage of pay to Stoker Wallace for being absent without leave a couple of days previously.

The order to weigh anchor and put to sea came early on the morning on 28th December. At 06.00, in company with the armed boarding vessels *Royal Scot* and *Duke of Cornwall*, the *King Orry* proceeded up the eastern coast of the Orkney Islands to patrol the sea area up towards the Shetland Islands.

*The Poop Deck of the **King Orry** following the removal of the after 12 pdr gun from the Promenade Deck and the installation of the two 4" guns during August 1915. (David Handscombe collection) .*

King Orry

*The **King Orry** at anchor in Longhope, Scapa Flow during 1915. (David Handscombe collection)*

The three ships were strung out in a long line, each one visible to their neighbour but covering a distance of nearly twenty miles.

At just after 15.00, the *Royal Scot* which was at the extreme left, spotted a steamship heading in their direction. The *King Orry* being the fastest of the three vessels immediately gave chase with a view to putting a boarding party on board.

The steamship was soon overhauled and ordered to stop with the forward 12 pdr trained on her bridge to deter her Master from attempting to run.

The vessel turned out to be the Norwegian steamship, *Margaret*, outward bound from Oslo to Santos in Brazil. With some difficulty, the boarding party pulled across to the steamer in the whaler and eventually confirmed that the Norwegian's papers were in order and that she was not carrying any contraband.

After being warned to look out for German submarines, she was allowed to proceed on her way. At 16.30, the trawler *A476* from Aberdeen was stopped and inspected before also being allowed to resume her voyage, this time to Lerwick in the Shetland Islands. The remainder of the day proved fruitless as far as sighting shipping was concerned.

After spending another night at sea, the three armed boarding vessels returned to Scapa Flow, anchoring in Longhope at just after 06.00. At 08.30, the collier *Mercedes* came alongside and commenced rebunkering the *King Orry*. This continued throughout the day and all through the night, finally finishing at 08.00 on 30th December.

The armed boarding vessels based at Scapa Flow were to have a very hard war. Most of them had been built for seasonal holiday traffic and as a result had not been designed for deep-sea service. Their crews were to suffer many hardships as they took on the ferocious gales that were common in these northern waters. In the early part of the war, they operated in three main patrol areas, known as the Eastern Patrol, Western Patrol and the Northern Patrol.

The Eastern Patrol reached out from Orkney towards the coast of Norway and Denmark and then down into the North Sea to a line approximately level with the Skagerrak, the entrance to the Baltic Sea.

The Western Patrol stretched from the Orkney Islands to beyond the Outer Hebrides while the Northern Patrol was the most unpleasant as it reached out to far beyond the Shetland and Faroe Islands.

In all these areas, especially in the winter months, the crews could expect continual gales and freezing weather. The mountainous seas that continually crashed down onto the decks, managed to find entry points into every part of the ship, leaving the mess decks awash with water.

The only consolation that the crew on the *King Orry* had was the knowledge that the destroyer and trawler crews fared much worse.

With the exception of some of the officers, the majority of the *King Orry's* crew were peacetime Royal Naval volunteer reservists, who prior to the war had probably only mustered at their training centre a couple of times a month. Now many of them were beginning to learn that life in the Royal Navy was not all the fun that they had believed it was when they paraded in their uniforms for a couple of hours in the evening, or attended the odd course at one of the navy's training ships.

The armed boarding vessels were hard pressed ships as they had a large area of the ocean to cover on a daily basis. The average time spent on patrol was usually two to three days, with often only 24 hours in harbour before commencing the next patrol.

After two or three consecutive patrols, a period of about 5 days in harbour was normally given. The *King Orry* put to sea again on the afternoon of 30th December in company with the elderly cruiser *Sappho*.

It had become common practice for an armed boarding vessel and a cruiser to work together, as it would provide the lightly-armed former merchant ships with a heavy backup should they encounter a disguised German raider.

The cruiser would position herself just over the horizon ready to race up and support the armed boarding vessel if required. As will be described later, the lack of this arrangement on 8th August 1915 was to have disastrous results on one of the *King Orry's* running mates.

1915

The two ships remained at sea throughout New Year's Eve without sighting another vessel, arriving back at Longhope in the early hours of New Year's Day 1915.

The bunkers on board the *King Orry* had only been designed for service in the Irish Sea and were therefore not particularly large and the requirement to take on coal every two or three days was to restrict the ship from taking part in extended patrols throughout her naval service. It was now common practice for a collier to meet the ship as soon as she anchored in Longhope.

On this New Year's Day she was met by the collier *Hollinside*. The next few days were spent swinging around the buoy at Longhope and it was not until 08.15 on 4th January that the *King Orry* proceeded to sea on patrol, once again with the cruiser *Sappho*.

The weather was still bitterly cold, although the sea state had calmed down slightly, compared with the severe gales encountered during the previous month.

FALSE ALARMS

At just after 11.00 the following day, 5th January, the steam ship *Colonia* was ordered to stop by the *King Orry*. The Captain of this vessel either failed to see the signal or decided to ignore it as the *Colonia* made no attempt to stop.

Fearing that the *Colonia* may be about to make an attempt to break the blockade being imposed against Germany and make a run for it, the *King Orry's* Captain gave the order to fire a shot across the bows of the suspect vessel. Within seconds of the shell exploding in the water, just a few yards ahead of the *Colonia*, the vessel indicated that she was stopping.

The boarding party was mustered and they were soon pulling away from the side of the *King Orry* in the 27ft whaler towards the now hove-to steamer. The heavy swell and bitter wind made the journey in the open sea boat miserable, although the seamen were wrapped up in their heavy oilskin coats, they were soaked to the skin by the time that they reached the suspect vessel.

After the boarding party had clambered on board and searched the ship, her papers were found to be in order and her cargo matched the manifest. The *Colonia* turned out to be Norwegian, bound from Oslo to New York with a cargo of wood pulp for making paper. On this occasion the search had revealed nothing that was classed as contraband and the *Colonia* was allowed to proceed on her way. The *King Orry's* crew settled down to another wet and cold night at sea, the heavy swell caused the vessel to roll heavily and only the seasoned members of her crew were able to sleep with any comfort.

Dawn on 6th January heralded a bleak overcast day but the rough seas still persisted. It was a fruitless day and as dusk approached the Captain decided to make one final sweep across Pentland Firth before returning to Longhope the following morning.

At just after 19.00, as the *King Orry* was approaching the southern tip of Hoy, the lookout on the port bridge wing spotted a darkened ship creeping through the water about 2 miles away on port side. The vessel was close inshore and also appeared to be heading towards Pentland Firth.

The Captain was called to the bridge and informed about the vessel, whereupon he studied the darkened ship through a signalman's telescope. The ship appeared to be a merchant vessel and as such was outside of the designated sea lane that merchant ships were required to travel in when passing down the coast of the Orkney Islands. Was this a disguised German raider attempting to approach Scapa Flow and cause havoc amongst the unsuspecting shipping that regularly moved in and out of the Orkney anchorage?

The *King Orry* increased speed to 15 knots and turned towards the suspect ship. The crew were already at action stations as it was policy to close up gun crews at dawn and dusk which were considered to be the most dangerous parts of the day as the twilight made it too difficult to see clearly over a long distance.

The clanging of the heavy greased breechblocks on the 12 pdr guns confirmed that shells had already been loaded. The searchlight crew on the bridge roof were given instructions to illuminate the suspect vessel at a given signal which would be followed immediately by two ranging shots from the *King Orry's* main armament. The *King Orry* had closed to within just under a mile and still there was no sign of the other vessel altering course or even noticing that the *King Orry* was closing in.

At the appropriate moment, the Captain yelled out the given signal, the searchlight came on and its powerful beam swept across the waves towards the other vessel. A split second later, both the forward and after 12 pdr guns exploded into life. The two shots had been aimed to land in front of the suspect vessel, their phosphorescent white waterspouts showing up in the darkness as the shells exploded in the water. The breaches clanged shut, as the guns were made ready to fire again.

Now, as the *King Orry* illuminated the other vessel with her powerful searchlight, a challenge was flashed on her Morse signal lamp. To everyone's surprise the correct reply came to the challenge and as the searchlight's beam played along the superstructure of the suspect vessel, it illuminated the red white and blue of a Royal Navy White Ensign as it fluttered from the ensign staff at the vessel's stern.

The order to cease fire was given a split second before the 12 pdrs released a second salvo towards the unfortunate ship. The searchlight was extinguished as a signal message flashed across the water from the other vessel, identifying herself as the armed boarding vessel *Fiona*.

Apparently, the lookouts on board the *Fiona* had failed to sight the *King Orry* as she closed in to inspect their darkened ship. This was indeed a major failure on their behalf and must surely have resulted in disciplinary action being taken. A brief exchange of messages followed before the two ships parted company, the *Fiona* into Scapa Flow and the *King Orry* to continue her patrol. Although inexcusable, incidents like this were not uncommon in wartime, but fortunately as the *King Orry's* two shots had been primarily used to establish the range between the two vessels, no damage or loss of life had occurred. After this brief period of excitement, the remainder of the patrol was uneventful and the *King Orry* returned to her anchorage in Longhope at a few minutes before 10.00 the following morning, 7th January.

The collier *Mercedes* supplied coal to top up the ship's bunkers throughout the remainder of the day, after which the crew cleaned ship and loaded stores in preparation for the next patrol. After 48 hours in Longhope the *King Orry* sailed for her next patrol in company with the cruiser *Sappho* at 09.00 on 9th January. This patrol took place to the north of the Shetland Islands and would prove to be a busy period but it would not result in any contraband being seized.

At midday the American freighter, the *William Dawson* was stopped and boarded, while at just after midnight the following morning, the Norwegian vessel *Rio Del Plata* was stopped and searched. Both vessels were subsequently found to be carrying legal cargo and allowed to proceed on their way.

A former Steam Packet running mate, namely the armed boarding vessel *Ramsey* joined company with the *King Orry* at 04.00 and remained until midday, when she resumed her own patrol. These two former Manx vessels were to operate together on many occasions and friendships were formed between the two ship's companies although some officers and ratings were long-established friends from pre-war days when they served together in the Isle of Man Steam Packet.

The patrol continued into 11th January until at just past 02.30 the shadow of a vessel loomed into view through the dark overcast night.

A large sea swell was running so the concept of stopping the ship and sending over a boarding party was considered to be too dangerous. The cold, wet members of the gun crews were roused and called out from the minimal shelter that they had found adjacent to their guns and instructed to train their two 12 pdr guns on the other vessel. Similar to the incident with the *Fiona* a few days before, the searchlight was suddenly turned on and the forward 12 pdr fired a shot across the vessel's bow.

This time there was no hesitation and the suspect vessel quickly signalled that she was stopping although this did not deter the vigilance of the *King Orry's* gunners and lookouts as the possibility of the vessel being a German raider playing the part of a hapless merchantman to fool the Royal Navy had not been ruled out.

The vessel identified herself as the *Eidsvagg* of 298 tons, proceeding from Bergen to Burntisland in the Firth of Forth. As boarding the vessel was out of the question, the *King Orry* continued to illuminate her with the searchlight and ordered her to follow on a parallel course.

Full daylight occurred at 09.00 but sending over a boarding party was ruled out again as the sea swell was still very high causing both vessels to roll heavily.

The *Eidsvagg* had now been identified as Norwegian but as it had still not been confirmed whether she was carrying contraband or not, the decision to order her to proceed to Kirkwall in the Orkney Islands for proper inspection was made. The Captain of the *Eidsvagg* was

Engineer Lieutenant John Keig standing on the **King Orry's** *Promenade Deck in March 1915. (David Handscombe collection)*

not happy with this, and complained that he had been detained by the Royal Navy for long enough and indicated that he was about to ignore the *King Orry's* demands and resume his original course.

As the *Eidsvagg* began to alter course away from the *King Orry*, Lt Cdr Selwyn Day gave the order for the forward 12 pdr to fire another shot across the *Eidsvagg's* bow, while the after 12 pdr was aimed at her bridge. The required compliance with the *King Orry's* directive was achieved as the waterspout from the shot across her bow fell harmlessly into the sea and the *Eidsvagg* made a noticeable change of course and fell in line with the armed boarding vessel. The thought of a 12 pdr shell through his bridge had convinced her Captain to proceed to Kirkwall after all!

It took 24 hours for the two vessels to reach the Orkney capital before the *King Orry* dropped her anchor at 06.00 on 12th January and had a boarding party put onboard the *Eidsvagg* by 07.00. Sadly all of the hard work of the previous day had been fruitless and as the *Eidsvagg* was found to have the correct documents and free from contraband, she was allowed to resume her voyage to Burntisland.

Incidents like this did little to enthuse the tired crews of the armed boarding vessels and no doubt did even less to stimulate good relationships with the neutral Norwegian seamen who were still trying to earn a living.

REST PERIOD

The *King Orry* was now given a short rest period from patrol and she remained at Longhope until 22nd January. Although classed as a rest period, the crew still had to work throughout the day and keep watches at night. Guns were overhauled, decks scrubbed, painting carried out on the hull and superstructure, and mess decks dried out and cleaned. As well as these chores, coal, water, ammunition and stores were taken on board. When all these jobs were complete, the crews of the armed boarding vessels had little to look forward to in the form of entertainment if they were allowed shore leave.

There was a fleet canteen at Longhope, but this was nothing very special. In January, the weather in the Orkney Islands could be described as terrible with a few bad days.

The ships inside Scapa Flow were protected from the rough seas, but they still received the brunt of the bitter winds, driving rain, blizzards and snow.

A stroll ashore followed by a beer in the fleet canteen was often put off due to the thought of going ashore on the exposed decks of the duty fleet tender which was little more than a converted fishing boat. At times the levels of boredom could be so acute that many people took up hobbies to keep themselves entertained. Chief Petty Officer Crispen Redshaw was one of these and took up photography, using his Wireless Office as a darkroom when he was not required to man it for watch keeping.

As the *King Orry* swung round her anchor, an incident occurred at Longhope, which brought the realities of war rushing home to the crews of the ships anchored there.

On 13th January, the minesweeper *Roedean* was dealing with a couple of mines, which had broken adrift from one of the minefields and drifted into Longhope. Nobody was really certain what actually happened, but there was a huge explosion and when the smoke had cleared, the remains of the *Roedean* were sinking below the waters of the anchorage. The *King Orry's* log book does not record whether there where any survivors, but it is probable that there were.

DOGGER BANK

The break from duty came to and end at 08.25 on 22nd January, when in company with the cruiser *Sappho*, she returned to her patrol duties. They were joined the following day by the *Ramsey* and all three ships returned to Longhope on 24th January.

Meanwhile, as the *King Orry* and her consorts were returning to their anchorage, elements of the Grand Fleet were poised to inflict another blow against the German High Seas Fleet in an area of the North Sea that was previously only known as being a fishing ground, the Dogger Bank.

Since the commencement of hostilities the previous August, German warships had been dashing across the North Sea and bombarding English coastal towns: Yarmouth on 3rd November 1914 and Scarborough, Whitby and Hartlepool on 10th December 1914 being the worst hit.

Early on 23rd January 1915, British intelligence informed the Admiralty that they believed the Germans were about to strike again. Sure enough at 17.45 that evening a large raiding squadron under the command of Rear Admiral Scheer left its anchorage and sped across the North Sea. This squadron consisted of battle cruisers *Seydlitz*, *Moltke* and *Derfflinger*, the heavy cruiser *Bleucher*, four light cruisers and nineteen destroyers.

The Admiralty alerted Vice Admiral Sir David Beatty and Vice Admiral Sir George Warrender, instructing them to put to sea with their respective squadrons of warships. Beatty left Rosyth with the battle cruisers *Lion*, *Tiger*, *New Zealand*, *Princess Royal* and *Indomitable* while Warrender provided a further six Dreadnoughts. Both squadrons were backed up with cruisers and destroyers.

The two opposing fleets met at dawn on the following morning, 24th January. In the battle that ensued, the

British, with Beatty's battle cruisers leading, won a decisive although not crushing victory over the Germans. The German battle cruiser *Seydlitz* was badly damaged while the slower *Bleucher* was sunk with heavy loss of life. On the British side, Beatty's flagship *Lion* was badly damaged but with minimal loss of life.

As the second major battle in the North Sea between the powerful fleets of Britain and Germany died away, the British rejoiced that they were the victors yet again. For a second time the Germans had left the battlefield leaving the Royal Navy as master of the North Sea. The news of the victory at the battle of the Dogger Bank soon flashed around the ships at Scapa Flow and gave a brief respite from the misery of the isolated northern base.

THE WEATHER WORSENS

The *King Orry* was now back into the regular patrol pattern of two or three days on patrol, followed by one or two days in Longhope, or one of the other Orkney Island anchorages, before returning to sea to repeat the patrol cycle. Crew training was paramount not only to maintain levels of efficiency but also to keep the crews from becoming bored with the monotonous patrol routine.

While on patrol on 26th - 27th January, instruction in the use of the cutlass was given to the Royal Marines, seamen and stokers. During the First World War when the revolver, rifle and machine gun were in regular use within the Royal Navy, boarding parties armed with cutlass' and clubs, clambering over the side of an enemy vessel in the Nelson tradition was still considered to be a viable proposition. To this end, regular training was carried out within the fleet and especially on board the armed boarding vessels.

The next patrol, which commenced on 30th January was another busy period. On the first day at sea, the *King Orry* stopped and boarded four vessels: the Grimsby trawler *Ontario (GY213)*, the Aberdeen trawlers *A60* and *A103* and finally a Danish freighter *Kronstad*.

All four vessels were found to be free from contraband and allowed to proceed. On the following day the Swedish tramp steamer *Imita* and the Aberdeen trawler *A614* were stopped and inspected.

As the *King Orry* was returning from patrol, the weather suddenly deteriorated and whipped up into a gale which blew in from the North Atlantic.

By midday on 3rd February, the seas were so rough that the Captain decided to put into Inganess Bay, to the east of Kirkwall, rather than attempt to round the southern tip of South Ronaldsay and enter Scapa Flow.

Large waves were breaking over the forecastle, the canvas awning, which covered the forward 12 pdr gun,

had been ripped away and water was pouring down into the lower decks. Having anchored with some difficulty, the *King Orry* remained in Inganess Bay until the evening of 4th February when, during a brief lull in the storm, she succeeded in rounding South Ronaldsay and made her way to the anchorage in Longhope.

The storm whipped up into a frenzy again during the following day and as a precaution the second anchor was dropped and the Chief Engineer was ordered to maintain steam in the boiler in case it was necessary for the *King Orry* to get under way should her anchors start to drag.

At the height of the storm at 00.30 on 6th February, there was a terrific crash which rocked the *King Orry* violently, followed by a grating of steel against steel as something was dragged down the port side.

As the first members of the crew tumbled out onto the upper deck, the dark shape of a ship could be seen disappearing astern into the darkness, having passed down the port side from the bow. A quick examination of the *King Orry's* hull was called and this subsequently revealed a large dent in the bow plates on the port side, scrape marks down the whole side of the ship and damage to the wooden belting. Fortunately this was not too severe and did not warrant immediate repair.

The mystery ship turned out to be the destroyer *Contest* which had dragged her anchors and was out of control before her crew had time to take any action. She subsequently ended up running aground on Crockness Taing on the northern shore of Longhope.

The Admiralty fleet tug *Alliance* was sent to assist the stricken destroyer only to succeed in going aground herself as she attempted to pull the destroyer off the rocks. Both vessels were eventually refloated and found to be undamaged a few days later. As if the collision with the destroyer was not sufficient, on the following night the Tribal class destroyer *Eskimo* narrowly missed the *King Orry's* stern as she attempted to anchor adjacent to the armed boarding vessel.

The storm persisted for a few days but this did not stop the *King Orry* from commencing her next patrol on 8th February.

Once clear of the shelter offered by the Orkney coast, she began to bury her bow into the mountainous waves and it was not long before the continual pounding from the waves began to affect the armed boarding vessel. The caulking between the planking on the forecastle suffered damage again while seawater found its way into the compartments below.

A particularly large wave hit the *King Orry's* starboard side and damaged the hull plating, level with the Promenade Deck. Although the water that washed around the lower decks did not represent any danger to the ship's stability, it made life on board very unpleasant for the crew. Unable to effectively continue with her patrol, the *King Orry* was forced to return to Longhope the following day, 9th February.

The patrols for the remainder of the month proved fruitless with only one ship being stopped and boarded, the American freighter *Hutton* on 15th February.

On 20th February, as the ship was passing the small island of Swona, one of the bridge lookouts reported three sinister floating objects which looked like mines. The *King Orry* was put about and approached the objects very cautiously before a boat was put into the water and sent to investigate. The objects turned out to be three oil drums which had probably been washed off the upper deck of a ship during the recent storms. Although the oil drums were harmless they presented an ideal opportunity for some gunnery practice and were dispatched with the 12 pdr guns.

RETURN TO THE MERSEY

The *King Orry* received orders to proceed to Cammell Laird's shipyard at Birkenhead for repairs to her bow plating and foredeck on the morning of 22nd February.

The journey South commenced at 09.00 and she secured alongside Princes Landing Stage at Liverpool at 23.20 on 23rd February. The short trip across the river to Cammell Laird's shipyard was undertaken at 09.00 the following morning.

The *King Orry* remained at Cammell Laird's until 7th March during which time the damaged plating on the port bow and starboard Promenade Deck was removed and replaced. The planking on the forecastle was recaulked and finally the whole ship repainted.

Until now the crew had been called to action stations by the ship's public address system, or tannoy as the Royal Navy tended to call it. This was a very inefficient system as it had not been installed throughout the ship, only in the areas that had previously been occupied by the passengers and places such as the Engine and Boiler Rooms had to be informed by telephone or word of mouth. To this end, Cammell Laird installed action station alarm bells throughout the ship which were operated from the bridge.

DOUGLAS BAY

Leaving the Cammell Laird shipyard during the early afternoon on 7th March, the *King Orry* set a course which would take her close to the Isle of Man, as she proceeded north to Scapa Flow.

She passed up the east side of the Island and steamed into Douglas Bay, sounding her siren before steaming out past Onchan Head and resuming her journey.

This was the first time that the Manx people had been given the opportunity to see one of their steamers in the guise of one of His Majesty's warships and no doubt the Manxmen amongst the *King Orry's* crew felt homesick as they passed so near to their homeland.

Following her return to Scapa Flow, the *King Orry's* crew were given no time to rest and coaling from the collier *Mercedes* commenced as soon as the anchor was dropped, to be followed by an ammunition barge coming alongside to top up the magazines with 12 pdr shells.

As soon as the ammunition replenishment was complete and the coal dust had been washed from the decks, the Engine Room received orders to build up steam in preparation for proceeding on patrol.

After less than 24 hours at anchor in Longhope, the *King Orry* passed through the Switha Boom at just after 18.00 on 10th March. During the next 36 hours, she patrolled off the coast of Cape Wrath and stopped three suspect vessels. The Danish schooner *Nashakia* and the Norwegian barque *Minor* were inspected and allowed to proceed, while at 18.10 on 11th March, a shot was put across the bow of the Danish freighter *Yung King*.

This vessel was indeed found to be carrying contraband, but unfortunately for the crew of the *King Orry* she had already been arrested and a prize crew from the armed boarding vessel *Calyx* was on board.

On 17th March, whilst at anchor in Longhope, a signal was received from the *Cyclops* ordering the *King Orry's* crew to commence an immediate abandon ship drill.

The crew were mustered on deck and the lifeboats were lowered. With the exception of the duty watch, all of the crew descended into the lifeboats and had to complete a circuit of the ship before being allowed to return on board. Drills like this were unpopular but were necessary to ensure that the crew all knew what to do if their ship suddenly began to sink below them and they had to abandon ship in a hurry.

The patrols continued on a regular basis for the next few weeks, most of them in appalling weather.

While patrolling off Sinclairs Bay on the western coast of Scotland on 21st March, the *King Orry* fired on a vessel that failed to return her challenge. Like the incident a few weeks earlier with the *Fiona*, the suspect vessel turned out to be an armed boarding vessel - the *Orvieto*. Had the *King Orry* been a German raider, it would probably have been the end of her and no doubt the cause of the *Orvieto's* failure to respond to the challenge was poor watch keeping. The *King Orry's* Captain recorded his comments in the log book: "Laxity in watch keeping must be treated as a very serious offence as it puts the safety of the whole ship's company at risk".

Two more freighters, the *Borgland* and the *Normandie*, were stopped on 22nd March, while the steamer *Japan* was escorted into Kirkwall on 26th March.

While passing out through the Switha Boom on 28th March, the *King Orry* had a confrontation with an old assailant when she collided with the destroyer *Contest*. The ship's log does not record who was at fault, but damage was caused to the *King Orry's* port side, including the Shelter Deck screen, although it did not stop her from proceeding on patrol.

The following day, 29th March was unusually calm with a sea fog. At 13.00, almost like the *Mary Celeste*, a barque loomed out of the mist a mere few hundred yards ahead of the *King Orry*, causing her to alter course rather quickly to avoid a collision.

The sailing ship turned out to be the Norwegian vessel *Anaconda* which was duly boarded and searched, and because there appeared to be a false bulkhead in one of her holds, she was escorted into Kirkwall for a thorough inspection. This revealed nothing sinister and she was eventually allowed to proceed.

In a period when trans-Atlantic liners were steaming across the seas at high speed and Super Dreadnoughts ruled the waves, sailing vessels such as the *Anaconda* seemed to belong to another world.

April 1915 passed without any incidents and included a 10-day break from patrol duty.

On 7th May 1915, as the *King Orry* lay at anchor in Longhope, an incident occurred that shocked the world. A German U boat operating in the Irish Sea off the coast of Southern Ireland torpedoed and sank the Cunard liner, *Lusitania*. In 18 minutes, the 32.000 ton liner disappeared beneath the Irish Sea taking 1.198 passengers and crew with her, many of them neutral Americans.

A SUCCESSFUL PATROL

Many of the U boats that were operating around the coast of Great Britain were based at Germany's Baltic Sea ports and entered the North Sea via the Skagerrak. As most of these U boats only had a limited endurance, it was suspected that German supply ships might be operating in the North Sea, especially off the coast of Denmark and Norway. In an attempt to seek out these supply ships, the *King Orry* and her consorts were given patrols further afield and were sent to cruise off the coasts of Norway and Denmark.

At 14.15 on the afternoon of 10th May, the *King Orry* was operating off the Skagerrak, the entrance to the Baltic Sea. The sea was rough but the visibility was good. A lookout, high up in the crow's nest on the foremast, informed the officer of the watch that he had spotted a ship, which appeared to be a tanker some distance away.

Having informed the Captain, the officer of the watch instructed the Engine Room to bring the *King Orry* up to 18 knots, while he plotted a course that would intercept the other ship.

The tanker's crew must have seen the *King Orry* approaching and she altered course away from the speeding armed boarding vessel, perhaps hoping to make the neutral waters of Norway. With black smoke billowing from her funnel, the *King Orry* soon began to overhaul the tanker and the Captain ordered the forward 12 pdr gun to put a shot across her bow.

Not surprisingly this achieved immediate results and the tanker stopped her engines and hove to. The *King Orry* circled the ship which was flying a Norwegian flag but had no port of registration on her stern, only the name *Energie*.

A boarding party consisting of Royal Marines and seamen was mustered, issued with rifles and sent across to the tanker in the 27ft whaler and a lifeboat.

In due course the Boarding Officer reported that although the tanker was full of fuel, her papers did not appear to be correct which led him to believe that she may be a German supply ship as most of the instruction posters displayed on board were in German and not Norwegian.

Had the *King Orry* really found one of the U boat supply ships that were rumoured to be operating in the area? Even if she was not, her papers did not reflect why she was full of fuel and so her cargo was contraband.

The Captain of the tanker and his crew were informed that they had been arrested and a prize crew would take their ship back to Kirkwall in the Orkney Islands.

Having ensured that all was well on board the *Energie* and that there was no chance of the prize crew being overpowered by the tanker's crew, the *King Orry* departed and resumed her patrol. With the successful seizure of thousands of tons of fuel oil to her credit, the *King Orry* did not have to wait for much longer before she added another vessel to her credit.

The *King Orry* began her return trip to the Orkney Islands on the morning of 19th May. At 07.00 another vessel was spotted sailing without lights in the direction of the Skagerak and Baltic Sea.

The *King Orry* manoeuvred into position and approached the suspect vessel from astern, quickly overhauling her as she had done with the *Energie*. The searchlight was then switched on and a shot was put across the bow of the suspect ship.

The searchlight illuminated her name and port of registration, which were painted in large white letters on her side. She was the *Llama* and registered in New York. As the sea state was rough, it was decided to board her in the morning and so the *King Orry* ordered the ship to remain hove-to all night while she circled around her and periodically illuminated her with the searchlight.

At dawn the sea state had subdued sufficiently to allow a boarding party to report that her cargo was 10.000 tons of wheat and that it was destined for German mouths. Needless to say, the Germans were no longer going to see it.

The crew of the *Llama* were arrested and a prize crew put on board to take her back to Aberdeen for unloading. This was the first and only occasion that the *King Orry* arrested a neutral vessel that was openly supporting the enemy. After completing what was to prove to be the most successful patrol that she would undertake, the *King Orry* returned to her anchorage in Longhope at 11.00 on 18th May.

While on patrol on 23rd May, the *King Orry* had her first contact with a probable German U boat. At 11.00, as she patrolled in the Pentland Firth, the crow's nest lookout called out that he had sighted a periscope on the port beam. There was no time to debate whether the submarine was German or British as if she was German a torpedo may already be aimed at the *King Orry*.

At the same time as pressing the action stations alarm, the officer of the watch ordered the *King Orry* to turn ninety degrees to port and instructed the helmsman to head directly at the periscope which could now be seen clearly from the *King Orry's* bridge.

As the armed boarding vessel raced towards the periscope, the forward 12 pdr gun opened fire and dropped a shell some thirty feet from the protruding object. Not surprisingly, the periscope promptly disappeared below the waves while the *King Orry* sped over the last reported position of the submarine and everybody on the bridge braced themselves for a collision.

There was no collision and the periscope was not seen again. Fearing that the submarine may be manoeuvring underwater to gain a position from which she could commence an attack, and that the "Orry' had no effective anti-submarine weapons on board, the Captain made the decision that his ship should leave the vicinity of the periscope sighting immediately. As she left the area at increasing speed, a signal was sent to the Commander In Chief at Scapa Flow advising him that a U boat may be operating in Pentland Firth.

No other vessel reported seeing a periscope and no British submarine reported being attacked by the *King Orry*. It can only be assumed that if the submarine was German, it made a hasty retreat. Unfortunately, I doubt that the true identity of the submarine will ever be known, assuming that it was a periscope that had been sighted.

Later on the same day, the *King Orry* fired a shot across the bow of the Admiralty armed yacht *Jason* - once again for failing to answer a challenge.

The next 11 days were spent at anchor in Longhope, the summer was finally beginning to arrive in the far north and the crew of the *King Orry* took advantage of being able to get ashore for recreation without being subjected to the possibility of catching hypothermia. Unfortunately, one department on board was kept very busy and did not have the opportunity of to relax like the other members of the ship's company.

During her previous patrol a fault had been detected on one of the turbines which after prolonged periods of running, was causing the bearings to over heat. Within the limitations of the maintenance that the Engine Room staff were capable of carrying out on board, they had been unable to identify and rectify the problem.

The Chief Engineer, Lt John Keig, informed the Captain that in his opinion the *King Orry* needed dockyard assistance to rectify the defect. This defect report was forwarded to the Base Engineer Commander on board the repair ship *Assistance* and when the *King Orry* sailed for patrol on 4th June 1915, his reply was still awaited. This patrol took the *King Orry* down into the North Sea where in company with a number of other warships they carried out a search for vessels carrying contraband.

The Norwegian barque **Anaconda**, *escorted into Kirkwall for inspection by* **the King Orry** *on 29th March 1915. (David Handscombe collection)*

They travelled across the North Sea as far as the German minefields which put them in a position approximately ninety miles off Heligoland. During the first day they stopped and searched numerous Dutch fishing boats but no contraband was found. The remainder of the patrol was just as fruitless and the *King Orry* returned to her anchorage in Longhope during the afternoon of 6th June. As she approached the Orkney Islands she encountered thick fog and although she found her anchorage safely, the armed boarding vessel *Duke of Albany* was not so lucky and ran aground on the Louther Skerry in Pentland Firth.

While the *King Orry* had been at sea, a decision on the repairs to the turbines had been made and sailing orders were sent on board shortly after she dropped anchor in Longhope. These orders, which were signed by Admiral Jellicoe on board his *Iron Duke*, instructed the Captain of the *King Orry to* proceed to Liverpool on return from their present patrol in order that repairs could be carried out in Cammell Laird's shipyard. The sailing order directed that the *King Orry* should sail down between the island of Skye and the Scottish mainland and pass through Loch Alsh, the Sound of Sleat, the Sound of Mull and the Sound of Islay. She was then to pass within two miles of the Mull of Kintyre and then down through the north Irish Channel to Liverpool. It went on to state that the Mull of Kintyre should be passed during the night and that the *King Orry* was to keep clear of the areas mentioned in the Notice to Mariners No 137 which probably referred to minefields.

Additionally the *King Orry* was warned to take every precaution against enemy submarines during the latter part of the passage when a high speed was to be maintained and a zig-zag course steered. No doubt the Captain and Chief Engineer hoped that the damaged turbine would cope with a high-speed passage. The forthcoming period in dockyard hands would also give the opportunity to repair the damage to the *King Orry's* port side and shelter deck, which had been sustained during the collision with the destroyer *Contest* on 28th March.

ENCOUNTER WITH JURA

The *King Orry* took on coal and water and was ready to proceed to Liverpool by first light on 7th June. She weighed anchor at just after 07.00 and headed out of Scapa Flow, turned to the west and made course for Cape Wrath and then down through The Minch and the Inner Sound towards the Isle of Skye and Loch Alsh.

The journey was uneventful until the morning of 9th June. At just before 09.00, the *King Orry* entered the narrow Sound of Islay, which separates the islands of Islay and Jura.

Maintaining a speed of 19 knots, with Jura on her port side and Islay on the starboard, she must have created a very impressive sight for those who watched her from the shore.

The Sound of Islay was well charted, but on this particular day, the *King Orry's* navigator was not as accurate as perhaps he should have been.

The American steamer **Llama**, *boarded by the* **King Orry** *on 15th May 1915 and found to be carrying 10,.000 tons of wheat bound for Germany. (David Handscombe collection).*

As the *King Orry* cleared the southern end of the sound, still at 19 knots, she suddenly hit a submerged reef. She first struck on her starboard side just forward of the stokehold and rolling heavily to port she struck the reef again, this time below the Engine Room.

Although the *King Orry* had struck the reef twice, she was still making headway and slid over the rocks to an accompaniment of screeching and grating steel.

After what seemed a lifetime, there was a final shock and she slid back into deep water. As she floated clear, the officer of the watch ordered the engines to be stopped and all watertight doors to be closed. The crew were mustered at their abandon ship stations and instructed to swing out the boats and prepare them for lowering as the extent of damage to the vessel was not yet known.

However, as the damage control parties reported their findings to the Captain, it soon became apparent that she was not in any immediate danger of foundering. In order to prevent her from drifting onto any more submerged rocks the anchor was dropped and a thorough inspection revealed that the hull appeared to be sound and she was not taking in any water.

Although the *King Orry* was not in any danger of sinking, she had been quite badly damaged. The final large bang as she slid off the reef had been the rudder striking the bottom which had resulted in the steering motors located above the rudder being jolted from their mountings. The starboard turbines were not responding and it was suspected that they too had been thrown off their mountings.

Having held a meeting with the First Lieutenant and the Chief Engineer, the Captain decided that the *King Orry* was still seaworthy and that they should make all haste in proceeding to Cammell Laird for repairs. As the *King Orry* was about to transit an area of sea where she had already been warned about possible German U boat activity, the Captain decided not to inform the Commander In Chief at Scapa Flow about the damage but would maintain wireless silence and wait until the *King Orry* reached the safety of the River Mersey before sending a signal. No doubt the Captain was aware that the Germans had the capability to intercept British signals and he did not wish to inform a prowling German U boat of his predicament.

Emergency repairs commenced, the wreckage of the steering gear was removed and emergency hand steering from the tiller flat established. During the removal of the damaged steering gear it was discovered that the rudder post had been bent.

It took three hours to fully inspect the vessel and prepare her for the passage to the Mersey. Despite the damage to the rudder and only running on the port turbine, the *King Orry* still managed to make 12 knots as she steamed south although her steering was a bit erratic and she was not capable of maintaining a zig-zag course.

Having completed the remainder of the passage fairly quickly, and fortunately uneventfully, she arrived off Cammell Laird's shipyard at 13.00 the following day and was immediately taken into dry dock.

Once the dock had been drained, an external inspection of the hull revealed a large dent under her stokehold and Engine Room while the rudder post and rudder were noticeably bent. A hole was found in one of her double bottom compartments but as the damage had not penetrated the inner plating, the ship had remained watertight.

On the engineering side, the starboard propeller shaft had been bent inside its stern tube and the starboard propeller badly damaged which no doubt occurred when the propeller struck the bottom and was brought to a violent stop. The starboard thrust block was also fractured.

As had been suspected following the inspection carried out immediately after the accident, the starboard turbine and its single-reduction gearing had been thrown out of alignment but miraculously neither had sustained any serious damage. The fact that the *King Orry* had survived this incident bore testament to her strong construction by Cammell Laird.

The repairs took until 28th July and included the damage caused during the collision with the destroyer *Contest*. During this prolonged repair period, the damaged bottom plates were removed and replaced, the starboard turbine and its associated gearing was stripped down and then remounted. The damaged propeller shaft and propeller were replaced and the rudder and steering gear repaired.

Cammell Laird's also took the opportunity to repair some other minor defects and make a few improvements to her accommodation areas. Two weeks leave was granted to both watches, which was the first time that anybody had taken more than a few days since the ship had commissioned in November the previous year.

On 29th July, with the repairs now completed, the *King Orry* was moved out of the dry dock and lay in the basin. A collier had moored alongside and the crew spent the whole day topping up the bunkers. This was a particularly arduous task as it was a very hot day and the temperature in the bunkers was almost unbearable. By 18.00 the task was complete and the crew washed away the coal dust from the decks and superstructure.

As she was due to sail from the River Mersey on the following day's morning tide, 29th July, night leave was granted from 19.30 but expired at midnight. The pilot, Captain Andrews, and an engineering inspector from Cammell Laird's boarded the *King Orry* at 06.45, the crew having been hard at work since 05.30 making the ship ready to proceed to sea.

She finally moved out of the basin and entered the Mersey at 07.45, immediately securing to a wharf at Wallasey. The crew were stood down and went for a welcome breakfast after which a few last-minute items of stores were taken on board.

As the crew were busying themselves with taking on these stores, the Chief Engineer, Lt John Keig and the inspector from Cammell Laird toured the Engine Room and checked that everything was functioning correctly. At just after 11.30, having been informed by the Chief Engineer that the engines were ready for sea, the Captain gave the order for the *King Orry* to move away from the wharf and proceed down river towards the Bar Lightship, which was passed at 13.00.

Once clear of the buoyed channel, the engines were opened up and a full power trial was commenced. This consisted of steaming north west for twenty minutes and then returning along the reverse course to the starting point. The turbines and steering gear was given a vigorous test as the *King Orry* sped along at just under 19 knots.

Having successfully completed various engine and steering gear evolutions during the full power trial, the Cammell Laird inspector informed both the Captain and Chief Engineer that as far as he was concerned the *King Orry* was now fully serviceable and fit to resume her naval duties.

At 13.40, with the Bar Lightship about a mile away, the *King Orry* dropped her anchor to allow for a compass swing to be carried out. Shortly after anchoring, a cutter came alongside and took off the pilot and the engineering inspector. By 15.00, the ship was ready in all respects to return to her patrol duties and so the anchor was raised and His Majesty's Armed Boarding Vessel *King Orry* commenced her journey back to the Orkney Islands.

The passage was uneventful and the *King Orry* dropped her anchor in Longhope at just after 07.00 on 1st August.

At midday the Captain, First Lieutenant, Navigating Officer and Chief Engineer were summoned to the *Cyclops* to attend a Board of Inquiry which had been convened to investigate the grounding of the *King Orry* in the Sound of Islay. Its findings are not known but as the ship's log does not record any officer or rating being dismissed from the ship, then it can be assumed that the *King Orry* did not run aground as a result of negligence.

She remained at Longhope for the remainder of the week, sailing for her next patrol at 08.00 on 8th August.

This patrol, which took her out beyond the Western Isles, did not result in any contraband being seized and the *King Orry* returned to her anchorage on 13th August.. However, while she was out on patrol an incident occurred which would alter the whole concept of armed boarding vessel operations.

As previously mentioned, the ideal combination of ships for a patrol was an armed boarding vessel accompanied by either a cruiser or destroyers, the latter being available to provide back up should the lightly-armed boarding vessels encounter a disguised German raider or warship.

On 8th August, the lack of a warship escort was to prove disastrous for one of the *King Orry's* running mates.

CHAPTER FIVE

Tragedy and Tumult

The armed boarding vessel HMS *Ramsey*, formerly the Isle of Man Steam Packet vessel *The Ramsey*, had left Longhope on the afternoon of 7th August 1915 and had headed out into the North Sea.

Just before midnight a signal was received informing the *Ramsey's* Captain that a suspected German blockade-runner was reported to be at sea and instructed him to keep a lookout for any vessels approaching from the east. Any such vessel should be boarded and searched for contraband.

At 05.00 on 8th August, as dawn broke, a vessel was sighted on the eastern horizon. The *Ramsey* altered course towards the suspect ship which appeared to be a tramp steamer.

It took about 30 minutes for the *Ramsey* to close the suspect vessel and as she drew within visual signal distance it was noted that she was flying a Russian flag.

The *Ramsey* hoisted a signal instructing the tramp steamer to stop and prepare to take on a boarding party who would search the ship for contraband. The signal was ignored and the tramp steamer continued on her way.

The *Ramsey* now drew alongside the suspect vessel and repeated her demands. As the *Ramsey* slowed to the speed of the other ship, and was no more than a couple of hundred yards away, the Russian flag was suddenly hauled down and the white, black and red battle ensign of the Imperial German Navy was hauled to the mast head.

Before the crew of the *Ramsey* were aware of what was happening, the German ship had opened fire with two 8.8 cm and two 37 mm guns which had been concealed by false deck houses and canvas covers.

Shells crashed into the *Ramsey's* hull and superstructure while machine gun fire raked her decks. One shell destroyed her bridge killing everyone who stood there including the Captain.

As the *Ramsey's* crew rushed to man their guns, the German ship fired a torpedo which struck the stricken vessel towards her stern. The *Ramsey's* crew had no time to respond; she had been caught completely by surprise and was now suffering the consequences. Many of her crew were still in their mess decks and were killed by the torpedo explosion. The gun crews on the *Ramey* had no time to return fire and with her stern destroyed, she quickly began to settle and within five minutes had rolled over onto her beam ends and disappeared below the waves.

Miraculously the crew managed to launch two lifeboats although one of them soon capsized. However as soon as it became apparent that their ship was doomed, the majority of the crew who had survived the gunfire did not wait around for the boats to be lowered but jumped straight into the sea.

As soon as the *Ramsey* had sunk, the Germans began to rescue her survivors. Out of a crew of ninety-eight, forty-six shocked and frightened British seaman were hauled from the cold sea by the crew of the German raider.

A large number of the *Ramsey's* crew were reservists from the Isle of Man and no fewer than 21 Manxmen lost their lives that morning. Many of those killed were from the engine and boiler rooms and had stood little chance as the ship's side had been blown apart and the cold sea rushed in.

The German raider turned out to be the auxiliary minelayer *Meteor* which had started out life as the British merchant vessel *Vienna*, built in 1903 and seized by the Germans at Hamburg when the war broke out. However the euphoria of the German victory was not to last for long.

Shortly after the *Ramsey* had received the signal informing her of the suspected blockade-runner, a cruiser force had sailed from Harwich to assist with the search and was now patrolling off the coast of Belgium.

The *Meteor's* Captain decided that it was time to return to port as he was aware that a signal reporting contact with a German raider had been sent by the striken ship and that the Royal Navy would now be out in force searching for him.

Unfortunately, the temptation to sink just one more ship before he returned to port was to be the *Meteor's* downfall.

As the *Meteor* headed towards the Belgian port of Zeebrugge she came across a Norwegian schooner which was bound for a British port with a cargo of pit props. It took an hour to sink her and rescue the crew; an hour that sealed the fate of the German ship.

In order to assist the *Meteor* with over-the-horizon surveillance, a Zeppelin airship had arrived and was now acting as her lookout. The Zeppelin's commander sent a frantic message to the *Meteor* informing her Captain that a large force of British cruisers was just over the horizon and was heading in his direction and it was inevitable that the German ship would be intercepted by the British warships.

As the cruisers approached, the *Meteor's* Captain realised that his ship did not stand a chance and rather than risk her being captured by the British, he decided to scuttle her.

Before setting the charges, he commandeered a neutral Danish fishing boat which was in the vicinity and transferred his crew and the survivors from the *Ramsey* and the Norwegian schooner. As the Danish fishing boat moved off to a safe distance, there was a loud explosion followed by sheets of flame leaping into the air as the *Meteor* blew up and sank. With the British cruisers now bearing down on their position, the Germans, having no desire to become prisoners of war decided to transfer the British survivors to a nearby Norwegian fishing boat while they made their escape in the Danish vessel.

The *Ramsey's* crew were eventually picked up by the British light cruiser *Arethusa* and later landed at Harwich.

CONSEQUENCES

The news of the loss of the *Ramsey* hit the crew of the *King Orry* very hard. Both ship's companies were well known to each other and many were close friends from their pre-war days in the Isle of Man. Her sinking in such a short time by another auxiliary warship, albeit German, was to have severe implications regarding the future use of the converted merchantmen in the role of armed boarding vessels.

On 14th August, Admiral Jellicoe (Commander in Chief Grand Fleet) wrote a letter to the Admiralty regarding the loss of the *Ramsey*. He pointed out that as the Germans were now using disguised merchantmen as auxiliary warships, then consideration must be given to ensuring that vessels which were required to intercept them were sufficiently well-armed to defend themselves especially when ships like the *Meteor* were armed with a minimum of two 3.45" guns and torpedo tubes. He went on to explain that it was doubtful whether a cruiser would have survived a torpedo attack at such close range, but with her larger calibre guns and armoured protection, she would probably have sunk the enemy vessel before it got a chance to fire a torpedo. Admiral Jellicoe concluded by stating that armed boarding vessels should be fitted with larger calibre guns as soon as possible and that in future they must be closed up at full action stations when approaching suspect shipping.

This directive was acted upon almost immediately as far as the *King Orry* was concerned.

On the evening of 15th August, the *King Orry* received orders to proceed to the River Tyne at first light the following morning. On arrival she was to be taken into dockyard hands and be fitted with two 4" guns.

She duly left her anchorage in Longhope at 06.30 arrived off the mouth of the River Tyne at 09.00 on 17th August proceeding up river to Jarrow.

At midday she berthed alongside Palmer's shipyard and work to install the new weapons commenced as soon as a meeting with the Dockyard Manager was over. With the installation of two 4" guns, it had been decided that the after 12 pdr gun was no longer necessary and this was removed that afternoon. The two 4" guns were to be installed on the Poop Deck (or Quarter Deck as it was known by the Royal Navy); one gun would be fitted on either side in order that their combined arcs of fire covered both the port and starboard quarter and forward to an angle of 45 degrees off the beam.

The locating of both 4" guns on the after end of the ship was not ideal as it meant that the *King Orry* could not bring her main armament to bear as she approached a suspect or enemy vessel from a bow-on angle, and when broadside on could only bring one 4" gun to bear on the target.

It had proved impracticable to replace the forward 12 pdr with a 4" gun as the latter was a much larger and heavier weapon and it would not fit into the small confines of the forecastle without a major reconstruction of that area. In fact, the fitting of the guns on the Poop Deck required considerable work as areas of the deck planking had to be removed and replaced by thick steel plating to support the heavy 4" gun mountings. Additionally, the rigid metal guardrails around the stern were removed and replaced by the collapsible Royal Navy pattern, to give the guns a clear field of fire when shooting astern.

Work also began on enlarging both of the magazines, the forward one to hold additional shells and the after one to accommodate the larger 4" shells and to provide stowage for two guns rather than one. The work to install the new guns and associated equipment took until 2nd September to complete.

As the installation work did not involve the majority of the ship's company, seven days leave was granted to each watch, the port watch going on leave on the day that the *King Orry* arrived at Jarrow and the starboard watch having leave from 26th August.

On 2nd September, with both watches now back on board, the crew commenced coaling ship and taking on ammunition for the new weapons.

As well as 4" ammunition, 12 pdr ammunition was also taken on board, as it had been necessary to land the shells from the forward 12 pdr magazine before work to enlarge it could commence. By the evening of 4th September the *King Orry* was ready to return to duty and at 08.00 the following morning, she left the River Tyne and proceeded north to the Orkney Islands.

DANGEROUS WATERS

The *King Orry* spent the next few weeks at anchor in Longhope or on Eastern Patrol which took her into the North Sea and towards the coast of Denmark and Norway. While at sea, every opportunity was taken to exercise the 4" gun crews with their new weapons.

In the early hours of 23rd September, the *King Orry* left her anchorage and passed through the Switha Boom to commence another Eastern Patrol. It was still dark and due to a thick fog, progress was very slow.

The lookouts on the bridge wings and the forecastle had to be extra vigilant and keep their ears and eyes open if they were to spot another vessel before a collision occurred.

At 04.00, as the *King Orry* moved away from Scapa Flow and passed the small island of Swona, a dark shape suddenly loomed out of the fog from astern. The torpedo boat destroyer *Christopher* had also been leaving Scapa Flow to commence a patrol but unfortunately she was not taking as much care as the *King Orry* and was perhaps travelling too fast to navigate safely in the prevailing weather conditions.

Before either ship could take any avoiding action, the destroyer caught up with the *King Orry* and struck her very hard on the starboard quarter, proceeding to scrape down the *King Orry's* starboard side before again disappearing into the fog. The Captain ordered the *King*

Orry's engines to be stopped and sent the damage control parties to inspect the starboard quarter. They soon reported that no serious damage had been sustained but some of her plating was dented and a few sprung rivets were allowing water to seep in.

The Engine Room also reported water seeping in but confirmed that they had started the pumps and the ingress was under control.

As the *King Orry* lay drifting in the fog, the destroyer having also stopped, slowly drifted into view. She had not been so lucky and had a large hole in her port bow and her port pom-pom mounting and also the 27ft sea boat had been damaged. Her crew were busy trying to rig a collision mat over the hole in an attempt to stem the flow of water that was pouring in but they were having problems as the damage to their sea boat prevented it from being used to assist in securing the collision mat to the ship's side.

The *Christopher's* Captain requested assistance and asked for the *King Orry* to put one of her boats into the water in order that its crew could help secure the collision mat to her side. It took until mid-morning before this was made secure and the flow of water into the destroyer was reduced to a rate that her pumps could control. By this time the fog was beginning to lift and the *King Orry's* navigator was able to confirm the exact position of the two vessels.

Fortunately they had not drifted very far and were in no danger of running ashore. The destroyer's Captain had sent a signal to Scapa Flow requesting a tug as his ship was no longer capable of making her own way and the damage to the *King Orry* prevented her from attempting to tow his vessel. The Admiralty tug *Stoic* arrived at just before noon and as soon as she had the destroyer connected to a towing hawser, the *King Orry* departed and made her way back to Longhope to enable a thorough inspection of her own damage to be carried out.

As soon as she was secure at her anchorage, a boat arrived carrying shipwrights from the repair ship *Assistance*. Before boarding the *King Orry*, they inspected the damage to the starboard quarter and once they were satisfied, they boarded the armed boarding vessel and were taken to inspect the damage from the inside. Their report was good news and although the *King Orry* would require to be dry docked at sometime in the future to replace the damaged plates, they could effect repairs that would make her watertight again and allow her to return to her duties. These repairs were completed by the evening of 24th September and the *King Orry* sailed at 07.00 the following morning to resume her Eastern Patrol.

The tedium of a couple of days at sea on either the Eastern or Western Patrols followed by a couple of days in Longhope continued through to the end of September and for the whole of October 1915. Her log book records that she only stopped one vessel suspected of carrying contraband during this period, this was on 30th September, when at 13.00 she stopped the Danish tramp steamer *Trumf*. Fortunately for the Danes, their cargo manifest was correct and she was allowed to proceed on her way.

The weather was now beginning to deteriorate as the winter closed in and an entry in the *King Orry's* log during October 1915 shows how this weather affected a young cabin boy on a trawler.

The *King Orry* had been on patrol for a couple of days and was on her way back to her base when she came across a trawler from Aberdeen that was flying a signal flag indicating that she required medical assistance.

The *King Orry* closed the trawler and, via a megaphone, established that a young cabin boy had been suffering from severe sea sickness for a couple of days and was now in very poor health. The *King Orry* did not carry a doctor but it was agreed that the boy should be transferred to the armed boarding vessel. This was achieved with some difficulty as the rough seas made a boat transfer a very hazardous event. Meanwhile, the *King Orry's* Captain had sent a message to the armed merchant cruiser *Ebro* which was in proximity and which carried a medical officer. The two warships rendezvoused later that day, and again with great difficulty a boat transfer was carried out and the

medical officer was transferred to the *King Orry*. On arrival he gave the young cabin boy medication which relieved his symptoms and advised that he should remain on board until she returned to Scapa Flow. The Doctor then made the perilous journey back to his own ship before the *King Orry* returned to Longhope the following morning and transferred the boy to the hospital ship from which he was presumably sent back to the mainland.

On 2nd November 1915, the *King Orry's* log shows that the patrol areas changed their names and instead of sailing for Eastern or Western Patrols, she now sailed for either Alpha, Bravo or Charlie Patrols. Unfortunately, the exact location of these areas is not known but entries in the *King Orry's* log indicate that they were similar to those that were mined during 1917 to form the Northern Barrage, the patrol areas Alpha, Bravo and Charlie becoming the minefields with the same name. The area occupied by the former Eastern and Western Patrol has also not been positively identified and was probably altered for each patrol. Sailing orders issued to the *King Orry* during 1916, which detailed her to patrol in areas X-Ray and Yankee, give different navigational positions for each time she carried out either of these patrols. It can only be assumed that although patrol areas now used letters of the alphabet, it did not necessarily mean that each Alpha, Bravo, Charlie, X-Ray or Yankee Patrol covered the same area although most of them were still in either the North Sea and southern parts of the Norwegian Sea or out towards the Hebrides and Western Isles.

*The **King Orry's** starboard 4" gun: Scapa Flow August 1915. (David Handscombe collection)*

At 07.00 on 23rd November 1915, the *King Orry* left Longhope to commence Patrol Bravo. As she passed through the Swaitha Boom, her starboard propeller fouled the cable that supported the boom marker buoys. The cable was dragged under the ship and caused much grating and screeching as the *King Orry* rode over it.

The propellers were immediately stopped and the *King Orry* drifted clear but on restarting the engines there was a slight vibration on the starboard shaft and the rudder was sluggish on the starboard helm. The *King Orry* was instructed to return to her anchorage and await an inspection by divers from the repair ship, *Assistance*.

This inspection was duly carried out during the afternoon and it confirmed that a blade on the starboard propeller had minor damage, the rudder post was bent slightly and there were more dented plates below the water line on the starboard quarter.

As on the previous occasion when an inspection was carried out by personnel from the repair ship, they stated that the damage could wait until a later date to be repaired and that the *King Orry* could still proceed to sea, although her starboard propeller could not be run at full speed.

As a result of the reduced speed aspect of the report, the patrol that she was about to embark upon was cancelled and the standby armed boarding vessel was detailed to undertake the patrol instead. The *King Orry* therefore remained at her anchorage until 27th November and no doubt the Captain was becoming embarrassed by the accumulation of minor incidents that his ship was involved in as on each occasion he was required to attend an enquiry on board the flag ship.

An entry in the log for 25th November records Sub Lieutenant Anderson being logged for insolent behaviour when asked by the Captain why he was late in securing the water carrier *Polmont* alongside. Further details of the incident are not included but it is possible that the water carrier was late because Sub Lieutenant Anderson did not have a securing party mustered at the appropriate time and his excuse failed to impress the Captain. Due to the recent damage to the propeller and rudder, the Admiral commanding armed boarding vessels decided that the *King Orry* should only be employed in local waters and that arrangements should be made for her to go to a shipyard for repair as soon as possible. To this end, she carried out an overnight patrol in Pentland Firth and the approaches to Scapa Flow between 27th - 28th November and 3rd - 4th December.

The order to proceed to Birkenhead for repairs was issued on the afternoon of 7th December and at 06.00 the following morning she left Longhope and made her way southwards towards the River Mersey.

THE MERSEYRE VISITED

The *King Orry* was ordered to follow the same route to Liverpool route to that she had taken on 7th June that year. However, on this occasion the passage through the Sound of Islay was uneventful, no doubt the Captain and Navigating Officer were extra cautious.

She arrived at the bar to the River Mersey at midday on 9th December and took on the pilot before proceeding up river to berth alongside Princes Landing Stage at 14.45 where she was to remain over night.

Princes Landing Stage was a familiar berth for the *King Orry* as she had used it many times during her pre-war days with the Steam Packet but sadly the noises and bustle of happy holiday makers were gone and her gleaming black hull, white superstructure and red and black funnel had now been replaced by rust-streaked drab grey paint. She must have looked a sorry sight for the Liverpool stevedores who remembered her steaming up the Mersey on her maiden voyage, only a couple of years before.

At 09.00 the following morning, two tugs arrived and took the *King Orry* across the river to Cammell Laird's shipyard at Birkenhead. She entered the dry dock at 11.25 whereupon the process to drain the dock commenced. It took until mid-afternoon to complete this and it was only then that the dockyard workers began to swarm on board to commence the *King Orry's* many repairs.

One of the first tasks to be undertaken was to land all of the ammunition from the magazines. With the ship in dry dock, her fire main and magazine sprays would not have a water supply and the last thing that anybody wanted was a fire in the vicinity of one of the magazines and no water available to put it out.

Scaffolding was placed around the stern and work began to remove the damaged plating on her starboard quarter. The rudder and starboard propeller were also removed and taken away for repair.

As the days progressed, engineers from the shipyard began to strip down and overhaul her turbines and machinery. The shipwrights made repairs to the planking on the forecastle and replaced any missing or damaged caulking. The frequent loss of this caulking must have been a contributing factor to the ever-present problem of water leaking into the *King Orry's* forward compartments during the violent winter storms.

Every item of equipment on board was checked, including the telescopes and binoculars, which were sent to the Liverpool firm of Sewill for servicing. As during the period that that the *King Orry* had spent in dock on the River Tyne, the majority of the ship's company were once again not involved in the repair or maintenance work. This gave the opportunity to send as many people away on leave as could be spared.

The first leave party departed for nine days leave as soon as all of the ammunition had been put ashore on 10th December while the second leave party went home ten days later.

With the war that would be over by Christmas 1914 about to enter another year, those that remained on board the *King Orry* over Christmas would not have had a very festive time. With the ship remaining in dry dock and the Engine Room shut down for maintenance, there would have been no heating on board and oil lamps would have provided lighting. Although the galley ovens were coal fired, the galley itself would not have been fully operational as no fresh water was available due to the fresh water pumps being shut down, likewise the toilets and bathrooms would not have been usable. No doubt some of those who were lucky enough not to be required for duty on Christmas Day were invited to the homes of the Cammell Laird employees and Birkenhead towns folk.

The repairs to the rudder, starboard propeller and plating on the starboard quarter were all completed by the morning of 27th December and later on that day work commenced to repaint the ship's bottom.

The second leave party returned on board on 29th December, and as the shipyard manager had already informed the Captain that the *King Orry* would be ready to leave the dry dock on 30th December, all hands were employed in preparing to refloat the vessel the following morning. A part of these preparations required the ship's engineers to check all of the intake and discharge valves that were located in the ship's side to ensure that they were still watertight and to check that the rudder and starboard propeller had been replaced correctly.

The Chief Engineer, Lt John Keig and the shipyard's engineering manager inspected all the areas where work had been carried out to confirm that everything was in order. Once this inspection was complete and Lt John Keig was satisfied, he informed the Captain that the *King Orry* appeared to be watertight and signed the log to that effect.

As 30th December dawned, the crew of the *King Orry* found themselves being roused early. The dry dock was due to be flooded at 08.00 and the final preparations, which included breakfast had to be completed by 07.30. One of these preparations was to place members of the ship's company in compartments

that were below the water line. These men were required to check the compartments for watertight integrity and to inform the bridge immediately if there was any sign of water seeping in, especially in compartments where work on the hull had been carried out. Fortunately, the report made by the Chief Engineer on the previous afternoon regarding the *King Orry* being watertight was confirmed, and the ship remained dry. The dry dock was flooded by 09.30 and shortly afterwards the dock gates were opened to allow the ship to be moved out. As she had no motive power of her own, she was towed by two tugs and secured to the north wall of the Cammell Laird basin.

The remainder of the day and most of the next day, which was New Year's Eve, was taken up with the loading of stores and ammunition. Some of the last items to be brought back onboard were the telescopes and binoculars, which had been refurbished and repaired by Sewill's. The crew worked hard throughout the morning and early afternoon of New Year's Eve to ensure that all stores and ammunition were loaded and stowed away. They had been informed that as soon as storing was completed, the *King Orry* would be moved out of the basin and taken down river to a basin in neighbouring Wallasey, where she would remain for a few days. While at Wallasey, she would take on coal and carry out basin trials on her main machinery.

The crew knew that if the *King Orry* missed the afternoon high tide, the next time that she could be moved was on the high tide at just after dawn on the following morning, New Year's Day. As many of them had already planned to attend one of the numerous New Year's Eve parties being held in the pubs ashore, it was in their interest to ensure that the *King Orry* was secure in the basin at Wallasey that evening as nobody wanted an early start on New Year's Day. The hard work paid off and the *King Orry* was secured alongside the basin wall at Wallasey by 19.00, having caught the high tide and been moved from the Cammell Laird basin by three tugs towards the end of the afternoon. Leave was granted to all but the duty watch at 21.00 and no doubt there were many sore heads the following morning.

1916

The first day of 1916 was cold, wet and miserable. The crew were not woken from their sleep until 07.00 although this did not mean that New Year's Day was to be a holiday. The engineers were busy preparing to carry out the various basin trials on the main engines. These would include putting full steam pressure into the boilers and turning the turbines, although the

*Lt Cdr Selwyn Day takes Sunday prayers on the **King Orry's** Promenade Deck: Scapa Flow 1915. (David Handscombe collection)*

propeller shafts would be disconnected as they wished the *King Orry* to remain stationary.

At some time during the basin trials the propeller shafts would be turned, but only very slowly, just enough to ensure that they functioned correctly. However, before any boiler pressure could be raised it was necessary to refill the bunkers as they were almost empty.

The stock of coal had been deliberately run down before the *King Orry* went into dry dock in order that the bunkers could be cleaned out and inspected by the shipyard.

Coaling ship commenced at midday and with the exception of the engineers, involved the whole crew. It was a particularly arduous task as the coal was delivered in railway wagons that drew up on the dockside alongside the ship and required to be unloaded one at a time. The process of coaling ship was completed by dusk on the following day, 2nd January, although it took until midnight to clean all of the grime and coal dust from the wooden decks and superstructure.

ANOTHER MISHAP

The basin trials commenced the following morning and were not completed until the evening of 5th January. Amongst the items tested were the repaired rudder post and starboard propeller shaft, both which functioned correctly. Having been declared fit for sea and capable of resuming her naval duties, the *King Orry* was ready to leave the basin at Wallasey on the morning high tide on 6th January but unfortunately, she was to add another entry to her growing list of accidents.

As it would be high tide slack water when the *King Orry* passed through the lock gates into the river, the Captain had decided that he would take the ship out of the basin under her own power, although a tug would stand by to render assistance if required.

She entered the lock at just after 09.00 with the tug ahead of her. At slow speed the *King Orry* had limited steerageway and could not alter course quickly and as she passed through the lock, a slight turbulence in the water caused her to drift over to starboard and she bumped against the lock wall. Normally this would not have caused any damage as the wooden belting would have protected the hull. However, when the Royal Navy had removed the centre sections of the belting, the leading edge of the remaining after section was not rounded off and as a resultof this it stood out at right angles to the ship's side.

As the starboard belting scraped along the lock wall, the leading edge of the after section snagged on a protruding piece of masonry. The *King Orry* continued to move forward, even though the after section of starboard belting was jammed hard against the piece of masonry. As the seamen tried to fend the ship off from the lock wall and lower large wicker fenders over the side, there was a resounding crack and a large section of the belting snapped off and fell into the water.

Having already spotted the *King Orry's* predicament, the tug quickly moved in and secured a line to the vessel and pulled her clear of the lock and out into the river, whereupon the *King Orry* stopped her engines and dropped anchor.

No doubt the Captain feared the worst as he waited for a report on the damage. Would the *King Orry* have to go back into dry dock to have her starboard quarter repaired again? When the report eventually reached the bridge the damage was not as bad as had been feared although the noise that had been made when the belting had broken away sounded as if the whole stern had been ripped off. The report confirmed that a 15ft section of the belting on the starboard quarter had been lost while a further 10ft was hanging loose but there did not appear to be any structural damage to the ship's side.

The Captain decided that the *King Orry* should return to the basin in order that repairs could be carried out as the loose section of belting needed to be secured before the ship put to sea. This time the *King Orry* wisely entered the lock with the assistance of the tug. Having safely passed back into the basin, she was berthed alongside by 10.00. Carpenters were summoned from Cammell Laird's and it took the remainder of the day to remove and replace the damaged sections of belting.

The river pilot boarded at 21.00 that night and half an hour later at high tide slack water, two tugs slowly moved the *King Orry* away from the wall and out through the lock into the River Mersey. The wind had now blown up so the tugs pulled their charge around and pointed her down river before releasing their towropes.

As the *King Orry* began to make headway and proceed towards the mouth of the river, she was accompanied by one of the tugs as the river pilot would need to be brought ashore once she had cleared the marked channel. The Bar Lightship was passed at 23.00 and the *King Orry* slowed down to allow the tug to come alongside and retrieve the pilot - not any easy task as the wind had blown the sea up into a heavy swell.

However, the pilot was duly transferred without mishap and after delaying her departure for a short while to adjust her compass, His Majesty's Ship *King Orry* bade farewell to the Mersey and headed north. As Liverpool and Birkenhead were left astern, few on board would have had any inclination that the *King Orry* would be returning to her birthplace a lot sooner than was expected.

GALES AND STORMS

As the *King Orry* cleared Liverpool Bay and headed up through the Irish Sea and North Channel, the weather began to deteriorate and by early morning she was pushing her way through a severe gale.

She made little headway throughout the day and had only reached the southern end of the Sound of Islay by dusk. The passage through the sheltered waters of the sound allowed the crew to have their first hot meal since leaving the Mersey, but this calm was not to last for long for as the *King Orry* cleared the northern end of the Sound, the full force of the gale hit her again.

As she struggled through the second night at sea, few of her crew had any decent sleep. Unlike the crews of warships who slept in hammocks, most of the *King Orry's* crew slept in makeshift bunks that had been erected in her former passenger saloons and as a result they were continually tossed from side to side. To make things worse, the old problem of water finding its way into every nook and cranny was very evident and few of the junior ratings had a dry mess deck.

With no sign of the storm abating, the Captain decided to seek shelter for a few hours to allow his tired crew to dry out their accommodation, eat another hot meal and catch up on their sleep. The *King Orry* had reached the sheltered waters of the Sound of Lorne by first light on 8th January, and at just after 08.00 she dropped anchor off Oban.

The Navigating Officer was sent ashore to see the Naval Liaison Officer in the hope that an up to date weather report could be obtained. On his return he informed the Captain that the gale was expected to subside by early afternoon, but more importantly he had information concerning a recent warship loss.

On 6th January the battleship *King Edward VII* had hit a mine off Cape Wrath and had sunk. At this moment of time it was not known whether she had hit a drifting British mine or whether the Germans had laid mines in the proximity of of the cape. All warships passing Cape Wrath had therefore been ordered to keep well out to sea.

True to prediction, by midday a message was received on board informing the Captain that the wind was dropping and that by mid-afternoon the sea state in the Minch and around the north of Scotland should be considerably calmer.

King Orry

*Members of the **King Orry's** crew pose for the camera on the after end of the Promenade Deck: Scapa Flow 1915. (David Handscombe collection)*

At 13.00, the *King Orry* weighed anchor and continued her journey north via the Sound of Mull, Sound of Sleat and Kyle of Lochalsh. With the sea now much calmer, she made good progress and entered Scapa Flow at 08.30 the following morning, having given Cape Wrath a wide berth.

The next few days were spent at anchor while the crew prepared the ship to return to patrol duties. The bunkers were topped up with coal, extra ammunition was stowed in the magazines and fresh meat and vegetables were brought on board.

At 08.00 on 13th January, the *King Orry* left her anchorage to commence what was expected to be a routine patrol in the North Sea. As she left Pentland Firth and headed eastward, the clouds began to darken and the wind increased.

By midday the sea state was very rough and the *King Orry* was heading straight into a storm. Large waves began to break over her forecastle and as she started to pitch and roll violently, the weather continued to deteriorate throughout the afternoon but, as she had

not yet reached her patrol area, there was no option but to continue steaming into the storm.

The *King Orry* was beginning to sustain damage as the seas pounded against her - the gales of a few days earlier were nothing compared with the conditions that she was now encountering. As the last specks of daylight disappeared, the oncoming waves could not be seen until they hit the bow and exploded in a sheet of white spray over the forecastle and bridge.

Speed had been reduced to slow ahead in an attempt to lessen the impact of the waves and although this helped to reduce the deluge of water that crashed over the forecastle, it increased the rolling motion and the inclinometer on the bridge frequently recorded more than 40 degrees of roll.

Reports were being received stating that the mess decks were awash and that some members of the crew had sustained injuries as a result of being thrown against bulkheads or hit by loose objects. As dawn approached on the following morning, the storm was at its worst and the log book recorded it as being storm force 10.

At 07.00 on 14th January, the *King Orry* was approximately 125 miles east of Duncansby Head. During the night, although the exact time was not known, the steel covers that fitted over the anchor cable and prevented water from entering the cable locker via the chain pipes (or naval pipes as they are as called by the Royal Navy) had been washed away. Each time a wave crashed over the *King Orry's* forecastle, water poured down into the cable locker and the bow was becoming noticeably lower in the water.

The pumps had been started but after about 10 minutes they suddenly stopped as something blocked the suction box within the cable locker. With the locker flooded, the *King Orry* became very heavy and inert forward and the helmsman was experiencing difficulty in maintaining the set course. It would not be safe to put men onto the forecastle to attempt repairs to the chain pipe covers with the *King Orry* still heading directly into the storm and so the Captain decided that his only option was to turn the ship around and hove to. The message was passed around the ship and her crew braced themselves for the heavy rolling that would occur as she turned about.

As the *King Orry* began to swing, her starboard side was exposed to the full force of the oncoming sea and when she was about half way through the manoeuvre, a huge wave suddenly rose up and hit her on the starboard side, washing over the upper decks and pushing the vessel over to port, onto her beam ends.

For a few moments it looked as if the *King Orry* might capsize. As everybody hung on and prepared for the worst, the *King Orry* gave a violent shudder and slowly returned to an even keel. Although the ship now was out of the immediate danger of capsizing, her problems were by no means over.

As the Captain and other occupants of the bridge regained their composure, reports began to arrive regarding damage that had been sustained throughout the vessel. The most reassuring report came from the Chief Engineer who reported that although water had entered the Boiler Room it had not affected the fires below the boilers and full steam pressure was still available, the watertight doors were all closed and the pumps were working to full capacity and coping with the water that had entered the ship.

This good news was soon overshadowed by the report that came in regarding the forecastle and Boat Deck. The canvas cover, which protected the forward 12 pdr gun, had been ripped off and the gun had been knocked off its traversing ring so that its barrel now pointed rather lopsidedly over the port bow.

The Boat Deck was a scene of total devastation and all boats had sustained some sort of damage. On the starboard side, the two lifeboats (originally No 5 and No 7 boats) had been smashed beyond repair while on the port side the 27ft whaler had completely disappeared while the aftermost lifeboat (originally No 8 boat) had been ripped out of its davits and deposited on the after end of the Boat Deck, directly above the Wireless Office. The damage caused by this boat was potentially the most serious as the terminals to the wireless aerials had been smashed when the lifeboat had crashed down onto the deck. This now meant that the *King Orry* could not communicate with the outside world or inform anybody of her predicament.

Only one boat was found to be serviceable, this was the foremost lifeboat (originally No 6 boat) on the port side. Unfortunately, although the boat was not damaged, it could not be lowered as the forward davit had been bent and would no longer swing outwards. A high percentage of the guardrails around the Boat Deck and after end of the Promenade Deck had also been washed away.

Over the next hour reports continued to arrive on the bridge, advising the Captain of additional damage that had been sustained elsewhere on the ship. The glass in some of the portholes (or scuttles) on the starboard side had been cracked and most of the crew's mess decks were now awash. Those mess decks and compartments that had remained dry were not much better off as they were littered with numerous items of broken furniture, crockery and the crew's personal belongings. The starboard edge of the Boat Deck had been wrenched away from its supports and was buckled

upwards. As well as the cable locker, the forward magazine was now flooded and there appeared to be many loose rivets in the bow plating as water continued to leak into the forward end of the ship. The starboard bridge wing house had lost its glass windows, while on the bridge roof, the binnacle, semaphore arms and searchlight were all damaged.

The *King Orry* was obviously no longer in a condition to remain at sea and the only sensible thing to do was abandon the patrol and head for the safety of a harbour.

The Captain made the decision at 09.00, but as the *King Orry* had drifted for most of the time since being hit by the wave, her exact position was not known. Her position at 07.00 had been approximately 125 miles east of Duncansby Head, but this had been worked out by estimating the distance that she had travelled since leaving the approaches to Scapa Flow the previous morning. The Navigating Officer was confident that the ship had drifted in a southerly direction and that she was now further down the North Sea.

After estimating the distance that she had drifted, he worked out an approximate position and then gave a course that would take the *King Orry* towards the coast of Scotland. If a good lookout was kept, it was hoped that when land was spotted they would be able to obtain sufficient bearings to work out their exact position.

Since the *King Orry* had turned around and assumed a course that would take her towards the safety of a port, the storm had abated slightly, although she was still rolling from side to side and taking waves over her bow.

However, now that she was running with the sea, she managed to maintain an average speed of 14 knots for most of the day. The crew were kept busy carrying out essential repairs and succeeded in clearing the suction box in the cable locker, enabling it to be pumped out. The forward 12 pdr gun and the remaining boats were all secured with rope to prevent further damage.

In the crew's mess deck, the broken port holes were covered from the inside with canvas and their heavy steel covers (deadlights) clamped down. As dusk approached, a lookout, who had braved the violence of the storm and climbed up to the crow's nest on the foremast, sighted land. It did not take long for the Navigating Officer to obtain sufficient information and compass bearings to be able to inform the Captain that the *King Orry* was approaching Tarbat Ness at the head of the Moray Firth.

Due to the damaged wireless aerials, the *King Orry* had been unable to inform anybody of her predicament or present position but when she had failed to send in her routine radio report, the navy had assumed the worst.

As a result of this concern, warships had been sent out from Scapa Flow and the base at Invergordon to search for the *King Orry*.

While the Captain was being informed of the *King Orry's p*osition, a lookout reported that a flotilla of destroyers was approaching at high speed from the north.

At this present moment of time the *King Orry* was following the naval practice of not showing any navigation lights when operating in waters where an enemy vessel could be lurking. The Captain of the lead destroyer obviously thought that the darkened *King Orry* looked suspicious and a signal lamp was seen to flash a message across the water, demanding to know the identity of the suspect vessel.

As it was now too dark to read signal flags, the Chief Yeoman of Signals used a hand held signal lamp to flash the *King Orry's* call sign back to the destroyer while at the same time a signalman was sent away to hoist a new White Ensign on the mainmast to replace the storm-tattered flag that presently flew there.

Obviously the destroyer's Captain was still suspicious as a searchlight beam shot across the water and illuminated the *King Orry*. The beam played along the ship's side and finally rose up the mainmast until it rested on the White Ensign that had been hoisted only a few moments earlier.

Now that her Captain was satisfied that the *King Orry* was neither a blockade runner nor a German raider, the destroyer approached the armed boarding vessel and drew up alongside. As the two Captains spoke to one another by megaphone, the saga of the *King Orry's* storm damage and the subsequent loss of wireless aerials were relayed. The destroyer's Captain said that he would send a wireless message ashore and advise the naval authorities about her condition. The *King Orry* was ordered to sail into the Moray Firth and anchor off Cromarty until daybreak when she was to proceed to the naval base at Invergordon.

INVERGORDON

At 07.00 the following morning, 16th January, the *King Orry* weighed anchor and proceeded into Cromarty Firth where she secured alongside Berth 26.

Rear Admiral Gaunt from the battleship *Collingwood* came on board at 10.00 to inspect the damage. The *King Orry* looked a pitiful sight as he walked around her Boat Deck surveying the remains of the boats and other deck fittings.

The Admiral left after about 45 minutes and shortly afterwards teams of shipwrights and carpenters arrived on board from the battleship. Temporary repairs were commenced, but the *King Orry* would have to proceed to a shipyard for more permanent repairs to her damaged forward 12 pdr gun, the buckled starboard side of the boat deck and the loose rivets in the bow plating. The two lifeboats on the starboard side that had been smashed beyond repair were put ashore, while the lifeboat that now lay over the Wireless Office was found to be repairable.

It was decided to delay the repair of this boat until the *King Orry* went into the shipyard and in the meantime the boat was lifted back between its davits on the port side and securely lashed down. Amongst the many essential repairs that were carried out was to erect new wireless ariels.

A Court of Enquiry into the incidents leading up to and including the damage caused by the large wave on 14th January was held at 10.00 on 19th January. The Captain, First Lieutenant, Navigating Officer and Chief Engineer reported to the battleship *Hercules*, where they were to remain until late afternoon answering questions about every aspect of the incident.

As the *King Orry* was very nearly overwhelmed by the storm, the Admiralty wanted to be sure that neither human error nor negligence was involved. As all four officers remained as part of the *King Orry's* crew, it can only be assumed that they were all exonerated.

The *King Orry* went out to anchor in Cromarty Firth on the afternoon of 21st January to allow replacement boats to be hoisted on board. Two spare lifeboats from the interned German merchantman *Paris* were hoisted into the davits that had originally held the two smashed lifeboats (No 5 and No 7) on the starboard side. A replacement 27ft whaler was provided from the spare boat pool at Invergordon as were two large carley floats that had been added to provide the *King Orry w*ith extra lifesaving equipment until her remaining damaged lifeboats were repaired.

As it had not been possible to repair the loose rivets in the bow plating or replace the cracked glass in the port-holes in the crew mess deck, the *King Orry* was ordered to remain in Cromarty Firth until the storm had completely abated.

REPAIRS IN THE MERSEY

With the storm in the North Sea having now subsided and all essential repair work completed, the *King Orry* received orders to proceed to Cammell Laird's shipyard at Birkenhead on the morning of 24th January.

While en-route, she was to call at Scapa Flow to take on coal. Having taken shelter in Tobermory Bay on the island of Mull for most of 26th January, the *King Orry* arrived off the Mersey Bar at 15.00 on 28th January.

After exchanging messages with a naval patrol vessel, she picked up the pilot at 16.30 and proceeded up river towards Birkenhead. Passage was slow and it was dark by the time that the *King Orry* approached the Perch Rock Lighthouse off New Brighton.

As she passed the lighthouse, a searchlight beam suddenly shot out from the New Brighton Battery and illuminated the *King Orry* while at the same time a gun fired and seconds later a tower of water shot up into the air adjacent to the starboard bow. The *King Orry* immediately hove to and hoisted the signal flags that spelt out her call sign. Messages were passed between the ship and the shore battery via signal lamp and it was established that the *King Orry* had failed to answer the recognition challenge that had been sent from ashore. The log does not give any explanation for this omission, but does record that she was eventually allowed to proceed and secured alongside the Cammell Laird wharf at 19.30.

The *King Orry* was taken into the basin by two tugs at 08.00 the following morning. She was due to enter the dry dock later that morning, but before this could happen the forward 12 pdr magazine had to be emptied and all of its ammunition placed in the after 4" magazine to allow the Cammell Laird workers to enter the forward magazine and repair the loose rivets in the bow plating.

The transfer of the ammunition was completed by 10.00 at which time the *King Orry* was taken into the dry dock. She remained there until the morning of 9th February and during this period the shipyard employees worked 24 hours a day to repair all the damaged aspects of the vessel.

The forward 12 pdr gun was removed and sent ashore for repair and while it was away the caulking between the planking on the forecastle was checked to ensure that it was watertight. A new set of metal covers were also manufactured and fitted over the chain pipes while on the bridge roof, both the binnacle and searchlight were found to be repairable although the broken semaphore arms had to be replaced.

For the first few days in dry dock the ship vibrated to the clatter of hammers as the riveters replaced the loose rivets in the bow plating. Work also commenced to repair the damage to the starboard side of the Boat Deck and to the lifeboats. With the assistance of a dockyard crane, all lifeboats and the two carley floats

that had been taken on board in Cromarty Firth were lifted ashore.

The two replacement lifeboats on the starboard side were smaller than the original boats and would therefore not be put back on board but new boats were provided by Cammell Laird. The aftermost boat from the port side was taken away for repair while the forward one was placed on the jetty to await the replacement of its damaged davit.

The 27ft whaler remained in situ, as no repairs were required. All davits and boat chocks on the starboard side were removed to allow the shipyard workers to carry out the necessary repairs to the buckled deck which entailed removing large areas of planking to expose the buckled steel supports. The work to repair the loose rivets in the bow plating was completed by the evening of 5th February and the opportunity was taken to install a higher combing around the hatch to the forward magazine. It was hoped that this would prevent water draining down into the magazine should it manage to find its way into the forward part of the ship again.

*Warrant Engineer Haigh RNR, joined the **King Orry** on 21st November 1914. (David Handscombe collection)*

All of the 12 pdr and 4" ammunition was transferred from the after magazine into the forward magazine the following day to enable a similar coaming to be fitted around the hatch to the after magazine. As the repairs to the *King Orry* neared completion, a new 12 pdr gun was delivered. When the damaged 12 pdr gun had been inspected at the Naval Ordnance Depot, the armourers discovered that it had been extensively damaged and had decided that it would be better to replace the gun rather than repair it.

A new 3 pdr Hotchkiss quick-fire gun was also delivered. The provision of this small calibre gun was welcomed as it would now give her a more appropriate weapon for shooting at small targets and would be useful for destroying drifting wreckage such as abandoned lifeboats and rafts. The gun was fitted onto the Promenade Deck in the same location as the after 12 pdr gun which had been removed the previous August.

The ladder leading down from the Promenade Deck to the Poop Deck, which is shown in some of Crispen Redshaw's photographs, may have been installed during this refit period as the new 3 pdr gun was much smaller than the 12 pdr gun that had previously been installed and its barrel did not overhang the after end of the Promenade Deck. Space to stow the ammunition for this gun would be made within the existing 4" magazine.

As the major repair work was completed, Cammell Laird concentrated on the smaller tasks such as replacing the broken glass in the portholes and the starboard bridge wing house windows.

The *King Orry* was ready to be moved out of the dry dock on the morning of 9th February but before she was moved, a crane lifted the lifeboat that had been left

*Warrant Engineer Haigh inspecting one of the **King Orry's** damaged lifeboats following the violent storm of 13th – 14th January 1916. (David Handscombe collection)*

sitting on the jetty back into its davits on the port side. The remaining lifeboats would be hoisted back on board once the *King Orry* was out of the dock, the two smashed lifeboats on the starboard side having now been replaced by the correct-sized boats which had been taken from the steamer *Prince*.

Once the boats had been hoisted on board, two tugs towed the *King Orry* out of Cammell Laird's basin and took her down river to the basin at Wallasey. She would remain there for four days during which time the crew were employed on repainting the hull and superstructure.

At 04.00 on 14th February, the *King Orry* left the basin at Wallasey on the morning high tide and proceeded down river to carry out a compass swing, returning to anchor off Wallasey at 14.00. During the latter part of the afternoon, a team of Admiralty officials boarded the steamer and carried out an inspection of the repairs. For the second time within a month, the *King Orry* was declared as fit to return to her naval duties and as a result weighed anchor at dawn the following morning and proceeded north towards her base at Longhope.

BACK ON PATROL

She made a fairly slow passage towards the Orkney Islands and did not arrive off the entrance to Scapa Flow until just before 08.00 on 19th February, although her journey north had not been without incident.

On the morning of 17th February, the cruiser *Achilles* had fired a shot across her bow when she had failed to give a prompt reply to the cruiser's recognition

*The **King Orry** was not a good sea boat and she rolled heavily in rough weather making life on board uncomfortable for her crew: North Sea 1915. (David Handscombe collection)*

signal, while on the afternoon of 18th February, she ordered a suspicious vessel to stop and put a boarding party on board.

The vessel turned out to be the neutral American ship *Polaine*, and as her cargo manifest was correct she was allowed to proceed on her journey to the United States.

While the *King Orry* lay at anchor in Longhope on 20th February, Engineer Sub Lieutenant A Garrett, a Manxman from Ramsey, was taken ill with severe stomach pains. He was subsequently transferred to the hospital ship *Plassey*, where he was diagnosed as having appendicitis.

Until now, the rifles that were carried on board were not the standard British Lee Enfield .303" rifle. When war commenced in 1914, supplies of the Lee Enfield rifle had fallen short of requirements and the priority for issue had been given to the army. The navy were provided with a variety of weapons, many of which were either obsolete or of non-standard design. The *King Orry* had been provided with Japanese Arisaka Type 38 (M1905) 6.5mm rifles, that had been purchased from the French Government. However, on 26th February they were replaced with a consignment of Canadian Ross .303" rifles. Although the Ross rifle used the standard .303" cartridge, the army had

rejected it, as it was prone to jamming when exposed to the mud of the trenches.

The *King Orry* left Longhope to commence an Eastern Patrol later that day. Although she did not encounter any enemy shipping while on patrol, she would come across the sad remains of yet another merchant ship that had been forced into naval service.

The 15.831-ton Royal Mail Line passenger liner *Alcantara* had been requisitioned by the Royal Navy at the outbreak of war and had been converted into an armed merchant cruiser. At midday on 28th February, the Captain of a British submarine operating off the Skagerrak had informed the Admiralty that he had spotted a ship that looked suspicious and that it may be a disguised German raider attempting to break out into the North Sea.

This ship, which turned out to be the German commerce raider *Greif* had left Hamburg at dawn on 27th February disguised as a Norwegian steamer. In answer to the intelligence report, the Admiralty had notified all warships in the area to watch out for the raider and these included the *Alcantara* and the *Andes*.

The *Alcantara* and her consort were patrolling in an area approximately 70 miles to the north east of the Shetland Islands. At 09.15 on 29th February the *Alcantara* intercepted the *Greif* which promptly

*The **King Orry's** Royal Marine Light Infantry detachment with C/Sgt Little standing on the left: Scapa Flow 1915. Notice the Japanese Arisaka Type 38 rifles. (David Handscombe collection)*

HMS Cyclops, *the headquarters and repair ship for the armed boarding vessels based at Longhope, Scapa Flow. (David Handscombe collection)*

identified herself as the Norwegian steamer *Rena* that was sailing from La Plata to Trondheim.

Although the *Greif's* appearance seemed to resemble the details given in the "Lloyd's Register", the fact that she had been heading away from Norway rather than towards it made the *Alcantara's* Captain suspicious. Captain T E Wardle ordered the suspect vessel to stop and informed her Captain that he was going to put a boarding party on board to carry out an inspection. At he same time he sent a signal to the *Andes*, which was some 14 miles away, informing her that they had stopped what was believed to be the suspicious ship.

Almost simultaneously with the message being sent, the *Greif* uncovered her 5.9" guns and opened fire on the *Alcantara* at a range of little more than 1,200 yards. The first few shots shattered the *Alcantara's* Boat Deck and disabled her steering gear. Although she was now out of control, the *Alcantara* began to hit back with her 6" guns and soon wrecked the *Greif's* superstructure and set her on fire. One by one the raider's guns were silenced as the superior British gunnery took its toll.

Dense black smoke began to pour out of the German ship and her crew was seen to be taking to the lifeboats.

When it looked as if the *Greif* was finished, as a final act of defiance she fired a torpedo which struck the *Alcantara* on the port side and ripped a huge hole in

her Engine Room and Boiler Room. The *Alcantara* immediately began to list heavily to port and within minutes she suddenly rolled over and sank.

By this time the armed merchant cruiser *Andes*, the light cruiser *Comus* and the M Class destroyer *Munster* had arrived on the scene. While the *Andes* dispatched the wrecked and burning *Greif* to the bottom, the *Comus* and *Munster* started to pick up survivors, both British and German. The *Greif* finally blew up and sank at 13.00.

The *King Orry* had been diverted from her Eastern Patrol to assist with the search for the German raider but, by the time that she arrived in the area, the incident was over.

At 09.30 on 2nd March, she arrived at the last position of the *Alcantara* and the *Greif* to find the sea covered with wreckage and the occasional floating body. In the centre of the wreckage, a solitary lifeboat was drifting and the *King Orry* drew up alongside to ensure that there were no survivors on board. It was one of the collapsible Englehart type, which had gained notoriety when Second Officer Charles Lightoller had attempted to launch similar boats from the deck of the sinking White Star liner *Titanic*. Although the boat was badly damaged and full of shrapnel holes, the faded name *Alcantara* could still be read on the scorched paintwork. A quick inspection of the lifeboat from the vantage point of the *King Orry's* port bridge wing confirmed that there were no survivors or bodies on board, although there were a couple of life jackets and some items of personal clothing floating in a film of slime in the boat's bilge. To ensure that there were no classified documents on board, one of the seamen was lowered into the boat to sift through the artifacts. Finding nothing of consequence he was hauled back on board the *King Orry*.

The lifeboat was considered too badly damaged to warrant recovery and as it may have become a danger to shipping, it was set adrift to be dispatched to the bottom with gunfire from the 3 pdr gun. After two shells had ripped through the waterlogged lifeboat's hull, the last remains of the *Alcantara* disappeared below the waves.

The *Alcantara* was the second British merchant ship, which had been converted into an auxiliary warship to be sunk by a torpedo fired at close range from a disguised German raider. The *King Orry* remained in the area for another half an hour before turning south and heading back towards the Orkney Islands.

The *King Orry* continued to be employed on patrol duties to the North of the Shetland Islands until 20th March. At this time of the year, these northern waters were usually very rough and snow squalls were frequent.

As the crew of the *King Orry* attempted to keep their mess decks warm and dry, hot food from the galley was often not available as it was too dangerous to light the galley ovens due to the constant violent rolling of the ship.

On one particularly rough day, the voice pipe that connected the 3 pdr gun mounting to the bridge was washed away by a large wave that had crashed over the port bridge wing but fortunately nobody was injured. On another occasion the *King Orry* took part in a fruitless search for a seaman who had been washed overboard from an armed trawler. Having returned to her anchorage in Longhope on the evening of 20th March, the *King Orry* was stood down from patrol duty for two weeks which allowed her crew to get ashore and enjoy the limited recreation facilities that were available at the base.

TECHNICAL PROBLEMS

In the early hours of 3rd April, a sailing order was dispatched from the flagship, *Iron Duke*. It detailed a cruiser and an armed boarding vessel to leave Scapa Flow and once past the Pentland Skerries, to proceed north, passing between the Orkney Islands and the Fair Isle to an area to the west of the Shetland Islands. The two ships detailed were the *King Orry* and the 10.850 ton Devonshire Class light cruiser *Hampshire*.

*Under the watchful eye of C/Sgt Little, members of the **King Orry's** Royal Marine Light Infantry detachment enjoy a session of physical training. (David Handscombe collection)*

They were ordered to patrol in two areas, known as X-Ray and Yankee and their task was to intercept blockade-runners. Patrol area X-Ray covered a box that spread from the coast of Norway to the north of the Faroe Islands, while area Yankee spread from the Norwegian coast out to the north of Iceland. Each area was split into four patrol lines, which were known as A, B, C and D, prefixed with either X -Ray or Yankee as appropriate. The patrol lines were to be transited in approximately 60-mile long zig-zags, commencing at the south west corner of the box at first light and working towards the eastern limits by dusk.

The two areas were to be patrolled on alternate days, using the cover of night to sail to the next area. At just after 07.00 that same day, the *King Orry* and her consort left the anchorage in Longhope and proceeded towards the Switha Boom. As far as the *King Orry* was concerned, the patrol was to get off to a bad start. As she passed through the boom, her Officer of the Watch misjudged the speed and course of the armed trawler that was guarding the entrance and before either vessel could take any avoiding action, the *King Orry* collided with the smaller vessel.

Although the damage to both ships was minimal, the *King Orry* was left with an embarrassing scrape mark that stretched from her port bow to just below her bridge wing. The remainder of the journey northwards was without incident, but a severe gale slowed down the progress of both ships. The sailing order detailed the ships to remain on station for four days and to continue for a fifth day providing the *King Orry* had sufficient coal.

The patrol appeared to be doomed as far as the *King Orry* was concerned. First there was the collision at the Switha Boom and then at just after dusk on 6th April, the armed boarding vessel was involved in a dilemma yet again. As she steamed astern of the cruiser *Hampshire*, she suddenly veered off course, completely out of control.

The helmsman swung the wheel in an attempt to bring the ship back onto her correct heading but it quickly became obvious that her steering gear had failed.

While the engineers rushed to the steering gear compartment to investigate the failure, emergency hand steering was initiated by using the two large wooden steering wheels that were located on her Poop Deck.

After a period of about 10 minutes, Engineer Lieutenant John Keig arrived on the bridge and informed the Captain that the steering telemotor had failed and that repairs could not be carried out without support from the repair ship *Assistance*.

At 21.30, a signal was sent to the *Hampshire* informing her Captain of the situation and that it was necessary for the *King Orry* to abort the patrol and return to Scapa Flow for repairs. The *King Orry* reached Longhope at 09.00 the following morning after a fast passage, but it had been hard work for the seamen who had spent all night struggling with the emergency steering.

Unlike the wheel on the bridge which turned the rudder with the assistance of the electric telemotor, the emergency steering wheels where connected directly to the tiller bar by a combination of ropes and steel cables which made any movement of the rudder extremely hard work and required at least two men on each steering wheel.

The repairs were completed within 24 hours but the *King Orry* was ordered to remain at her anchorage to wait further sailing orders. They came on the evening of 12th April and the *King Orry* sailed at first light the following morning once again in company with the cruiser *Hampshire*.

The two ships were ordered to carry out a sweep down into the North Sea as far south as Peterhead and then eastward towards the coast of Denmark. Both ships were back at Longhope on the morning of 15th April, having encountered no enemy shipping or vessels acting suspiciously.

The remainder of April and early May 1916 saw the *King Orry* operating from the Shetland Islands.

Along with her running mate *Hampshire*, she was based in the Olna Firth. The areas that the two ships would operate in were the same X-Ray and Yankee patrol areas of the previous month, the only difference being that their base was now the Shetland Islands.

This northern base was very bleak and made the limited facilities that were available in Longhope, look like the centre of civilisation. Although the ships were

*Looking down into the hold of the collier **Mercedes** as bags of coal are craned aboard the **King Orry** to replenish her bunkers on 30th November 1914. (David Handscombe collection)*

protected from the storms that raged in the open sea, the weather was very cold with frequent snow squalls. On the odd occasion the weather did permit shore leave, but the small fishing communities in Voe and Busta had little to offer that would tempt the *King Orry's* crew away from the warmth of their mess decks.

The ordeal of operating from the Shetland Islands came to an end on 9th May when orders were received to proceed back to Longhope.

The patrols of the past few weeks had achieved little as far as stopping blockade runners was concerned, although many ships had been stopped and inspected, none of them had been carrying anything that warranted prize crews being put on board and the ships being taken to a British port.

However, on the morning of 10th May, as the *King Orry* sailed back towards the Orkney Islands, she came upon the Dutch steamer *Nieuw Amsterdam*. The vessel was ordered to stop and a boarding party put on board.

It was established that she was homeward bound from New York and heading towards her namesake port in Holland. A search of her cargo revealed nothing that was considered to be contraband but suspicions were raised when her Captain was unable to produce a cargo manifest.

The *King Orry's* Captain, Lt Cdr Selwyn Day, decided that this ship required further investigation and much to the disapproval of the Dutch Captain, he ordered the *Nieuw Amsterdam* to proceed into Kirkwall for inspection by the naval authorities. The *King Orry* arrived in Longhope later that day.

In company with two destroyers, the *King Orry* left Longhope to commence her next patrol at 05.00 on 14th May but she was not to remain at sea for very long. She had been ordered to proceed into the North Sea and carry out a sweep towards the Dutch coast but as she passed Duncansby Head, the hand of fate struck again.

Without warning, the *King Orry* suddenly veered off course: the steering gear had failed yet again. She immediately hove to and signalled her escort to inform them of the dilemma. As the problem again appeared to be related to the telemotor, the patrol was aborted and with emergency steering being carried out from the Poop Deck, the *King Orry* headed back to Longhope for repairs.

The artificers from the repair ship *Assistance* boarded the *King Orry* as soon as she arrived at her anchorage. At first the problem with the steering gear could not be identified as the telemotor was found to be serviceable but a more thorough inspection of the system revealed some corroded electrical wiring which

had been missed during the repairs that were carried out during April.

Unlike the previous repairs, which only took 24 hours, it took nearly a week to repair the defect as it was necessary to inspect the whole wiring system for similar corrosion.

The next set of sailing orders for the *King Orry* were issued from the flagship *Iron Duke* on 23rd May.

Along with the Monmouth Class cruiser *Donegal*, the *King Orry* was detailed to patrol off the Norwegian coast in the vicinity of Stadlandet, in the hope they would intercept blockade-runners. As well as carrying other contraband goods, it was suspected that ships were sailing from Narvik to Rotterdam with cargoes of iron ore that would eventually end up in the hands of the Germans.

As well as looking out for such vessels, the Captains of the two warships were warned about the possibility of encountering disguised German raiders that were accompanied by U boats. The two ships were to be in position off the coast of Stadlandet by daybreak on the morning after sailing from Scapa Flow.

On arrival, they would cruise in the area for three or four hours then withdraw to the west. They were to return to the patrol area at irregular intervals varying between twenty-four and forty eight hours for four days at a time. It was predicted that the most likely time to catch a blockade runner would be during misty weather, at dawn, dusk or during the night. Additionally, it was suspected that any ship attempting to break through the blockade would sail very close to the border of Norwegian territorial waters, thus allowing them to slip into the safety of Norway's neutrality should they be approached by a British warship.

On the morning of the fifth day, the *King Orry* and *Donegal* proceed to the Olna Firth in the Shetland Islands for a two-day rest period. No doubt the King Orry's crew received the prospect of returning to the Olna Firth with little enthusiasm.

The *King Orry* and the *Donegal* weighed anchor and sailed from Longhope at 07.00 on 24th May and proceeded north to their allotted patrol area. Having arrived off the Norwegian coast at dawn the following morning, the next five days were spent creeping in and out of the Stadlandet patrol area in the hope of catching a blockade-runner. Numerous Norwegian and Danish fishing boats were encountered as the two warships cruised up and down their patrol line.

It was known that many Norwegians and Danes were sympathetic to the German cause, so great care had to be taken to ensure that the true intention of the two warships was not given away to anybody who may have been observing them.

To this end, the *King Orry* and the *Dinegal* never arrived at the same time and always approached and departed from the patrol area in opposite directions. Once they had disappeared over the horizon and were out of sight from any suspicious observer, they would meet up and prepare for the next sortie. They only came across one suspect vessel; at dusk on 28th May.

The suspect ship appeared to be a large tramp steamer, which had drawn attention to itself by steaming with no lights in a southerly direction very close to the border of Norwegian territorial waters. Her Captain must have been warned about the possibility of encountering British warships for as soon as the *King Orry* increased speed to shorten the distance between the two vessels, the steamer turned sharply to port and disappeared into the night and the safety of Norway's territorial waters.

Chasing the vessel would have been a fruitless exercise and may have caused an embarrassing international incident had the Norwegians spotted the two British ships blatantly violating the sovereignty of their neutrality and territorial waters. After all, the Royal Navy had enough problems with the German navy, let alone provoking a confrontation with the small but efficient Norwegian navy.

The *King Orry* and the *Donegal* terminated their patrol on the morning of 29th May and with the coal bunkers on board the *King Orry* nearly empty, they both anchored within the Olna Firth in the Shetland Islands at 06.00 the following morning.

The two ships were scheduled to remain at anchor until 1st June but their stand down was interrupted towards the end of the afternoon on 31st May. As dusk approached, there was a sudden hive of activity amongst the other warships as orders to proceed to sea were received from the Rear Admiral in Command of the ships operating from the Olna Firth. The *King Orry* and *Donegal* were ordered to raise steam and to remain at immediate notice to put to sea. Although the reason for this flurry of action was still unclear, unconfirmed reports of a massive sea battle were beginning to reach the ears of the *King Orry's* crew.

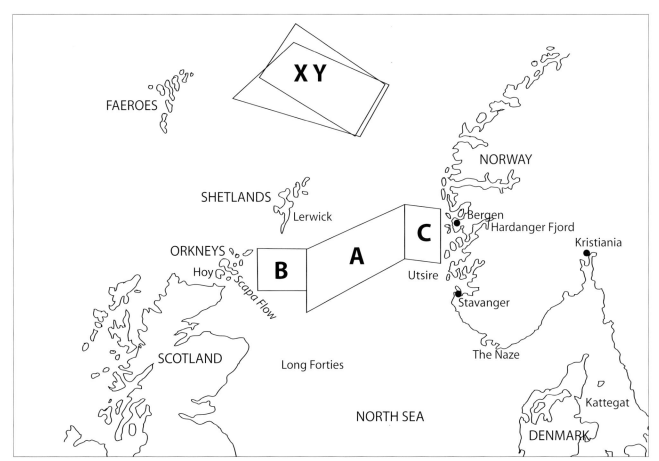

Armed Boarding vessel Patrol Areas Orkney and Shetland 1914-1918

*Looking foreward from the **King Orry's** Poop Deck, showing the 12 pdr gun on the after end of the Promenade Deck: Scapa Flow 1915. (David Handscombe collection)*

CHAPTER SIX

With the Grand Fleet

JUTLAND

On 31st May, while the crew of the *King Orry* busied themselves with preparing their ship to proceed to sea, the rumours of battle that had reached their ears were indeed a reality and were taking place some 420 miles south east of the Shetland Islands.

Often referred to as the "clash of the Titans", heavy units of the Royal Navy and the German High Seas Fleet were engaged in a confused and violent confrontation that developed into what is now known as the Battle of Jutland.

During the first few months of 1916, both the British and German fleets had been trying to lure each other into battle and inflict catastrophic damage on the opposition's ships and therefore claim supremacy at sea.

At dusk on 30th May, Admiral Sir John Jellicoe sailed from Scapa Flow with his battleships while Vice Admiral Sir David Beatty left the Firth of Forth with his battle cruiser squadron. A second battleship force left Cromarty Firth under the command of Vice Admiral Sir Martyn Jerram.

With their guns cleared for action, the British warships raced through the night towards the Skagerrak, where is was hoped they would find the ships of the German High Seas Fleet.

At just after 14.00 the following afternoon, the British light cruiser *Galatea* sighted a merchant ship that was stopped and blowing off steam and as this looked unusual the *Galatea's* Captain decided to investigate.

As the cruiser approached the suspicious vessel, two destroyers that were easily identifiable as German appeared from behind the merchant ship and scurried away towards the horizon. The *Galatea* gave chase and opened fire, at the same time sending a signal to the flagship, "enemy in sight".

As the *Galatea's* signal was being decoded on board the British flagship, the Germans had sent a similar signal to their fleet commander. The events that took place over the next few hours are well documented and have been the subject of numerous books, needless to say only a brief outline of the battle and its outcome is appropriate as part of the *King Orry's* story.

Approximately one hour later, the battle cruisers of Vice Admiral Beatty and Rear Admiral Hipper engaged in combat. The exchange of fire was confused, but the German gunnery was far superior and devastatingly effective. At just after 16.00 the German battle cruiser *Von Der Tann* hit the British battle cruiser *Indefatigable* with a full salvo and moments later she erupted into a ball of fire and smoke and blew up with only two of her crew surviving.

With the first major kill to the Germans, they were soon to prove that dispatching the *Indefatigable* to a watery grave was not just a lucky hit. Twenty minutes later, a second British battle cruiser, the *Queen Mary* took a combined salvo from the German *Seydlitz* and *Derfflinger* that penetrated her upper decks and detonated one of her magazines. A dull red glow appeared amidships and seconds later the *Queen Mary* blew up and sank in a similar manner to the *Indefatigable*.

As the battle continued, the Super Dreadnoughts of Admiral Jellicoe and his opponent Vice Admiral Scheer arrived, both Admirals having steamed at high speed after being informed of the whereabouts of each other's forces.

The 15" guns and 13.5" guns of Jellicoe's battleships were soon wreaking havoc amongst the German warships. The *Seydlitz* was hit by 22 shells and one torpedo but despite extensive damage managed to survive the onslaught and limp home.

Just as the might of Jellicoe's battleships was beginning to inflict severe damage on the Germans, a third catastrophe occurred. The battle cruiser *Invincible* was repeatedly scoring hits on the German *Derfflinger* and as the damage was beginning to take its toll on the German ship, she fired two salvos at her British assailant. The first salvo straddled the *Invincible* but the shells from the second plunged into the British ship's hull and shrouded her in smoke. As this began to clear and the *Invincible* came into view again, flames suddenly shot up from her midships section and to the amazement of the German onlookers, the third British battle cruiser to fall victim to German gunnery exploded and sank within two minutes. All that was left of the *Invincible* were the pathetic remains of her bow and stern sections.

Later in the action, Rear Admiral Hipper was forced to abandon his flagship *Lutzow* as she had been so badly damaged by gunfire that she was no longer capable of acting as a fighting ship. The two fleets continued to manoeuvre and pound one another as the daylight drifted into darkness

By midnight, the whereabouts of each other's ships had become confusing and Vice Admiral Scheer took advantage of the situation by withdrawing his warships into the darkness and running for home. The last contact with the German High Seas Fleet was at just after 02.00 just as the first streaks of dawn began to appear on the horizon.

The British fleet continued to patrol the North Sea well into the morning of Thursday 1st June, hoping to locate any damaged German warships that had fallen behind the main force. All they found was pitiable flotsam, bits of wood and paper, cork life preservers and floating corpses in the uniforms of both navies. At midday, saddened by the loss of so many fine ships and men, Admiral Jellicoe ordered the Grand Fleet to return to its bases: the "clash of the Titans" was over.

Both sides claimed victory, the British claim based on the fact that the German High Seas Fleet had run for home and the German claim based upon the loss of British warships being greater than their own. The Grand Fleet had indeed suffered a greater loss, loosing three battle cruisers, three armoured cruisers and eight destroyers, with a total loss of life of 6,097 men.

On the German side the High Seas Fleet lost one pre-Dreadnought battle ship, one battle cruiser, four light cruisers and five destroyers, with a total of 2,545 men.

It could be said that the Germans were justified in claiming victory based upon the greater loss to the British fleet but the mere fact that the German High Seas Fleet never attempted to challenge the might of the Grand Fleet again during the remainder of the First World War must support the claim that the Royal Navy once again ruled the waves.

BACK ON PATROL

On the evening of 31st May, the *King Orry* was in the Olna Firth in the Shetland Islands. She had raised steam by 19.30 and at 20.00 her Captain was summoned to a meeting on board the cruiser *Donegal*, returning some thirty minutes later.

As soon as he was back on board, the crew were called to harbour stations and the *King Orry* was made ready to proceed to sea. As the final preparations for sailing were taking place, the Captain called for the officers to muster in the wardroom where they were presumably briefed on the current situation and given the details of the *King Orry's* sailing orders.

At 21.00, with her crew closed up at action stations and in company with her consort, the *Donegal*, the *King Orry* weighed anchor and left the Olna Firth.

The two ships had been ordered to sail back towards the coast of Norway and patrol areas X-Ray and Yankee, the same area where they had spent the previous few days. The sailing order does not mention the Battle of Jutland but informs the two ships to be on the look out for enemy vessels that may be attempting to reach the neutral ports of Norway. Presumably, the term "enemy vessels" must refer to blockade runners or possibly disguised raiders as neither the *King Orry* nor the *Donegal* would have been any match for heavy units of the German High Seas Fleet.

The two ships remained on patrol until the evening of 3rd June when a signal instructed them to return to Longhope. Fortunately, they had not sighted any German warships or suspect vessels during their patrol and finally anchored within Longhope at 17.00 on 4th June.

The log records that the Captain mustered the ship's company at 09.00 on 4th June and officially informed them of the Battle of Jutland and its outcome, although at this stage the battle had not been given a name.

The atmosphere within Scapa Flow was one of jubilation but it was also very evident that the Grand Fleet had sustained considerable damage during the battle. Many of the ships showed signs of battle damage with shell holes pepper-potting their hulls and superstructure, while the sombre news of the loss of the three battle cruisers and the other warships cast a shadow on the celebrations that were taking place in the many pubs and naval canteens ashore.

While the men of the Grand Fleet boasted that they had swept the seas clear of German warships, a German naval mine was about to inflict a blow that would rock the hierarchy of the War Office and Government, and shock the nation as a whole.

The morning of 5th June 1916 was blustery and as the day progressed a gale blew up from the north east. There was an air of secrecy within Scapa Flow as firstly at about midday when the Commander In Chief's dispatch vessel, the destroyer *Oak* arrived and then at 17.30 when the cruiser *Hampshire* left the Flow via the Hoxa Sound, escorted by two destroyers.

As the rumours spread around the *King Orry* regarding the secretive movements of the *Oak* and the *Hampshire*, orders were received that instructed the Captain to take the *King Orry* down to Birkenhead for an overhaul at Cammell Laird's shipyard and if the workload permitted, to give leave to each watch. The *King Orry* had been ordered to sail for the River Mersey at dawn the following morning, 6th June.

She weighed anchor at just after 07.00 and set course for the River Mersey. The passage south was uneventful and after passing the Bar Lightship at 10.00 the next day, the *King Orry* secured alongside Princes Landing Stage in Liverpool one hour later. Soon afterwards, the port watch was sent on ten days' leave.

LOSS OF THE HAMPSHIRE

The secrecy surrounding the arrival of the Commander In Chief's dispatch vessel at Scapa Flow on 5th June and the subsequent departure of the cruiser *Hampshire* was still a mystery to everybody on board the *King Orry*. However, when the evening newspapers were published, they carried a numbing headline on the front page, "Lord Kitchener Drowned".

It was only now that the cloud of secrecy was lifted and the sad facts revealed. Lord Kitchener, the British War Minister had been despatched by the Government for a secret meeting with Tsar Nicholas of Russia during which he would inspect various aspects of the Russian war machine and discuss future military co-operation between the British and Russian Governments. After dining with Admiral Jellicoe on board his flagship *Iron Duke*, Lord Kitchener transferred to the cruiser *Hampshire* to begin his journey to Archangel in Russia where he was due to arrive on 9th June. For obvious reasons this mission was being kept a tight secret.

Due to the NE gale that was now pounding the Orkney Islands, Jellicoe suggested that Lord Kitchener should delay his departure until the following morning, when it was predicted that the storm would have abated. But Kitchener being an impetuous man would have none of this and demanded that plans be made for his departure that evening.

The usual route taken by ships travelling northwards from the Orkney Islands was via the east coast channel which was regularly swept for mines and was considered to be relatively safe. However, because of the north easterly gale, Jellicoe made plans for the *Hampshire* to travel up the inner channel on the western coast of the Orkney islands which would allow the cruiser to be in the lee of the land for the first part of the journey.

The cruiser and her escorting destroyers sailed at just after 17.30 and met mountainous seas as they buffeted their way around the southern tip of Hoy and up the western coast of Orkney. The gale had suddenly shifted and was now blowing from the north west and the shelter of the coast was no longer available to the three ships. At just before 19.00, the *Hampshire's* Captain ordered the two destroyers back to Scapa Flow, as they were not making any headway in the heavy seas. Some forty minutes later the *Hampshire* met her doom. As she drew abreast of Marwick Head, she struck a mine. Within fifteen minutes the cruiser had rolled over to starboard, capsized and sunk. The lookout point on Birsay witnessed the sinking and a message had been sent to the naval headquarters. Unfortunately, due to poor telephone links and confusion there, when they finally received the message it was some hours before rescue ships were dispatched to the scene.

Sadly, by the time that they arrived all but twelve of the *Hampshire's* crew had perished in the mountainous seas, including Lord Kitchener and every member of his staff.

After the war was over and German naval records were made available to the British Government, it was revealed that the western coast of Orkney had been mined by the submarine *U75* over the night of 28th - 29th May. Although the Germans knew nothing of Lord Kitchener's mission, they had hoped to catch units of the Grand Fleet putting to sea in response to the High Seas Fleet challenge to battle, which resulted in the Battle of Jutland.

The news was received on board the *King Orry* with disbelief; Lord Kitchener was a national hero who had risen to fame during the Sudanese War when he had commanded the British and Egyptian forces, which had finally beaten the fanatical Dervish army at the Battle of Omdurman. Since the outbreak of the First World War he had been Secretary of State for War and his face adorned the recruiting posters with the famous "Your Country Needs You" slogan. After the public euphoria following the Battle of Jutland, Kitchener's death was received with genuine sorrow.

REFIT

With the port watch away on leave, the *King Orry* remained at Princes Landing Stage until 9th June, when at midday she was moved by tugs across the River Mersey to Cammell Laird's shipyard.

During the course of the afternoon all the ammunition was put ashore and she entered the dry dock which was drained by 19.30 when the *King Orry* sat high and dry on the wooden blocks.

Work began the following morning to clean the grime and barnacles from the ship's bottom in preparation for a new coat paint being applied. The cleaning and subsequent repainting took until the afternoon of 13th June to complete.

The dock was then reflooded during the following morning and at midday the *King Orry* was moved into the basin and secured alongside the south wall. As soon as she was secure, shipyard workers piled on board with various items of equipment and tools. Now that her bottom had been repainted and she was afloat again, work commenced on the other items of work that had been programmed into the short refit period. Amongst the major items of work that were commenced were the enlargement of the Chart Room and the installation of mine laying and depth charge rails onto the Poop Deck.

The Chart Room on the *King Orry* was very small and it was probably too cramped for the amount of chart work that was carried out by the Navigating Officer and watch keeping officers during patrols. This enlarged Chart Room was one of the few alterations that was not returned to its original condition when the *King Orry* was returned to the Steam Packet at the end of the war.

The installation of the mine laying and depth charge rails on the Poop Deck caused speculation amongst the crew that the *King Orry* was going to be employed as a minelayer, possibly in a covert role similar to the merchant vessels that the German navy was using as raiders. However, the role that these mine laying rails would play would be far less sinister and would have little effect on the future role of the *King Orry*.

Unfortunately, no photographs exist which show the rails in position but it can only be assumed that the rails were little more than small tracks that were bolted directly onto the *King Orry's* Poop Deck for portable items that could be removed when not in use. The installation of anything larger would not have been possible on the Poop deck due to the amount of room that was already taken up by the two 4" guns and the emergency steering wheels. Although the artificers from the repair ship *Assistance* had carried out repairs to the steering telemotor while the *King Orry* was at Longhope, Cammell Laird took the opportunity to completely strip the system, overhauling the hydraulics and surveying all the associated electrical wiring. Routine maintenance was also carried out on the turbines and gearing.

The port watch returned from their ten days leave at 08.00 on 17th June, which allowed the starboard watch to proceed on leave at midday, returning on 27th June.

The *King Orry* remained at Birkenhead until 28th June. As all work had been completed two days earlier, the remaining time was taken with loading ammunition and taking coal on board.

At 07.00 on 28th June the *King Orry* embarked the pilot and moved out into the River Mersey. The Bar Lightship was passed an hour later and shortly afterwards the *King Orry* dropped her anchor to carry out a compass swing. This was successfully completed by 11.00 at which time the pilot disembarked and the armed boarding vessel commenced her journey back to the Orkney Islands where she safely arrived on 1st July.

While en-route to her northern base, a drifting mine was spotted floating in the vicinity of Dunnett Head but was duly dispatched with rifle fire.

Over the next few days the crew were kept occupied with taking onboard various items of stores, more ammunition and topping up the bunkers with coal.

LONGHOPE MISHAP

At dawn on 5th July, the *King Orry* weighed anchor and proceeded slowly towards the entrance to Longhope as she commenced yet another routine Eastern Patrol.

There was a strong tide running and as she approached an anchored steamer, the *Valhynia*, the combination of the tide and the suction caused by the *King Orry's* propellers swung the stern of the anchored vessel towards her. With no time to take avoiding action, the *King Orry's* starboard quarter collided with the *Valhynia* and this was followed by a long grating noise as the *King Orry* scraped down the side of the steamer and rode up over her anchor cable.

The *King Orry* stopped as soon as she was clear of the anchor cable and a hurried inspection to ascertain how much damage had been caused was carried out. The damage to her starboard quarter was minimal and she was not taking in any water. The Captain sent a signal to the headquarters ship *Cyclops*, informing the Admiral of the incident and that all was well. Soon afterwards the armed boarding vessel got under way, passed through the Switha Boom and entered Pentland Firth.

Shortly after 10.00, a signal was received from the destroyer *Mandrake* requesting that the *King Orry* stood by a disabled trawler until a tug arrived from Scapa Flow. Fortunately this did not delay the *King Orry* for very long as a tug arrived an hour later and took the trawler in tow.

While on patrol, the Captain took the opportunity to carry out gunnery practice with the 12 pdr gun. Although her log does not contain exact details, it contains a statement that during the gunnery practice the gun's breechblock malfunctioned, rendering the weapon unserviceable.

On her return to Longhope on 7th July, armourers from the repair ship *Assistance* inspected the gun and decided that it would have to be taken ashore for repair at the nearby Naval Ordnance Depot. The damage that the breechblock sustained is not recorded, but it must have been fairly significant as the 12 pdr had not been returned by the time that the *King Orry* commenced her next patrol.

Minus her forward armament, the *King Orry* left Longhope to carry out an Eastern Patrol on 12th July, returning two days later. Upon her return, she was reunited with the repaired forward 12 pdr gun. Divers from the *Assistance* carried out an underwater inspection of the *King Orry's* hull on 17th July and discovered that the starboard bilge keel had been badly bent when the *King Orry* had scraped over the *Valhynia's* anchor cable a couple of weeks earlier but as the damage did not interfere with her seaworthiness, repairs were delayed until her next routine dry-docking period.

The *King Orry* continued with her patrol routine throughout July and it remained fruitless until the afternoon of 28th July. The ship had sailed from Longhope the previous morning in company with the armed boarding vessel, *Dundee*.

At 13.30, the Captain of the *Dundee* asked the *King Orry* to take over the tow of a Dutch trawler *SCH 124*, which had been arrested by the *Dundee* earlier in the day for having an excessive amount of petrol on board. Apart from the petrol, suspicion had also been aroused, as the trawler did not have an engine. It was suspected that the petrol was contraband and that the trawler was attempting to smuggle it into Germany. With an armed boarding party put on board, the *King Orry* towed the trawler towards Kirkwall until 17.00, when she was relieved of her charge by a naval tug. The *King Orry* then resumed her patrol, returning to Longhope early the following morning.

Q SHIPS

The next few days were to prove to be very busy for the armed boarding vessel's crew. The Admiralty had used armed merchant ships disguised as peaceful traders for some time, as had the Germans. The British called the ships submarine decoy vessels or as they were more commonly known, Q ships. The main function of Q ships was to lure German submarines into thinking that they were attacking a peaceful merchant ship.

When the submarine surfaced and ordered the ship to stop, the outwardly-looking peaceful merchant ship would drop its disguise and reveal her guns, hopefully sinking the U boat before its crew realised what was happening. Unfortunately, one of the knock-on effects from this tactic was that German U boat commanders began to ignore the code of chivalry and stopped surfacing and ordering the crews of merchantman to abandon ship before they attacked their vessel.

However, in July 1916 the Admiralty were still happy with the results of the Q ships and now decided to use similar tactics to lure merchant vessels carrying contraband for Germany into thinking that they were being approached by another peaceful merchant ship.

On 3rd August, work commenced to disguise the *King Orry's* weapons and to return her appearance to that of a peaceful merchantman while similar work also commenced on board the *Dundee*.

It is possible that other armed boarding vessels were involved in this exercise, although record of their involvement has not been found. To disguise the *King Orry*, her Poop Deck railings were covered in canvas to give the effect of being solid bulwarks. A boom was attached to the front of the foremast, parallel with the barrel of the 12 pdr gun and rigged to look like a derrick. The gun was then covered with a canvas awning and ropes were hung over the boom in sufficient length as to completely cover the gun mounting. From a distance this effect resembled that of a cargo derrick on a tramp steamer. The two 4" guns were similarly disguised with canvas, while another artificial boom was fitted to the rear of the mainmast to disguise the 3 pdr gun sited on the after end of the Promenade Deck.

The exposed after end of the Shelter Deck was covered in with canvas awnings and then the hull and superstructure up to deck level on the Promenade Deck was painted black. There is no record of whether the remaining superstructure was repainted white, although it probably was. The funnel was repainted yellow with a black top. The embossed name letters on either side of her Bow were enhanced with the addition of the letters V and I, thus making her name read *Viking Orry*.

As the name 'Viking' was common in Scandinavian waters, it was thought that the name *Viking Orry* might allow the armed boarding vessel to easily pass as a peaceful merchant ship.

However, before the *King Orry* sailed on her cloak and dagger mission, she was tasked to assist with the disposal of a defective depth charge. This had been returned to the repair ship *Assistance* by one of the warships after the depth setting regulator had been damaged during the arming process. The regulator could no longer be returned to the safe position, resulting in the fuse being jammed at a predetermined depth.

Rather than tamper with the device, the ordnance artificers from the *Assistance* had decided to take the depth charge out to sea and drop it over the side utilising the *King Orry's* recently-installed mine laying and depth charge rails. Once dropped over the side, the depth charge would explode when it reached the depth to which the fuse was set.

The *King Orry*, albeit now partially disguised as *Viking Orry*, left Longhope at 08.00 on 8th August and disposed of the defective weapon in Pentland Firth later that morning. The dropping of a depth charge over the stern of the *King Orry* must have been a precarious exercise that necessitated her travelling at high speed if she was not to blow her own stern off when the charge exploded. The *King Orry* then returned to Longhope to allow her crew to continue with the work on her disguise.

At 06.00 on the morning of 16th August, the *Viking Orry*, in company with the similarly disguised *Dundee*, sailed from Scapa Flow and headed eastward towards Norway. The two ships were to patrol off the Norwegian coast, the *King Orry* in the vicinity of Stadlandet, an area in which she had previously operated with the cruiser *Donegal*, while the *Dundee* would patrol in the vicinity of Utsira Island and an area known as the Utsira Patch.

The *King Orry* arrived in her patrol area the following morning and cruised slowly up and down in a predetermined pattern. Due to her disguise as a peaceful merchantman, she did not fly the Royal Navy White Ensign from her masthead and the log does not give any indication of any particular national flags that may have been flown. It has always been assumed that she flew a Norwegian flag while disguised as the *Viking Orry*, but an undated wartime photograph of her Poop Deck clearly shows the Red Ensign (or perhaps the Blue Ensign) being flown from her ensign staff which

suggests that she may have disguised herself as a British vessel at some time during this period.

She encountered no suspect vessels on the first day but had a submarine scare when a periscope was sighted during the afternoon which necessitated the *King Orry* to increase her speed to 19 knots in order that she could out run the U boat before it had time to move into an attacking position although it was never established whether this submarine was British or German.

During the hours of darkness the *King Orry* would steam with no navigation lights showing which would allow her to get up close to any suspect vessel without drawing attention to herself. She would then take a close look at the other vessel and providing nothing suspicious was detected, sail away into the darkness again leaving the other steamer in total oblivion to the fact that an armed boarding vessel had given her a close examination.

The following morning, 18th August, was misty with a fairly calm sea state. As the *King Orry* cruised through the mist at about 8 knots, a large steamer loomed into view at a distance of no more than two miles. The *King Orry* gently altered her course until she was on a similar heading to that of the other vessel and increased her speed slightly in order that she would eventually overhaul her.

All of the *King Orry's* movements had to be very casual so that they did not alarm the crew of the suspect vessel. The steamer was flying a Norwegian flag and had the name *Britannic* painted on her stern (not to be confused with the White Star Liner) but her port of registration was not visible.

The omission of this small detail aroused the suspicion of the *King Orry's* Captain and he decided to investigate in more detail. As it was necessary to uncover the *King Orry's* 4" guns without alarming the crew of the *Britannic*, the *King Orry* slowly altered her position until she was directly astern of the suspect vessel thus putting her Poop Deck and 4" guns out of view. Unfortunately, this manoeuvre must have made the Captain of the *Britannic* realise the armed boarding vessel's true purpose for the *Britannic* suddenly altered course and attempted to run for the cover of the mist and the safety of Norwegian territorial waters.

As soon as it became apparent what the *Britannic* was attempting, the *King Orry's* Captain ordered the White Ensign to be hoisted to the masthead and gave chase.

There was little competition between the two ships and the relatively calm sea state allowed the *King Orry* to increase her speed to 18 knots and she soon overhauled the other vessel. At the same time as she drew alongside the *Britannic* and ordered her to heave to, the port 4" gun fired a shell across the steamer's bow.

The Captain of the *Britannic* was obviously now fully aware of the situation and his future predicament if he ignored the British ship's demands and so wisely slowed down and stopped. Once stationary, she let off steam to indicate that she was complying with the armed boarding vessel's orders.

The boarding party of Royal Marines swiftly made their way over to the stationary steamer in one of the *King Orry's* boats and on arrival climbed up the jumping ladder, which had been lowered down the steamer's side.

An inspection of the vessel revealed that the *King Orry's* Captain had good cause to be suspicious as the *Britannic's* holds were full of iron ore and examination of her cargo manifest indicated that it was not bound for an allied cause. The ship was promptly arrested and under the supervision of an armed boarding party, she was dispatched to Kirkwall for proper inspection by the contraband authorities.

An account of this incident published shortly after the First World War mentions that the *Britannic's* Captain knew that the *King Orry* (albeit the *Viking Orry*) was not a peaceful merchantman as soon as he had seen her as her rakish design made her appear warlike and menacing.

When the *King Orry* had first come into sight, he had been warned by a member of his crew about the true identity of vessel that now stalked them as he had apparently worked on the Birkenhead ferries before the war and recognised the Manx steamer at once.

The *Britannic* had been hugging the coast of Norway and had used the numerous small islands to hide her progress but when the mist had closed in the Captain had decided to seek the safety of deeper water further out to sea. This had been his downfall and he blamed the mist for his capture. The *Britannic* was dispatched to the Orkney Islands shortly after midday while the *King Orry* continued her patrol for a further 24 hours and returned to Longhope at 07.10 on 20th August. She carried out one further patrol to the east of the Orkney Islands on 23rd - 24th August.

THE LESSONS OF JUTLAND

The return of the *King Orry* to Longhope on 24th August heralded the end of her duties against blockade runners and on contraband patrol. The vessels that operated these blockade and contraband duties were part of the Northern Patrol and although they were

*The after end of the King Orry's Boat and Promenade Decks and may show her being repainted as the **Viking Orry** at Scapa Flow in August 1916. (David Handscombe collection)*

denied the glamour that was given to the battleships and destroyers of the Grand Fleet, their role was a vital one.

Since 1914, the Northern Patrol had guarded an area of sea that covered some 800 miles stretching from the Orkney Islands to Iceland and across the North Sea to Norway. Until now it had intercepted over 14,000 ships and the patrol was so effective that less than 4% of the vessels attempting to break through the blockade actually succeeded. The *King Orry*, often rust-streaked and showing signs of storm damage, had proved to be a valuable asset to the unsung heroes of the Northern Patrol.

Following the Battle of Jutland, the Admiralty had analysed the outcome of the battle and the performance of its ships and men. The controversial enquiry into the loss of the three battle cruisers finally concluded that a design fault in their magazine construction and inadequate upper deck armour had caused their demise.

However, these design faults were compounded by the greater accuracy of the German gunners when compared with their British counterparts. The large guns of the German navy were brought onto target by a far more sophisticated gun sight than that used by the Royal Navy. British warships ranged their guns by firing salvos to obtain what was known as a straddle. This meant that a salvo was fired over the target, followed by a salvo being fired short of the target. The distance between the two falls of shot was then calculated and the range of the enemy ship established. This method was time consuming and was often inaccurate if the enemy ship was manoeuvring, whereas the German gun sight was designed to establish a ship's range with the first salvo, giving the German gunners a distinct advantage.

Another factor that was revealed during the investigation was that British gunners had little experience in shooting at fast moving targets, as the Royal Navy tended to practice its gunnery against large battle targets which were towed behind slow-moving tugs.

Two battleships approaching each other could have a closing speed of nearly fifty miles per hour, whereas two cruisers or destroyers could close on each other at between sixty and seventy miles per hour. Another aspect of the battle that was discussed in the enquiry was the confusion caused by signals either being missed or not understood when being passed around the fleet. The proposals to rectify the shortcomings in the Grand Fleet's gunnery practice and passing of signal messages was to affect the future use of the *King Orry*.

Having returned from patrol on 24th August, the *King Orry* remained at anchor within Longhope and awaited further sailing orders. On 2nd September, Lt Cdr Selwyn Day temporarily stood down as the *King Orry's* commanding officer and was relieved by Captain Basil V Brooke RN.

Captain Brooke had arrived in the Orkney Islands a few days earlier to take command of the light cruiser *Blonde*, but unfortunately during a severe gale on 10th August, she had run aground on the Louther Rocks in Pentland Firth and suffered considerable underwater damage. Following emergency repairs to make her watertight, she had been dispatched to Cammell Laird's shipyard for dry-docking and permanent repair.

At the time of the grounding, the *Blonde* had been under the Command of Lt Cdr Alexander Burton. He had been the *Blonde's* Executive Officer and had been given temporary command of the light cruiser as there was a gap of a month between her previous Captain leaving and Captain Brooke joining. Lt Cdr Burton had now returned to Scapa Flow to attend the enquiry into the grounding incident and to meet Captain Brooke. As the repairs to the *Blonde* were expected to take a few weeks to complete, both officers had been temporarily appointed to the *King Orry*.

*The forward 12pdr gun being disguised by covering it with canvass and then draping ropes over a temporary boom suspended above the gun on board the **Viking Orry** during August 1916. (David Handscombe collection)*

This must have been an awkward arrangement as an officer with Captain Brooke's seniority would not usually be appointed to such a minor vessel as the *King Orry*, especially as his previous appointment had been second in command of the 30.000 ton battleship, *Emperor of India*.

A few members of the *Blonde's* crew had remained at Scapa Flow when the light cruiser had sailed for repair and they also now joined the *King Orry*.

The *King Orry's* engineers had been experiencing problems with the ship's dynamo (electrical generator) for the past few weeks. These problems became critical on 6th September and necessitated the Chief Engineer, Eng Lt John Keig calling on the Fleet Engineer Officer in the repair ship *Assistance* to discuss methods of rectification.

It was decided to order a new dynamo and replace the troublesome item. The defective dynamo obviously affected the use of the *King Orry* as a disguised Norwegian merchantman and her log records that on 6th Septemberher crew were instructed to remove the disguise and return her appearance to that of an armed boarding vessel. Over the next few days the artificial derricks and bulwarks were removed and the hull, the superstructure and funnel were repainted and returned to the traditional Royal Navy dark grey. This task was completed on 14th September.

The replacement dynamo arrived on board on the afternoon of 16th September, Artificers from the *Assistance* came on board the following morning and spent the next few days removing the old unit and installing the replacement. This was completed by 20th

September and the *King Orry* proceeded to sea for 48 hours to allow the new equipment to be tested under operational conditions. The result of the trial is not recorded in the log but following her return to Longhope on 22nd September she did not proceed to sea again until 26th October when she was ordered to proceed to Cammell Laird's ship yard. It can only be assumed that all was not well.

Although the crew of the *King Orry* was not granted any home leave during extended periods at anchor within Longhope, they were given the opportunity to get ashore although facilities were relatively spartan. Compared with the cramped mess decks on board the warships anchored within Scapa Flow, however, they provided a very welcome alternative for relaxation.

The victualling rations that were provided to the warships were wholesome and provided the crews with a nutritional diet but the variety of vegetables was somewhat limited. To offset this shortcoming, many of the warship crews took to growing their own produce and small gardens or allotments were a familiar sight on the land that surrounded the port facilities.

The crew of the *King Orry* were no exception to this practice and as a result had a good selection of home-grown vegetables in their provision room. Many of the *King Orry's* crew befriended local Orcadian families and enjoyed a few brief hours of relaxation in a family environment during their shore leave which was mainly at the weekend.

The sailing orders, which instructed the *King Orry* to proceed to Liverpool on 26th October arrived on board on the afternoon of 24th October. They also instructed that Captain Brooke, Lieutenant Commander Burton and the remaining members of the crew from the *Blonde* should take passage to Liverpool where on arrival they were to rejoin their ship and Lieutenant Commander Selwyn Day would reassume command of the *King Orry*.

THE MERSEY AGAIN

At 08.00 on 26th October the confidential books were taken across to the headquarters ship *Cyclops* for safe keeping and an hour later the *King Orry* commenced her journey to the familiar waters of the Irish Sea and River Mersey.

She made a fast passage and picked up the pilot at the bar at just after midday on 27th October, securing alongside the wharf at Cammell Laird's yard by mid afternoon. Having disembarked her passengers, the *King Orry* moved into No 5 dry dock the following morning.

After the dock had been emptied, both anchors and their cables were lowered to the dock bottom. The ammunition magazines were emptied on the 30th October and the ammunition was put ashore allowing a general overhaul of the whole ship to commence later that day.

Considerable work was to be carried out on the vessel to repair defects, improve living conditions and prepare her for the new role which she would commence once she returned to the Orkney Islands.

Following the realisation that the Royal Navy's gunnery was inferior to that of their German counterparts, the Admiralty had decided to employ fast target-towing vessels. The *King Orry* had been selected for this role as her powerful turbines would allow her to pull the heavy battle targets at a speed that was more comparable with that of a moving warship.

The heavy targets were towed at the end of a steel cable which would be secured to the existing bollards on the *King Orry's* Poop Deck but, as it would sweep from side to side when the vessel manoeuvred, it was necessary to modify the collapsible guardrails that had been fitted when the two 4" guns had been installed the previous summer.

With the *King Orry* in dry dock, it was now possible to examine the damage that had been sustained to the starboard bilge keel when she had steamed over the anchor cable of the *Valhynia* on 5th July. The damage was found to be more extensive than had been originally reported and necessitated much of the bilge keel being replaced.

Over the next few weeks the dockyard workers completed the long list of jobs. The mine laying and depth charge rails that had been fitted onto the Poop Deck in June 1916 were removed and replaced with a modified version, while the forward 12 pdr gun was put ashore to enable repairs to be carried out on the deck fittings which secured it to the forecastle.

The ammunition for the *King Orry's* 12 pdr and 4" guns was carried from the magazine to the gun by hand which involved excessive manpower and resulted in a slow supply of ammunition. To rectify this problem, mechanical shell hoists were installed to move ammunition from both magazines to their respective guns. Whilst the ship was in the dockyard, both 4" guns and the 3 pdr gun were removed for overhaul.

The replacement dynamo that had been installed on board by the artificers from the repair ship *Assistance*, was stripped down and inspected by the shipyard engineers and following rectifications it was soon made fully serviceable.

This new dynamo was more powerful than the original and was more capable of supplying electricity to the numerous additional items of equipment that had been placed on board by the Admiralty.

Work on board continued throughout November and December and once the essential jobs were completed, work commenced to improve facilities within some of the accommodation areas.

A sound-proof bulkhead was constructed within the Captain's sea cabin as its proximity to the bridge no doubt made it a noisy place to sleep when the ship was at sea. The wardroom and senior ratings' mess were refurbished with new bunks being fitted in the latter.

Although misdemeanours and the crime rate amongst the crew were minimal, a small cell was built above the forward magazine. Its position so far forward in the ship, must have made it a very unpleasant place to be locked up in rough weather.

A tragic accident occurred on the evening of 3rd December. At 21.05, Stoker D C Gray returned on board in a very drunken condition. As he staggered over the gangway, he swayed and fell against the guardrail. Before anybody had time to rush forward and grab him, he toppled over and fell down between the dock wall and the ship's side.

By the time that the quartermaster and officer of the day had clambered down into the dock, Stoker Gray had died from his head injuries. This was the first fatality within *King Orry's* crew since she had been taken over by the Royal Navy in November 1914. Stoker Gray's funeral took place on the morning of 9th December and with the exception of the dutywatch, all of the ship's company attended.

Lt Cdr Selwyn Day, the Captain of the *King Orry* since the beginning of the war, relinquished command on 7th December and handed over to Captain Edwin H Edwards.

Captain Edwards was a retired Royal Navy captain who had volunteered to be recalled for war service but due to his age he had not been given command of a cruiser or battleship, which would have been the usual command given to an officer of his rank and seniority.

Lt Cdr Selwyn Day was appointed to take command of the armed boarding vessel *Dundee*, a ship with which the *King Orry* had been in company many times. He was subsequently awarded the Distinguished Service Order (DSO) while in command of the *Dundee* for his ship's involvement in the destruction of the disguised German raider *Leopard* on 16th March 1917.

The extended period at Cammell Laird's shipyard gave an opportunity for the ship's company to be granted leave, each watch being given seven days during December.

The *King Orry* was ready to move out of the dry dock by 16th December with all the equipment that had been removed for overhaul, including the 3 pdr, 12 pdr and 4" guns having now been returned back on board. The dock was flooded by mid-morning, but due to a thick fog it was decided that she should remain in situ.

The fog continued throughout the next day and is was not until late on the afternoon of 18th December that she was finally towed out of the dock and secured to the north wall in Cammell Laird's basin. Over the next couple of days, both coal and ammunition were taken on board.

Following a successful engine basin trial, the *King Orry* was ready to proceed back to her northern base on 22nd December 1916.

She left Cammell Laird's shipyard at 09.00 and almost immediately commenced a full power trial down towards the Bar Lightship where she arrived and anchored at just after 10.30. Following the compulsory compass swing, the river pilot was dropped and the *King Orry* left the River Mersey at 17.00.

The journey north was uneventful and she arrived at her anchorage in Longhope at 19.00 on Christmas Eve. The weather was bitterly cold and a blizzard was in full force.

Many of the crew may have hoped that Christmas Day would be left for the festivities, but they were to be disappointed. At 09.00 on Christmas Day the confidential books arrived back from the *Cyclops*, while at 10.00 the collier *Mercedes* came alongside and unloaded 108 tons of coal into the *King Orry's* bunkers.

It was well after dark before all of the coal had been taken on board and the coal dust had been washed off the decks and superstructure and although it was still Christmas Day, most of the crew were too exhausted to consider celebrating the festive season, preferring to climb into their bunks or hammocks and go to sleep instead.

However, there was some respite on Boxing Day as the crew were not called from their slumber until 08.00 and a relaxed routine was worked throughout day. The remainder of 1916 was spent swinging around the anchor cable and apart from those members of the crew who were required to go ashore on duty, few ventured far from the warmth of the *King Orry's* mess decks.

The long warm summer days had been replaced by the now frequent rain, gales and snowstorms which are so familiar to these Northern Isles during the winter months.

1917

New Year's Day 1917 was spent at Longhope and final preparations were made for a period of training for the ship's company that was to include gunnery practice and target towing exercises for her new role.

In the midst of a snow storm, the *King Orry* left her anchorage and proceeded out into Pentland Firth at 10.00 the following morning. Once clear of the approaches to Scapa Flow, the gun crews were closed up and a gunnery shoot with both her 4" and 12 pdr guns commenced. Although no targets were provided, the gun crews were drilled to improve their rate of fire utilising the recently installed shell hoists.

On 5th January, the ship acted as a target for a submarine torpedo exercise. It must have been unnerving for the crew as they watched the phosphorescent torpedo tracks racing towards their ship. On 8th January the *King Orry* acted as a target for a gunnery ranging exercise that was carried out by the battleship *Royal Oak*. Her log does not record whether this exercise involved the *Royal Oak* shooting 15" shells weighing one ton towards the *King Orry*, or whether it was just a exercise for the gunnery director crews. If it was the former it must have been a frightening experience.

The *King Orry's* duties as a target-towing vessel began on 10th January, when at 10.30 she left her anchorage in Longhope and met up with the Admiralty tug *Stoic* in the approaches to Pentland Firth.

The *Stoic* had left her anchorage within Longhope shortly before the *King Orry* and had towed the massive battle target out through the boom. These targets consisted of large wooden latticework frames that measured some sixty feet long by forty feet high. The structure was erected on top of an equally large wood and steel catamaran. In order that the target could be seen at a great distance, the lattice framework was covered with a canvas awning that was rolled up when not in use. A heavy keel made of pig iron was fitted below the catamaran to keep the target upright in a heavy sea swell.

The target on its own was of considerable weight but when it was connected to a wire hawser and towed at a distance of about half a mile behind the target-towing vessel, the target's overall weight was many tons.

Previous to the *King Orry* being detailed for target-towing duties, the battle targets had been towed behind Admiralty tugs, such as the *Stoic*. Although they had considerable pulling power, they lacked the speed to tow the target at anything that approached the speed of a warship. As a result the targets often appeared to be stationary when viewed from a fast-moving warship and tended to give the gun crews and director crews an unrealistic scenario to shoot at. Compared with the slow moving tugs, the single reduction geared steam turbines installed in the *King Orry* would allow her to pull the targets at speeds averaging 15 knots.

Having met up with the *Stoic*, it took the *King Orry's* crew over an hour to attach the target to its wire-towing hawser and then to secure the inboard end of the hawser to a bollard on the Poop Deck. As soon as the tow was connected, the *King Orry* bade farewell to the *Stoic* and moved out into Pentland Firth where she was due meet the cruiser *Duke of Edinburgh* for a gunnery shoot at midday.

To avoid breaking the wire hawser that connected the *King Orry* to the target, it was necessary for her to build up speed very slowly as a breaking wire whiplash across the *King Orry's* Poop Deck could cut down any unfortunate sailor who happened to be in its path.

Having picked up speed with no mishaps and with the target now trailing astern, the *King Orry* signalled the cruiser that she was ready to commence her first gunnery shoot, while at the same time a large red flag was hoisted to the head of her foremast to warn other ships to keep clear.

As both ships steamed towards Cape Wrath with the *Duke of Edinburgh* only just visible on the horizon, the first indication that she had opened fire with her 9.2" guns was when their muzzle flashes were observed. Within seconds the high-pitched whistle of the incoming shells filled the air and the sea around the target suddenly erupted as huge columns of white water indicated where they had landed.

Warships carrying out gunnery shoots employed one of two methods for taking aim on the target. The first method was simply taking aim on the target and then open fire but the second method was far more complicated and if it went wrong could be disastrous for the target-towing vessel.

The vessel carrying out the shoot would be informed of the distance between the towing vessel and the target which would be calculated to the nearest foot. The gunnery director would then take aim on the towing vessel rather than the target, the distance between the ship and the target being added as a deflection on the gun's bearing. When the director was locked onto the towing vessel, the order to open fire would be given and providing the gunnery officer's calculations were accurate, the shell would fall harmlessly around the target.

The crew of the *King Orry* would learn to dread this latter method, especially as a miscalculation could easily seal their fate and the reality of this danger would be experienced before the war was over.

Following exercising her 9.2" gun crews, the *Duke of Edinburgh* continued the shoot using her 6" guns. The shoot was completed by 14.30 and both ships headed back towards Scapa Flow. As the *King Orry* approached the Switha Boom she was met by the *Stoic*, which was waiting to take the target back through the boom. It was not an easy task to transfer the target and as the *King Orry* did not have the capability to retrieve the towing hawser, it had to be passed back to the tug. Once the tug had retrieved the wire, the heavy target was hauled alongside the *Stoic* and secured to her side. Both vessels then proceeded back through the boom to the safety of the Longhope anchorage.

The log for 10th January records that the *King Orry* towed the battle target at 18.5 knots, whereas referral to the log on subsequent days indicates that the target was towed at an average of 15 knots. It can only be assumed that as this was the first target-towing exercise and that the Captain put the *King Orry* through her paces to see what speed could be achieved. Bearing in mind the heavy sea swell that could be encountered in these waters during January, the target must have been bouncing across the waves with the wire-towing hawser sweeping from side to side across the *King Orry's* Poop Deck. Perhaps a slightly slower towing speed was deemed prudent.

The *King Orry* was not employed on target-towing duties every day and when she was not needed for Grand Fleet gunnery training, she was often employed as a gunnery training ship for both the Royal Naval Volunteer Reserve and the gun crews from defensively armed merchant ships.

When training such gunners, the *King Orry* would leave Scapa Flow early in the morning, the sailing time altering throughout the year depending upon the time of dawn and dusk. Once at sea the gunners would be trained on both the 4" and 12 pdr guns. Unlike the RNVR gunners who had received peacetime instruction on naval gunnery, most of the other gunners were merchant seamen and had never seen a gun close

up, let alone fired one, until they arrived on board the *King Orry*.

A NEW ROUTINE

The *King Orry's* crew now settled down into another routine. Gone were the long days on patrol in the inhospitable waters off the coast of Norway, the only relief being a few days at anchor in the Olna Firth in the remote Shetland Islands. She now adopted a much more routine schedule which was based upon the fact that the Royal Navy could only carry out gunnery training during daylight hours. Although a night action had been fought at the Battle of Jutland with the aid of searchlights to illuminate enemy ships, to carry out night action training against a target towed by a vessel such as the *King Orry* was considered far too dangerous to be attempted.

The time that the *King Orry* would sail for target towing duties with units of the Grand Fleet was dependant upon the time of dawn and dusk. Over the next couple of months the *King Orry* acted as a target-towing vessel for most of the major units of the Grand Fleet. Battleships such as the *Iron Duke*, *Emperor of India*, *St Vincent*, *Queen Elizabeth* and *Royal Oak* all exercised their guns crews at targets towed by the little Manx steamer.

Occasionally minor mishaps occurred such as on 22nd January when the tow parted and the wire hawser wrapped around the port propeller. Although no damage was caused it took divers from the battleship *Marlborough* four days to unravel it.

The training that was provided for gunners also caused a few minor problems, the main one involving the troublesome forward 12 pdr gun mounting. The continual firing of this gun caused the rivets that secured the mounting to the deck to loosen once again, The ordnance artificers from the repair ship *Assistance* were to become regular visitors.

Due to the exposed and isolated areas in which the *King Orry* was required to operate, the Captain had repeatedly asked the Fleet Medical Officer if a doctor could be appointed to the ship. Eventually he relented, and on 20th February, Temporary Surgeon Lieutenant Cyril Williams RNVR joined the armed boarding vessel. No doubt, the addition of a medical officer pleased the ships company.

On 1st March, the ever-present threat of German mines raised its ugly head again when the destroyer *Pheasant* struck a mine off the Old Man of Hoy and sank with heavy loss of life.

However, revenge for her loss may have been swift for on 10th March the destroyer *G13* torpedoed and sank the German submarine *UC43*. It is possible that

One of the large battle targets towed by the **King Orry**. *(David Handscombe collection)*

this submarine may have been the mine-laying vessel. As far as the *King Orry* was concerned, most of the month of March 1917 was spent at anchor within Longhope to allow various improvements and repairs to be carried out on board.

The artificers from the *Assistance* returned although on this occasion their work was not focused on the forward gun mounting. When a gunnery shoot was carried out the warship conducting the shoot would send a gunnery officer and a couple of ratings over to the *King Orry* to witness the fall of shot. The bad weather that frequented the waters around the Orkney Islands often prevented them from being transferred back to their own ship at the end of the day. On occasions like this they would have to remain on board the *King Orry* overnight or at least until the ship arrived back at Longhope.

As accommodation on board the *King Orry* was at a premium, extra officers' bunks were constructed within an empty store room on the Promenade Deck although there were no problems accommodating the ratings as they could sling a hammock in one of the seaman's mess decks.

Problems had also been encountered with the bollards on the Poop Deck that were used to secure the towing hawser. The *King Orry's* bollards had never been designed for towing at high speed and as a result they were being slowly pulled out of the deck. To rectify this problem, heavy-duty towing bollards were installed in their place. A large cable reel was also installed on the Poop Deck to allow the *King Orry* to recover the wire-towing hawser at the end of each shoot. Along with the two 4" guns and the depth charge rails that had already been installed on the Poop Deck, this latest addition must have made the deck a very cluttered area, compared with when she was a peacetime passenger vessel. Another item of equipment that was put on board during this period was an 18ft motor boat which replaced the 27ft whaler that was stowed in the davits belonging to the former No 4 life boat on the port side.

The ship's medical officer sent Captain Edwards to the hospital ship *Soudan* on 25th March after he had complained that he was suffering from abdominal pains but fortunately it was nothing serious and he returned on board on 2nd April.

While at sea on 1st April, towing a target for the battleship *Erin*, an extremely improbable event occurred.

At 10.45 one of the 13.5-inch shells fired from the battleship's main armament hit the wire-towing cable and severed it. The shoot was temporarily postponed while a replacement-towing hawser was connected to the target and recommenced at 11.30. Within minutes of the battleship recommencing her gunnery shoot, yet another shell severed the wire.

As the morning progressed, the weather had begun to worsen and a gale now swept through Pentland Firth. With the target now wallowing about in a heavy swell the decision to cancel the shoot was made and the *King Orry* set about attempting to retrieve it.

It took nearly three hours to secure a new wire to the target as each time the *King Orry's* sea boat approached the pitching and rolling structure, a wave would pitch the target against the boat and threaten to smash it to pulp and throw the crew into the cold and hostile water.

Another incident that involved a drifting target occurred a few days later. On 20th April at 02.00, the *King Orry* was ordered into the Pentland Firth to retrieve a large battle target that had been reported to be drifting near the island of Stroma. Due to its size it was an obvious hazard to shipping. The target was quickly located and secured to the port side of the armed boarding vessel, whereupon she returned to Longhope, arriving at 05.00.

While the *King Orry* was busily involved in her target-towing duties, the month of April 1917 finally brought the might of the United States of America into the war against Germany.

On the 4th April, after nearly two and a half years watching the slaughter of the armies of Britain and her allies in the mud of France and Belgium, President Woodrow Wilson was finally forced to commit the United States to fight for the common cause.

One of the major factors that forced him into making this decision was Germany's declaration of unrestricted U boat warfare on 1st February. This declaration put the previously neutral American merchant ships under the same threat of attack as the ships of Britain and her allies.

Although America had now committed her armed forces to fight alongside the allies, it would not be until the end of the year that the battleships of the United States Navy would arrive in British waters to support the Grand Fleet.

REPEATING SHIP

Another role that now fell upon the *King Orry* was that of repeating ship for the Grand Fleet.

In 1917, the main source of communication used to pass messages between ships at sea was still the signal flag.

When at sea a squadron of warships, such as Admiral Jellicoe's battleships, would stretch out in line ahead and there may be a distance of many miles between the flagship and the rear ship in the line.

Even with the aid of a telescope it was often not possible for the signalman on the rear ship to read the signals that were hauled up on the flagship's masts. To rectify this problem, vessels such as the *King Orry* would be employed to relay the flagship's signals to the other warships. The *King Orry* would be stationed near the flagship and when a signal was hoisted, she would hoist the same signal and then sail down the line of warships to ensure that they all received the message.

If a reply was required, she would bring this back to the flagship by flying the appropriate signal flags. The first time that the *King Orry* was employed on such duties was between 26th April and 4th May, when the Grand Fleet carried out a sweep down into the North Sea and out towards the enemy coastline.

At just before midday on 3rd May, the lookout in the *King Orry's* crow's nest spotted a submarine's conning tower a short distance from the line of warships.

As no British submarines had been reported as operating in the area, it was immediately assumed that the submarine was a German U boat.

As the signal "enemy in sight" was hauled up on the *King Orry's* foremast, she altered course towards the conning tower and increased speed to 19 knots. The lookouts on the submarine did not spot the armed boarding vessel's approach and their first indication of impending danger was when a shell from the *King Orry's* forward 12 pdr gun whistled over their heads and plunged into the sea a few feet away.

As the gun's crew slammed the breech shut on the 12 pdr gun and informed the bridge that they were ready to fire again, a frantic message was passed from the submarine's conning tower informing the *King Orry* that she was attacking a British submarine.

The cease fire order was immediately given and no doubt a very worried submarine crew relaxed, knowing that they had only just escaped a very watery grave. The circumstances of the incident were passed back to the flagship and it is assumed that the Captain of the submarine was asked to report his reasons for failing to spot the *King Orry* until she was close enough to open fire.

When the *King Orry* was not at sea, her ship's company were often entertained by one of the Royal Marine bands that were carried on board the battleships and battle cruisers. One such band was carried on board the battleship *Vanguard* and they entertained the crew of the *King Orry* on the evening of 18th May. Sadly this band would suffer a tragic demise before the summer was over. While the *King Orry* lay at anchor in Longhope on 8th June, the motor boat that had been installed on board earlier in the year

suffered an unfortunate mishap. To allow routine maintenance to be carried out on the propeller shaft it had been necessary to remove the boat's propeller but unfortunately as it was being replaced it was accidentally dropped over the ship's side and disappeared into the murky depths of Longhope. As a result, the motor boat sat idle in its davits for a couple of weeks awaiting the arrival of a replacement propeller.

Target towing duties, interrupted by short periods acting as Grand Fleet Repeating Ship, continued throughout the next few weeks. A former member of the crew of the battleship *Monarch*, Manxman Mr W Banham recalled how unpleasant life on board the *King Orry* could be during a gunnery shoot:

" *Four seamen with an officer in charge would be sent over to the King Orry to record the splash of the shells so that the range and correction could be reported and from it find out where the firing ship was going wrong. Volunteers were called for from the fleet and I found it was a welcome change from being stuck below in a gun turret magazine on board the Monarch, a Super Dreadnought. The King Orry was not a perfect 'Lady', at times it was difficult to stand as she would roll, pitch and yaw. On she would go for a few yards and then come to a jerky halt as the target pulled her back. The tow hawser flew from side to side, it would slacken and then wham, up it would spring bar taut. Advantage was taken of fleet movements and the island's little vessel would be there on the spot with her target veered astern, ready for the detached ships to have a go. I think that her Captain used to smell out the winds and the sea, for calm or gale found her in place. Never at any time did she hold up units of the fleet or let the side down. It was not always just a case of popping a few miles out of Scapa Flow, sometimes it meant two or three days at sea off the Shetland Islands, Cape Wrath, Invergordon or Firth of Forth. The weather, seas and her appendage made no difference, she was always there. The King Orry probably did more sea time than any other unit of the Grand Fleet, for she was by the nature of her calling the first ship out of harbour and the last in*".

On 10th June, while at anchor in Longhope, the *King Orry's* log records an incident that resulted in the Court martial of one of her officers.

At 14.00, Sub Lieutenant Cyril Reardon is entered as proceeding ashore, even though shore leave had not been granted as the ship was at six hours notice to proceed to sea. At midnight another entry records him as having failed to return on board and he was therefore classed as being absent without leave which is considered a very serious offence on board a ship that

*The **King Orry** at anchor in Longhope, Scapa Flow. As there is a 6 Pdr Hotchkiss Anti-Aircraft gun on the after end of her Promenade Deck, the picture was taken between 20th July 1917 and 12th May 1918. (David Handscombe collection)*

is under notice to proceed to sea. By dawn the following morning the *King Orry* had received a message informing her Captain that the offending officer had been seen with officers from the naval auxiliary vessel *Ruthenia* on the previous evening.

This ship was employed as the headquarters ship for the victualling and naval stores officer who supplied the numerous ships based at Scapa Flow.

The *Ruthenia* also acted as the fleet mail office, receiving and despatching the mail for the ships under her care. At 06.00 the navigating officer, Lt Cdr Charles Champness and a party of seamen were dispatched by boat to the *Ruthenia* where a search of the ship revealed Sub Lieutenant Reardon laying on the deck of a spare cabin in a drunken stupor. He was returned to the *King Orry* and placed under close arrest in his cabin. The log also records that A/B Chadwick was placed under close arrest at 20.00, having returned on board after being absent without leave for 24 hours.

As there is no entry in the log book to connect these two offenders, it is presumed that they were isolated incidents. The Court Martial of Sub Lieutenant Reardon took place on board the *Assistance* between 10.00 and 11.30 on 18th June, although the charge against him and the verdict is not recorded. He was

dismissed his ship and sent to the depot ship *Vivid* the following day.

ROYAL VISIT

His Majesty King George V sailed into Scapa Flow on board the light cruiser *Castor* on 21st June.

After spending the night on board Admiral Jellicoe's flagship *Queen Elizabeth*, he witnessed a gunnery shoot at a target towed by the *King Orry* the following day. Fortunately the gunners on board the *Queen Elizabeth* gave a good account of themselves and after instructing Admiral Jellicoe to splice the mainbrace, the King returned to the mainland on 25th June, once again on board the cruiser *Castor*.

The *King Orry* remained at Longhope for the next couple of weeks, which allowed the crew to get ashore and relax. The seamen challenged the signalmen to a whaler race on 27th June; needless to say the seamen were victorious.

At 23.20 on 9th July, a violent explosion rocked Scapa Flow. In the semi darkness that covered the anchorage in the summer months, a sheet of flame had shot up from one of the battleships anchored to the north of Flotta Island. For a few seconds the whole of Scapa Flow was illuminated by an eerie green light, this very quickly changed into a column of dense black smoke.

The alarm bells on board the *King Orry* brought the crew from slumber to their action stations while reports of a German U boat gaining access to the Grand Fleet's anchorage and torpedoing a battleship spread around the ship. While the crew remained at action stations, rescue boats from nearby ships raced to the disaster site but all they found were three badly injured survivors amongst the flotsam while the great battleship had completely disappeared. The order to stand down came at 02.00. Details of the disaster began to filter through to the *King Orry* while the crew were at breakfast the following morning. The warship that had tragically blown up and sunk was the *Vanguard*, a 23.000 ton battleship which had only arrived in Scapa Flow on the previous afternoon. There were reports that huge pieces of burning debris had rained down upon the decks of the ships that surrounded her, a complete 12" gun turret, weighing nearly 400 tons had been found on the island of Flotta.

As the rescue boats continued to sift through the wreckage, a 50ft steam pinnace was found floating upside down. Apart from being upside down it

North Sea 1916: a destroyer takes station astern of the **King Orry** *(David Handscombe collection)*

appeared to have suffered no damage. As the day went on it was confirmed that 864 officers and men had perished, although 24 officers and 71 men had had a lucky escape by being on board the battleship *Royal Oak* for a Royal Marine Band concert. Sadly none of these were members of the Royal Marine Band from the *Vanguard*, which had entertained the crew of the *King Orry* only a few weeks earlier.

Although the immediate cause for the loss of the battleship was put down to a U boat attack, it was soon realised that the warship had been lost as the result of an internal explosion.

The official enquiry eventually put her loss down to a magazine explosion caused by old, unstable and deteriorating cordite. The cruiser *Natal* had blown up in similar circumstances in the Cromarty Firth on 31st December 1915.

A survey of the *Vanguard's* wreck was carried out some years ago. All that remains of the once-mighty ship is approximately 80ft of her bow section and 60ft of her stern. The remainder of her 536ft long hull lies between these sections in a mass of twisted and broken metal. Close examination of the jagged ends to the bow and stern show that the plates are blown outwards, confirming that her demise was from an internal explosion.

For a few days after the loss of the *Vanguard*, the boats' crews from the *King Orry* were tasked to row along the shoreline of Longhope and retrieve any bodies that were found washed up on the rocks or beach. This must have been a very grim task, as many of the bodies would have been dismembered by the blast from the explosion.

On 12th July, three days after the *Vanguard* had blown up, the warships anchored within Scapa Flow were ordered to fly their ensigns at half-mast while a memorial service was held ashore at St Magnus' Cathedral in Kirkwall.

TYNE REFIT

The *King Orry* continued on her target towing duties until 17th July, when she was ordered to proceed to the River Tyne for a period in dry dock. Divers from the *Assistance* had carried out an underwater survey of the *King Orry's* hull a few weeks previous and had reported that her rudder, propeller shafts and areas of the hull were showing signs of corrosion and so no doubt this maintenance period had been scheduled to rectify this problem.

The *King Orry* sailed from Longhope at 07.00 on 17th July and arrived at the mouth of the River Tyne at just before 14.00 on the following day. She was taken up river by a tug and secured alongside the wharf at Swan Hunter's shipyard by 16.00.

Before the *King Orry* could be put into dry dock it was necessary to take the ammunition out of the magazines. This was achieved on the next day and it was put on board the pre-Dreadnought battleship *Illustrious*, which had been completed in 1898 and had been disarmed and converted into a store ship during 1915.

The *King Orry* was moved into the dry dock during the afternoon and once all was secure on board, 50% of the crew were sent on 8 days leave, the remaining crew being given their leave on 28th July.

To allow the shipyard workers to remedy the corrosion problems on the hull, the rudder and both propellers were removed, the rudder being taken to a workshop while the propellers were placed on the dock bottom.

While repairs to the hull were being carried out, other items on board also received attention. All the signal halyards were replaced, improved equipment was put in the wireless office and the four lifeboats that remained on board were landed onto the jetty to allow them to be surveyed and repainted. The 12 pdr and 4" guns were completely stripped down and overhauled, while the 3 pdr Hotchkiss quick-fire gun that had been placed on the after end of the Promenade Deck during January 1916, was removed and replaced with a 6 pdr Hotchkiss anti-aircraft gun. Although ships were unlikely to be attacked by German aircraft, the threat of being bombed from a Zeppelin was very high.

The removal of the corrosion from the lower hull plating took longer than had been anticipated, and it was not until the afternoon of 8th August that the repainting of the lower hull plating, ship's side and superstructure were finally completed.

Resplendent in her new coat of paint, she was removed from the dry dock and berthed alongside Swan Hunter's tidal wharf the following morning.

The ammunition that had been sent to the *Illustrious* when the *King Orry* had arrived at Swan Hunter's ship yard three weeks earlier was re-stowed into the magazines on 11th August, while on 13th August, Rear Admiral Grant visited the ship to inspect the repair and improvement work that had been carried out. Once this visit was over, the crew started to coal ship and preparations to sail from the River Tyne on the following morning's high tide commenced.

The *King Orry* left Swan Hunter's shipyard and sailed down the River Tyne towards the North Sea at 09.00 the following morning, 14th August having been ordered to proceed to the Naval Dockyard at Rosyth to await further instructions.

At 14.30, she passed St Abb's Head and by 15.30 she was off May Island at the entrance to the Firth of Forth before altering course and sailing up the firth towards Rosyth.

ROSYTH

As she passed the small island of Inchkeith, the Forth railway bridge came into view through the afternoon haze.

To those members of the crew who had never seen it before, the massive three red-painted arches created an impressive spectacle as they towered above the *King Orry* and the surrounding countryside. The armed boarding vessel passed under the northern span and shortly after 18.00, secured to a buoy off Rosyth dockyard.

The Firth of Forth was very busy compared with the remoteness of the Orkney Islands. Battleships of the 4th Battle Squadron, under the command of Admiral Sir Doveton Sturdee were secured to buoys in line ahead in the centre of the river, while tenders and picket boats rushed to and fro, busy about their everyday business.

The *King Orry* did not receive any orders until the evening of 19th August when her Captain was informed that Admiral Sir Doveton Sturdee would inspect the ship's company the following morning.

Having been at work since the crack of dawn to ensure that she was prepared for an Admiral's inspection, the crew were all fallen in at 09.45. The famous Admiral arrived alongside in his barge at 10.00 and quickly clambered up the accommodation ladder. After meeting the Captain and his Officers, he inspected the ship's company and took time to speak to many of the assembled crew.

Following the inspection, he presented CPO William Bate with the Distinguished Service Medal (DSM). The presentation of this prestigious award by Admiral Sturdee was in itself an honour for he had been the commander of the battle cruiser squadron that had sank the German cruisers of Vice Admiral Graf von Spee's squadron at the Battle of the Falkland Islands in December 1914.

On 27th August, the *King Orry* entered a whaler crew in the 4th Battle Squadron's sailing regatta but unfortunately they were no match for the well-practised crews from the battleships.

Orders were received on 3rd September to unload all the 12 pdr ammunition to the Royal Naval Ordnance Depot at nearby Crombie and then to proceed into the basin at Rosyth Dockyard to allow an inclining test to be carried out.

Since the *King Orry* had commissioned as an armed boarding vessel in November 1914, many items of equipment had either been removed or installed on board. During target towing the *King Orry* had been observed to heel over rather alarmingly and then take a long time to come back to an even keel. The Fleet Engineering Officer had therefore decided that an inclining test should be carried out to ensure that the many alterations had not made her unstable, which was probably the reason why she had been ordered to proceed to Rosyth.

The inclining test required all items of equipment to be securely lashed down before all the crew was put ashore. This latter requirement was for safety reasons in case the *King Orry* failed the test and capsized.

The ship was moved away from the harbour wall and secured between two tugs, one forward and one aft. A dockyard crane then lowered a succession of weights, weighing many tons onto first one side and then the other causing the *King Orry* to list depending on which side they were placed. The maximum angle that the *King Orry* was capable of heeling over before she became unstable had already been calculated and so this test was to prove whether it was accurate and the *King Orry* was still safe to put to sea. The test was carried out on 6th September and it was obviously successful as the *King Orry* returned to the buoy in the Firth of Forth on 7th September with sailing orders to proceed to the Orkney Islands on 16th September.

The days between returning to her buoy and sailing for Scapa Flow were taken up with taking on supplies, ammunition and coal. On the evening of 14th September, the Royal Marine Band from the battleship *Collingwood* came on board to entertain the ship's company.

ORKNEY AGAIN

The *King Orry* slipped her buoy at 06.10 on 16th September and steamed slowly down the Forth towards the sea. Her log mentions that the Forth rail bridge was shrouded in mist, similar to how it had appeared when they had arrived in mid-August. She made a slow passage to the Orkney Islands and steamed into Longhope to resume her duties at 06.30 on 18th September.

Having taking on more coal, she returned to target-towing duties on 20th September, when the ships of the 2nd light cruiser squadron exercised their 6" guns at her target.

Now that she was back on towing target duties and occasionally acting as the repeating ship for units of the Grand Fleet, the crew of the *King Orry* soon settled down into the familiar routine. Only one noteworthy incident is recorded in the log book during this period when on 8th October the towing hawser could not be released from the target requiring the *King Orry* to tow the target back into Scapa Flow.

With the target trailing at a distance of about half a mile behind the *King Orry*, manoeuvring through the Switha Boom proved to be a tricky exercise. Once inside the safety of Scapa Flow, the towing hawser was cut and the target was towed away by the Admiralty tug *Stoic*. A replacement hawser was brought on board the following day.

On 31st October, one of her former Steam Packet Engineers, Engineer Sub Lieutenant Allen V Garrett left the *King Orry*. He had been a popular member of the Engine Room staff and apart from a short period in hospital during February 1916, had been on board since the ship commissioned.

Engineer Sub Lieutenant Hugh McIntyre RNR, who had joined the *King Orry* the day before, replaced him. Another new face in the wardroom, albeit only temporary, was Lt Cdr Kinnell from the United States Navy. He joined the *King Orry* as a gunnery observer on 3rd November and was no doubt assessing the Royal Navy's gunnery techniques in order that he could report back to his American superiors. He left the ship on 11th November.

Although nobody on board the *King Orry* was aware of it at this moment, the provision of this officer was to herald the arrival of the American battleships at Scapa Flow a few weeks later.

The assessment of the Grand Fleet's gunnery was to be further enhanced by the provision of photographic equipment on board the *King Orry*.

On 10th November, a team of artificers from the *Assistance* arrived on board and started to convert the former Chief Steward's cabin on the Shelter Deck into a photographic dark room. The conversion work only took a few days to complete and finished on 14th November, Commander Curzon RNVR and a team of sailors arrived on board from the *Cyclops* to install the photographic equipment.

The provision of this photographic equipment would allow Commander Curzon and his team to photograph the fall of shot from the warships carrying out gunnery shoots. After studying the images, the Grand Fleet's gunnery officers would then take appropriate action to rectify any deficiencies in their particular ship's gunnery.

When the *King Orry* returned to her anchorage from a gunnery shoot on the afternoon of 16th November, she was ordered to take on coal from the collier *Mercedes* and prepare to put to sea again early

the next morning in company with the 1st Battle Squadron, led by the battleship *St Vincent*.

Under the cover of the early morning twilight, the ships slipped out of Scapa Flow at 05.00 and steamed down into the North Sea. With the *King Orry* acting as their signal repeating ship, the warships patrolled the Dogger Bank area of the North Sea for most of 18th November in the hope of catching unsuspecting units of the German fleet. Unfortunately for the British warships, the German navy was not at sea and the order to return to Scapa Flow was given shortly after dusk.

The *King Orry's* arrival back in Longhope on the evening of 19th November marked the end of Captain Edwards's period in command of the Manx steamer. At 09.00 the following day, Commander Harry T Mosse RNR arrived on board and assumed command.

In some previous accounts of the *King Orry's* war service, it has been noted that Commander Mosse has been incorrectly named as Captain Harry T Norse RN but scrutiny of the official Admiralty navy list for the First World War confirms that the new commanding officer's surname was definitely Mosse, not Norse and that he was a Commander, not a Captain.

Having taken Commander Mosse on a tour of the ship and introduced him to the various Heads of Department, Captain Edwards was piped ashore at

*The Boat Deck of the **King Orry** following her conversion into an armed boarding vessel: Scapa Flow 1915. (David Handscombe collection)*

10.30 and left the *King Orry* to take over command of the cruiser *Boadicea* which was undergoing conversion into a minelayer and would recommission at the end of December 1917.

The *King Orry* continued with her target towing duties throughout December until Christmas Eve, when at 17.00 her crew were informed that the ship had been stood down until the morning of 31st December. Festive decorations were quickly hung up in the various mess decks and at midnight the whole crew mustered in the Dining Room for a Christmas carol service. Relaxed daily routines were worked for the next few days, although on Christmas Day and Boxing Day only the duty watch were required to turn to.

December 1917 had finally seen the arrival of the United States Navy. At midday on 7th December, along with other vessels, the *King Orry* had been ordered to anchor adjacent to the anti-submarine boom in Hoxa Sound. At 14.00 the crew had been mustered on the Boat Deck and shortly afterwards four American battleships and their destroyer escorts steamed through Hoxa Sound into Scapa Flow.

The crews of the assembled British ships cheered their new allies, as they steamed slowly past. These four battleships, the *Texas, Delaware, Florida* and *New York* would be formed into the Grand Fleet's 6th Battle Squadron and would be augmented by additional American battleships during early 1918. Ironically, the date of 7th December would mark the entry of the United States Navy into another war in 1941.

The year 1917 had seen the war drag on and the death toll rise on both sides without any obvious sign of peace being any nearer. The armies, which had endured campaign after campaign, were now bogged down in the mud of France and Belgium.

Unrest within the French army had resulted in a mutiny in April and Russia was now in turmoil as the country was gripped by a bloody revolution that had overthrown the Tsar.

Although the heavy units of the German High Seas Fleet had not dared to challenge the might of the Royal Navy since its severe mauling at the Battle of Jutland, the Kaiser's warships still poised a major threat which kept the Grand Fleet on full alert. Each time that the British thought the German navy was defeated, a raiding force would break out into the North Sea and attack unsuspecting shipping. The Grand Fleet would rush out from Scapa Flow, Invergordon and Rosyth only to find that the Germans had returned to the safety of their home ports before the British arrived in the area.

With Christmas Day 1917 now just a memory, the crew of the *King Orry* returned to target-towing duties

at 07.45 on New Year's Eve when they left Scapa Flow for a gunnery shoot with the 1st Battle Squadron led by the battleship *St Vincent*.

The shoot was uneventful and the *King Orry* was back at her anchorage by dusk.

1918 - A DIRECT HIT!

Another change took place amongst the engineers on 6th January 1918, when Sub Lieutenant John Pealing RNR relieved Sub Lieutenant John McMenemey RNR.

The *King Orry* continued her target-towing duties without incident until the morning of 29th January when at 07.00 she left her anchorage to commence a gunnery shoot with the 2nd Light Cruiser Squadron.

At 10.00, Rear Admiral Ferguson ordered his squadron, which consisted of the cruisers *Dublin, Yarmouth* and the two Australian light cruisers *Melbourne and Sydney* to form up in line ahead behind his flagship, *Birmingham*.

The *Birmingham* opened fire at 11.00 and was followed in succession by the remainder of the squadron.

The *King Orry's* log book records that at 11.25 one of the light cruisers appeared to be having difficulty with finding the correct range as her 6" shells were landing dangerously close to the ship.

At 11.31 the inevitable happened. The *King Orry* was suddenly rocked violently to starboard as a large explosion on the ship's port side sent a cloud of water and smoke up into the air, followed almost immediately by a cloud of smoke on the starboard side. A 6" shell had hit the ship.

As confused reports of damage arrived on the bridge, the Captain gave the order to close all watertight doors and standby to start the pumps. The signals to cease fire and for immediate assistance were hauled up on the foremast as the *King Orry* stopped her engines and came to a standstill in the heavy swell of Pentland Firth.

Fortunately, the 6" shell was only a practice shell and was therefore not fitted with an explosive charge, although it had still caused considerable damage to the *King Orry*.

It had entered the hull approximately 2ft above the water line on the port side and had passed straight through the after seamen's mess deck, which was located in the former Second Class sleeping cabin. The shell then exited the mess deck through the starboard side at water line level.

Miraculously, even though shrapnel had whizzed round the compartment, none of the handful of off-duty seamen who had been present had been hurt.

However, seawater now poured into the mess deck through the hole that had been punched through the starboard side when the shell made its exit.

Damage control parties were summoned and were soon wading through the water that had risen to waist deep. Fortunately, with the *King Orry* now stopped and wallowing in the swell, the water only rushed into the mess deck when she heeled over to starboard. Hammocks and mattresses were pushed into the two holes and in a fairly short time the ingress of water was under control.

The chief shipwright organised the erection of wooden shoring to hold the hammocks and mattresses in place and the pumps soon began to lower the level of water.

The light cruiser *Birmingham* now came alongside and asked if assistance was required. She departed soon afterwards having been informed that the situation was now under control. Shortly after the *King Orry* had hove to, the target and its cable had been cut loose and was now drifting with the wind and tide and in danger of becoming a navigational hazard.

Having been summoned from Scapa Flow, the Admiralty tug *Viper* soon arrived on the scene and sped off in pursuit of the wayward target. Fortunately, the ingress of water into the *King Orry* had not flooded the Boiler Room which meant that she was able to proceed back to Scapa Flow under her own steam. She was escorted back to the Switha Boom by the Admiralty tug *Stoic*, which had also hurried to the scene. The *King Orry* secured alongside the repair ship *Cyclops* at 15.20 and was immediately boarded by a team of shipwrights who inspected the damage.

No serious structural damage was found but on yet another occasion since the *King Orry* had been taken over by the Royal Navy, it became apparent that Cammell Laird's strong construction had saved her from a watery grave.

Over the next few days, teams of shipwrights and blacksmiths from the *Cyclops* and the battleships *St Vincent* and *Hercules* toiled in the mess deck to repair the two holes in the hull and return the area to a habitable condition.

An enquiry into the incident was held on board the battle cruiser *Tiger* at 10.00 the following morning and a misjudgement by a light cruiser's gunnery officer was subsequently recorded as the cause of the accident.

Unfortunately, neither the *King Orry's* log book, or those of of the vessels that comprised the 2nd Light Cruiser Squadron reveal which ship was guilty.

Temporary repairs were completed by 2nd February and the *King Orry* returned to her anchorage in Longhope where she remained until 11th February when she recommenced her duties by towing a target for the 2nd Battle Squadron. Unfortunately this shoot was abruptly curtailed at 10.30 when the first 12" shell to be fired scored a direct hit and totally destroyed the target. After retrieving the remains of the cable, the *King Orry* was back in Longhope by 13.00.

The remainder of February, all of March and the first week of April 1918, the *King Orry* was employed on target- towing duties for units of the Grand Fleet.

During this period, two mishaps occurred. Having completed a gunnery shoot with the light cruisers *Royalist, Castor, Phaeton, Inconstant* and *Yarmouth* on 20th February, the *King Orry* was returning to Scapa Flow when she was struck by a freak wave.

The wave broke over the forecastle and stove in her bridge windows wrecking the binnacle on the bridge roof. Fortunately, nobody was injured and the bridge windows were replaced the following day while a replacement binnacle was installed on 27th February.

The second mishap occurred when the *King Orry* was entering Scapa Flow after a gunnery shoot with the battleship *Queen Elizabeth* on 9th April. As she approached the Switha Boom, the officer of the watch misjudged his position and the *King Orry* ran over the steel cables that supported it. With a screeching of metal, the armed boarding vessel scraped over the boom and continued on her way into Longhope.

Divers from the *Cyclops* subsequently inspected her hull plating the following morning and reported that there was some damage, but it could wait until her next period in dry dock before it was repaired.

On 19th - 20th March, the gunners of the United States Navy were given the opportunity to fire at the *King Orry's* target. The battleships of the newly formed 6th Battle Squadron each took their turn to shoot but achieved disappointing results with their rather erratic fire. History records that it took a while for them to bring their gunnery up to the standards of the remainder of the Grand Fleet, much to the embarrassment of the American gunners as they had boasted that they were more than an equal to gunners of the Royal Navy.

While at anchor in Longhope on 11th April, there was some disgruntlement amongst the seamen regarding the amount of leave that was being allowed. This increased as the day wore on and at 17.00 the Royal Marines were instructed to muster with their rifles. Shortly afterwards the whole ships company were ordered to fall in on the after end of the Promenade Deck.

The Master at Arms from the headquarters ship *Cyclops* had been summoned to read the articles of war to the ship's company and inform them that their actions could be regarded as mutinous. It is assumed that their reading and the subsequent warning about mutiny defused the situation, as there is no further record of the incident within the *King Orry's* log book.

THE FORTH

The *King Orry* put to sea at 08.00 the following day in company with the 1st Battle Squadron, sailing southwards into the North Sea and acting as the signal repeating ship once again. The 1st Battle Squadron then met up with the 5th Battle Squadron on the morning of 13th April and together they steamed into the Firth of Forth towards the end of the afternoon.

The *King Orry* was ordered to anchor off Charlestown, which is to the west of Rosyth Naval Base and where an incident occurred which resulted in the Navigating Officer being dismissed from the ship.

Lt Cdr Charles Peyton Ventris RNR had only joined the *King Orry* on 21st January 1918 and on the evening of 14th April, the officer of the day had noticed his cabin door open with a collection of official-looking documents on his bunk, On closer examination, these documents were found to be Grand Fleet signal code books ie, secret documents.

The discovery was reported to the Captain and Lt Cdr Ventris was subsequently disciplined. His name appears in the log book for 15th April which records that in contravention to King's Regulations and Admiralty Instructions, article 724, "He had left in his cabin, in a place accessible to anybody, a collection of information likely to be of use to the enemy."

This was indeed a serious offence and a major breach in security but fortunately, the documents had been discovered before any unauthorised person had been given a chance to view them. Unfortunately for Lt Cdr Ventris, his act of carelessness resulted in him being dismissed from the ship on the morning of 18th April. Lt Guy Cooper RNR replaced him as Navigating Officer.

The *King Orry* moved to No 3 buoy, which was opposite Rosyth Naval Base on the morning of 16th April and apart from a few hours acting as the repeating ship for the 4th Battle Squadron on 1st May, she remained at this buoy until the evening 12th May.

On the 19th April, Rear Admiral Nicholson took the opportunity to cross over from his flagship, the battleship *Colossus*, to inspect the *King Orry's* ship's company and then witness them drill at both action stations and abandon ship stations. Both drills passed without mishap and impressed the Admiral.

When not required for duty, the *King Orry's* crew were granted shore leave during the evenings and at weekends, After the isolation of the Orkney Islands, the public houses in Rosyth, Inverkeithing and Dunfermline had much to offer the sailors. No doubt the more ambitious members of the ship's company took the train from Inverkeithing and crossed the Forth bridge to Edinburgh.

ZEEBRUGGE

While the *King Orry* had lain at her buoy in the Firth of Forth, a daring raid had taken place on the enemy coastline that had the aim of blocking the entrance into the North Sea that was being used by German U boats based at the inland port of Bruges in occupied Belgium.

Although the heavy units of the German High Seas Fleet were bottled up in their home ports and were poising an increasingly reduced threat, German U boats were still causing havoc to allied shipping.

At dawn on St George's Day, 23rd April 1918, a large landing force stormed the harbour defences at Zeebrugge. The fighting was fierce and loss of life amongst the sailors and marines was considerable. While the hand-to-hand fighting was taking place ashore, three obsolete warships, the cruisers *Intrepid*, *Thetis* and *Iphigenia* were scuttled in the entrance to the canal.

After hours of bitter fighting, the mauled survivors who had not been taken prisoner by the German defenders were shipped back to Britain on board a fleet of destroyers, motor launches and the converted Mersey ferries *Iris* and *Daffodil*.

As the raid on Zeebrugge was taking place, a similar attack had been made on the canal entrance at Ostend but although block ships were sunk in the mouth of the canal, a large landing force had not been included.

The news of the battle reached the crews of the warships a couple of days later. Sadly the initial euphoria, which accompanied the news of the attack, was short lived when it became evident that despite the heroism and sacrifice of the attackers, the canals had not been adequately blocked and German U boats were still able to get out into the North Sea.

Late in the afternoon of 11th May, a picket boat from the battleship *Queen Elizabeth* came alongside the *King Orry* with a sealed envelope for the Captain. This contained her sailing orders and instructed Commander Mosse to take the *King Orry* down to the River Tyne at 20.00 the following day, Sunday 12th May.

They also warned her Captain to keep a good lookout for the submarine *K12* that was patrolling in an area that the *King Orry* would pass through. Having taken on coal from the collier *Transporter*, the *King Orry* slipped her buoy at just after 19.30 and steamed slowly down river towards the open sea.

TYNE REPAIR AND OVERHAUL

The passage south was uneventful, and without sighting the submarine *K12*, the *King Orry* arrived off the mouth of the River Tyne at 05.00 on 13th May.

Having identified herself to a patrol vessel, she steamed slowly through the early morning mist and proceeded up the Tyne, finally berthing alongside the wharf at Brigham and Cowan's shipyard in South Shields.

The crew were fallen out from harbour stations and went for breakfast before being mustered again at 08.00 when they were detailed off for their daily work commitments.

The major task for the day was to unload all the coal from the bunkers into a lighter that had arrived alongside. Although the task was still incomplete at 14.00, it was essential that the *King Orry* be moved into the dry dock on the afternoon high tide. After the coal lighter had been towed away, a tug was secured alongside and the armed boarding vessel was moved into the dock.

As soon as the caisson was put back into position in the dock entrance, the water began to be pumped out and the *King Orry* was sat high and dry on the wooden blocks by 17.50. The remainder of the coal was put ashore on the following morning although on this occasion it was lifted out by crane and put into railway wagons which had been placed on the dockside.

The port watch were then sent on a well-deserved two weeks leave later in the day, while Lt Richard Thomas joined as a replacement for Lt William Cowling, who proceeded on leave and draft along with the port watch.

No doubt, the granting of this leave quelled the disgruntlement that had resulted in the articles of war being read to the ship's company on 11th April. With the unloading of the coal from the bunkers finally completed, shipyard workers arrived on board on the morning of 16th May and commenced to repair the damage that had been sustained to the ship's bottom when she had run over the anti-submarine boom in Switha Sound on 9th April. It only took 48 hours to repair the damage and the *King Orry* was refloated and returned to the tidal wharf on the morning of 18th May.

Work now commenced on a general overhaul of the ship and her machinery. With the exception of the gun sights for the 4 inch and 12 pdr gun being taken ashore for recalibration on 4th June and permanent repairs being carried out on the two 6" shell holes in the forward seamen's mess deck, there is no mention within the ship's log book of any specific work carried out.

However, there is mention that the shipyard painters were kept busy giving the armed boarding vessel a new appearance. Apart from the short period when she was disguised as the *Viking Orry*, the *King Orry* had been painted dark warship grey since she had been commissioned in November 1914.

Now, in an attempt to make it difficult for German warships, especially U boats, to establish the identity and course of British vessels, the Admiralty had decided to camouflage or dazzle paint all warships and naval auxiliary vessels. To this end, the *King Orry's* hull, funnel and superstructure was repainted in a bizarre multi-coloured paint scheme, her sleek lines being completely disguised by a confused pattern of yellow, dark blue anddull red.

The starboard watch was sent on leave at midday on 29th May, the port watch having returned on board that morning. With the assistance of a tug, the *King Orry* was moved away from the wharf and secured to a buoy in mid river early in the morning of 8th June and shortly afterwards the collier *Rynhope* came alongside and replenished the empty coal bunkers.

With half the crew away on leave, coaling ship was particularly arduous and was not completed until late in the afternoon on the following day. To allow a spare propeller to be put on board for shipment back to Longhope and for the returning starboard watch to re-embark, the *King Orry* was moved back onto the wharf for a couple of hours at 05.00 on 11th June. She was back at the buoy by 08.00 and the crew spent the remainder of the day cleaning the ship and preparing to sail from the River Tyne on the high tide the following morning.

RETURN TO LONGHOPE

The morning of 12th June was bright and sunny with a light breeze. The river pilot boarded the *King Orry* at 08.00 and after allowing for a full head of steam to be raised in her boilers, she slipped the buoy and proceeded down river at just after 11.30.

Shortly after she cleared the mouth of the river and disembarked the pilot, the *King Orry* turned north and built her speed up to 19 knots as she steamed towards her Orkney Island home.

She arrived in Longhope at 11.50 the following day and immediately secured alongside the collier *Fullerton* to allow her bunkers to be topped up. Later in the day, an ammunition barge was brought alongside to replenish her magazines with 4" and 12 pdr shells.

Resplendent in her new colour scheme, the *King Orry* returned to target towing the following morning, 15th June. She continued on these duties until the last week in July and during this period the battleships of the American 6th Battle Squadron frequently fired their guns at her target.

Since they had arrived in Scapa Flow during December of the previous year and had subsequently demonstrated that their gunnery was not as accurate as that of the Grand Fleet, the American ships had undergone intensive gunnery training. Now some seven months later, they were now demonstrating that they were capable of achieving the same level of accuracy as their British counterparts although, unlike their British and French allies, they could not boast that they had ever fired their main armament in anger.

At 10.00 on 29th June, the ship's company were fallen in on the after end of the Promenade Deck and inspected by the Captain in preparation for a visit by Rear Admiral Nicholson on the following day. He had previously visited the *King Orry* while she was at Rosyth in April.

The *King Orry* operated from her Orkney Island base for most of July although her duties of target-towing and acting as repeating ship to the Grand Fleet were now becoming somewhat tedious to her ship's company.

The possibility of a major fleet action between the Grand Fleet and German High Seas Fleet was becoming increasingly unlikely. Although there had been a few skirmishes involving light units of the High Seas Fleet, their battleships and battle cruisers had not sought to challenge the might of the Royal Navy since the Battle of Jutland.

Even though the *King Orry's* duties were monotonous and seemingly mundane when compared with the glory that often accompanied the actions of destroyers and light cruisers, the crew of the *King Orry* was not demoralised.

News was beginning to reach the ears of sailors at Scapa Flow that all was not well within Germany. The German army had launched attacks which became known as the Ludendorff offensive at St Quentin, Lys and on the Aisne during the preceding couple of months but although these had initially been successful, the allies had counter attacked and stopped the German progress.

The **King Orry** *was painted in this dazzle camouflage scheme in May 1918. (Imperial War Museum)*

The effect of four years of maritime blockade and the entry of America into the war was now taking its toll on the German economy. There was political unrest within the country and now it looked as if it would be impossible for Germany to win the war.

The Kaiser's Government was secretly seeking a honourable end to the hostilities as elements of the German navy and army were becoming disillusioned. Many had not been paid for months and supplies of food were often infrequent. These stories filled the British servicemen with optimism and to many of them the thought of an allied victory was no longer just a dream but a forthcoming reality

FORTH ROYAL REVIEW

The *King Orry* was ordered to accompany the 1st Battle Squadron as repeating ship on the afternoon of 21st July. At 13.20 she left her anchorage and proceeded south into the North Sea. The battle squadron arrived off May Island at 08.00 the following morning and by 10.35 the *King Orry* was secured to a buoy opposite Rosyth Dockyard.

Shortly after the securing to the buoy, a signal was received on board informing the Captain that the King would review the assembled warships at 11.30 and that ships crews were to man and cheer ship. The crew were instructed to don their best uniforms and muster on the forecastle, Boat Deck and Poop Deck by division.

At 11.40, the Commander-in-Chief's despatch vessel, the destroyer *Oak* came into view flying the Royal Standard from her foremast. As she steamed past, the *King Orry's* crew gave three cheers for the King, each time raising their caps above their heads.

As well as reviewing the warships from the bridge of the *Oak*, the King wanted to meet as many officers and men as possible. To this end, the Captain and forty members of the crew went over to the battleship *Hercules* at 08.00 on 23rd July. The King arrived on board at 08.30 and inspected the assembled officers and men who had been drawn from the numerous ships anchored within the Firth of Forth.

The *King Orry* was to be based at Rosyth for the next seven weeks, no doubt much to the satisfaction of her crew.

The Fleet Surgeon came on board and inspected the ship's company on 30th July. An Influenza epidemic was beginning to grip the country and all crews were being given health checks to ensure that they were fit.

At 09.00 on 22nd August, the *King Orry* was ordered to sea to act as the repeating ship to the 1st Battle Squadron but no sooner had the ships left the shelter of the Firth of Forth than they encountered a severe gale.

The gale continued into the next day and increased in severity as the hours passed. By midday on 23rd August, the sea state was so rough that the *King Orry* was unable to keep station with the other warships and began to fall astern. As she plunged her bows into the mountainous waves, water began to pour into the compartments below and into the cable locker. As it had become necessary to start the pumps to control the ingress of water, the Captain sent a signal to the flagship informing the Admiral of the *King Orry's* perilous predicament.

Much to everyone's relief, the Admiral's reply ordered the *King Orry* to return to Rosyth for repairs. She passed under the Forth bridge just before 09.00 the following morning and secured to a buoy opposite the Naval Dockyard some thirty minutes later.

Shortly after her arrival, a boat came alongside and the warrant shipwright from the battleship *Superb* clambered on board to inspect the storm damage. Having completed his inspection, he informed the Captain that one of the major contributing factors to the water ingress had been some loose rivets in the forepeak plating and damage to the steel covers that fitted over the chain pipes, (the pipes that allowed the anchor cable to pass down from the forecastle into the cable locker). These were the same troublesome covers that had broken loose and nearly caused disaster in the severe storm of January 1916. Provided that she did not proceed to sea in a storm, he advised that the *King Orry* was still seaworthy and that repairs would be commenced when shipwrights could be released from more essential work on board other vessels.

On 27th August, Major Dutton RMLI inspected the *King Orry's* Royal Marine detachment while on the following afternoon, the *King Orry* was invited to enter a crew to race in the 4th Battle Squadron Sailing Regatta. Unfortunately, despite much hard work and enthusiasm, they failed to win any prizes.

The morning of 29th August found the *King Orry* being employed as a target-towing vessel once again. She picked up a battle target from an armed trawler at 09.15 and proceeded to sea with the American battleships *Texas* and *Florida*.

The shoot was carried out off Fidra island and was completed by mid-afternoon. As the American ships steamed back towards Rosyth, the unfortunate *King Orry* had to remain on station to commence another shoot with the recently-commissioned aircraft-carrier *Furious*. She had been laid down as a light battle-cruiser whose main armament had been two massive 18" guns, each gun being mounted in its own turret, one forward and one aft.

However, she was never completed to her original design and was subsequently converted to operate aircraft, entering service in her new role in March 1918. On this particular afternoon, she fired at the *King Orry's* target with her remaining armament, which consisted of ten 5.5" guns. This second shoot was completed by 18.00 and the *King Orry* was secure to her buoy off Rosyth Dockyard by 22.00.

Despite their failure in the recent sailing regatta, the *King Orry's* sea boat crew proved their worth on the afternoon of 1st September. At 14.25, the 27ft whaler from the light cruiser *Undaunted* passed by the *King Orry*. As the whaler drew astern, for reasons that are not explained in the *King Orry's* log book, it suddenly capsized and deposited its six man crew into the Firth of Forth. Having witnessed the incident, the officer of the watch ordered the *King Orry's* sea boat to go to the rescue of the stricken crew, and within ten minutes the bedraggled sailors from the *Undaunted* were safely on board the armed boarding vessel. Having been given dry clothing, they were taken back to the *Undaunted* later in the afternoon.

The *King Orry* received orders on the morning of 2nd September to proceed into the main basin at the dockyard and to secure alongside the repair ship *Assistance*, which had moved down from Scapa Flow. After waiting for the next high tide, she slipped her buoy at 14.20 and after passing through the lock gates was secure alongside the *Assistance* by 16.30. Repair work was to be carried out on her bow plating but before this work could commence, it was necessary to transfer all of the ammunition from the forward 12 pdr magazine into the after magazines. With the assistance of sailors from the repair ship, this task was completed within a couple of hours.

A team of shipwrights arrived on board at 08.00 the next day and commenced repairing the forepeak hull plating and the chain pipe covers.

While the repairs were being carried out, a team of divers took the opportunity to carry out an underwater inspection of the ship's bottom plating, rudder and propellers. The repairs were completed on 7th September and by 17.00 the ammunition was transferred into the forward magazine. She remained alongside the *Assistance* until the morning of 10th September, when she moved back into the river and secured to B3 buoy to await further orders.

Sailing orders arrived on board on the afternoon of 16th September having been issued by Admiral Beatty from his flagship, the battleship *Queen Elizabeth* earlier in the day. They instructed the *King Orry*, along with units of the 4th Battle Squadron and the cruiser *Boadicea* to proceed to Scapa Flow on the following

afternoon. Destroyers from the 14th Flotilla would provide an anti-submarine screen. The *King Orry* slipped her buoy at 12.30 and passed through the Bridge Gate anti-submarine boom, which was below the Forth bridge, at 13.00. During the afternoon, the *King Orry* suffered a mishap when she lost her patent log which was attached to a bracket on the stern railing. The torpedo-shaped propeller was trailed astern and attached to the log via a long line. The spinning motion of this propeller recorded the distance travelled on the patent log's clock face.

Although the ships had been advised that they might meet a convoy in the proximity of Rattery Head, the *King Orry* arrived in Scapa Flow at midday on 18th September, having sighted no other vessel outside of those with whom she was in company.

The units of the 4th Battle Squadron operated from Scapa Flow for the next couple of weeks and carried out various exercises and gunnery shoots. The *King Orry* was employed as both a repeating ship and target-towing vessel.

They departed from the Orkney Island anchorage on the afternoon of 30th September, arriving back in the Firth of Forth the following day.

Before the *King Orry* departed from Scapa Flow, a member of her crew who had been on board since she had commissioned as an armed boarding vessel left the ship for the last time. Having joined her on 21st November 1914, Chief Petty Officer (Wireless Telegraphist) Crispen Redshaw left the *King Orry* and transferred to the depot ship *Cyclops*. He would remain on board the *Cyclops* until he was demobilised from the Royal Naval Reserve on 9th February 1919.

After spending a week and a half at Rosyth, orders were received on the afternoon of 11th October, instructing the *King Orry* to proceed to sea the following day in company with elements of the 4th Battle Squadron. As preparations were being made to put to sea, a medical officer from the nearby naval base came on board and with the assistance of the *King Orry's* medical officer, Temporary Surgeon Cyril Williams, gave every member of the crew a vaccination against Influenza which was now sweeping through the United Kingdom and claiming many lives. In these crucial days with the end of the war in sight, the last thing that the Admiralty wanted was that its ships were forced to remain in harbour as their crews were incapacitated by disease.

A LAST VISIT TO SCAPA FLOW

The *King Orry* slipped her buoy at 16.00 the following day and steamed under the Forth Bridge and out towards the North Sea, astern of the battleship

Agincourt. The ships arrived in Scapa Flow at midday on 13th October, with the *King Orry* anchoring in B3 anchorage. At 07.00 on 15th October, the *King Orry* left her anchorage and picked up a battle target from the Admiralty tug *Stoic* before steaming out into Pentland Firth and carrying out a gunnery shoot with battleships from both the 2nd and 4th Battle Squadrons.

The next few days were spent at anchor in Longhope and members of the crew took the opportunity to proceed ashore and renew friendships with local inhabitants.

Orders were received instructing the *King Orry* to proceed to sea at 07.00 on 21st October, and after exercising her own 12 pdr and 4" guns crews, she was to proceed to Rosyth. As she steamed out through the Switha Boom and entered Pentland Firth, nobody on board was aware that this was to be the last time that the *King Orry* would operate from Scapa Flow, the long bleak winters in this northern outpost were to be a thing of the past.

ROSYTH AGAIN

The *King Orry* secured to B2 buoy, opposite Rosyth Naval Base at just before 08.00 the next day and would remain there until the morning of 30th October when she proceeded to sea to tow a target for a squadron of light cruisers in the vicinity of the islands of Elie and Fidra.

At 11.35, while she manoeuvred into position to begin her target-towing run, her steering gear jammed with 20 degrees of port wheel on the helm causing her to veer straight across the bows of the light cruiser *Cardiff* and narrowly avoiding what might have been a fatal collision.

Fortunately, the *Cardiff* swung away from the rapidly approaching armed boarding vessel. Temporary repairs were carried out and the *King Orry* was ordered to proceed back to Rosyth, Artificers from the repair ship *Assistance* came on board later in the day and repaired the defective equipment.

This near disastrous day was to be the last time that the *King Orry* proceeded to sea during the First World War.

As the crew of the *King Orry* rose from their bunks and hammocks on the morning of 1st November, the newspapers were full of the news that Turkey had signed an armistice on the previous day and that hostilities had ceased against the Ottoman Empire. The country rejoiced and many now predicted that as Germany no longer had the support of Turkey, she could not expect to stand up against the might of the allies for much longer.

On the morning of 4th November, thirty stokers from the battleship *Bellerophon* arrived on board and assisted with cleaning the *King Orry's* boilers, a task which was not completed until 7th November.

The situation within Germany worsened over the next few days with elements of the German army and navy now in open revolt. On 9th November, the Kaiser was forced to abdicate and the Government gave way to a socialist regime.

Just after 05.00 on Monday 11th November 1918, the German Government signed the document that ended the First World War.

CHAPTER SEVEN

The Armistice, Internment and Peace

As the crew of the *King Orry* awoke from their sleep on the morning of 11th November 1918, they were still unaware that the armistice had been signed and the war would be over in a few hours time.

At 09.00, the crew were mustered by division on the after end of the Promenade Deck where the Captain told them that a signal had arrived on board from the Commander-in-Chief of the Grand Fleet informing them that at 05.10 that morning, the Government of Germany had signed an armistice and that at 11.00 all hostilities against Germany and her allies would cease.

Although this news had been expected for some time, to hear the news officially resulted in jubilation and cheering from the assembled sailors. After this had died down the Captain held a short church service and no doubt a few tears were shed as the tension of four long years of carnage finally disappeared and memories of lost relatives and comrades flooded back.

However, in the best traditions of the Royal Navy, once the service was over the crew were given a period of physical training followed by the administration of more influenza prophylaxis.

Once this had been completed, the ship's company were sent back to work within their various departments for the remainder of the morning. Although it had not been officially sanctioned by the Captain, the crew began to muster on the upper decks as the eleventh hour approached. At precisely 11.00, a saluting gun fired from somewhere ashore and the whole fleet erupted into a mass of cheering sailors, accompanied by the sounding of ships' sirens.

Leave was granted to the non-duty watch at 12.30 and the crew of the *King Orry* streamed ashore to take part in the rejoicing that was taking place in nearby Dunfermline and Inverkeithing, although they were under orders to be back on board by 17.00.

At 19.00 the crew were mustered again and informed that Admiral Sir David Beatty; Commander-in-Chief Grand Fleet had sent a signal ordering all ships to splice the mainbrace and celebrate the end of hostilities with Germany. Even though the war was now over, the *King Orry's* log book records that at 21.00, darken ship took place.

At 11.30 the following morning, the crew were mustered yet again on the after end of the Promenade Deck. On this occasion, a personal message from His Majesty King George V to every member of the Grand Fleet was read aloud by the Captain. The *King Orry* remained at her buoy for the next few days and during this time everybody on board was speculating about what the future had in store for them. They did not have to wait for very long as one of the initial terms of the armistice would effect the future employment of the *King Orry*.

The allies anticipated that it might take many months to finalise the terms of the armistice and decide upon the future of the German Empire but in the meantime it was necessary to prevent Germany from waging any form of warfare should they decide that they were unhappy with any of the terms that were forced upon them.

Although the German navy was in disarray, the ships of the High Seas Fleet still poised a significant threat, especially if they should fall into the hands of one of the extremist movements that were now fighting for power within Germany. The allies therefore decided that the majority of the High Seas Fleet should be interned within a neutral port to await the outcome of the post war peace settlement. This settlement, or to be more appropriate the directives that the allied powers would force Germany to abide by would eventually be signed on 28th June 1919 and would come to be known as the Treaty Of Versailles. Germany was ordered to prepare 10 battleships, 6 battle cruisers,

8 light cruisers, 50 destroyers and all U boats for internment.

The ships of the High Seas Fleet that were nominated for internment were to have their ammunition put ashore before they sailed from their bases and only carry sufficient fuel to take them to their place of internment.

On 13th November, the allies decided that as no neutral power had offered the facilities of any of its ports to intern the German warships, the U boats would be sent to various British ports and the surface ships would proceed to Scapa Flow. All ships nominated for internment were to be ready to proceed to the United Kingdom within 7 days.

As the German Naval High Command was complying with these orders, the ships of the Grand Fleet awaited their orders from the Admiralty. It was known that many of the German warships were in a neglected state and the Admiralty wanted to display that the Grand Fleet was still in a high state of efficiency and that its moral was high.

To this end, all ships within the Grand Fleet were ordered to repaint their hulls and superstructure and remove all signs of rust and weathering. The crew of the *King Orry* commenced painting ship on 13th November and finished the task on 18th.

At 07.00 on 19th November, she was ordered to proceed to sea and take part in fleet exercises acting as the repeating ship. After being at sea for only a couple of hours, a signal was received which cancelled the exercise and instructed all ships back to Rosyth to await further orders: the *King Orry* was secured to her buoy again by midday.

VICTORY REVIEW

During the afternoon, the Captain briefed the crew that His Majesty King George V was due at Rosyth the following morning and that he would review the Grand Fleet from the bridge of the Commander-in-Chief's despatch vessel, the destroyer *Oak*. As the anchorages and moorings within the Firth of Firth did not permit all ships to be ranged in line, some ships, including the *King Orry*, would be required to slip their moorings and steam slowly past the *Oak* in line ahead.

The *King Orry* was in position to steam past His Majesty by 10.30 the following morning and shortly afterwards the column of ships began to move slowly towards the *Oak* in line ahead. The *King Orry* drew abreast of the destroyer at 11.40 and as she steamed past her crew raised their caps from their heads and gave three cheers for His Majesty.

The review was over by midday and all of the ships involved returned to their respective buoys and

anchorages shortly afterwards. His Majesty then went on board the flagship, the battleship *Queen Elizabeth* to have lunch with Admiral Beatty.

Later that afternoon, the *King Orry* received a signal from the flagship, which gave the awaited instructions for escorting the High Seas Fleet into internment.

The signal was code named Operation ZZ and detailed how the Grand Fleet would meet the High Seas Fleet between 08.00 and 09.00 the following morning, 21st November 1918. The German ships would then be escorted into the Firth of Forth for inspection before being escorted north to Scapa Flow. The *King Orry* had been detailed to take part in the operation.

SOLE REPRESENTATIVE

There is a popular story that has been recalled in many publications about the Isle of Man Steam Packet. This relates that the *King Orry* was personally selected to take part by Admiral Sir David Beatty and that she was to be the sole representative of the Merchant Navy. The story also mentions that she led the ships of the German High Seas Fleet into internment at Scapa Flow.

Although it would be nice to believe that such an honour was bestowed upon the little, but proud Manx vessel, examination of official Admiralty records and the signal Operation ZZ confirms that this story is an adaptation of the true facts.

The *King Orry* was indeed detailed to form part of the Grand Fleet's reception committee which would lead the German ships into internment but only into the Firth of Forth: she was not involved in their subsequent move to Scapa Flow. It is also a fact that the *King Orry* was the only former merchant vessel to take part in Operation ZZ but there is no documented evidence to support the claim that she was invited to attend at the personal request of Admiral Beatty.

However, the fact that Admiral Beatty personally signed the fleet operation order could be interpreted that he asked for the *King Orry* to attend. The role of the Manx steamer during Operation ZZ was to act as one of the five repeating ships, the other vessels being the cruisers *Blonde*, *Fearless*, *Blance* and *Boadicea*. As the *King Orry* had acted as a repeating ship for the Grand Fleet on many previous occasions, she was an obvious choice and ideally suited for this role.

It is possible that the myth of her leading the German ships into captivity has arisen from a painting displayed in the Manx Museum. This picture was painted by Mr Arthur Burgess shortly after the First World War and shows the *King Orry* leading a column of British and German warships at the surrender of the German High Seas Fleet. Many people have stated that the painting depicts the *King Orry* leading the British light cruiser *Cardiff* and a column of German battle cruisers into internment at Scapa Flow. It is true that the cruiser *Cardiff* did lead the surrendered German warships into internment, but into the Firth of Forth and not Scapa Flow.

Unfortunately, the *King Orry* was not positioned ahead of the *Cardiff*, as has been claimed, but was half way down the centre column of the German warships. It is probable that this painting has mistakenly given the impression that the *King Orry* was the lead ship when the allied warships escorted the High Seas Fleet into internment and that the ships astern of the *King Orry* have been mistaken for the cruiser *Cardiff* and the three German battle cruisers, *Seydlitz, Moltke* and *Derfflinger.*

The exact position of the *King Orry* is further complicated by a document called Der Tag (The Day) which was sold to the general public as a souvenir shortly after the event. It shows the positions of all of the British, allied and German warships as they steamed into the Firth of Firth. The *King Orry* is shown at the rear of the centre column - again an incorrect position.

Admiralty records confirm that the *King Orry's* correct position was in the centre of the middle column of warships. Immediately ahead of her, and at a distance of one and a half miles was the German battleship *Grosser Kurfurst* while astern of the *King Orry*, again at a distance of one and a half miles, was the British light cruiser *Phaeton*.

Close examination of Arthur Burgess's painting does in fact reveal that it gives an accurate portrayal of the position of the *King Orry* on 21st November 1918. The British light cruiser astern of the *King Orry* is the *Phaeton*, not the *Cardiff*. The misinterpretation of this painting has given ammunition to the claim that the *King Orry* led the High Seas Fleet into internment.

SURRENDER

Having raised steam, the *King Orry* slipped her buoy at 03.00 on the morning of 21st November. After slowly manoeuvring into her allotted position, she left harbour some fifty minutes later in company with the 4th Battle Squadron. All of the ships involved in escorting the Germans into the Firth of Forth were required to leave their anchorages and moorings off Rosyth very early in the morning as they were all required to be in position off May Island, which sits in the entrance to the Firth of Forth, by 08.15, ready to meet the High Seas Fleet at just after 09.00.

The first vessels that were required to be in position were those of the 1st Light Cruiser Squadron which had to be off May by 04.30, while the last ships were those of the 7th Light Cruiser Squadron which had to be on station by 08.15. It was necessary to stagger the departure of the Grand Fleet from Rosyth and their arrival off May Island over a four-hour period to minimise the risk of collision.

Once all of the ships were on station, the various squadrons of battleships, battle cruisers and light cruisers would form up into two lines, each steaming out into the North Sea in an easterly direction. The northern line would be known as the Red Fleet and would fly a red burgee, while the southern line would be known as the Blue Fleet and fly a blue burgee.

After the Grand Fleet met up with the High Seas Fleet, a third or centre line would be formed which

*With her crew mustered on the Upper Deck and signal flags flying from her masts, the **King Orry** steams past the battleship **Queen Elizabeth** in the Firth of Forth during early November 1918. (Imperial War Museum)*

Chapter Seven

would be made up from the German warships steaming in line ahead and four British warships.

The light cruiser *Cardiff* would be stationed at the head of the centre column with the German battleships and battle cruisers astern of her, the light cruiser *Phaeton* would be stationed ahead of the German light cruisers, while the light cruiser *Castor* would lead the German destroyer flotillas. All these three British ships would be flying a Blue Ensign at their masthead. The fourth British warship within the centre column was to be the *King Orry* in her capacity as repeating ship. She would position herself behind the last German battleship and ahead of the cruiser *Phaeton*.

The whole fleet was under the Command of Admiral Sir David Beatty on board his flagship *Queen Elizabeth*. Having formed into column and now steaming out into the North Sea, the Grand Fleet created an impressive sight.

The northern column consisted of some 40 warships, while the southern column totalled 37 (which gave a combined total of 77 warships).

The High Seas Fleet had been ordered to steam in line ahead and as it approached, the northern and southern line of ships would steam past them before, at a given signal reverse their course 180 degrees and form up on either side of the German fleet at a distance of 3 miles on their port and starboard beams.

The cruisers *Cardiff, Phaeton, Caster* and their destroyer flotillas had been sent ahead of the Grand Fleet and would be the first ships to make contact with the Germans. On meeting the German warships, the three light cruisers would take their allotted positions within the German column and, with the *Cardiff* ahead, would then lead the High Seas Fleet towards the waiting Grand Fleet.

The *King Orry* and the other four repeating ships would initially steam between the northern and southern lines of the Grand Fleet and after it had reversed course, the repeating ships would also turn about and move into their allotted positions behind or abeam of the German ships.

The *King Orry* and the 4th Battle Squadron passed through the Black Rock Gate anti-submarine boom at 05.00 and arrived off May Island at 07.00, ten minutes later than their programmed time.

Having detached herself from the 4th Battle Squadron, the *King Orry* was in her allotted position, equidistant between the northern and southern line of the Grand Fleet by 07.30.

As the darkness gave way to daylight, the Grand Fleet waited for the arrival of the High Seas Fleet. As a precaution against German treachery, the Grand Fleet had been ordered to close up at action stations,

ammunition was to be available at each gun but turrets were to be ranged fore and aft. To avoid any provocation, gun crews in exposed positions were to keep out of sight. The *King Orry's* 4" and 12 pdr gun crews crouched down behind the bulwarks on the forecastle and Poop Deck.

Daylight on Thursday 21st November 1918 revealed a cool misty day, the wind was coming from the south west and the *King Orry's* log book recorded the sea state as Force 3. The Grand Fleet was moving eastward on a course of 90 degrees, at about 12 knots.

At just after 09.10 the cruiser *Cardiff* suddenly loomed out of the mist and steamed towards the *King Orry*. As she drew near, the ghostly shapes of the German High Seas Fleet appeared out of the mist behind her. The *King Orry* passed down the starboard side of the *Cardiff* and approached the first German battle cruiser, the *Seydlitz*. She was followed by four more battle cruisers that included the infamous *Derfflinger* which had been credited as having fired the shells that destroyed the British battle cruisers *Invincible* and *Queen Mary* at the Battle of Jutland.

As the last of the rust-streaked German battle cruisers steamed past, the battleship *Freidrich Der Grosse* loomed into view. She was flying the flag of Rear Admiral von Reuter who had been given the unenviable task of commanding the High Seas Fleet and taking it into captivity. Another eight battleships steamed past before the *King Orry* made a 180 degree turn to port and took up station one and a half miles astern: the time was 09.40.

At almost the same time as the *King Orry* reversed her course, Admiral Beatty ordered the two columns of the Grand Fleet to turn outwards and make a 180 degree turn and then to form up on either side of the defeated Germans. The three columns of warships, which spanned a distance of nearly nineteen miles from front to rear ship, then steamed westward on a course of 270 degrees and headed back towards the Firth of Forth.

The High Seas Fleet no longer poised a threat and Britannia once more ruled the waves.

At 10.40, Admiral Sir David Beatty sent the following signal to the Admiralty:

The Grand Fleet met this morning at 09.30, 5 battle cruisers, 9 battleships, 7 light cruisers, 49 destroyers of the High Seas Fleet which surrendered for internment and are now being brought to the Firth of Forth.

The *King Orry's* log records that she passed May Island at 12.07 while at 14.30, as the ships approached the small Island of Inchkeith, the *King Orry* was instructed to leave the German column and take station astern of a French cruiser, the *Amiral Aube*, and then to follow her through the Black Rock anti-submarine boom. The boom was cleared by 14.42 and she passed under the Forth Bridge at 15.20.

Her duties for this memorable day now completed, the proud Manx steamer was secured to B2 buoy, adjacent to Rosyth Dockyard at just after 16.00. Although her duties during the day had been uneventful, the fact that she had been part of the mighty fleet that had brought the German navy into captivity would become the most remembered aspect of her service with the Royal Navy during the First World War, and no doubt would be recalled over many a pint of beer by her former crew members in the forthcoming years.

The remaining ships of the Grand Fleet went to various anchorages over the next couple of hours. Under the watchful eyes of the Royal Navy, the ships of the once proud High Seas Fleet were anchored in parallel lines from a position just off North Queensferry (approximately underneath the present Forth road bridge) to a position some five miles up river, opposite the Naval Armament Depot at Crombie.

At 18.00, a Divine Service and Thanksgiving for the Victory of the Allies was conducted by Commander Mosse on the after end of the Promenade Deck and all off-duty crew members attended. The Germans were given a final humiliation as dusk approached when Admiral Beatty sent them the following signal:

The German ensign will be hauled down at sunset today, Thursday, and will not be hoisted again without permission.

As the men of the *King Orry* went to their bunks and hammocks that night, they knew that peace had finally arrived and that the menace of the High Seas Fleet was securely locked away within the confines of the naval anchorage in the Firth of Forth.

Following their arrival in the Forth, all German ships were inspected and the breech blocks from their guns removed as was the wireless equipment. A limited amount of fuel was left on board, sufficient to get the ships to Scapa Flow, and then to provide power for essential services such as heating, lighting and cooking. Once the inspections were completed, the ships were escorted to internment within Scapa Flow.

The participation of the *King Orry* at the surrender of the German High Seas Fleet had not gone unnoticed by the Manx press as an article written by Mr J C Christian appeared in the "Isle Of Man Examiner" on 23rd November 1918.

THE DEVIL SHIP OF THE NORTH SEA.

Your readers may be interested in an incident I witnessed in the North Sea last Thursday, when I was one of a number of London journalists at the surrender of the German navy to the British Grand Fleet. That story, which is probably destined to become one of the most historic events in the annals of Britain, has already been told, so I will not trouble your readers by repeating it here. The story, however that I am going to write about has not been told. I should explain that each pressman was allocated to a different ship, so that there was only one civilian on each Man o' War. I myself, had the good fortune to be drawn for HMS Warspite, perhaps the finest ship in the battleship squadron and a sister ship of the flagship, HMS Queen Elizabeth.

We were roughly sixty miles out to sea, it was nine o' clock in the morning and I was looking out of the gun control tower from where one gets an ideal view. We had just received a message from the flagship that it was expected that we should sight the German ships at 9.25. Looking away on our starboard side, I saw a ship in the grey mist of the North Sea. I casually pointed to the object on the horizon, "That" said the Lieutenant Commander who had been deputed to look after me, "That is the King Orry, an armed mercantile cruiser". "Really" I replied, for this was very interesting. I am afraid my enthusiasm aroused his curiosity. Perhaps I had heard of her? Ra-ther! Did I know her? Did I not, well well. One felt proud of being a Manxman and prouder still that a Manx vessel was taking part in the reception of the Hun ships. Later in the evening, when we had got back to our anchorage in the Forth, just below the famous bridge, a dreadful looking ship passed through the line, three cables away. I stood on the Quarter Deck and looked at her, for she was an object of much curiosity. In fact she might have been one of those devil ships that came out of the pages of Dante. The Lieutenant Commander ran up to me, "That's the King Orry" he said, pointing to the phantom thing that was silently passing us at about 10 knots. Nonsense! Oh yes it was, but I was suspicious. Officers of His Majesty's navy have a habit of sometimes pulling a civilian's leg. I appealed to the Quartermaster - The King Orry he replied decisively. So there was the Manx liner, superbly camouflaged. Her sides were painted in three colours, yellow, dark blue and a kind of dull red. The colours were painted diagonally, and I was told that at a distance, a Hun submarine Commander would have difficulty, not so much as discerning her, as in judging her course and speed.

If ever the King Orry should come to the Island in all the glory of her war paint, I am quite certain she will give my Manx friends a great fright. She is known to the men of the Grand Fleet as the Devil Ship, and I am sure that

King Orry

*Arthur Burgess' painting of the **King Orry** which suggested that she may have led the German fleet into internment.*

the people of Manxland would like to see her as she really is. There used to be some seamen in the Island, especially at Ramsey who could tell the name of a ship passing many leagues out to sea. I defy any of them to name the King Orry. If ever she comes around Maughold Head with her war paint on, the Promenade, I fear, would soon be cleared. While on board the Warspite, I heard a Lieutenant tell a fine humorous story about the King Orry, but that will keep.

The Manx people would indeed have an opportunity to see the Devil Ship of the North Sea in a few weeks time.

With the events of the previous day still paramount in their minds and the thought of being demobilised from the Royal Navy about to become a reality, the crew of the *King Orry* were given little time to relax.

Having been roused from their slumber at 05.00 on 22nd November, the crew commenced coaling ship from a barge that was brought alongside by a tug at 06.30.

Although the naval war was definitely over, the Admiralty obviously wanted to ensure that all of its ships were ready to proceed to sea if required. It took most of the day to unload the barge; although when it departed the *King Orry's* bunkers were still not full. The next two days were spent swinging around the buoy, and the crew was given shore leave during the evening.

At 11.00 on 25th November, the 4" and 12 pdr gun crews were drilled and to some if must have appeared to be a pointless exercise as there was no enemy to shoot at any more. The *King Orry* moved to number A4 berth in the dockyard the next day and commenced taking on the remainder of the coal that was required to top up her bunkers.

*Robert Lloyd's fine painting of the **King Orry** (3) shows her at the surrender of the German High Seas Fleet east of the Firth of Forth in November 1918. This event represented one of the Steam Packet's greatest hours. (By kind permission of Stan Basnett)*

INTERNMENT OF GERMAN HIGH SEAS FLEET
THURSDAY, NOVEMBER 21, 1918
POSITIONS AT 10.0 A.M. OF SHIPS BOUND FOR THE FIRTH OF FORTH

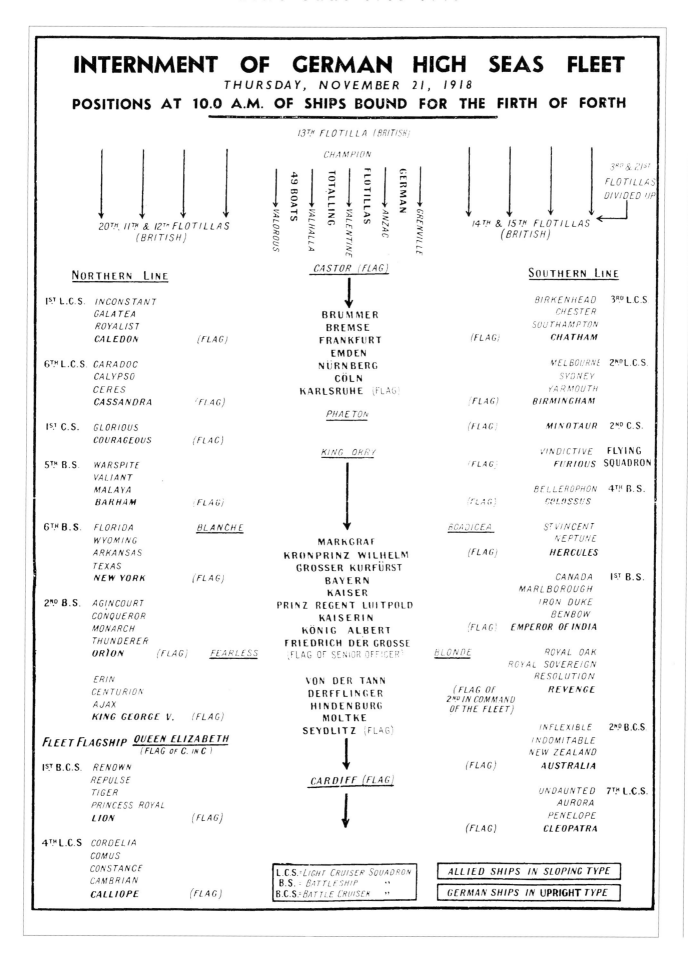

13TH FLOTILLA (BRITISH)

CHAMPION

20TH, 11TH & 12TH FLOTILLAS (BRITISH)

49 BOATS

VALOROUS / VALHALLA / VALENTINE / ANZAC / GRENVILLE

TOTALLING / FLOTILLAS / GERMAN

3RD & 21ST FLOTILLAS DIVIDED UP

14TH & 15TH FLOTILLAS (BRITISH)

NORTHERN LINE

1ST L.C.S. INCONSTANT
GALATEA
ROYALIST
CALEDON   (FLAG)

6TH L.C.S. CARADOC
CALYPSO
CERES
CASSANDRA   (FLAG)

1ST C.S. GLORIOUS
COURAGEOUS   (FLAG)

5TH B.S. WARSPITE
VALIANT
MALAYA
BARHAM   (FLAG)

6TH B.S. FLORIDA   BLANCHE
WYOMING
ARKANSAS
TEXAS
NEW YORK   (FLAG)

2ND B.S. AGINCOURT
CONQUEROR
MONARCH
THUNDERER
ORION   (FLAG)   FEARLESS

ERIN
CENTURION
AJAX
KING GEORGE V.   (FLAG)

FLEET FLAGSHIP QUEEN ELIZABETH
(FLAG OF C. IN C.)

1ST B.C.S. RENOWN
REPULSE
TIGER
PRINCESS ROYAL
LION   (FLAG)

4TH L.C.S. CORDELIA
COMUS
CONSTANCE
CAMBRIAN
CALLIOPE   (FLAG)

CASTOR (FLAG)

BRUMMER
BREMSE
FRANKFURT
EMDEN
NÜRNBERG
CÖLN
KARLSRUHE (FLAG)

PHAETON

KING ORRY

MARKGRAF
KRONPRINZ WILHELM
GROSSER KURFÜRST
BAYERN
KAISER
PRINZ REGENT LUITPOLD
KAISERIN
KÖNIG ALBERT
FRIEDRICH DER GROSSE
(FLAG OF SENIOR OFFICER)

VON DER TANN
DERFFLINGER
HINDENBURG
MOLTKE
SEYDLITZ (FLAG)

CARDIFF (FLAG)

SOUTHERN LINE

BIRKENHEAD   3RD L.C.S.
CHESTER
SOUTHAMPTON
(FLAG)   CHATHAM

MELBOURNE   2ND L.C.S.
SYDNEY
YARMOUTH
(FLAG)   BIRMINGHAM

(FLAG)   MINOTAUR   2ND C.S.

VINDICTIVE   FLYING
(FLAG)   FURIOUS   SQUADRON

BELLEROPHON   4TH B.S.
(FLAG)   COLOSSUS

BOADICEA   ST VINCENT
NEPTUNE
(FLAG)   HERCULES

CANADA   1ST B.S.
MARLBOROUGH
IRON DUKE
BENBOW
(FLAG) EMPEROR OF INDIA

BLONDE   ROYAL OAK
ROYAL SOVEREIGN
RESOLUTION
(FLAG OF   REVENGE
2ND IN COMMAND
OF THE FLEET)

INFLEXIBLE   2ND B.C.S.
INDOMITABLE
NEW ZEALAND
(FLAG)   AUSTRALIA

UNDAUNTED   7TH L.C.S.
AURORA
PENELOPE
(FLAG)   CLEOPATRA

L.C.S.=Light Cruiser Squadron
B.S. = Battleship   ,,
B.C.S.= Battle Cruiser   ,,

ALLIED SHIPS IN SLOPING TYPE

GERMAN SHIPS IN UPRIGHT TYPE

PAYING-OFF

While she was alongside, Admiralty officials and dockyard workers came on board to inspect the ship and establish what work would need to be carried out on the *King Orry* before she could be handed back to the Steam Packet. To the hostilities-only members of her crew, this must have been a good sign as it indicated that the *King Orry* might not be required for naval service for much longer. After remaining at her berth for a further day, the *King Orry* moved away from the naval base at 14.00 on 29th and steamed up river to secure to J1 buoy off the small town of Burntisland. More gunnery drill was carried out the next day, although on this occasion it involved the gun crews from the 12 pdr and 6 pdr anti-aircraft gun.

Maintaining fighting efficiency was still a requirement of the navy and the *King Orry* resorted to her role as a target-towing vessel the next day. She left her buoy at 05.00 and proceeded to sea with the 5th Light Cruiser Squadron to carry out a gunnery shoot. This was completed by mid-afternoon and the *King Orry* returned to the same berth that she had occupied in the dockyard a few days earlier.

She again proceeded to sea on 11th and 18th December, on both occasions towing a target for the 5th Light Cruiser Squadron, although on the second occasion the shoot was cancelled due to bad weather.

This was to be the last occasion that the *King Orry* proceeded to sea as an active unit of the Royal Navy for when she returned to harbour, she was ordered to proceed into the Naval Dockyard and to start making preparations to unload the numerous items of naval equipment that had been installed on board.

At 09.00, shipwrights from the battleships *Bellerophon* and *St Vincent* arrived on board to start stripping out the photographic equipment from the darkroom. At 13.15, two tugs moved the *King Orry* through the lock gates and took her into the basin. As the afternoon wore on a working party of one Petty Officer and six Junior Ratings came on board from the battleship *Neptune* and took the photographic equipment ashore.

Once all of this equipment was ashore, the same working party commenced removing the smaller items of target-towing gear. The next few days were taken up with removing the heavier items and the depth charge/mine-laying rails. The heavy-duty towing bollards were removed and the type of bollards that had originally been fitted at Cammell Laird's were put back on board. All work was stopped on Christmas Day and Boxing Day to allow everybody to enjoy the first Christmas at peace since 1913.

The last items of equipment that had to be put ashore before the *King Orry* left Rosyth were removed by late afternoon on 27th December. The guns, searchlights, signal and wireless equipment would be retained on board until the *King Orry* finally decommissioned. The long awaited sailing orders for the *King Orry* to pay off arrived on board on 28th December. She was to proceed to the River Mersey, and after destoring would be taken in hand by Cammell Laird's shipyard where work would be carried out to convert her back into a passenger vessel.

The *King Orry* was ready to leave Rosyth on the morning of 30th December. At 07.00 all of her secret Grand Fleet documents were taken to the Fleet Mail Office for onward dispatch to the battleship *Colossus*. At just after midday, the mooring ropes were cast off and, assisted by two tugs, the *King Orry* moved across the basin and entered the lock. She was clear by 13.00 and as she turned down river towards the North Sea, the traditional pennant used by warships to indicate that they were paying off was raised to the head of her foremast. This pennant, known as the paying-off pennant, was by tradition at least the length of the ship and the *King Orry's* pennant was no exception.

As she steamed between the lines of anchored warships with her crew lining the guardrails, she was greeted with cheers and messages of good luck from the warship crews. For the *King Orry* to attract so much attention must have made her crew very proud. She passed under the massive structure of the Forth bridge for the final time and was clear of the Black Rock Gate anti-submarine boom by 14.00. As May Island disappeared astern at just before 16.00, the Manx steamer turned north and began her journey back to the once familiar waters of the Irish Sea and River Mersey.

1919 - ISLAND BOUND!

The Girdle Ness lighthouse near Aberdeen was passed at 23.00, Duncansby Head and Cape Wrath were passed during 31st December while New Years Day 1919 found the *King Orry* heading south towards the Irish Sea. The Isle of Skye was passed early in the morning and she passed through the Sound of Mull at 13.00. Having reduced speed, the *King Orry* steamed through the narrow waters of the Sound of Islay between the islands of Islay and Jura during the afternoon. Members of the crew who had been on board since 1915, no doubt remembered the near disastrous grounding incident when the *King Orry* had steamed over a reef at the southern end of the sound on 9th June 1915. Fortunately, on this occasion she passed through the sound without mishap.

The flashing light from the Mull of Kintyre lighthouse was seen at 19.00 and shortly afterwards the *King Orry* set a course into the Irish Sea, towards the Isle Of Man. The comments relating to the impact that the dazzle-painted *King Orry* would make upon the Manx people, should she venture into Manx waters that had been written by Mr J Christian in his newspaper article of 23rd November, were about to be put to the test.

Having steamed slowly down the west coast of the island, the *King Orry* arrived at its southern point, the Calf of Man at 12.45 and then hove to. Having drifted away from the island with the tide for nearly four hours, she got under way again at 05.00 and set course for Douglas Bay.

With her service within the Royal Navy having only a matter of a few hours to run, the *King Orry* was to suffer one final mishap. Although the war was over, the thousands of mines that had been laid by both the allies and the Germans still poised a significant threat to shipping.

Operations were already being undertaken to clear the minefields that had been laid by the allies and Germany had also handed over details on where they had laid their mines. Once a minefield was identified, it was relatively safe as shipping could be advised to keep clear of the area. The danger came from mines that had dragged their moorings or broken adrift. As these mines drifted with the tide, they could be encountered in areas that were thought to be mine-free. As a precaution, warships were still required to trail paravanes which were buoyant bomb-shaped floats pulled astern of a ship. They were attached by a heavy wire that incorporated a cutting device and so if a mine was snagged, it was dragged towards the cutter which would hopefully snap its securing cable, allowing it to float to the surface. The mine would then be sunk or detonated by gunfire.

As the Manx ship steamed past Langness Point, towards Douglas, her paravanes were being trailed astern. She was only a matter a few hundred yards away from the dangerous rocks that surrounded Langness but as she drew level with the lighthouse, the wires suddenly snagged on an underwater object and snapped. The jolt of the wires snapping was felt throughout the ship, and the Captain ordered the *King Orry* to heave to.

No sign of the paravanes could be found and it was assumed that they had been caught up in the rocks and pulled below the waves. After about half an hour, the search was abandoned and the *King Orry* continued on her course towards Douglas. She rounded Douglas Head at 06.45, just as daylight was beginning to break,

and anchored in the middle of Douglas Bay. She remained at anchor until 10.45 and a report in the "Isle Of Man Examiner" dated 4th January 1919 recalls her visit to the Island and the impression that she made upon on the onlookers from ashore:

HMS *KING ORRY* - NEW YEAR CALL AT DOUGLAS

On Thursday, Douglas people were pleasantly surprised to see HMS King Orry at anchor in the bay. The good ship, since she was requisitioned by the Admiralty from the Isle of Man Steam Packet Company's fleet, has rendered fine service to the navy as an auxiliary cruiser and has borne a distinguished part in operations carried out in the North Sea and elsewhere having for object the blockage of Germany, the blockade that has so greatly contributed to the allied success. One of the last services of moment engaged in by the King Orry was the guiding of the German light cruisers to their inglorious internment in terms of the armistice. She was on a voyage to the Mersey, when she put into Douglas Bay in the small hours of Thursday. She remained until about 11 o'clock, when she weighed and steamed for her appointed destination. While she lay in the bay, she was regarded with affectionate curiosity by many towns' folk, who were much gratified with what they conceived was the first outward and visible sign of holiday reconstruction. It was freely stated that the King Orry will be dismantled at Birkenhead of her war armament and will then be refitted for engagement in the peaceful occupation of carrying pleasure seekers to and from the island next season. The vessel, it was observed was dazzle painted by way of camouflage and her masts had been adapted for the purpose of wireless telegraphy installation. Otherwise she presented the same beautiful appearance as of yore. As the SS Douglas left Douglas for Liverpool, she accorded the King Orry the salute with which British ships of war are customarily greeted by British Merchant Ships.

Many people took the opportunity to look upon the *King Orry* and a fairly large crowd assembled on the promenade. The Steam Packet vessel, *Douglas* left the harbour a few minutes before the *King Orry* weighed anchor. Both ships were heading towards Liverpool, the *Douglas* remained in sight for a couple of hours before she finally fell astern and disappeared over the horizon. The Bar Lightship was passed at 15.30 and the *King Orry* eventually dropped anchor opposite Cammell Laird's shipyard at about 16.00.

*The **King Orry** going astern as she leaves Douglas harbour in 1919. (Manx National Heritage)*

She had just completed her last voyage as a warship and had created an impressive sight as she steamed past New Brighton in her camouflage and with her paying-off pennant once again flying from her foremast. As Commander Mosse moved the Engine Room telegraph handle to "finished with engines", her career with the Grand Fleet was effectively over.

At 09.30, the following morning, 3rd January, the *King Orry* was taken into the Alfred Basin in Birkenhead by two tugs and secured to the south wall. She remained there until 13.15, when she was taken into the Wallasey Dock and secured to the north wall. Destoring commenced the next morning, one of the first jobs being the return of the remaining confidential books to the Admiralty agent.

Dockyard workers arrived on board at midday and commenced removing the guns. While they were being removed, the crew began to move all of the ammunition out of the magazines and load it into a lighter which was secured alongside. On 8th January, the paymaster from the local naval headquarters came on board and paid the crew their outstanding wages. On completion, the regular Royal Naval personnel were sent on leave with orders to report to their respective depots when their leave expired, which meant that the *King Orry* was now manned by the remaining hostilities-only ratings, who were all waiting to be demobilised from the navy.

It took until 10th January to unload all the Admiralty stores and the last items to be put ashore

were the comprehensive medical stores that had accompanied her medical officer when he had joined the ship in February 1917. Once all the stores had been put ashore, the Admiralty agents came on board and inspected the vessel. The crew now began to clean the ship in preparation for handing her back to the Steam Packet.

The *King Orry* finally paid off at 08.00 on 13th January 1919. The White Ensign was hauled down and the Red Ensign hauled up in its place. Her ship's log records:

08.00 - HMS King Orry paid off out of Admiralty service. Isle Of Man Steam Packet Company took charge of SS King Orry.

This was the last entry in her Royal Navy ship's log book. With the exception of the members of her crew who were former Steam Packet employees, all remaining naval personnel now left the ship. The proud little Manx steamer was no longer one of His Majesty's ships. She had done everything that had been asked of her, survived the violence of hostile weather and had been instrumental in stopping many tons of much-needed supplies reaching the German war effort. It is estimated that she steamed some 52.000 miles while flying the White Ensign from her masthead.

CHAPTER EIGHT

At Peace Again - The Inter-War Years

Although the *King Orry* had been decommissioned as a warship and handed back to the Steam Packet on 13th January 1919, she was retained on Government charter and employed as a troop transport.

On 14th January, she was moved into Cammell Laird's shipyard where essential refurbishment to allow her to operate as a passenger vessel was carried out. Her guns and the two 27ft whalers were put ashore and the lifeboats and davits, which had been removed from the forward end of the boat deck, were replaced. The search light and signal arms were removed from the bridge roof, as were the bunks that had been erected in the saloons.

The only items of equipment that had been installed during her time as an armed boarding vessel which were not removed were the reinforced deck plates on which her guns had sat, the bridge wing houses, the crow's nest and the powerful long-range wireless transmitters. The Admiralty had directed that these items should be retained on board until the *King Orry* completed her duties as a transport. Cammell Laird's had painted out her dazzle camouflage scheme but rather than repainting her in the Steam Packet colours, they had simply given her an all-over warship grey appearance.

Her ship's log records that the Merchant Navy crew signed on, on 27th January 1919 under the command of Captain William Cain.

Captain Cain had just been promoted Commodore of the Steam Packet fleet and no doubt his encounter with a German U boat during the war had some bearing on his selection for this position. He had been in command of the paddle steamer *Mona's Queen* that was employed on trooping duties between Southampton and Le Havre.

On 6th February 1917, while the *Mona's Queen* was en route to Le Havre with over a thousand troops on board, a German U boat, the *UC26*, suddenly surfaced some 500 feet in front of the vessel, virtually dead ahead. As the *Mona's Queen* was travelling at 15 knots, she was on top of the U boat within seconds. Captain Cain did not attempt to alter course but rammed the submarine just forward of the conning tower, catching it with the port paddle wheel, causing catastrophic damage to both the paddle wheel and the U boat.

The U boat scraped down the port side and drifted astern, disappearing below the surface almost immediately. At first it was thought that the U boat had been sunk and when the now badly damaged *Mona's Queen* limped into Le Havre some hours later, Captain Cain and his crew were duly treated as heroes.

However, German naval records released after the First World War revealed that the *UC26* had survived the collision and although she was extensively damaged, she had managed to limp into Ostend two days later. Her Captain had crashed-dived the submarine, which gave the impression that she had been sunk. The *UC26* had only been given a brief reprieve, for British destroyers sank her while operating in the Thames estuary only two months later, and this time her crew did not escape.

Many of the *King Orry's* crew were former Royal Naval reservists who had been part of her ship's company when she had been employed as an armed boarding vessel. These included her Manx Chief Engineer John Keig and Warrant Engineer Haigh, who had signed on as Third Engineer. Thirteen other crew members are recorded as having served on board the armed boarding vessel, eight of them were Manxman and are presumed to be former Steam Packet employees who joined the Royal Navy for the duration. The *King Orry's* 1913 crew agreement shows that one of them, Fireman John Flynn had served on the *King Orry* prior to the war. Another reservist who joined her crew was 25 year old Able Seaman Phillip (Ginger)

Bridson but, although he would pay-off at the end of the 1919 season, he was to return to the *King Orry* in 1929, this time in a far more exalted position.

TROOPING

The *King Orry* left Cammell Laird's shipyard on 28th January and crossed the River Mersey, securing alongside Princes Landing Stage at Liverpool. She remained there until 30th January, when in an unladen condition, she proceeded to Southampton to commence transporting troops back across the English Channel from France and Belgium.

She lay at Southampton for eight days until 8th February when she proceeded across the Channel to Cherbourg and embarked her first consignment of troops.

This work pattern continued for the next six and a half weeks although the port of call in France varied between Le Havre and Cherbourg. Having made a total of fourteen trips from France to England, loaded to capacity with jubilant but tired troops returning home, she was finally released from Government service on 27th March 1919.

Having discharged her last cargo of troops, the *King Orry* steamed back to Liverpool and thence to Birkenhead, arriving on 29th March. Her crew, including the remnants of her naval ship's company, were all paid-off by 1st April at which time she was taken back into Cammell Laird's yard for refitting and complete refurbishment to bring her back to the pre-war Steam Packet standards.

Four years of war had taken their toll on the *King Orry*: much of her varnished woodwork had been painted over and this now had to be stripped down to bare wood and brought back to its former lustre. The saloons, which had been used as mess decks by the Royal Navy had been stripped of many of their fine furnishings, both as a necessity of war and it some cases as a result of vandalism.

The carpenters and upholsterers did a fine job in restoring them to their former glory. To the layman, the rebuilt saloons looked much the same as they had been pre-war, but in the immediate post-war period some of the original expensive furnishings were not yet available and so they were replaced with cheaper substitutes. The bridge wing houses were removed, as was the crow's nest on the foremast, the reinforced deck plates for the gun mountings and the powerful radio transmitters. The collapsible guardrails that had been fitted around the stern during her target-towing days were now all replaced with the original, ridged steel pattern. On either side of the hull, the midships

sections of belting that had been removed early in the war as a safety precaution to avoid damage to her two 27ft whaler sea boats, was also restored.

Towards the end of her naval service, a vibration had been noted on the starboard propeller shaft and as the refurbishment included a period in dry dock, this provided the opportunity to inspect it. No defects were found but one of the blades on the propeller was slightly bent. As this was obviously the cause of the vibration, a new propeller was fitted.

It took some two months to complete most of the work required to refurbish the *King Orry*. Finally, as the month of May came to a close, her hull was repainted black, the superstructure repainted white and her tall funnel restored to the distinctive black and red colours of the Isle of Man Steam Packet.

READY FOR SERVICE

The *King Orry* was now ready to rejoin her running mates in the Steam Packet fleet, but many of the familiar names were missing. The pride of the fleet, the *Ben-my-Chree* had been lost to enemy action, as had the *Snaefell* and *The Ramsey*, while the *Empress Queen* had run aground on rocks off Bembridge on the Isle of Wight and became a total loss.

The *Queen Victoria*, *Mona's Isle* and *Prince of Wales* were never returned to the Company and disposed of by the Admiralty. Luckily, the powerful *Viking* had survived and she was returned in April 1919, but due to the need to reconvert her from a seaplane carrier back into a passenger ship, she did not enter service until June 1920.

The remaining two vessels requisitioned for war service, the *Peel Castle* and *Mona's Queen* were returned in May 1919, although the *Mona's Queen* did not recommence her Steam Packet duties until the following year. Throughout the war, the service to the Isle of Man had been maintained by the ageing *Tynwald*, *Fenella*, *Douglas* and the small cargo ship, the *Tyrconnel*.

Now in June 1919 as the holiday makers started to return to the Island, the need for ships like the *King Orry* once again became paramount. To ease the workload on the reduced Manx fleet during the 1919 season, the Steam Packet purchased the former Laird Line steamer *Hazel* (1907) in May 1919, renaming her the *Mona.*.

Her refit completed, the *King Orry* was ready to recommence her peacetime duties on 6th June 1919 and duly entered service with the 10.30 sailing from Liverpool to Douglas. She was once again under the command of Captain William Cain, although John

Cormish had relieved Thomas Quayle as the First Mate. The last remnants of her non-Manx Royal Navy crew had paid-off prior to the refit, but one of her former naval officers now rejoined her.

Engineer Lieutenant A V Garrett RNR, a Manxman from Ramsey who had recently been discharged from the Royal Navy joined her crew as 2nd Engineer. He had served on board the *King Orry* as an Engineer Sub Lieutenant from 1914 until 1916; no doubt Chief Engineer John Keig was pleased to have him as a member of his department again.

The *King Orry* now commenced what was to become her standard operating schedule for the next twenty years. She would maintain the daily service between the Island and Liverpool, with periodic trips to Dublin, Belfast, Ardrossan, Fleetwood and Llandudno during the summer season and lay up at either Birkenhead or Barrow during the winter.

As the *King Orry* arrived at Douglas on the evening of 21st June, having completed the afternoon sailing from Liverpool, there was debate and discussion being carried out ashore relating to an incident at Scapa Flow that afternoon. News had just been released that the interned German High Seas Fleet had been involved in an act of treachery. The exact details were unknown, but one rumour was that the Germans had attacked the British fleet and had escaped to sea and hence back to Germany.

As the following day dawned, the correct details were now being released to the press; the German High Seas Fleet had not attacked the British, but had scuttled itself and now lay on the bottom of Scapa Flow. There had been unrest and near mutiny within the German navy ever since the terms of the armistice had interned it at Scapa Flow in late November of the previous year. The armistice was due to expire at 12.00 on 21st June and Germany was dragging her heels on signing the final peace agreement as it was not happy with some of the terms of the Treaty of Versailles. The British Government therefore issued an ultimatum stating that if Germany did not sign by 12.00 on 21st June, then the British were prepared to resume hostilities. This ultimatum gave the German Government and the commander of the interned German fleet, Admiral Ludwig von Reuter, an immense feeling of unease as the German ships in Scapa Flow could not defend themselves and would inevitably be taken over by the Royal Navy.

Therefore, secret messages were passed between Berlin and Admiral Reuter informing him to prepare to scuttle his fleet, as the dishonour incurred by the German ships being taken by the British was far greater than their actual loss. The ships were all secretly prepared for scuttling and told to wait for a prearranged code signal to be raised by the flagship.

At 11.20 on the morning of 21st June, forty minutes before the armistice was due to expire, the secret signal code was hoisted on the flagship's foremast – "commence scuttling". To the British onlookers nothing appeared out of the normal until 12.16, when the battleship *Friedrich Der Grosse* suddenly took on an alarming list, rolled onto her beam ends and sank. Within minutes every German warship was repeating the same spectacle. The Royal Navy was powerless to intervene and by late afternoon, the German High Seas Fleet was no more. A total of fifty-one ships had been sunk. The allies were outraged, the Germans now content that their fleet was no longer in threat, moderated their demands and finally signed the Treaty of Versailles on 28th June. The threat of war was finally over.

The news of the demise of the German fleet was met with some with indifference, although to people like Chief Engineer John Keig on board *King Orry* and former Chief Petty Officer Crispen Redshaw, the news must have bought back many memories.

As the passengers on board the *King Orry* read about the events at Scapa Flow and discussed it amongst themselves, few would have had any idea that the vessel on which they were travelling had been involved in the great procession up the Firth of Firth seven months earlier.

The date that the *King Orry* ceased service in 1919 is not known as the relevant page from her log is missing, although it is presumed that it was in late September. With the exception of routine monthly lifeboat drill for the crew, no incidents such as collisions or grounding are recorded, and so, as this was her first pre-war season, it was also the first season where she had not been involved in some sort of accident.

During the period of winter lay-up at Birkenhead, more work was carried out by Cammell Laird to restore the *King Orry* to her original pre-war condition, replacing some of the cheap substitute furnishings that were hastily put on board during her refit in April and May.

One passenger who remembers sailing on the *King Orry* during this first post-war summer season is Cecil Mitchell. As a 14-year-old boy, young Cecil made his first sailing on the *King Orry* on the morning service from Liverpool to Douglas on 25th September 1919. He recalls that she was a very comfortable and modern ship, compared with the old *Tynwald* and the *Douglas*, both of which he had travelled on during the previous four years of war. Over the next 20 years he made a further 35 sailings on the vessel. When Cecil grew up

*The **King Orry** approaches the Queen's Pier at Ramsey. (Richard Danielson collection)*

he went on to establish Silverdale Glen near Ballasalla on the Isle of Man: he still lives there.

During this first post war holiday season, some 343,332 holiday-makers flocked back to the Island. Although this was down on pre-war totals, it reassured the Steam Packet and Manx tourist trade that the British population were returning to their annual holiday routine following the four previous years of carnage and death.

As the Manx fleet was somewhat reduced during the 1919 season, the Steam Packet chartered the paddle steamer *La Marguerite* from the Liverpool and North Wales Steamship Company. Although *La Marguerite* was an old vessel, she had a large passenger capacity and was extensively used during her period of charter from 28th June until 16th September.

1920

To boost their passenger carrying capacity back to its pre-war levels, the Steam Packet purchased three second-hand vessels during the early months of 1920. The first two of these vessels were bought in March; the *Manxman* (1904), which had been previously owned by the Midland Railway Company, was bought

direct from the Admiralty, while the *Snaefell* (1906), formally the *Viper*, came from G and J Burns. The third ship in the trio, the *Mona's Isle* (1905) came along in May having been operated by the South Eastern & Chatham Railway Company as the *Onward*.

As the 1920 summer season began to materialise, the addition of these three ships, plus the re-entry into service of the *Viking* and *Mona's Queen*, gave the Steam Packet the assurance that they could now meet any demand to carry passengers during the anticipated busy holiday period, although the loss of their mini-Cunarder, the *Ben-my-Chree* was still mourned. One further ship purchase was made during 1920, although this was not a passenger vessel. The small coaster, the *Ardnagrena*, which had been operated by Humber Steam Coasters, entered Steam Packet service as the *Cushag*.

Having had her Board of Trade certificate issued, the *King Orry* came out of winter lay up on the morning of 20th May 1920, making her first sailing to Liverpool the following day. Once again she was under the command of Captain William Cain who had spent the winter season as Master of the *Mona*. A new First Mate, First Officer Richard Crellin had also joined he ship and like Captain Cain, he had also spent the winter on board the *Mona*.

The Engine Room department was once again led by the longest-serving member of her crew John Keig, who by now had firmly established himself as the father figure of the *King Orry*. Having drilled the crew at lifeboat stations, Captain Cain and the *King Orry* were ready to begin what was hoped to be an uneventful summer season.

With the exception of return sailings from Douglas to Fleetwood on 9th and 19th June, return sailings to Ardrossan on the 19th and 26th July and a return sailing from Liverpool to Morecambe on 10th August, the *King Orry* maintained the Douglas to Liverpool service for the whole of the 1920 summer season.

Although she was not involved in any more embarrassing collisions or groundings, two tragic events cast a black shadow on the holiday atmosphere for 1920.

At 23.15 on 3rd July, while the *King Orry* lay at the Victoria Pier in Douglas, Assistant Steward Joseph Green suffered what proved to be a fatal accident. As he returned on board in a somewhat drunken state, he declined all offers of assistance and decided not to wait for the night watchman to put the gangway ashore. Instead he staggered down the concrete steps on the side of the pier and attempted to step onto the ship's belting with a view to climbing up the ship's side.

A strong easterly wind was blowing which caused the *King Orry* to move about quite violently at her berth. Not being aware of this motion, he slipped and missed his handhold, falling backwards onto the steps. He then rolled forward and fell between the ship and the pier. At this precise moment the *King Orry* was blown against the pier and pinioned him between the concrete and the belting, crushing his legs and lower body. The wind then took her away from the pier allowing him to drop into the water.

The quick actions of the night watchman and another member of the crew resulted in him being pulled from the water before he drowned. An ambulance was called and he was conveyed to Nobles Hospital in Douglas but, due to the severity of his injuries, he died at 03.00 the following morning. An inquest held on 6th July recorded a verdict of accidental death.

The second tragic incident happened just over a fortnight later. On 05.35 on the morning of 19th July, the *King Orry* was nearing the end of an overnight passage from Douglas to Ardrossan. When still was some 5 miles from Ardrossan, a male passenger was observed to walk down from the Promenade Deck onto the Poop Deck. He walked through the midst of some crew members who were preparing the after berthing ropes for the ship's arrival at Ardrossan when suddenly, and before any of then could stop him, he climbed up onto the guard rail and leapt over the side. An officer immediately alerted the bridge while a seaman threw one of the cork lifebuoys into the vessel's boiling wake. With her siren wailing to alert other vessels of the incident, the *King Orry's* helm was put hard over as she reversed her course in an attempt to spot the passenger and rescue him from the cold water.

She reduced speed to dead slow and cruised around for half an hour but despite extra lookouts being posted all around the Upper Deck, no sign of the passenger was seen. Eventually, it became obvious that he had drowned and after stopping to recover the lifebuoy the decision was made to proceed to Ardrossan. A search of the passenger saloons revealed some unclaimed belongings, including a wallet.

The drowned man was identified as 34-year-old William Wardroph, who lived at 11 Waverley Terrace, Bellshill, Lanarkshire. On arrival at Ardrossan, the Captain informed the police of the tragic incident and handed over Mr Wardroph's effects. The outcome of their investigation and coroner's inquest is unfortunately not recorded in the *King Orry's* log, but no doubt Mr Wardroph's death was suicide. The remainder of the year went without further incident. The only other entries of note in her log are that the crew were drilled at lifeboat stations on 30th July, 31st August and 15th September 1920.

Captain Cain had relinquished command of the *King Orry* on 8th July as he had been appointed to the newly-refurbished *Viking*, which had just re-entered service.

Now that the *Ben-my-Chree* was gone, the *Viking* became the flagship of the Manx fleet although at the end of August there had been a glimmer of hope that the "Ben" might have been able to re-enter Steam Packet service.

The Admiralty had appointed the Ocean Salvage Company Ltd to raise her wreck and report on the viability of repair. After being salvaged on 18th August 1920 and towed to Piraeus by the tugs *La Valetta* and *King Lear*, the initial hull survey reported that her machinery and boilers were in good condition and the damage to her structure was repairable. However, subsequent reports confirmed that although repair was feasible, the cost would outweigh the value of the vessel. Sadly the *Ben-my-Chree* ended her days in 1923 when she was towed from Piraeus to Venice for demolition.

The new Master of the *King Orry* was Captain Henry Quine, who at an age of 54 joined the vessel after commanding the *Tynwald*. He was to see many years service in command of the *King Orry*.

Her final passenger service for 1920 was from Liverpool to Douglas on 18th September after which she proceeded to Barrow for winter lay-up. Her catering department had been paid-off after she had arrived at Douglas, leaving the remainder to be paid-off on 20th September at Barrow.

The year 1920 had been a busy year for the Isle of Man Steam Packet; some 561,124 passengers had arrived on the Island, almost all of them being carried by one of their vessels. This record remained unbroken until 1937, when 583,037 passengers were recorded as being carried to the island.

1921

As 1921 dawned, with the *King Orry* still lying at Barrow, the world had now adjusted to peace once again. On the Isle of Man the hotels and glens had eventually all been refurbished following fours years of neglect during the war, while the atmosphere on the Island was returning to its pre-war relaxed state. In

Douglas, the shops in Strand Street and Victoria Street were now full of goods again and everybody was looking forward to a prosperous summer holiday season.

The *King Orry* left Barrow for Liverpool at the crack of dawn on 19th June, her entry back into service being delayed by nearly a month when compared with 1920. This was due to an unexpected drop in passengers, rather than the anticipated increase.

The bulk of her crew had joined on 16th June, under the command of Captain Henry Quine. First Officer Richard Crellin and Chief Engineer John Keig completed the ship's hierarchy. On arrival at Liverpool, the *King Orry* immediately took on sufficient coal for a return sailing to the Isle of Man, leaving for Douglas as soon as it was on board. The *King Orry* was scheduled to recommence service with a 16.00 sailing back to Liverpool. As the trip from Barrow and the taking on of coal at Liverpool had all been very hurried, the crew spent much of the voyage to the Island cleaning the coal dust from her decks and preparing the saloons for passengers. However, once the first day of service was behind her, she continued to ply the Irish Sea between Douglas and Liverpool for the majority of the season,

High and dry: the **King Orry** *beached at New Brighton on 19th August 1921. (David Handscombe collection)*

*The **King Orry** aground near the Perch Rock lighthouse, New Brighton, on 19th August 1921. (David Handscombe collection)*

although she did visit Belfast on 8th and 18th July, Ardrossan on 14th and 16th July and Dublin on 21st July.

One unusual event that has been gleaned from scrutiny of her ship's log is that the lifeboats were not tested and the crew not drilled at lifeboat stations until 23rd June, some 4 days after she had returned to passenger service. The reason behind this cannot be explained, especially as the crew joined three days before she left Barrow.

The summer was progressing well, although the passenger figures had still not reached the numbers that the Steam Packet had hoped for. An entry in the "Lloyds Weekly Casualty Report" records that on 28th June 1921 a minor collision occurred while the *King Orry* was berthing alongside the landing stage at Liverpool. She had left Douglas with the morning sailing and had made a slow passage through a very rough Irish Sea. As she approached Princes Landing Stage, at just after 14.30, a sudden gust of wind caught her and pushed her forward, which resulted in her overshooting the berth. Unfortunately, the *Mona's Isle* was berthed ahead and the *King Orry* struck her stern

with some force. Although no serious damage was sustained to either vessel, it left the *Mona's Isle* with a large dent in her port quarter. As the *King Orry* remained on service and returned to Douglas the following day, it is assumed that the damage to her was minimal.

However, this minor incident was soon to be overshadowed by a much more serious event which occurred on 19th August. This time disaster nearly struck the *King Orry*.

She had left Douglas at 09.00 bound for Liverpool with 1,300 passengers on board and had made most of the passage in dense fog. Having made a slow crossing, she approached the River Mersey at just after 13.00 and proceeded up river at a very slow speed. The visibility was only a few yards in front of her bow and the risk of hitting another vessel or colliding with one of the channel marker buoys was very high.

At just after 13.45, a white lighthouse suddenly became visible through the pall of mist and at the same moment a strange vibration, followed by a jerking motion ran through the ship. Almost immediately the *King Orry* came to a grinding halt. It did not take very

*Onlookers gather around the stern of the **King Orry** as she sits on the beach at New Brighton on 19th August 1921. (Manx National Heritage)*

long for Captain Quine to realise that his vessel had run aground and that the lighthouse was probably the Perch Rock light at New Brighton.

The watertight doors were closed and Chief Engineer John Keig was ordered to put the *King Orry's* engines astern, but this had no effect other than to fling clouds of mud and sand into the air. Distress flares and a signal gun were fired, accompanied by long blasts of the siren as attempts to summon assistance were made. While all of this was going on, the mist suddenly began to lift and within a few minutes the sun was shining on the *King Orry* as she lay like a beached whale on the New Brighton Beach.

The distress flares and gun had attracted many boats and they could now be seen hurrying to render assistance. Amongst these was the Wallasey ferry *Royal Daffodil* and the Mersey Docks and Harbour Board buoy tenders *Salvor* and *Vigilant*, the former having been quickly requisitioned by the Steam Packet to see if it was possible to transfer the *King Orry's* passengers. The New Brighton steam lifeboat had also been launched.

As the tide was on the ebb and rapidly dropping, none of these vessels could approach the *King Orry* for fear of grounding themselves although a few small rowing boats did manage to take some passengers off before they too had to retire. Within an hour the *King Orry* was high and dry.

Now that the mist had cleared it was possible to assess the vessel's predicament: she was laying with her bow pointing up river while some 10 to 12 yards away on her port side sat the Perch Rocks and it was only now that it became apparent just how close to disaster the *King Orry* had came.

As the *King Orry* had crawled up river, the beach at New Brighton had been crowded with holidaymakers, even though it was shrouded in mist. Many of them later reported that they had heard the whistle of a large steamer mingling with the mournful note of the lighthouse fog bell. When the *King Orry* had run aground, they had also heard the slow grating noise as she beached herself but were uncertain as to the noise's origin.

It was different for those holiday makers who were standing on the New Brighton battery as they too had heard the steamer's whistle followed by the grating noise, but to their surprise the bow of the vessel suddenly loomed out of the mist a few yards in front of them. As the mist lifted slightly they could clearly read her name which was painted on the bow.

Now that the mist had completely cleared, thousands of people swarmed onto the beach or lined the promenade at New Brighton, all keen to look upon the unexpected spectacle that now sat in front of them. Captain Quine ordered one of the engineers and the carpenter to climb down onto the sand and walk around the ship to establish if there was any damage to her hull plating. It did not take more than a few minutes before they were hauled back on board and reported that the hull appeared to be sound.

The next priority was what to do with the passengers remaining on board. The *King Orry* had left Douglas with some 1,300 passengers and although a few had left the ship via the small rowing boats that came alongside before the tide receded, the vast majority were still on the ship.

The idea of placing a ladder over the stern was considered around 15.00, but not acted upon until 16.25 when a towering ladder was put over the ship's side. The first passenger to swing a leg over the gunwale and climb onto the ladder received a roar of cheering from the large crowd of onlookers who had mustered on the sands and promenade to watch the spectacle. When he finally reached the safety of the sand, he turned and saluted his laughing audience.

Half an hour later another ladder was placed against one of the gangway doors. Finally, the Wallasey fire brigade arrived on the scene and placed their wheeled escape ladder against another gangway opening in the ship's side. As the passengers began to descend to the sands, their luggage was attached to ropes and lowered to them by members of the crew.

Children were brought down grasped in the arms of members of the crew, while the womenfolk who were nervous had a secure rope tied around their waists before they started to descend.

The press interviewed many of the passengers; amongst these were Mr A.H.Sykes, a secondary schoolmaster from Widnes. He had just been appointed to a school in Douglas and was returning to the mainland to collect his family. Another passenger, Mr W.J.Duffle from Macclesfield, commented that he had been talking to one of the crew at the precise moment the ship grounded.

Seconds before she ran onto the sands, he had gasped as the lighthouse loomed out of the fog and uttered " By George, we are cutting it a bit fine." The crew man who was also alarmed, just stared at the lighthouse and simply replied "Yes". Neither of them had any idea that the ship had drifted out of the Crosby Channel.

A large majority of the passengers remarked that they were not even aware that the *King Orry* had grounded until the message was passed around the ship by the crew. The impact was so slight that few felt it, and those that did had not associated it with anything out of the ordinary.

About a thousand passengers descended to the New Brighton sands and struggled up the beach with their luggage to the waiting line of taxis and buses which had been summoned by the Steam Packet to convey people to the railway and bus stations. Some 300 passengers decided to remain on board the *King Orry* and return to the landing stage with the ship once she had been refloated. These were mainly people who lived far away and had missed their train connections, so had no hope of arriving home that night. The *King Orry* refloated on the rising tide at about 23.00, and it was just after midnight before she secured alongside Princes Landing Stage, having been towed up river by four tugs.

As soon as she was alongside the remaining passengers were disembarked. For those who intended to spend the remainder of the night in a Liverpool hotel, the Steam Packet provided them with taxis to take them to their accommodation.

The *King Orry* remained at her berth until the following morning when she was taken into the dry dock at Cammell Laird's yard for a thorough inspection of her hull plates. Little or no damage was found; she had a very lucky escape. The scenario surrounding this grounding was almost identical to her previous grounding incident on the Isle of Man in July 1914. It took a couple of days to check that her hull was still watertight and that there was no damage to her turbines and gearing and so she did not return to service until the morning of 24th August, when she took the 10.30 sailing back to Douglas.

For the remainder of the 1921 season, the *King Orry* plied between Douglas and Liverpool, making her final passenger sailing from Liverpool to Douglas on 5th September. She remained at Douglas for a couple of days to off-load stores and pay-off the bulk of the catering staff, before departing for Barrow and winter lay up on 8th September.

Captain Quine and the remainder of the crew paid-off the following day.

When the Steam Packet board of Directors met at the end of the 1921 summer season, they expressed disappointment at the passenger figures which revealed that there had been a significant drop in trade; only 427,923 passengers had travelled to the island compared with 561,124 the previous year. The Company had hoped that the passenger boom in 1920 had heralded a return to the pre-war influx of tourists to the island and ultimately an increase in their trade.

*The **King Orry** disembarks the soldiers from the Sherwood Foresters Regiment at Peel on 27th July 1924. (David Handscombe collection)*

1922

The *King Orry* remained at Barrow until 30th May 1922 when once again under the command of Captain Quine, she sailed down to Liverpool to rebunker and take on provisions.

The daily routine that the *King Orry* was now to adopt was to remain similar for the next few years, although the date she entered service and paid-off for winter lay up altered marginally each season.

To continue an in-depth detail of her service year by year would make this account very repetitious and so the remainder of this chapter will concentrate on a brief outline of each year's service, and only mention points of interest.

The *King Orry* operated on the Liverpool to Douglas route for the majority of the 1922 season, although she made two trips to Belfast, one to Dublin, three to Ardrossan and one return sailing between Liverpool and Ramsey. Her final passenger service was from Liverpool to Douglas on 10th September, she proceeded to Barrow for winter lay up the following day. Captain Quine had taken a weeks leave between 12th and 19th June, being relieved by Captain William Gawne.

1923

The 1923 season started on 18th May with a passenger sailing from Liverpool to Douglas, the *King Orry* having left Barrow the previous day. However, she only remained on service to cover the Whitsun holiday passenger traffic. During this short period, she made a trip from Liverpool to Ramsey and back again but, as this was not a regular Steam Packet route, it is probable that she was employed on a day excursion. As the Whitsun passenger traffic subsided, she was laid up at

Liverpool from 21st May until 27th June. On re-entering service on 27th June, she undertook the Liverpool to Douglas route, remaining on this service until being withdrawn for winter lay up at Barrow on 11th September 1923.

At the end of the 1923 season, the Steam Packet purchased another second-hand passenger vessel. Formerly called the *Caesarea* and operated by the Southern Railway Company, she entered Manx service as the *Manx Maid*. She had been acquired as a replacement for the steamer *Douglas*, which had been lost in a collision in the River Mersey on 16th August 1923. Prior to entering Steam Packet service she had been refurbished at Cammell Laird's yard and converted to burn oil fuel to heat her boilers. She was to be the second vessel operated by the Steam Packet to use this type of fuel, as the *Manxman* had been similarly converted during 1921.

1924

The *King Orry* was not required for the 1924 Whitsun passenger traffic and did not leave Barrow until 16th June, when, once again under the command of Captain Quine, she proceeded to Liverpool. As in previous years, she spent the majority of her time on the Liverpool to Douglas service, although the now familiar excursions to Belfast, Dublin and Ardrossan were undertaken.

On 27th July, the *King Orry* was chartered by the war department to convey a battalion of soldiers from the Sherwood Foresters Regiment to the island for a summer training camp. Embarking the troops at Liverpool, the *King Orry* proceeded to Peel on the west coast of the Isle of Man, instead of the more usual port of Douglas. Peel was sometimes used as an alternative port of call when an easterly gale was battering the Island, making it too dangerous to attempt entering Douglas Harbour. However, on this occasion there is no report of bad weather and it must be assumed that unloading the troops at Peel was for logistic purposes, possibly their camp was within marching distance from this particular port.

Her log records no incidents apart from routine lifeboat musters on 26th June, 25th July and 26th August. On 20th August while at Liverpool, one of the firemen, J Coyle, who had joined the *King Orry* only the day before, is recorded as being absent on sailing and therefore presumed to have jumped ship.

As another season drew to a close, the *King Orry* proceeded to Barrow for lay up on 15th September, having completed her last passenger service from Liverpool to Douglas the day before.

When the Steam Packet Directors met for the end of season board meeting, they were disappointed by the passenger report. Although there had been a small increase in passengers, the annual income had been lower than had been expected. This was due to the swing of passengers from First Class to Second Class which was no doubt a direct result of the depression that gripped the United Kingdom.

1925

Regrettably the log for 1925 has been lost, so details of the date that the *King Orry* entered and finished service during this year are unknown. However, it is known that during September, she was required to take over the services being run by the *Viking* which had suffered an engine defect and was withdrawn from service prematurely and laid up for the winter.

1926

The *King Orry* was laid up at Barrow again during the winter of 1925/26 and reappeared for service on 31st March 1926. This was the first year that she had been brought out of lay up for the Easter holiday traffic.

Captain Quine was in command, First Officer Richard Crellin served as Mate while John Keig commenced his twelfth consecutive year as the *King Orry's* Chief Engineer. She was only required on service for a few days and was laid up again at Liverpool on 10th April. During this brief interlude she was employed solely on the Liverpool to Douglas route.

The year 1926 will always be remembered for the General Strike in the United Kingdom that nearly crippled the nation. This strike also had grave effects on the Island and Steam Packet, especially regarding the provision of coal for the steamers and the marked reduction in passenger traffic.

During this chaotic year the number of passengers using the Company's vessels dropped to 384,705. Due to the lack of coal, the cargo vessels *Fenella*, *Tyrconnel* and *Cushag* were taken out of service and cargo was carried on the passenger vessels. A number of proposed charter sailings were also cancelled.

It has been recorded that during this period the Liverpool to Douglas service was maintained by the two oil-burning vessels *Manxman* and *Manx Maid* and that on 20th May the Steam Packet reduced these sailings to a single passage each way. Although this report is obviously based on fact, examination of the *King Orry's* log tends to contradict it.

The *King Orry* was brought back into service on 2nd July and immediately commenced the Liverpool to

Douglas passenger service. She remained in service until 14th September when she was laid up at Barrow for the winter. During this 75 day period, the *King Orry* made a total of 68 passenger sailings between Liverpool and Douglas - 34 in each direction. The remainder of her time in service was taken up with sailings between the Island and Belfast, Dublin, Ardrossan and Fleetwood. Obviously the work carried out by the *King Orry* during 1926 had been overlooked, or more probably not researched, as the Maritime History Archive at the University of Newfoundland, Canada now keeps all her Half Yearly Agreements and Account of Voyages and Crew.

However, as the General Strike ended, the Steam Packet began to look to the future.

In 1926 they possessed a motley fleet of vessels. The majority had been bought second hand as war loss replacements while the newest, the *King Orry*, was already 13 years old.

The Board of Directors had been debating obtaining a new vessel for some months but had withheld their order because of the General Strike and coal shortage. Finally they decided to take a gamble and as the 1926 season came to an end, they placed an order for a new ship with Cammell Laird's at Birkenhead. The keel was laid on 29th November and the ship slid down the slipway on 5th April 1927. To everyone's delight the company had decided to name the vessel *Ben-my-Chree*. She was slightly larger than her famous predecessor; her tonnage was 2,586 tons compared with the 2,250 tons of her 1908 namesake. Surprisingly though she was some 20 feet shorter, measuring only 355 feet long. She was also 2 knots slower, only being able to make 22.5 knots compared with the mini-Cunarder's 24.5 knots. It was here that all similarity ceased, the new "Ben' was an enlarged and improved design based on the *King Orry's* layout of compartments and machinery spaces, although she had double-reduction steam turbines instead of the single-reduction type installed in the *King Orry*.

The major improvement in her design was that she was the first vessel to be built for the Company that was an oil burner and so coal shortages like those experienced the year before would not affect her. The new "Ben" made her maiden voyage on 29th June 1927 under the Command of Captain William Cain, the Fleet Commodore who had been Master of the *King Orry* in 1919 and for a brief period in 1920.

The new steamer was an immediate success and sadly the *King Orry* had to accept second place, as she could no longer boast being the Steam Packet's most technically advanced vessel.

1927

The *King Orry* came out of winter lay up on 26th May 1927 and, as in previous years, proceeded to Liverpool to take on coal and fresh stores. Captain Robert Clucas had taken over from Captain Quine as her Master although Richard Crellin and John Keig still filled the positions of Mate and Chief Engineer. Of all the Masters that the *King Orry* had during her Steam Packet service, Captain Quine will be remembered for being the longest serving, commanding the vessel from June 1920 until September 1926.

The following morning, 27th May, saw the *King Orry* commence the summer season with the morning sailing from Liverpool to Douglas and as in previous years this route was to form the majority of her passenger sailings.

She recorded another personal first this year when on 3rd August she sailed from Douglas to Holyhead and took day-trippers on a cruise up towards the Menai Bridge. On 8th September while she was alongside at Liverpool, one of her crew deserted - Fireman J Pidduck from Lyon Street in Barrow.

The 1927 season ran on for a couple of weeks longer than previous seasons and the *King Orry* is recorded as proceeding to Barrow for lay-up on 25th September. Amongst her crew that paid-off for the last time was the Mate, Richard Crellin. His service on the *King Orry* had lasted just over 7 years, having joined her in May 1920.

1928

The *King Orry* left Barrow on 17th May and proceeded to Liverpool in preparation for entering service the following day. Her new Mate or First Officer was an old friend of the *King Orry*.

At 51 years of age, John Quirk had already served on board as her Mate, having been part of her original crew under the command of Captain John Bridson in 1913.

Having left the *King Orry* in 1914, he had served on board the majority of the Steam Packet's vessels, the most recent of which had been the *Manxman*. Captain Clucas was in command while John Keig was still Lord and Master of her gleaming Engine Room.

Returning to the Liverpool - Douglas service, the *King Orry* left Princes Landing Stage with the morning sailing on 18th May and continued on this route for the majority of the season, making the odd excursion to ports such as Ardrossan, Dublin and Fleetwood.

First Officer John Quirk did not remain on board the *King Orry* for very long, being paid-off on 4th June and replaced by Chief Officer Radcliffe Duggan. With the joining of Chief Officer Duggan, the first use of the

The **King Orry** at speed during the 1930s. (David Handscombe collection)

title Chief Officer is recorded in her crew agreement. Prior to this, the second in command had always been referred to as the Mate, or occasionally First Officer.

During September 1927, the London, Midland & Scottish Railway Company had ceased their service between Heysham and the Island, allowing the Steam Packet to take over the route in 1928. As the LMS now had no requirement for the ships which had maintained the Heysham to Douglas route, the Steam Packet purchased two of them although both vessels were rather old. The older, which had been built in 1898 as the *Duke of Cornwall* entered Manx service as the *Rushen Castle.*

The second ship was only slightly newer, being built in 1904 as the *Antrim*, and she entered service with the Steam Packet as the *Ramsey Town*. This latter vessel did not remain in service for very long and was disposed of in 1936, although the *Rushen Castle* survived until 1946 and was one of the vessels that maintained the vital lifeline between the Island and Fleetwood during the Second World War. A third vessel was purchased in mid-1928. This was the former Southern Railway steamer *Victoria*, which had been built in 1907 and was a later sister of the *Onward/ Mona's Isle.* On entering

service with the company, she retained her original name and was the first ship to sail on the Steam Packet's new Heysham to Douglas route on 23rd June 1928.

The *King Orry* made her final passenger sailing of the 1928 season on 24th September between Douglas and Liverpool after which she steamed to Barrow arriving on the afternoon of 25th September. The remaining crew were paid-off on the following day.

Although the *King Orry* was still a valuable asset to the Steam Packet, she was beginning to be overtaken as a prime passenger carrier by the larger vessels that the Company had acquired in recent years. The year 1928 was to be the last year that she would enter service for the early season holiday traffic, and for the remainder of her career she would be regarded as a peak-season vessel and usually not enter service until June, or occasionally July.

1929

The 1929 season began on 12th June when the *King Orry* proceeded from Barrow to Liverpool to take on board stores and coal before taking the morning sailing to Douglas on 14th June. With the introduction of the

Ben-my-Chree, the *King Orry* began to undertake more sailings on the company's secondary routes.

Sailings to Ardrossan, Dublin, Belfast and Fleetwood began to appear more regularly on her weekly sailing schedules than had done in previous years. Captain Clucas was still in command assisted again by Chief Officer Duggan and the stalwart Chief Engineer John Keig. Chief Officer Duggan did not complete the season and paid-off on 28th June to be replaced by Chief Officer Philip (Ginger) Bridson. It will be remembered that as an Able Seaman, Chief Officer Bridson had served on the *King Orry* during 1919. He had gained his Master's Certificate during 1927 and the *King Orry* was his first appointment as Chief Officer. To rise from Able Seaman to Chief Officer in just 10 years is a feat that he must have been very proud of.

As the 1929 season progressed, the Board of Directors were looking towards celebrating the centenary of the company the following year. They decided that there would be no better way of celebrating this event than by introducing a new steamer, and a running mate for the *Ben-my-Chree*.

On 3rd July, an order was placed with Vickers Armstrong at Barrow for a new super steamer; she would be similar in design to the "Ben", but slightly larger and more luxuriously fitted out. To add esteem to her introduction, she was to be called the *Lady of Mann*.

In May 1929, a month or two before work began on the new vessel, another ship had entered service with the Company. She was the first purpose-built cargo ship to be owned by the Steam Packet and carried the name *Peveril*.

Two old faithfuls were to be retired at the same time; these were the Steam Packet's last paddle steamer the *Mona's Queen* of 1885 and the *Fenella* of 1881. Both vessels made their last voyage to the breaker's yard before the year was over. The *Fenella* had been a revolutionary ship, as was the *King Orry* when she entered service, being the first twin-propeller driven vessel that the Steam Packet had owned.

No incidents marred the *King Orry's* service in 1929 and on 27th September, she sailed to Barrow from Liverpool for another period of winter lay up.

1930

The year 1930 heralded the centenary of the Isle of Man Steam Packet Company Limited. The occasion was to be dominated by the introduction of the *Lady of Mann*. She had been launched on 4th March 1930 and entered service on 28th June, just two days short of the hundredth anniversary of the launch of the Steam Packet's first vessel, *Mona's Isle*.

The "Lady", as she was soon nicknamed, was an immediate success and along with her running mate the *Ben-my-Chree*, put the Steam Packet back into the limelight as a leading ferry company in United Kingdom coastal waters. The *Lady of Mann* would go on to give the Royal Navy valuable service as a troop transport during the Second World War and would remain flagship of the Manx fleet until her disposal in 1971. She would remain the largest vessel ever built for the Company until the *Ben-my-Chree* (6) in 1998.

The *King Orry* was now 17 years old and beginning to show her age. Apart from the refit and refurbishment in 1919 at the completion of her war service, she had not undergone any form of major overhaul, apart from routine dry-docking and maintenance during her periods of winter lay up. At the end of the previous season, Captain Clucas had relinquished command and was superseded by Captain John Comish who took her over on 18th June 1930, while she still at lay-up in Barrow. Captain Cormish was no newcomer to the vessel as he had served as her First Mate in 1919. Chief Officer 'Ginger' Bridson was again second in command.

As the 1930 season dawned, a very familiar face was no longer to be seen on board, Chief Engineer John Keig had decided to pay-off for the last time and he had said farewell to the *King Orry* after her arrival at Barrow the previous September.

John Keig had joined the *King Orry* in October 1914, just after she had been taken over by the Royal Navy as an armed boarding vessel. Since then he had given 15 years continuous service as her Chief Engineer and is without doubt her longest-serving officer. Although the records are vague, it is believed that he retired to his home in Barrow, having moved from the Isle of Man many years previously. No doubt he would keep a keen eye on the *King Orry* when she was at Barrow for winter lay up over the next few years.

Her new Chief Engineer, like her new Captain was no stranger to the *King Orry* and was an old friend of John Keig. Chief Engineer A Garrett had served on board the *King Orry* as an Engineer Sub Lieutenant RNR during the war and briefly as 2nd Engineer in 1919 at the same time as Captain Cormish had been First Mate.

With her new crew settled in on board, the *King Orry* left Barrow on 19th June 1930 and sailed to Liverpool where she was quickly prepared for the sailing to Douglas on the following morning. The pattern for 1930 differed little from the previous year, Ardrossan being the main port for this season.

The *King Orry* had left Douglas late on 29th June and as the sun rose on the following day she was approaching the port of Ardrossan after a slow

*Inward bound from the Isle of Man. the **King Orry** moves towards her berth on the Princes Landing Stage at Liverpool. (Ray Pugh)*

overnight passage. She berthed just after 07.00 and was scheduled to return to the Island just after noon. During the morning her crew had been kept busy preparing for the return trip, dressing the *King Orry* overall with rows of signal flags flying from both her fore and mainmast.

Two passengers who were on board for the sailing to Douglas on this fine sunny day were William McDonald and his wife Ruby. They had been married only two days earlier and were now embarking on their honeymoon.

William was familiar with ships as he worked as a carpenter at the famous John Brown shipyard but Ruby was very apprehensive about the sailing as she had never been to sea before. William was keen to get a good view of the Scottish coastline as they sailed down towards the Isle of Man and had decided that they should proceed up to the Promenade Deck. The last passengers boarded just before 12.00 and the gangways were pulled ashore.

Suddenly, the whole world seemed to explode as the *King Orry* let out a long blast on her steam whistle followed by two or three short blasts of her siren. Ruby nearly died with fright and William now admits that the sudden noise and hiss of steam gave him a shock as he had completely forgotten about their position's proximity to the ship's whistle and siren. Having calmed Ruby down and persuaded her to remain on the

Upper Deck, they once again settled down to enjoy the trip and relaxed in the two deck chairs that William had found nearby. About an hour after leaving Ardrossan and with Ruby now having fallen asleep, a two funnelled pleasure steamer was seen approaching the *King Orry* from ahead, William assumed that it was one of the Clyde steamers and did not give it a second thought. Then to his horror, he saw a cloud of steam shoot up from the pleasure steamer's forward funnel, accompanied seconds later by the shrill blast of her siren. Before he could warn Ruby, the *King Orry* replied to the greeting and gave a succession of blasts on her own siren. Ruby leapt up into the air and then ran off down the Promenade Deck with her hands over her ears before disappearing down one of the stairways to the deck below.

William ran after her and eventually found her in the Second Class Saloon, Ruby told him firmly that she was not going on deck again until after they arrived in Douglas and, what was worse, neither was he. The remainder of the trip was uneventful.

Although there did not appear to be anything special laid on by the Company to celebrate their anniversary during the *King Orry's* passage to the island, the atmosphere on board was jovial and many of the crew who would normally have been in their quarters, when not required for duty, remained on deck talking to the passengers. William remembers talking to

King Orry

an old sailor who had been a survivor from the *Ben-my-Chree* when she had been sunk during the First World War.

The *King Orry* arrived at Douglas at just after 18.30 and as she approached the harbour, William asked Ruby if could they go on deck and watch the vessel berth alongside, remembering this time to warn his wife that the whistle and siren may be used again. Ruby declined the suggestion, but said he was free to go if he wished.

The harbour was full of activity as small craft bustled about. The *Ben-my-Chree* and the new centenary ship *Lady of Mann* were both alongside as were the *Manxman* and the *Snaefell*. The *King Orry* gave the customary warning of her arrival to the Harbour Master by sounding her whistle as she approached the harbour entrance. True to William's predictions, the vessels that were already in Douglas gave the *King Orry* a rapturous welcome with their whistles, followed by the *King Orry's* very enthusiastic reply.

So ended the centenary sailing for the *King Orry* and the voyage to the Isle of Man for William and Ruby McDonald. They travelled back to the mainland seven days later, via Liverpool on board the *Ben-my-Chree* as they were going to see some relatives in Manchester.

The remainder of the season was uneventful. An entry in the log for 16th August mentions that Purser Arthur Harris was taken ill while at sea between Douglas and Liverpool. Although his condition was not life-threatening, he was seen by a doctor on arrival at Liverpool and subsequently declared medically unfit to return to the ship and was paid-off. Purser S Cain took his place on board, having been transferred from the *Snaefell*.

The *King Orry* completed her last passenger sailing for 1930 on the Liverpool to Douglas service on 6th September, slightly earlier than in the previous year, arriving at Barrow for winter lay up on 8th September. It was common practice for Steam Packet Masters to take over command of one of the winter season boats while their usual vessel was laid up for the winter. This particular year was no exception and Captain Cormish took over as Master of the *Peel Castle* until the following summer.

As the result of an accident to another of the Steam Packet's vessels, a navigational improvement was made to the approaches to Douglas Harbour during 1930. In the early hours of 2nd July, the *Mona* was in-bound to Douglas and as she approached the harbour entrance, her Master had difficulty in distinguishing the Tower of Refuge on Conister Rock from the grey stone background of the Victoria Pier. As a result, he misjudged his approach and ran up his ship onto the Conister Rock. Fortunately the *Mona* was not badly damaged and she was pulled clear later in the day. As a result of this incident, it was decided to paint the outer face of the Victoria Pier white in order that the Tower of Refuge could be more easily seen in poor visibility.

1931

The *King Orry's* crew rejoined her at Barrow on 17th June. On the following day the crew were exercised at lifeboat drill with all the boats being lowered into the water. She left Barrow later on in the day and proceeded to Liverpool still under the command of Captain Cormish. Her principal officers remained unchanged from 1930, although Chief Officer Albert Whiteway relieved Chief Officer 'Ginger' Bridson on 1st July.

This particular year marked a significant change in the *King Orry's* sailing schedule. Influenced by the introduction of the *Lady of Mann* on the Liverpool to Douglas service, the *King Orry* was not to frequent the River Mersey very often during this season. She made a total of 89 passenger sailings during 1931 and of these, 43 were in bound from various ports to Douglas. Of the remaining 46 sailings, 28 were from Douglas to Ardrossan, 4 from Douglas to Dublin, 4 from Douglas to Belfast, one from Douglas to Fleetwood and only 9 sailings to Liverpool.

Obviously the *King Orry* was falling from the limelight although her introduction onto the secondary routes marked a significant improvement in comfort for the passengers who used them. She made her final passenger sailing for 1931 on 31st August when she took the midnight sailing from Douglas to Liverpool. After disembarking her passengers and allowing the members of crew from Liverpool to pay-off, she sailed at 09.00 the same morning for Barrow, arriving just before 13.00. The remainder of the crew was paid-off on 1st September, proceeding either back to the Isle of Man or to their homes in the local area. It will be noted that this season was even shorter than its predecessor.

1932

Sad news preceded the start of the 1932 season for the Steam Packet. Just as they were preparing for the holiday trade, their Commodore, 68-year-old Captain William Cain collapsed and died. His exploits with the German U boat during the First World War had made him a folk hero within the Company and he was greatly missed by his colleagues. It was under his impeccable command that the *King Orry* had re entered Steam Packet service in summer 1919. Captain Henry Quine, who had himself been in command of the ship a few years earlier, superseded him as Commodore and as the Master of the *Ben-my-Chree.*

The *King Orry* emerged from Barrow on 8th June, just in time for the Whitsun trade. She was still under the command of Captain John Cormish who had only recently rejoined her after spending the winter season as Master of the *Mona.* Chief Officer Radcliffe Duggan had also rejoined the *King Orry*, having left her in June 1929 to become the Mate of the *Mona's Isle.*

Having left Barrow, the *King Orry* proceeded to Liverpool for bunkering and stores. Her first passenger sailing was an overnight passage to Douglas on 10th June. Following sailings on the 11th and 12th June, she returned to Liverpool and was laid-up again until 30th June, obviously only being required for the Whitsun traffic.

The crew were paid-off on 14th June and signed on again on 28th June. On returning to service, the *King Orry* returned to Douglas in order that she could commence the summer sailings to Ardrossan on 1st July. The remainder of the season was spent on the Ardrossan route, although she would make a weekly sailing to either Dublin or Belfast. Captain Cormish did not complete the season, handing over command of the *King Orry* on 28th August to Captain J Quayle, who had previously been Master of the *Rushen Castle.* Her last passenger sailing was the midnight service from Ardrossan to Douglas on 2nd September, arriving at Douglas at 07.40 the following morning.

She remained at Douglas for a short while to unload excess stores and pay-off the Manx members of her catering staff, before sailing for Barrow at 09.20 for winter lay up.

It was during the 1932 season that the famous pre-Second World War white livery carried by some Manx steamers was introduced. During early spring, the Diocese of Blackburn had chartered the "Ben" in order that a party could attend the Eucharistic Conference in Dublin. For this occasion, her hull was painted white with green boot topping. Unfortunately the charter was cancelled, but the all-white appearance was so impressive, that the Company decided it should remain. The colour scheme proved to be so popular with passengers, that the Steam Packet decided to repaint the *Lady of Mann* likewise during the winter lay-up period of 1932-1933.

As 1932 progressed, the Steam Packet decided to replace the ageing *Tyrconnel* by purchasing the *Abington* of 1921 from Cheviot Coasters Ltd of Newcastle, and renaming her the *Conister.* As well as the fleet changes during 1932, another familiar item was to disappear from the Steam Packet vessels.

The Isle of Man Government and the Steam Packet had both been advised that the *Three Legs of Mann* emblem that defaced the British Merchant Navy Red Ensign, as flown by the company's vessels, constituted an offence under the 1894 Merchant Shipping Act, and that a fine of £500 would be levied on every occasion that the flag was used. New ensigns were quickly obtained and it was not until September 1971 that the Manx Government finally obtained permission for Manx vessels to fly the Red Ensign defaced with the "Three Legs" emblem.

During the winter of 1932 -1933, the *Victoria* was taken into the Cammell Laird shipyard at Birkenhead and converted to oil fuel.

1933

On the morning of 14th June 1933, Captain C A Kinley joined the *King Orry* at Barrow and assumed command, having previously been Master of the *Peel Castle.* Chief Engineer A Garrett and most of his department had been on board for a few days and had already confirmed that the engines were fully serviceable and that sufficient coal was on board to sail the vessel to Liverpool.

As the day progressed, the bulk of the crew were signed on, although most of her catering staff were not due to join the ship until her arrival in Liverpool. One of those who joined at Barrow was Chief Officer Radcliffe Duggan. The engineers had an early start the following morning, as the *King Orry* was due to sail to Liverpool at just after first light. A full head of steam was available by 05.30 and at just after 06.30, the *King Orry* slipped her mooring and proceeded towards Morecambe Bay and Liverpool, arriving at Princes Landing Stage at 11.10. The remainder of the day was spent taking on stores for her catering facilities, signing on the remaining catering staff and topping up the bunkers with coal.

In previous years, the *King Orry* would usually commence her passenger service with the morning sailing from Liverpool to Douglas, but this year was to be an exception. She slipped away from Princes Landing Stage at just after midnight on the morning of Saturday 16th June, bound for Douglas with a full load of passengers, all keen to get the most out of their Whitsun weekend break. After her arrival in Douglas at 05.30, she was quickly unloaded and prepared to return to Liverpool with the routine 08.30 sailing.

Following the Whitsun weekend, the *King Orry* became surplus to requirements for the normal daily passenger traffic and was therefore laid-up in the Brunswick Dock at Liverpool from 19th - 29th June.

On re-entering service, she sailed to Douglas in order to commence the season's sailings to Ardrossan the following morning.

The remainder of the 1933 season now fell into line with that of recent years with the *King Orry* carrying out most of the sailings on the Ardrossan, Dublin and Belfast services. Chief Officer Duggan and 2nd Officer Cannell did not complete the full season on board the *King Orry* and both were paid off on the 4th July being replaced by Chief Officer James Callister and 2nd Officer Lyndhurst Callow, who joined from the *Ramsey Town* and the *Peel Castle*.

The *King Orry's* last passenger service during 1933 took place on 2nd September, when she undertook the midnight sailing from Belfast to Douglas. She left Douglas at 07.05 on 4th September and sailed to Barrow for winter lay up. Apart from the bulk of her catering staff who had been paid-off in Douglas on 3rd September, her crew were all paid-off on arrival at Barrow.

During 1933, the Steam Packet decided to dispose of the ageing *Tynwald*, which had been laid up for a couple of years. She was finally sold in 1934 to the Manx entrepreneur Mr R A Colby Cubbon, who eventually converted her into a yacht with the new name of *Western Isles* .

The passenger traffic was now beginning to return to the pre-First World War levels with 502,329 people travelling to the Island during 1933. Taking advantage of this influx in trade, the Steam Packet decided to invest in another new ship and an order was placed with Cammell Laird at Birkenhead. The new vessel was to be an improvement on the already successful steamers, the *Ben-my-Chree* and the *Lady of Mann*. She was to be called the *Mona's Queen* and was slightly larger than the "Ben", although not as long.

In order to give her additional space for passengers, which included 20 private cabins, the *Mona's Queen* was given an extra deck forward of her main superstructure. This put her forecastle one deck higher than was usual and it was now level with the Promenade Deck rather than the Shelter Deck. This feature, which gave her a rather odd, but distinctive appearance, was to greatly enhance her sea-keeping qualities in rough weather. The *Mona's Queen* was launched on 12th April 1934 and she entered service towards the end of the 1934 season. The *Mona's Queen* was painted white all over from the beginning, and along with the "Ben" and the "Lady," gave the Steam Packet a very impressive trio of modern passenger steamers.

1934

Whitsun 1934 heralded the *King Orry* re-entering service again. She left Barrow at midnight on 13th June for a slow overnight passage to Liverpool under the command of Captain Thomas Woods. Chief Officer William Crellin and 2nd Officer John Craine were her principal deck officers, while Chief Engineer Barwell had replaced Chief Engineer Garrett.

Now that Chief Engineer Garrett had left the ship, the last member of the *King Orry's* crew who had served on board her during the First World War had finally departed.

Passenger service commenced with the 12.10 overnight sailing from Liverpool to Douglas on Friday 15th June. However, she only remained on service for two days, returning to the Mersey in an unladen condition on the evening of Saturday 16th June, where on arrival she was laid up in the Alfred Basin at Birkenhead.

She remained there until the afternoon of 28th June when she crossed the river to the Princes Landing Stage and collected passengers for the 15.00 sailing to Douglas.

The morning of 29th June found the *King Orry* on the 08.30 service to Ardrossan. At just after 09.20, as she cruised by Laxey Head on the Isle of Man, an urgent message was passed to Purser Robert Addie.

A 62-year-old passenger by the name of Mr Thomas Barrie from Falkirk in Scotland had collapsed in the First Class saloon with a suspected heart attack. After ensuring that Mr Barrie was being cared for, Purser Addie informed Captain Woods of the incident. A message was quickly sent ashore by Mr W Ross, the Marconi Wireless Operator, requesting immediate medical assistance and advising that the *King Orry* would berth in Ramsey at about 09.50.

On arrival alongside the Queens Pier at Ramsey, Dr Cocker, who had been alerted to render assistance, boarded the vessel and examined the patient. Sadly, Mr Barrie could not be resuscitated and was pronounced dead, his body being removed from the *King Orry* before she resumed her voyage to Ardrossan.

The remainder of the season was uneventful with the *King Orry* carrying out the now familiar routine of covering the Ardrossan, Belfast and Dublin sailings. However, the *King Orry* did not retire from service during September, as in previous years. The reason for this is not certain, but is probably due to the passenger traffic into the Island during 1934 being up by 31,000 from the previous year. She remained in service until 30th October and was employed solely on the daily Douglas to Liverpool service from 15th September.

During 1934, the *King Orry* had begun to have problems with her turbines and, at high speed, the bearings on the single-reduction gearbox began to vibrate and became hot.

The decision was therefore taken to put the *King Orry* into the Vickers Armstrong shipyard at Barrow when she was withdrawn from service for a major engine overhaul and refurbishment. She entered the shipyard in January 1935 and it took some two months to complete the necessary work. The turbines and gearbox were stripped down, repaired and reassembled, although the exact details on what took place is not known as neither Vickers Armstrong nor the Steam Packet now have any official records that cover this refurbishment period.

A long-standing complaint about the *King Orry* was that in rough weather, her Shelter Deck took a lot of water, which usually ended up in her forward saloons. In order to resolve this problem, 16 glass windows were fitted to each side of the ship at the forward end of the Shelter Deck. Her external appearance was also altered slightly when her funnel was cut down by 4ft from 36ft to 32ft, as no doubt the top had rusted away.

The final task carried out by Vickers Armstrong was to replace worn furnishings in the saloons and paint her hull and superstructure. Surprisingly, the one thing that was not done during the refit, was to convert her boilers to use oil fuel, rather than coal.

1935

As Whitsun 1935 approached, the newly refurbished *King Orry* was once again brought back into service.

Captain George Woods had taken command, assisted by Chief Officer William Crellin and 2nd Officer W Cowley. Chief Engineer S Cowley was now in charge of the refurbished Engine Room.

Unfortunately the sailing schedule for 1935 has been lost, so details of her service are not known. However, an incident, which involved the ship, has come to light after scrutiny of the "Lloyds Weekly Casualty Reports" for 1935.

On the morning of 17th September, the *King Orry* was laying alongside Princes Landing Stage, with her bows towards the sea. She was scheduled to sail at 10.30 with the morning sailing to Douglas.

A fine picture of the **King Orry** *arriving in Liverpool. (John Clarkson collection)*

*The **King Orry** at speed in the River Mersey following her 1935 refurbishment. (Raymond Brandreth collection)*

*Hundreds of holidaymakers stream ashore in Douglas as they disembark from the recently arrived **King Orry** (furthest from camera) and the **Manxman** during the 1920s. (Ferry Publications Library)*

At the allotted time, Captain Woods eased the *King Orry* away from her berth and she began to move slowly down the river. Unknown to Captain Woods, at the very same moment the Clyde Shipping Company's steamer, *Rockabill* was about to enter the river from the lock leading out of Princes Dock. Giving no advance warning of her intention, the *Rockabill* suddenly shot out of the lock in front of the *King Orry*, a mere one hundred yards ahead of her bow.

Captain Woods ordered the helm to be put over to hard a port and her engines to be put full astern. At the same time an equally startled Captain on board the *Rockabill* saw the impending collision and took similar evasive action. But it was too late, the *King Orry* struck the *Rockabill* hard on her port quarter, seriously damaging her stern plating at water line level. The *King Orry* suffered minor damage to her stem. The damage to the *Rockabill* necessitated her being taken into dry dock for repairs, while the repairs to the *King Orry* were delayed until after she went into winter lay up.

The subsequent enquiry blamed the Captain of the *Rockabill* for causing the collision stating that he should have been more cautious when entering a busy shipping channel and should have given way to the *King Orry* as she was already under way in the river. At

the end of the 1935 season, the *King Orry* retired to her usual winter berth at Barrow.

One person with memories of the *King Orry* during the mid 1930's is Mr Ron Cretney. As a young boy aged 10, Ron helped his father and elder brothers with the family grocery business which was run from a shop on the North Quay in Douglas.

During the 1930s, the crew of Steam Packet vessels still had to provide themselves with their own daily rations and Ron's father had a good trade with them, supplying their needs.

As each Steam Packet vessel arrived in Douglas, Ron's elder brother Clifford would go down to the pier and once the passengers had disembarked, would board the ship and seek out the crew and take orders for their modest requirements. He would then give the order to one of his younger brothers, who would then rush it back to the shop; the order would then be prepared and wrapped up in brown paper. These orders often consisted of items such as bread, eggs, bacon, condensed milk, cheese, butter, tea and sugar. Should one of the crew ask for items such as sausages, chops or stewing meat, Ron's father would arrange for them to be collected from the butcher and include them in the parcel. Ron and his brothers would then take the parcels down to the individual ships, give them to the crew and collect the necessary payment.

As there was usually a large amount of parcels, they would be taken down to the ship in the wicker basket which was attached to the front of his father's delivery bicycle. Ron mentions that he had to push the bicycle as he was not tall enough to ride it. He recalls that the *King Orry* was a design all of her own as far as the crew's quarters were concerned, although the *Ben-my-Chree* and the *Lady of Mann* had some similarities. He remembers that, as the *King Orry* was still a coal burner, he would dread descending the ladder down into the firemen's (or stokers') mess. They would be covered in coal dust and to a young boy this presented as a frightening spectacle. He recalls that they all appeared to be hard, rough men from Liverpool but once you got to know them, especially after they had washed off the black grime, then they were no different to anybody else.

As the *King Orry* regularly carried out the Sunday midnight sailing to Liverpool during the summer season, she would often berth in Douglas on the Saturday afternoon to allow the Manx members of her crew to get a night at home. As they returned to the ship early on Sunday evening, they would often push pieces of paper with an order on it under the shop front door. The Cretney family always attended the evening church service but once this was over they would go back to the shop and prepare any orders that had been left. The boys would then rush them down to the ships before they sailed. Frequently, the orders were delivered so near to departure time that they would have to be handed over to the seaman at the top of the gangway and payment would be collected when the ship was next in Douglas. On occasion, although it never happened to Ron, one of his elder brothers would be still be on board the vessel when she sailed and they would get a free trip. Ron often suspected that his brothers did this on purpose.

1936

Captain George Woods brought the *King Orry* out of winter lay at 09.00 on 17th June when he took her to Liverpool to begin the season's work. She sailed with a skeleton crew, which comprised of mainly deck and Engine Room personnel; the majority of the catering personnel joined the ship when she berthed in Liverpool at just after 15.15.

The following day was spent alongside Princes Landing Stage as stores and coal were taken on board. The main members of her crew remained unchanged from the previous year.

Her first passenger sailing departed from Liverpool for Douglas at the unusual time of 03.00 and she made a very fast passage, arriving in Douglas at 06.50. She remained alongside in Douglas until 18.10 when she took the evening sailing back to Liverpool. It did not take very long before the *King Orry* was employed on the now normal routine of the Ardrossan, Dublin and Belfast sailings, the first trip to Ardrossan being made on the evening of 22nd June.

Chief Officer Crellin and 2nd Officer Cowley left the ship on 30th June, to be replaced by Chief Officer Thomas Corkill and 2nd Officer T E Cubbon, although Chief Officer Corkill only remained on board until 8th September, when Chief Officer Walter Cubbon relieved him.

The *King Orry* continued on regular passenger sailings for the whole season, although on the 19th, 20th and 27th August, she undertook Round the Island cruises.

The 1936 season was another very long one, with the *King Orry* remaining in service until 30th October. The continued increase in passenger traffic to the Island necessitated the Steam Packet keeping their summer vessels in service for yet another very welcome extended holiday season, just as they had done during 1934 and 1935.

With the possibility of another war being out of the question at this moment in time, the Directors of the Steam Packet believed that the boom in holiday traffic was back for good. They therefore decided to rejuvenate their fleet and replace some of the older vessels. Along with the fairly new *Ben-my-Chree*, the centenary vessel *Lady of Mann* and the new *Mona's Queen*, the addition of two new ships would put the Steam Packet into an unrivalled position amongst other United Kingdom coastal trade passenger ship companies.

In March 1936, two orders were placed with Vickers Armstrong Shipbuilders at Barrow. The design and layout of the new vessels was revolutionary and did not resemble any other vessel already in service with the Manx fleet.

The ships were to be called the *Fenella* and *Tynwald*, being named after two of the vessels that maintained the service to the Isle of Man during the First World War. Their machinery was similar to that of the *Mona's Queen* but their hull design was to incorporate a raked bow and cruiser stern instead of the traditional straight bow and counter stern fitted to all previous Steam Packet vessels.

A distinctive feature of both vessels was their funnel tops which were not raked back towards the stern in the traditional manner but were parallel to the waterline. This unusual funnel design had previously only been seen on large motor vessels, many of which had been built at the Belfast shipyard of Harland and Wolff, the most famous being the White Star liners *Britannic* and *Georgic*, of 1930 and 1932.

The *Fenella* and the *Tynwald* were both launched on the same day, 16th December 1936 and were to enter service in May and June the following year. Unlike the "Ben," the "Lady" or the *Mona's Queen*, they would be painted in the Steam Packet's traditional colours of black hull and white superstructure.

While the two ships were almost identical, they could easily be told apart as the bulwarks around the forecastle of the *Fenella* were painted black while those on the *Tynwald* were painted white. The design of these two ships was to form the basis of the design used by the Steam Packet when they ordered new ships in the post Second World War period to replace war-time losses.

Other changes to the fleet during 1936 were to include the withdrawal of the *Ramsey Town*, which was sold and broken up.

In October 1936, the Isle of Man Harbour Board installed a recent invention the Marconi TW3 Wireless Directional Beacon on the Victoria Pier. This had been influenced by the succession of vessels that had grounded on the Conister Rocks over the years which had included Steam Packet vessels. Early in 1937, the Steam Packet entered negotiations with Marconi and shortly afterwards every Steam Packet vessel was fitted with the special receiver required to be used in conjunction with the directional beacon. This device would greatly assist vessels entering Douglas in bad visibility.

1937

The entry into service of the new *Fenella* on 1st May and the *Tynwald* on 18th June affected the requirement for the *King Orry*. She was no longer needed for the

*A fine shot of the **King Orry** at speed in the River Mersey following her 1935 refurbishment and the installation of glass windows in her Shelter Deck. (Raymond Brandreth collection)*

*The **King Orry** steams into Douglas with another load of passengers looking forward to enjoying their forthcoming holiday on the Isle of Man. (David Handscombe collection)*

busy Whitsun period and did not leave Barrow until afternoon of 15th July.

For the first time, the *King Orry's* new Master was to be her Chief Officer from the previous year. Chief Officer Walter Cubbon had been promoted to Captain in late 1936 and had taken command of the cargo vessel *Peveril*. He was duly reappointed to the *King Orry* when she re-entered service. Her new Chief Officer, also from the *Peveril*, was Thomas Cain, who had been awarded the Distinguished Service Cross (DSC) while serving as a Lieutenant in the Royal Naval Reserve during the First World War. Second Officer Tom Corteen completed her Deck Officer team.

Unlike every previous year, the *King Orry* did not proceed to Liverpool to rebunker. Coal was taken on at Barrow and she sailed directly to Douglas at 16.00 on 15th June, arriving at 20.35.

Her first passenger service commenced at 16.00 on the following day when she took the afternoon sailing to Liverpool. As a direct result of the two new steamers, the *King Orry* only operated 23 passenger sailings during the 1937 season, which included two sailings to Fleetwood and two sailings between Ramsey and Liverpool. These latter two trips were to transport territorial army troops over to the Island for their summer training camp.

She was withdrawn from service some two months earlier than in 1936, carrying out her last passenger service from Douglas to Liverpool at 09.00 on 21st August, proceeding to Barrow for winter lay up the following day.

Although the *King Orry* did not complete the whole season, 1937 marked the busiest year for the Steam Packet during the inter-war years. A total of 583,037 passengers travelled to the island, the bulk of which were carried on Steam Packet vessels.

As the Isle of Man was enjoying the prosperity brought to its shores by the influx of tourists, a black cloud was once again beginning to cover Europe. A reborn Germany, under the control of its new leader Adolf Hitler, was beginning to flex its muscles and apply pressure to some of its less-powerful neighbours.

Despite the Treaty of Versailles and the London Naval Conference of 1930, Germany had secretly ignored the terms imposed upon her and had rebuilt her armed forces, bringing them up to a very formidable level of manpower. The German navy, army and air force were supplied with the latest type of arms and equipment, which in some cases were far superior to that used by the United Kingdom and her European allies.

In March 1935, Germany began to openly contravene the terms of the treaty of Versailles and moved her troops into the demilitarised zone, which formed her border with France, the Rhineland. France reacted immediately and demanded that Germany withdraw but when the French Government found that a cautious Britain considered that the problem was one for France to solve on their own, France did little more that than voice her objection.

In March 1938, Hitler made another bold move in his plan to reunite all of the former German-speaking territories and re-establish a German Empire. Austria was in the middle of political upheaval and crisis, having suffered similar sanctions as those placed upon Germany after the First World War. Hitler took advantage of the situation and moved his army across the Austrian border, the jubilant troops entering Vienna on 12th March.

Once again France and Britain did little more than object through the political circles. It must be appreciated that both Britain and France were only just recovering from the mass Depression of the previous decade and neither country was in the position or had the desire to be thrust into another costly and devastating conflict, such as the First World War. Therefore, the cautious stance taken by both Governments can be understood; after all, perhaps Germany might stop expanding now that it had occupied the Rhineland and Austria.

1938

As 1938 moved towards the summer, the Steam Packet resumed its seasonal holiday trade. The year 1938 was to prove to be the shortest season on which the *King Orry* was ever employed, being two days shorter than the previous year.

Once again she entered service in mid-July, leaving Barrow under the command of Captain Walter Cubbon at 11.00 on 14th July and proceeding directly to Douglas.

Having taken on her full crew after arriving at Douglas, she was ready to commence passenger traffic with the 16.00 sailing to Liverpool the following day. With the exception of a sailing to Fleetwood on 19th July and a three day period alongside there before she returned to Douglas, the *King Orry* was employed solely on the Douglas to Liverpool route.

On the morning of 20th August, she undertook the 08.30 sailing to Liverpool for the last time that season. On arrival at Prince's Landing Stage the bulk of her catering staff were paid-off and she proceeded to Barrow for winter lay up, arriving there at 18.20.

Her crew had remained unchanged throughout this short season, with Chief Officer Thomas Cain, 2nd Officer Harold Collister and Chief Engineer Stanley Cowley forming the hierarchy of her crew.

At the other end of the scale, two former crew members of the *King Orry* remember what life was like

as a fireman and a pantry boy during 1938. Twenty-year-old Stanley Gale from Peel on the Isle of Man, joined ship as a fireman at Barrow on 13th July 1938 - it was his first ship. As a fireman (or stoker), Stanley was employed way down in the bowels of the ship, in the stoke hold.

He was a member of a of the 14-man team, whose job it was to shovel the coal from the ship's stoke hold into each of her 15 furnaces, thus supplying heat to her two double-ended and one single-ended boiler. Stanley remembers it as being a very dirty and arduous task, although the team spirit was second to none. His quarters on board were located on the lower deck, adjacent to the galley and passenger sleeping saloons.

The furniture in the firemen's quarters was very basic and his bed consisted of no more than a wooden bunk with no springs and a rather dirty straw palliasse. It has already been mentioned that the crew of the *King Orry* had to supply his own victuals and Stanley was no exception. His mother would give him a food parcel at the beginning of each period of duty on board although he would often top-up his supplies from Ron Cretney's father's shop on the North Quay in Douglas. One particular memory that Stanley Gale has of 1938, occurred after the ship was laid up in Barrow.

The crew had been paid-off on 23rd August and the Manx members were preparing to leave the ship to travel back to the Island. Second Steward D Vondy, a Liverpool man, had also been paid-off and as no one had seen him for some time, it was assumed that he had already left the ship. As the day progressed, Chief Officer Thomas Cain was walking around the ship checking that all was secure and that all of the crew's cabins and quarters had been left in a tidy condition.

As he passed the Second Steward's cabin, he noticed that the door was closed but through an air vent in the door he observed that the lights had been left on. Opening the door to rectify the minor misdemeanour, he found that he had to push it very hard, as something appeared to be jammed behind it. When he finally gained access to the cabin, he was in for a shock.

Slumped behind the door, half on the bunk and half on the deck, was the body of the Second Steward and a quick glance at his bloated face was all that was needed to establish that he was dead.

Chief Officer Cain closed the cabin door and went to the Captain's cabin to inform him of the sad news, catching Captain Cubbon, as he was about to leave the ship. In due course a doctor was summoned on board to confirm death, as were the local police. Foul play was ruled out, and the doctor recorded the death of the 41-year-old Second Steward as being due to a heart attack.

With the formalities over, the next problem was to get the body ashore to an undertaker.

A local undertaker, Mr Robertson Fox, was contacted and asked to come to the *King Orry* to remove the body. When he eventually arrived, he asked Chief Officer Cain if two of the crew could be provided to assist him. Stanley Gale and his friend R A Kenna, also a fireman from the Isle of Man, were quickly volunteered to give Mr Robertson Fox a hand. Stanley remembers that the body was starting to go black and that rigor mortis had already set in. Once the unpleasant task was complete and the body was placed inside the undertaker's small van, both Stanley and his friend were surprised when Mr Robertson Fox paid them both the sum of 2/6d. Although Stanley Gale was pleased with his reward, the Second Steward had been a friend of his, and he was upset by the experience.

Cabin Boy John Cooil from Castletown on the Isle of Man was the youngest member of the *King Orry's*, crew being 15 years and 4 months old when he joined the ship at Douglas on 14th July 1938.

As the youngest member of the Catering Staff was invariably given all of the dirty tasks, his standard of living on board the *King Orry* was somewhat better than that of Stanley Gale. The stewards had their quarters adjacent to the Dining Saloon and Pantry on the Shelter Deck. Although the stewards' quarters were fitted with the same basic furniture as was used within the firemen's quarters, they were much cleaner and brighter.

Two unofficial perks that the stewards often benefited from were the use of the sheets and bedding which were provided for the passengers and the opportunity to acquire a meal from the galley. In 1938, John Cooil's duties consisted mainly of cleaning the passenger saloons and cabins at the end of each voyage and assisting the stewards in various other tasks when they were busy. John paid-off from the *King Orry* at Liverpool on 20th August and was therefore not on board when Second Steward D Vondy died at Barrow. Being a cabin boy, he had worked for the Second Steward and like Stanley Gale was upset when he was informed of his death.

As the *King Orry* lay at Barrow, the situation in Europe took another disastrous step towards conflict.

From March 1938, Germany had begun to put pressure on Czechoslovakia over the border territory known as the Sudetenland, which was mainly populated by German-speaking people. As Czechoslovakia formed the keystone of France's defensive alliance in Eastern Europe, both France and Britain suddenly woke up to the increasing threat that Germany now offered to European peace.

By August 1938, Hitler was demanding that Czechoslovakia gave the Sudetenland to Germany and that if they did not yield, his army would march. In September 1938, the situation had become so volatile, that Britain finally reacted, and what was to be known as the Munich Crisis followed. The Prime Minister, Mr Neville Chamberlain flew to Germany to meet Adolf Hitler in an attempt to defuse the powder keg that looked like it was about to explode. This was just the reaction that Hitler had hoped for. During the discussions that followed, he assured the Governments of Britain and France that if they agreed to his right to occupy the Sudetenland, then in return he would guarantee that he would not take any further action that was likely to cause a confrontation between the three countries that might result in war.

Although this agreement spelt the end for Czechoslovakia, the British Prime Minister returned to London waving the famous 'peace in our time' letter. Peace in Europe appeared to be secure again.

To the Isle of Man Steam Packet, the Munich Crisis had not just been a problem between the British, French and German Governments. As a precaution, in September 1938 the Director of Sea Transport had been directed by the British Government to prepare to provide various Merchant ships to support the Royal Navy should a conflict ensue. As a result of this directive, the Steam Packet had received formal notice that both the *King Orry* and the *Manx Maid* were requisitioned for urgent Government service and that they should be handed over at the earliest opportunity.

Fortunately, Mr Chamberlain's visit to Germany eased the tension and the Company were subsequently informed that the requisition order had been 'suspended'. As the *King Orry's* Half Yearly Crew Agreements show no details of a crew being provided for the vessel's requisition, it is presumed that no formal action was taken regarding the handover of the vessel to the British Government.

At the end of the 1938 season the Steam Packet decided to dispose of two of their older vessels, which had both seen better days, and were now made surplus to requirements by the introduction of the new *Tynwald* and the *Fenella*. The *Mona* of 1907 was sold for breaking up in December, while the *Peel Castle* of 1894 was sold to the breakers in February 1939.

The uneasy peace in Europe continued throughout the winter of 1938/1939 and Germany did not make any new attempts to dominate their neighbours until March 1939.

Hitler then encouraged a rebel Slovak leader, Father Tiso, to form an independent Slovak State, Bohemia. As soon as this was announced on 14th March, Hitler demanded that the Czechoslovakian Government recognise the new state as being part of Germany. When the Czech Government refused, this gave Hitler the excuse he needed to invade Czechoslovakia; his armies marched over the border and entered Prague the following day.

Here indeed was a reason for Britain and France to declare war on Germany, as they had both guaranteed the independence of what remained of Czechoslovakia after the Munich Crisis and the loss of the Sudetenland.

However, much to everyone's surprise and relief, the British Prime Minister announced that even though he deplored Hitler's actions, as Bohemia had asked to become an independent state, this destroyed the basis of the guarantee to protect Czechoslovakia as a sovereign state. There was therefore no cause for war to be declared, France followed a similar ploy.

Although war was not declared, the British Government was preparing for what now seemed the inevitable. The *King Orry* and the *Manx Maid* were still under their suspended requisition order.

OIL BURNER

Early in March 1939, the *King Orry* was taken into the Vickers Armstrong shipyard at Barrow, the decision to convert her to oil burning having been made. There has always been speculation as to why the vessel was converted to oil burning at this late stage in her life, for she was now 26 years old and could not be expected to serve for many more years. The official Steam Packet records have sadly been destroyed and the surviving Vickers Armstrong engineering details give no indication of who authorised the conversion.

It has been rumoured that the Director of Transport instructed the Steam Packet to convert the vessel, although whether the Steam Packet or the British Government paid for the conversion to be carried out, sadly remains a mystery. Indeed, as Britain was not an oil-producing country, but had large coal reserves, it is doubtful that the Steam Packet would have made the decision on their own to convert the vessel to a fuel which had to be brought in from overseas, especially when war and oil shortages might be imminent.

The work carried out by Vickers Armstrong consisted of converting all of the coal furnaces to the Wallsend - Howden Pressure System of oil burners. Two burners were fitted into each of the fifteen furnaces, making a total of thirty burners.

With the exception of No 8 Bunker, which was located on the Main Deck, all of the coal bunkers were converted to oil fuel tanks. The one remaining coal bunker, No 8, contained the only coal that was left on board the *King Orry*: fifteen tons that provided fuel for the galley ranges.

A maximum of 194.16 tons (at 35.96 cub ft/ton) of fuel oil was now carried in the converted bunkers, which was slightly lighter than the previous maximum of 210 tons of coal. In order that new load marks could be worked out, an inclining test was carried out in Vickers Armstrong's Devonshire Dock on the morning of 11th April.

Due to the combination of the work that was carried out in 1935 and the work just completed, her fully laden displacement had decreased from 2,885 tons (March 1913) to approximately 2,769 tons, while her Net Registered Tonnage went down from 762.22 tons to 759.91 tons. The conversion from coal to oil also meant that a reduction in her crew was necessary as the firemen who shovelled coal from the bunkers into the furnaces were no longer required.

The *King Orry's* Half Yearly Crew Agreement dated 30th June 1939, records a reduction of 13 men, making the crew 59 instead of the previous 72. Fireman Stanley Gale was retained and is recorded in the Crew Agreement as still being a fireman, although he no longer shovelled coal. The most noticeable aspect of the *King Orry's* conversion to oil fuel was that she no longer belched black smoke from her funnel. This feature had always been a trademark of the coal burning vessels within the Steam Packet fleet. Stanley Gale records that as well as no longer coming off duty looking like a coal miner, his quarters were now considerably cleaner although they now smelt of oil fuel rather than coal dust.

On 31st March, the British Government issued a statement to the effect that Great Britain would offer Poland any support that was required to ensure that her independence was not threatened by Germany. This complete change to British policy caught Hitler by surprise, especially as an equally surprised France was persuaded to follow Britain's example. Unfortunately, this united show of force did little to dissuade Hitler from his rampage within the European mainland.

1939

The *King Orry* entered service for the 1939 season on Saturday 15th April when she left Barrow and sailed to Liverpool to take on oil and stores. The bulk of the crew had signed on the day before while she lay at Barrow. Captain Thomas Woods had assumed command although Chief Officer Thomas Cain remained from the previous year. Along with fireman Stanley Gale, cabin boy John Cooil commenced his second season on board, although he became a pantry boy on 1st July.

The *King Orry's* 1939 passenger season commenced with the 10.45 Liverpool to Douglas service on Monday 17th April and she continued to carry out the daily return sailing to the Isle of Man for the next few weeks. Captain T C Woods relinquished command on 15th May and was reappointed as the Master of the *Lady of Mann*. Captain Archie Holkham assumed command, having previously been the Master of the *Fenella*. As the season progressed, the *King Orry* became involved in the routine sailings between the Island and Belfast, Dublin and Ardrossan on a more regular basis, usually sailing to each of these ports at least once a week.

The sailing between Douglas and Liverpool on the morning of Thursday 1st June is one that is remembered well by both Stanley Gale and John Cooil.

The *King Orry* had left Douglas at 09.00 and had crossed the Mersey Bar at just after midday. As she began to steam up the buoyed channel towards Liverpool, she was hailed by the tug *Grebecock*, which belonged to the Liverpool Screw Towing and Lighterage Company. She was on charter to Cammell Laird's yard and was acting as escort to a new vessel that was undergoing sea trials.

The *King Orry* was advised to proceed with caution as the new submarine *Thetis* was heading down river. The news quickly spread around the *King Orry* and both Stanley Gale and John Cooil crept away from their work place to have a look at the new submarine. The *Thetis* was one of the new "T" Class submarines, which had a length of 270ft, and displaced 1090 tons. Her crew would normally consist of 59, but today she had 103 persons on board, many of them Cammell Laird and Admiralty officials.

The *Thetis* was given a noisy welcome with a few blasts from the *King Orry's* siren, before she passed astern into the sunny haze that now covered the river. Once out of sight, the passengers and crew members that had lined the *King Orry's* guardrails returned to their own business or duties and thought no more of the submarine.

The *King Orry* left Princes Landing Stage at just after 15.30 to commence the return voyage to Douglas; it was still a warm sunny day. As she steamed out of Liverpool Bay and into the Irish Sea, the tug *Grebecock* could be seen on the horizon a few miles to the south.

Unknown to anybody on board the *King Orry*, one of the worst disasters in the history of Britain's submarine service was unfolding. The *Thetis* had submerged on what was supposed to be a routine test-dive earlier in the afternoon but she had failed to surface at the appointed time and had not been heard of since.

As the *King Orry* disappeared over the horizon, the *Grebecock* began to ask all ships that passed to proceed with extreme caution and keep a sharp look out for any sign of the missing vessel. Sadly, no evidence of the missing submarine was seen for the remainder of the day.

As dawn broke on the following morning, one of the vessels that was searching for the *Thetis* came across her and found her in a very grave and precarious position. The bow and conning tower were out of sight below the water. All that could be seen was the stern portion of her hull which stuck out of the sea like a tomb stone. At this point of time the reason for her precarious position was not known, but as the tide was rising and the *Thetis* appeared to remain static and not move with the tidal swell, it was assumed that her bow was resting on the bottom of Liverpool Bay.

Over the next few hours, as many attempts were made to bring the stricken vessel to the surface, four of her crew managed to escape. One of them, a Royal Navy Captain informed the rescue teams that somehow the rear door on one of the bow torpedo tubes had been opened, while the outer door was open to the sea. The sea had rushed in to the forward torpedo compartment before any attempt to shut the inner door could be made. The weight of the extra water in the forward end of the submarine had caused the bow to crash into the seabed. Fortunately they had managed to shut some of the watertight doors before the whole submarine flooded, hence her precarious position.

Numerous resue attempts failed, and it became obvious that the trapped submariners and officials were doomed.

As the weather began to worsen, the *Thetis* suddenly broke free from the salvage vessels that were now connected to her stern and slowly slipped below the waves, taking 99 people to a cold and watery grave.

As the *King Orry* left Douglas at 09.00 that morning and set course for Ardrossan, sadly the news of the submarine's predicament had already been passed around the ship. The Admiralty had advised all shipping in the Irish Sea to keep clear of the *Thetis'* position as attempts to rescue her crew had commenced. Both Stanley Gale and John Cooil recall that they were stunned by the news, as all had seemed so well as they had waved to the *Thetis'* crew who had been standing on her casing as she sailed out into the afternoon haze that hung over the Mersey.

For the *King Orry*, the remainder of June and July 1939 were busy. As the news of the *Thetis* disaster began to disappear from the front-page headlines, the *King Orry* and her crew busied themselves with scheduled sailings to Liverpool, Belfast, Dublin, Ardrossan, Fleetwood and Heysham. She also undertook her fair share of charter trips and took the employees of various companies and organisations for a day trips into the Irish Sea.

The first excursion took place only a couple of days after the *Thetis* sank. On the morning of Saturday 3rd June, the *King Orry* left Douglas and headed towards Barrow in Furness. On arrival, she took on board a large party of employees who worked for the ship builder Vickers Armstrong. Leaving Barrow at 13.00, she sailed back to Douglas and landed her passengers for a few hours of enjoyment amongst the many attractions in the Island's premier resort. The return trip to Barrow commenced at 22.30. No doubt the saloons on board were full of happy, but tired people.

On Wednesday 14th June the employees of McCartneys from Belfast enjoyed a cruise to the Island on board the Manx steamer, returning to Belfast on board the *Fenella*, leaving Douglas at 19.15. On 28th June, the *King Orry* commenced the first of two sailings between the Island and Fleetwood while on Thursday 6th July she made a single trip to Heysham.

It was rare for the *King Orry* to visit either of these ports, as now that she had been converted to burn oil, she became a useful asset to the Steam Packet again and her sailings in 1939 nearly doubled those of the previous year.

The *King Orry* was chartered to carry out excursions from Belfast for McClures on 12th July and the York L.O.L on the 13th July. These excursions, which were very popular with the employees of the companies concerned, usually left Belfast at 08.00, arrived at Douglas just before lunch and returned to Belfast at about 19.00. As with day trips to other Irish Sea ports, the Steam Packet vessels were always filled to capacity with happy, laughing holidaymakers, all of them enjoying the few hours that they had ashore on the Island. However, John Cooil recalls that on the return passage to Belfast with the McClures day trip on 12th July, some of the happy holidaymakers became violent in the Steerage Bar and started to fight amongst themselves. It was only when Thomas Cain, the Chief Officer threatened to close the bar and hose it down with a fire hose that the fighting ceased.

The situation in Europe had not been stabilised by the British and French guarantee of support to Poland, should she be invaded. In fact it exacerbated Hitler more.

As early as January 1939, the German leader had approached the Polish government about the Polish Corridor that separated Germany from East Prussia and the return of the old German town of Danzig which lay within the corridor. Now that Britain and France appeared to be standing up to the rapidly expanding German Empire, the resolve of Adolf Hitler and his henchmen to rule Europe, became fanatical.

As in the summer of 1914, the war clouds gathered again and Britain began to plan for the worst. In February, the Board of Trade and Department of Shipping had issued orders that merchant seamen were to be given instruction in air raid precautions. The Steam Packet responded to this directive by arranging for officers from the Isle of Man Constabulary to give lectures to the crews of the company's vessels. Many of the Steam Packet's officers and ratings were members of the Royal Naval Reserve or Royal Naval Volunteer Reserve and these men were required to confirm that they were still eligible to be called up, although none of them were given orders to report to the various barracks at this stage.

Hitler, for his own reasons, was prepared to play a game with the British Government, in that he believed that the British were a coldly realistic people, and that, despite what they might say, they would never dream of going to war in the defence of Poland. To ensure that this was the case, he met with the Russian leaders and came up with a treaty that guaranteed that Russia would not enter a war in support of any British or French action. In return he agreed to split Poland with Russia and allow them to occupy the Baltic States. On 23rd August, a bewildered world heard that Russia and Germany had signed a non-aggression pact; the stage was now set for Germany to act as she wished.

Unlike the summer of 1914, the holiday traffic to the Isle of Man during August 1939 remained consistent. The Steam Packet had planned passenger sailings as far ahead as 10th September with the *King Orry* playing a full part.

However, after the German announcement on 23rd August, the British Government feared the worst and decided to put their war plans into action and began to mobilise both the regular and reserve forces. On the morning of 24th August, the Admiralty sent a signal to all of the warships in the Home Fleet, both those at sea and in harbour, instructing them to proceed to their allotted war stations. The battleships and battle cruisers of the mighty Home Fleet prepared to proceed north to its former World War One base of Scapa Flow in the Orkney Islands. At the same time as the Admiralty instructed its warships to prepare for war, the Director of Sea Transport was instructed to issue requisition orders for various merchant vessels which would be required to support the Royal Navy.

As the *King Orry* sailed out of Douglas at just after 08.30 and headed towards Belfast on the morning of

Monday 21st August, nobody on board had any idea that this was to be her last week in service as a passenger vessel. Before the week was out the *King Orry* would be ordered to prepare for war and the Merchant Navy's Red Ensign would again be replaced by the Royal Navy's White Ensign.

This final week of service as a Steam Packet vessel is recorded in detail in the Steam Packet's Way Books. These meticulously maintained books, which are now in the possession of the Manx Museum, record each voyage completed by the Company's vessels and give details about the weather, sailing times and number of passengers and details of any cargo carried. They record that on this particular Belfast trip there was a moderate north easterly wind with moderate sea state and slight haze. Having called at Ramsey at 09.40 to pick up a few more people, the Way Book records that she carried a total of 571 passengers during this voyage.

The return trip to the Island commenced at 17.05. After calling at Ramsey at 21.24, the *King Orry* arrived back in Douglas at 22.18 She is recorded as carrying 522 passengers on this return and trip. The following morning saw her depart from Douglas for Ardrossan, leaving the Victoria Pier at 09.07. The sea state was slight and the visibility is recorded as being good with a moderate breeze blowing for the north west. Having stopped at Ramsey to collect more passengers, she passed Ailsa Craig at 14.12 and arrived in Ardrossan at 15.44. A total of 481 passengers are recorded as being on board. The return sailing to the Island was overnight, with the *King Orry* leaving Ardrossan at just after midnight with 85 full-paying passengers and a child. Passing Ailsa Craig at 01.38, she arrived back in Douglas at 06.00. There is no mention of her stopping at Ramsey on the way back, so it must be assumed that she sailed directly to Douglas.

The Steam Packet weekly sailing schedule shows the *King Orry* as being due to return to the Island from Ardrossan at 12 noon on Wednesday 23rd August, not at midnight as recorded in the Way Book. It is possible that there was a printing error in the Weekly Sailing Schedule and that it should read midnight, not midday. The *King Orry* remained in Douglas throughout the remainder of Wednesday 23rd and did not sail again until the early hours of Thursday 24th. She slipped out of Douglas at 00.32 and headed for Liverpool. The sea state was calm, although a dense fog was encountered as she approached the Mersey. She passed the Bar Lightship at 03.55 and the Rock Lighthouse off New Brighton at 05.30; her slow progress up the river was obviously due to the fog. After eventually berthing alongside Princes Landing Stage at 06.00, her 944 passengers were put ashore. On an overnight sailing,

this large number of passengers must have made it difficult for many to find somewhere to lie down and go to sleep, especially in steerage which totalled some 637 people. The *King Orry* returned to Douglas with the 15.30 sailing, although the Way Book records that she was five minutes late leaving the berth. With 207 passengers on board, she arrived at Douglas at 19.50. The dense fog had diminished to a slight haze and did not impede her journey.

ROYAL NAVY

On the morning of Friday 25th August, the Steam Packet received a telegram informing them that the *King Orry*, *Mona's Isle* and *Manx Maid* had been requisitioned by the Royal Navy and that they were to proceed to nominated British ports within 48 hours. The *King Orry* was to report to Sandon Dock in Liverpool.

The *King Orry* had already departed from Douglas by the time that the telegram was received, having sailed to Dublin at 08.37 with 890 passengers on board. Rather than risk a breach in security by sending a message to the Captain of the *King Orry* via the Steam Packet's agent in Dublin, it was decided to await the return of the ship to Douglas before informing Captain Holkham of the news. After all, it was general knowledge that some citizens from the Irish Republic would sooner support the Germans than the British.

The weather on the crossing from Douglas to Dublin was good and is recorded as being a slight to moderate easterly wind with a smooth sea, but no haze. This allowed the *King Orry* to make good time and she arrived alongside the Sir John Rogerson Quay in Dublin at 13.37. The return journey back to the Island began at 17.00 and with 399 passengers and a child on board, she arrived in Douglas at 22.00.

As soon as the ship was secure, Captain Holkham was summoned to Imperial Buildings and informed of the *King Orry's* future. As she was not required to be at Sandon Dock in Liverpool until Sunday 27th August, the Steam Packet decided that she could continue with her scheduled programme until Saturday evening. At this moment in time the Steam Packet had not publicised that the *King Orry*, *Mona's Isle* and the *Manx Maid* had been requisitioned by the Royal Navy and only a few key personnel within the company and on board the three ships had been informed.

However, it did not take very long before the rumours began to spread amongst the *King Orry's* crew. Fireman Stanley Gale recalls that although he did not know the precise details regarding the *King Orry's* future he was aware that her programme for the following week had been cancelled, as a friend of his had overheard the Chief Engineer discussing it with the Second Engineer.

Although it would be the last day that the *King Orry* would be employed on her peacetime duties, Saturday 26th August appeared to be just another routine day as the crew busied themselves with the preparations for leaving harbour and the passengers boarded for the 09.00 sailing to Heysham.

As she went astern out of Douglas with 1,384 passengers on board, only a handful of her crew were aware of her departure to serve King and Country once again on the following day.

As the *King Orry* sped across a smooth sea towards Morecambe Bay and the port of Heysham, her complement of passengers was the largest number that she had carried for some considerable time. It was almost as if everybody on board knew about her impending withdrawal from service and wanted a last trip before she went away to an uncertain future.

She arrived off the Lune Buoy, which marks the beginning of the channel that leads into Heysham Harbour at 11.45 but she did not berth alongside until 13.44. The reason for this delay is not recorded in the Way Book, although it does mention that she encountered poor visibility during the passage from Douglas. Perhaps Heysham harbour was fogbound?

The return journey to Douglas and the beginning of her final passenger sailing (although most people on board were still unaware of this) began at 15.37. With a greatly reduced amount of passengers, only 117, the *King Orry* passed the Lune Buoy at 16.07 and arrived in Douglas at 18.58. Little did her passengers realise that they were to be the last fare-paying passengers that the *King Orry* would ever carry. Once they had disembarked, the crew were officially informed about the *King Orry's* future. She would sail to Liverpool the following morning with only a steaming crew on board and the vast majority of the catering staff would be left in Douglas. Only those that lived in Liverpool would be allowed to sail. Pantry boy John Cooil recalls that the next few hours were very hectic and were spent unloading dozens of items of stores and equipment that were of either no use to the Royal Navy, or the Steam Packet deemed that it was inappropriate for the Navy to acquire them. These included much of the silverware and bone china crockery from the Dining Saloons.

As soon as the *King Orry* had been prepared for her hand over to the Royal Navy, the crew who were not required for the voyage to Liverpool were paid-off and amongst these was pantry boy John Cooil.

The *King Orry* slipped out of Douglas Harbour at just after a quarter past midnight on Sunday 27th August. As she set course for the Mersey and steamed away into the darkness, nobody on board realised that this would be the last time that the *King Orry* would see the Isle of Man.

The crossing over to Liverpool was uneventful with a calm sea and good visibility, although it did start to rain as she approached the Bar Lightship. She steamed up river and berthed alongside Princes Landing Stage at 04.25. She was then ordered to move to Sandon Dock at just after midday and after passing through the lock gates was berthed alongside an old friend, the *St Tudno* of the Liverpool and North Wales Steamship Company. As soon as the gangways were put ashore, officials from the Admiralty came on board and the *King Orry* was formally handed over to the Royal Navy. Shortly afterwards swarms of dockyard workers began to stream on board and in no time at all, the vessel began to resemble a building site.

As the engines on a merchant ship were somewhat different to the high-performance engines of a warship, her four engineer officers which consisted of Chief Engineer Stanley Cowley, 2nd Engineer Laurie Quine, 3rd Engineer Griff Hughes and 4th Engineer Reggie Scarffe were offered temporary commissions in the Royal Naval Reserve and requested to remain as part of her crew.

Fireman Stanley Gale also volunteered to remain on board, but at a medical examination he was found to have varicose veins and was not accepted. Another Manxman who remained as part of the naval crew was donkeyman George Campbell, although he no longer lived on the Island and now resided in Barrow. He had joined the *King Orry* in the spring of 1923 and had served on her ever since. Although George Campbell had seen 16 years service on board the *King Orry*, he was not the longest serving member of her crew. This honour went to carpenter Thomas Gawne who at the age of 47 had joined the vessel on 27th January 1919. Thomas Gawne and the crew who were not retained by the Royal Navy, were all signed-off, on 29th August.

MOBILISATION

The progression towards war now began to swing into full force and on 29th August, just as the *King Orry's* crew were being put ashore, the Admiralty ordered the Royal Navy to mobilise for war, while two days later on 31st August 1939, all naval reserves were mobilised.

The final tragic piece to the saga occurred on 1st September 1939, when in the early hours of the morning, German troops crossed the borders into Poland. The British Government was paralysed by shock and horror and for 24 hours remained uncertain what to do. Then, on the morning of 2nd September they issued an ultimatum to Berlin, followed shortly afterwards by one from France.

Both countries demanded that German forces withdrew from Poland within 24 hours and, if Germany ignored this demand, she could consider herself to be at war with Britain, France and their allies. As the morning of Sunday 3rd September dawned, there was no evidence of Germany complying with these demands, in fact the German army had advanced further into Polish territory.

Later that morning at just after 11.00, the Prime Minister Neville Chamberlain made a radio broadcast to inform the British people of the demands that had been made and that regrettably, the German Government had ignored. As a result, it was his sad duty to announce that Britain and her allies were at war with Germany.

As the *King Orry* lay at Sandon Dock in Liverpool, the few members of her crew who were on board listened to the Prime Minister's broadcast on the ship's wireless set. Each of them was very quiet as they wondered what the future held in store for them.

The *King Orry*, *Mona's Isle* and the *Manx Maid* were not the only Steam Packet ships to be called up. The *Mona's Queen*, *Viking*, *Tynwald*, *Fenella*, *Manxman*, *Lady of Mann* and the *Ben-my-Chree* all received similar orders to proceed to war.

By the second week of September 1939 the Steam Packet had lost its ten best ships, leaving the humble *Rushen Castle*, *Victoria* and *Snaefell* to continue with the passenger service, although the *Victoria* would receive her call-up papers before the war was over.

On 8th September, the Steam Packet sent a letter to their Liverpool agent informing him of the provisional sailing arrangements for the next few days. The company would maintain a daily service in one direction only between Douglas and Liverpool using the *Rushen Castle* and the *Victoria* with the *Snaefell* as the standby vessel.

The Company's cargo vessels, the *Peveril*, *Conister* and the *Cushag* were not required by the navy and remained in Steam Packet service throughout the war, although the *Cushag* would be sold for scrap in 1943.

As the war progressed and Liverpool became the centre for controlling the North Atlantic and its associated convoys, the Admiralty closed the port to all but essential war-effort shipping. To this end, the Steam Packet ceased sailings from Liverpool in December 1940 and moved its operations further up the coast to Fleetwood where they maintained a daily one-way sailing to the Island until April 1946.

Stanley Gale, fireman aboard the King Orry during 1938–1939. This photograph was taken after he joined the Royal Navy in 1939. (David Handscombe collection)

Post Script:

Although Fireman Stanley Gale had been unsuccessful in joining the Royal Navy at his first attempt, his wish to do his bit for the country did not prevent him from going to war with the Manx fleet. He succeeded in transferring to the Lady of Mann *and served on board her during her time as a troopship for the remainder of 1939 and the first half of 1940. He was wounded during the fall of France and the evacuation of the British Expeditionary Force from Dunkirk and was subsequently invalided back to the Isle of Man.*

Soon becoming bored at being ashore, he tried for the Royal Navy again and was successful at his second attempt. Having been kitted out in his naval uniform, he travelled to Chatham to join the coal-burning former Manx steamer Mona's Isle *that had been recently commissioned into the Royal Navy as an escort anti-aircraft ship. Unfortunately, after a couple of years his wound from Dunkirk started to cause problems and he was invalided out for a second time. Still not deterred, he immediately rejoined the Merchant Navy, where no medical was required, and eventually joined the troopship,* Ben-my-Chree, *remaining on board her until the end of hostilities.*

King Orry

The Phoney War

As August had drawn to a close and everybody on board the *King Orry* waited for the inevitable declaration of war, the Admiralty had begun to draft members of the Royal Naval Reserve to the Manx steamer. The *King Orry* was to be commissioned as an Armed Boarding Vessel, a role that she had last carried out twenty years earlier. When the White Ensign had been lowered in January 1919 and the *King Orry's* war paint had been replaced by the Steam Packet's distinctive livery, nobody in the Isle of Man Steam Packet would have believed that the Company's vessels would be required to defend the nation's seaways again.

Amongst those drafted to the *King Orry* was 18-year-old Joseph Jones from Connah's Quay in North Wales. He had joined the Royal Naval Reserve in May 1939 and had been ordered to report to the Royal Naval barracks at Portsmouth when the Admiralty had mobilised the reserves in late August. Three other reservists who had received their orders to mobilise were Ray Hughes, Sam Jones and Jimmy McCallum. Ray Hughes and Sam Jones also hailed from Connah's Quay and like Joe Jones had also joined the Royal Naval Reserve in May 1939. Jimmy McCallum was a Scot who came from Paisley near Glasgow. The Welshmen soon became friends with Jimmy McCallum and having had their kit checked at the naval barracks, all four travelled to Liverpool to join the *King Orry* on the day after war was declared.

Having arrived at Lime Street station in the early hours of the morning, the four intrepid sailors eventually found the *King Orry* lying in Sandon Dock. The berth ahead of the *King Orry* was occupied by the Liverpool and North Wales Steamship Company's *St Tudno* which was well known to the three Welshman as they had often seen her at one of the North Wales ports during the summer months. Like the *King Orry*, she had been taken over by the Admiralty for conversion into an armed boarding vessel. Compared with her pre-war days, the *King Orry* looked a sorry state. Her hull and superstructure were in the process of being repainted dark grey; scaffolding had been erected on the Forecastle and Poop Deck, while dockyard workers swarmed about her upper decks.

Although the work to convert her to an armed boarding vessel was based upon her First World War configuration, there were a few changes that had been initiated as a result of the lessons learnt during her previous war service. The most obvious change was that her main armament was not mounted directly onto her Forecastle or Poop Deck as it had been during the First World War. Her main armament consisted of two 4" guns (Quick Fire Mk IV) and one 12 pdr gun, although this latter gun was of dubious antiquity. The forward 4" gun was mounted on top of a raised platform which was known as a band stand. This meant that the gun was some 7ft above the Fore Deck, roughly level with the forward end of the Promenade Deck. Locating the gun on top of the band stand meant that it was now well clear of the seawater that had often flooded the forecastle during her previous naval service. The supports to this raised mounting were bolted onto a reinforced steel deck that had replaced part of the wooden planking.

This method of attaching the gun mounting to the forecastle would hopefully prevent the problem of the caulking between the deck planking working loose as a result of the vibration caused by the recoil of the gun when it was fired. The other 4" gun was mounted on the after end of the Promenade Deck, as was the 12 pdr gun. During the First World War, the *King Orry* had two 4" guns, which were mounted one on either side of the Poop Deck. Like the 12 pdr gun that had been mounted on the forecastle, they too had suffered from constant immersion in seawater during heavy weather.

To rectify this problem, a steel extension was now fitted to the after end of the Promenade Deck which protruded out over the Poop Deck for some 18ft and was supported by steel legs. The after end of this deck extension finished just above the emergency steering position. The after 4" gun was located on this deck extension, although its weight was supported by a mounting that was bolted onto the Poop Deck below, in a similar manner to that below the forward 4" gun. The 12 pdr gun was mounted directly onto the Promenade Deck, forward of the 4" gun, in more or less the same position as the after 12 pdr gun (replaced by a 3 pdr anti-aircraft gun) had been during the First World War. The raising of the *King Orry's* gun mountings to the level of the Promenade Deck not only prevented them from being engulfed in seawater but also meant that they had a greater arc of fire.

During the First World War the two 4" guns on the Poop Deck could each only traverse through some 90 degrees, with only one gun being able to bear on a target that was lying abeam. Now on its raised platform, the after 4" gun could traverse through nearly 200 degrees, with both the forward and after gun being able to fire at the same target, if it was laying abeam.

The only other guns that were fitted to the *King Orry* were two .303" Lewis light machine guns which were positioned on either side of the Boat Deck, just aft of the bridge.

A gunnery range finder was installed on top of the bridge roof in the position that had bee occupied by the search light during the First World War. The remainder of the conversion work carried out on the *King Orry* followed the pattern that had been undertaken in 1914, although on this occasion it had been decided that bridge wing houses would not be required. The saloons and sleeping cabins were converted into mess decks for the senior and junior ratings, while the officers occupied the cabins on the Promenade Deck. Unlike her previous conversion into an armed boarding vessel, the forward two pairs of davits on either side of the Boat Deck were not removed and she retained her full complement of eight lifeboats. A crow's nest was again fitted to the foremast.

The *King Orry's* crew was made up almost entirely from reservists and numbered some 85 officers and men, the majority coming from the Clyde and Sussex Divisions of the Royal Naval Volunteer Reserve.

Her commanding officer was Commander J Elliott RNR; he was a professional Merchant Navy officer who hailed from Deal in Kent. The *King Orry's* second in command or First Lieutenant was Lieutenant Commander E Gleave RNR, who, like his commanding officer, had also served in the Merchant Navy before the war.

The former Steam Packet engineers who had remained on board were also commissioned into the Royal Naval Reserve under the T124 scheme which

Fourth Engineer "Reggie" Scarffe standing alongside the **King Orry's** *after 12 Pdr gun at Sandon Dock, Liverpool in September/ October 1939. "Reggie" is still wearing his Steam Packet engineer's uniform. (Bernard Scarffe collection)*

meant that they volunteered to serve with the Royal Navy for the duration of hostilities. They wore naval uniform and came under naval discipline, although they retained their Merchant Navy rates of pay and conditions of service. This scheme was also open to Merchant Navy ratings.

Chief Engineer Stanley Cowley was commissioned as a Lieutenant (Engineer), while Second Engineer Lawrence (Laurie) Quine became a Sub Lieutenant (Engineer). The two remaining Manx engineers, Third Engineer H G (Griff) Hughes and Fourth Engineer J Robert Reginald (Reggie) Scarffe also entered the Royal Naval Reserve but the rank they were given is uncertain. They were not commissioned as engineer officers as their names do not appear in the navy list, the Admiralty publication that records all commissioned officers of the Royal Navy and its reserve elements.

A photograph that was taken of Reggie Scarffe a few weeks after the *King Orry* was requisitioned by the Royal Navy shows him still wearing his Steam Packet uniform while a photograph that was taken at a later date shows him in what appears to be a Royal Navy warrant officer's uniform. There were two other

Manxmen on board who came from the *King Orry's* Steam Packet crew and these were donkeyman George Campbell and greaser Arthur Corlett.

The dockyard workers took another couple of weeks to complete the *King Orry's* transition into an armed boarding vessel and, as work progressed, the remainder of the crew joined and provisions and ammunition were stowed on board in preparation for putting to sea.

Having been commissioned into the Royal Navy as an armed boarding vessel the previous day, His Majesty's Ship *King Orry* left Sandon Dock and steamed towards the Bar Lightship on the morning of 28th September 1939.

As she left the Bar Lightship astern, nobody on board had any indication that the River Mersey would never see the Manx steamer again.

When the *King Orry* had left the Mersey as one of His Majesty's Ships in November 1914, she had made her way north to the windswept Orkney Islands and Scapa Flow. Now, some twenty-five years later, and with the White Ensign once again flying from her mainmast, the *King Orry* turned to port and followed the North Wales coastline as she headed south into the Irish Sea. She had been ordered to proceed to the English Channel where she would join the Dover Patrol.

During the passage, the chief gunner's mate took the opportunity to exercise his gun crews and test the recently installed guns.

DOVER PATROL

The Dover Patrol had its Headquarters at Dover Castle in Kent. The officer in command was Vice Admiral Bertram Ramsey who had only recently rejoined the Royal Navy, having been placed on the retired list during 1938.

Vice Admiral Ramsey was well aware of the importance of patrolling the Straits of Dover as he had been part of the previous Dover Patrol during the First World War when he had been in command of the fleet destroyer *Broke*.

The *King Orry* would join a small fleet of auxiliary vessels that would patrol the English Channel and the Straits of Dover. Although her crew would not be subjected to the isolation and harsh weather conditions that their forebears had endured during the previous war when the *King Orry* had operated from Scapa Flow, operating in the English Channel was not to be a picnic.

The *King Orry* would operate between the ports of Dover and Ramsgate, although her main employment would be as either the South Downs or North Downs guard ship. In this role she would patrol the area to the north or south of the Goodwin Sands and stop any vessel that was suspected of carrying contraband or attempting to enter restricted waters.

The term 'South Downs guard ship' is not to be confused with the range of chalk hills bearing the same name which run through most of Sussex. The Downs is the name given to an area of sea off the eastern coast of Kent in proximity to the towns of Ramsgate and Deal. To the seaward side of the Downs lay the treacherous Goodwin Sands and the ships carrying out the duty of either North or South Downs guard ship were positioned to the north or south of this area, their main function being to assist with enforcing the Contraband Control Zone.

The Straits of Dover were classed as restricted waters and had been blocked by a series of mine-fields that stretched from the Goodwin Sands to Dunkirk in France.

Access through the mine fields and through the Straits of Dover was controlled by the British and French navies. Any merchant ship, including foreign and neutral vessels, wishing to pass through the straits were liable to be inspected to ensure that contraband was not being smuggled to the axis powers. Ships awaiting clearance to proceed would be escorted into the Downs to await inspection by contraband control officers, whose main base was at Ramsgate.

The *King Orry* would spend an average of seven to ten days on patrol, followed by a couple of days on stand down. During these periods she would anchor off Dover, Deal or Ramsgate and take on board stores, fuel and ammunition. If the crew were lucky, they might be granted a few hours shore leave when all work was completed, although consultation with former members of her crew has established that the luxury of a few hours ashore was not always forthcoming.

The first few months of the war were fairly quiet and are now often referred to as the phoney war. Although the German army had not begun its campaign against France and the Low Countries, and its air force had not started its heavy air raids over the English mainland, the German navy had demonstrated that it meant business from the commencement of hostilities.

On the very day that war was declared, and without warning, the 13.000-ton Donaldson liner *Athenia* was torpedoed by the U boat *U30* in the north west approaches. While the British were still debating whether the unprovoked attack on an unarmed passenger liner was a lawful act of war, the German navy struck again, this time a disastrous blow against the Royal Navy. On 17th September, as the ageing aircraft carrier *Courageous* was on patrol in the south west approaches, the *U29* sank the First World War veteran with a salvo of torpedoes.

The Royal Navy had moved its major units back to the safety, or so they thought, of Scapa Flow during late August 1939 but unfortunately the German navy soon demonstrated that its impregnability during the previous war was no longer so.

At just after midnight on 14th October, a daring U boat Commander manoeuvred the *U47* into the impregnable anchorage and sank the 29.000-ton battleship *Royal Oak* with just three torpedoes, with a loss of over 800 officers and men. The sinking of the *Royal Oak* within the so called safety of Scapa Flow, and the subsequent large loss of life, shattered the myth of the Royal Navy's invincibility and numbed the population of Portsmouth, the *Royal Oak's* home port.

Although the role of the *King Orry* and her consorts was tedious and repetitious, there were occasions when they would have to enforce the Contraband Control Zone regulations by threatening to open fire on ships that were reluctant to comply.

Ordinary Seaman Jimmy McCallum.joined the King Orry in September 1939 and was wounded during Operation Dynamo. (David Handscombe collection)

To the Captain of a merchant ship, even during wartime, any delay in delivering his cargo could result in financial penalties and the possible loss of a cargo for the return trip home. To this end, many foreign Captains were reluctant to obey the demands of the Royal Navy and would attempt to outrun the patrol vessels. When this occurred the *King Orry* would give chase and attempt to stop the absconding vessel by firing a few shells across the bow.

Once the merchant ship had been stopped, an armed boarding party would be put on board to ensure that the demands of the Royal Navy were obeyed. The anchorage where the suspect vessels were grouped prior to inspection was approximately one and half miles of shore the town of Deal and was often very crowded. Due to the proximity of the notorious Goodwin Sands and the sandy nature of the sea bed, there was always the risk that a ship might run aground.

GOODWIN SANDS

Able Seaman Joseph Jones recalled such an incident on the evening of 6th October 1939, when the Brocklebank Line's 6.690 ton steamer *Mahratta* ran onto the treacherous sands in the failing daylight as her Captain attempted to manoeuvre around the ships already at anchor. Dawn on 7th October revealed the *Mahratta* aground on the Fork Spit, which is at the western-most extremity of the Goodwin Sands, approximately three miles from Deal.

Over the next few days attempts were made to remove the stricken vessel and some progress was being made until disaster struck on 11th October. During the afternoon, a south-westerly gale developed and waves soon began to pound the side of the beached steamer. As the afternoon progressed, sounds of straining steel began to emulate from within the ship. Suddenly, at just before 16.00 the *Mahratta* began to tear apart, rivets snapped and her hull plates began to separate. Within thirty minutes the steamer had broken her back and became a constructive total loss, joining the long list of ships that had met their end on the Goodwin Sands.

Joe Jones recalls that the *King Orry* had left the scene of the grounded *Mahratta* on the morning of 8th October but when she returned on 12th, he found it hard to believe that the *Mahratta* had been transformed into a mass of twisted steel in such a short time.

As the weather slowly deteriorated over the next couple of months, the *King Orry* continued with her duties without major mishap until the morning of 1st December.

King Orry

A severe gale was blowing and the *King Orry* was attempting to shelter in the lee of the breakwater at Ramsgate. Poor visibility added to the difficulty in manoeuvring in the heavy swell and unknown to the *King Orry's* captain, the tanker *British Councillor* was also trying to seek the shelter offered by the breakwater.

Suddenly the tanker loomed out of the murky weather and began to bear down on the *King Orry*. Before either ship could take any evasive action, the *British Councillor* struck the *King Orry* amidships on the port side, the collision causing considerable damage to her hull plating and superstructure. She had a large hole in her port side, which extended from just above the water line at Main Deck level and reached up as far as the Shelter Deck. The bulwark on the Shelter Deck had been ripped away for a distance of some twelve feet, with the bulwark on the Promenade Deck suffering similar damage. The steel supports to all three decks had been buckled and the deck planking had suffered consequential damage.

The extent of damage sustained by the *British Councillor* cannot be confirmed, but an entry in the "Lloyds Weekly Casualty Report" dated 1st December 1939 records the following:

*Able Seaman Alf Haines examines the damage to the **King Orry's** Shelter Deck on 1st December 1939. (David Handscombe collection)*

*The damage to the port side of the **King Orry's** Shelter Deck caused during her collision with the tanker **British Councillor** on 1st December 1939. Leading Seaman Kemp is seen leaning over the side. (David Handscombe collection)*

British Councillor in collision off Ramsgate today - Starboard anchor and cable carried away, Stem bar bent and several plates badly twisted.

A further report records that the *British Councillor* arrived at Grangemouth (Firth of Forth) on 6th December, still carrying the scars of her confrontation with the *King Orry*. What happened to the *British Councillor* after the collision is not recorded, but the *King Orry* limped into Ramsgate Harbour and secured alongside the breakwater to allow an assessment of the damage to be carried out.

The hull below the water line was found to be watertight but some of the plates were buckled and would have to be replaced when the more obvious damage was repaired. Following emergency repairs to ensure that the hole above the water line remained watertight, the *King Orry* was ordered to proceed to West India Dock on the River Thames to enable a thorough inspection of the damage to take place.

LONDON

The *King Orry* arrived off the entrance to West India Dock twenty four hours later and after waiting for tugs, was moved into the basin and secured alongside the wall, adjacent to warehouse J.

Unlike the naval dockyards or shipyards such as Cammell Laird, the West India Dock did not have extensive repair facilities and a dry dock was not immediately available and so she had to remain secured to the dock wall until one became available.

Civilian contractors came on board at 08.00 the following morning and inspected the damage. They confirmed that the ship would have to enter a dry dock to allow repairs to the hull plating to be completed but work would begin on the damaged Shelter Deck and Promenade Deck within a few days, as soon as manpower could be moved from other ships that were also under repair.

This unscheduled repair period was also utilised to install degaussing equipment. The Germans had introduced a magnetic mine that was dropped by parachute and then sank to the seabed. The mine was detonated by the magnetic field that is created by a ship as it moves through the water and degaussing equipment reduced this magnetic field and allowed ships to pass safely. Unfortunately, it did not render the mine safe and any ship not fitted with degaussing equipment could still detonate it.

Although the temporary non-availability of the *King Orry* for patrol duties no doubt frustrated the hierarchy of the Dover Patrol, her crew rejoiced at the opportunity of a prolonged period of shore leave.

*Able Seaman Ray Hughes joined the **King Orry** in September 1939 and was wounded during Operation Dynamo. (David Handscombe collection)*

With the centre of London being only a few stops away on the tram, the crew took every opportunity to get ashore. The Luftwuffe had not yet commenced its blitz against London and so, apart from the black out, the city could still offer the sailors a night on the town.

Good news came a few days before Christmas when it was announced that one watch would be given leave over Christmas and the other would have leave over the New Year.

Joe Jones and Ray Hughes were fortunate enough to be given a few days leave over the Christmas period, while Jimmy McCallum from Paisley went home to Scotland for Hogmanay. Joe and Ray travelled to their home town of Connah's Quay in North Wales together, both of them carrying a small present. Joe would give his present to his aunt while Ray would give his to his fiancée Alice.

Unbelievably, even though the country was at war, organisations such as the NAAFI (Navy Army and Air Force Institute) were still able to supply servicemen with items of jewellery made out of silver. The presents that both Joe and Ray carried were small silver brooches that had been made in the form of a ship's crest. They depicted the three legs of Man emblem enclosed within a rope wreath and surmounted by a naval crown. A scroll beneath the rope wreath carried the name HMS *King Orry*.

*Able Seaman Joe Jones joined the **King Orry** in September 1939 and survived her sinking on 30th May 1940. (David Handscombe collection)*

Chapter Nine

Both brooches still survive: Joe now has his aunt's, while Ray's is still in the possession of his wife. Admiralty records reveal no record of an official crest ever being allocated to the *King Orry* during the Second World War and it is therefore probable that the small silver brooches are the only example of what the *King Orry's* Royal Navy crest may have looked like, had it ever been issued.

1940

New Year's Day 1940 found the *King Orry* still berthed adjacent to warehouse J in the West India Dock.

Joe Jones, Ray Hughes and the remainder of the first leave party had returned on board a couple of days after Christmas, which had allowed the second leave party to reach their homes in time for the New Year celebrations.

Although the work on repairing the collision damage was progressing, it was not progressing very quickly. The damaged hull plating above the water line, bulwarks and deck supports had all been removed as had sections of the wooden planking. While these sections were being removed, electricians had been busy installing power cables and items of equipment

The aft 12 pdr gun being loaded by A/B Hester, Sam Jones and Bill Dorwood. (David Handscombe collection)

that would be used when the degaussing gear was installed.

The Captain eventually informed the crew that the *King Orry* would enter dry dock on the afternoon of 4th January but before this could happen all ammunition would have to be put ashore. Ordnance artificers from the naval dockyard at Chatham arrived on the morning of 3rd January and commenced defusing all ammunition before it was taken ashore for storage.

The crew was mustered at 13.00 the following day and began to make preparations to move the *King Orry* into the dry dock. The dock pilot arrived on board at 14.00 and twenty minutes later two tugs were secured.

By 15.30, the *King Orry* had been moved into the dry dock and the pumps had begun to empty it of water. The following morning, 5th January saw work begin to remove the remainder of the damaged hull plating and once it had been replaced, the ship's bottom was cleaned and given a new coat of anti-fouling paint. One of the last jobs that was undertaken before the *King Orry* was ready to be moved was the installation of the degaussing loop that surrounded the hull.

With *King Orry* in dry dock, facilities on board were not very good. The crew had to use toilets on the dockside and bathrooms on board another ship. Due to

*The **King Orry's** ship's crest in the form of a silver brooch. These were purchased by members of the crew from the ship's NAAFI at Christmas 1939. They are the only known portrayals of the King Orry's Royal Navy crest. (David Handscombe collection)*

the boilers being shut down, there was no steam to supply any form of heating and as a result the ship was very cold.

Within a few days of entering the dry dock, scaffolding surrounded the *King Orry's* hull and she had a gaping hole in her port side. The whole ship echoed to the sound of hammers beating against the ship's side as rivets were inserted to hold the new hull plating in place. Although dockyard workers swarmed over the ship, there was very little work for the crew to carry out. Adding this lack of employment to the hardship of living on board a barely habitable ship prompted the Captain to send the majority of the ship's company on an extra ten days leave, commencing on 19th January.

The work to repair the damage to the hull plating was completed on 23rd January although the repairs to the damaged Shelter Deck and Promenade Deck were to take a few days longer. Now that the hull plates were repaired, a team of contractors finished repainting the ship's bottom. With the hull repairs completed and the bottom repainted, the *King Orry* was ready to leave the dry dock on 29th January.

The crew had returned from leave that morning and were immediately set to work to bring the *King Orry* back into a ship-shape condition. The decks were scrubbed and parties of men began repainting areas of rust-streaked superstructure. The degaussing equipment had been installed but could not be tested until the vessel was afloat with her engines and generators working.

The dry dock was flooded at 07.30 the following morning and by 10.00, the *King Orry* had been towed from the dock and secured alongside the foundry shed in the Blackwall Basin although contractors were still working on board, completing the finishing touches to the Shelter Deck and Promenade Deck.

The *King Orry* remained in the Blackwall Basin until the morning of 7th February. An oil barge had delivered 110 tons of fuel oil on 2nd February and the ammunition was brought back on board on 5th February. Even though the *King Orry's* boilers were now heated by fuel oil, a small quantity of coal was still required on board as the ovens in the galley were still heated by coal fires and 4 tons of coal was taken on board once the ammunition had been secured within the magazines and lockers.

On the afternoon of 6th February, the Flag Officer in charge of the Pool of London, Rear Admiral Black, visited the ship and inspected the repair work for a couple of hours, after which he returned to his office to initiate the issue of sailing orders.

The orders duly arrived in the early evening and instructed the captain to take the *King Orry* to sea on the morning high tide, the following day. The weather on the morning of 7th February was clear but bitterly cold. The crew enjoyed an early breakfast and was mustered at 07.00 to make the final preparations for the *King Orry* to leave the Blackwall Basin and proceed down the Thames to open water.

The log records that a full head of steam was reported to the officer of the watch at 08.00 and the degaussing equipment was switched on for the first time.

The dock pilot, Mr Anderson arrived on board at 09.00, which coincided with the arrival of two tugs. The *King Orry's* crew were already fallen in at their harbour stations and they had the two tugs secured fore and aft within a few minutes, the *Crag* on the bow and the *Beam* on the stern.

The head and stern ropes were let go at 09.15 which allowed the tugs to pull the *King Orry* into the basin's south west lock. Having bid farewell to the dock pilot and the two tugs, the *King Orry* cleared the lock at 10.40 and entered the river, whereupon she was met by the river pilot, Mr Marshall, who boarded her from the tug *Vespa*.

Having assisted the *King Orry* with pointing her bow down river, the *Vespa* took up station astern and both vessels then moved forwards toward the estuary. Having spent such a long period immobile within the West India Dock complex, it was necessary for the *King Orry* to have her compass recalibrated before she entered the open sea and to this end, she anchored off

The ***King Orry's*** *4" gun - April 1940 (David Handscombe collection)*

Erith at just after midday in order that a swing could be executed.

The compass adjuster, Mr Griffith, had been waiting in a launch for the arrival of the *King Orry* and clambered on board as soon as the anchor had been dropped. While the compass swing took place, the crew went for lunch.

Unfortunately, as lunch was being served, one of the cooks lacerated his left forearm with a carving knife and as the wound was fairly deep, a Red Cross launch was summoned to take him ashore for treatment at the nearby Erith Hospital.

With the compass swing successfully completed, the *King Orry* weighed anchor at 13.30 and recommenced her journey towards the sea. Having rounded Cold Harbour Point, she stopped off Gravesend to allow both the river pilot and the compass adjuster to be transferred to the tug.

RETURN TO DUTY

The *King Orry* then started making her own way back towards the Straits of Dover to recommence patrol duties. As she passed Sheerness, a naval launch came alongside and passed over route instructions for the remainder of her journey. The Nore Light Ship was passed at 15.30 and, as dusk approached, she anchored for the night off the Shivering Sands buoy, some 7.5 miles to the north of Herne Bay.

Having spent so many nights ashore in London, the gun crews and lookouts were given an abrupt reawakening to naval routine when they were ordered to remain closed up at first degree of readiness all through the night.

The *King Orry* weighed anchor at 07.20 the following morning and proceeded eastward along the Knob Channel until she rounded the Shingles Bank and turned south into the Edinburgh Channel, passing Margate at 08.30.

Having rounded Foreness Point, the northern-most tip of the east Kent coast, she headed towards the North Foreland. As she drew abeam of the headland, she encountered heavy fog and had to reduce her speed to dead slow. Fortunately, this reduced visibility did not prevent her from making her prearranged rendezvous with the armed boarding vessel *Lormont* at 10.00 and, having exchanged courtesies, the *King Orry* relieved the other vessel and took over duty as the North Downs guard ship.

The anchorage most frequently used for this role was near to the North Goodwin buoy, some three and a half miles south east of Ramsgate and four miles south west of the North Goodwin Lightship.

Unfortunately, the fog grew worse as the day progressed and the *King Orry* was forced to remain at anchor. As 9th February dawned, the *King Orry's* first full day as the North Downs guard ship began.

The thick fog that had hampered her movements on the previous afternoon persisted and she was yet again forced to remain at anchor throughout the day. Apart from keeping fog lookout, and being ready to close up at action stations at a moment's notice, the only activity of note that occurred during the day was when an Admiralty drifter, the *Lord Rodney*, eventually found the *King Orry*.

She had spent most of the morning creeping about in the fog asking each ship she encountered if they were the North Downs guard ship. Her arrival however brought good news as she had bags of mail on board for the crew and also returned the cook who had been sent ashore for treatment at Erith Hospital a couple of days earlier.

No doubt as the day progressed, some members of the crew thought that they had returned to the same tedious patrol routine that they had endured during October and November of the previous year. Prior to the collision with the *British Councillor*, the King *Orry* had spent a lot of time swinging around her anchor cable, just watching and waiting for something to happen.

However, dawn on the next morning, 10th February revealed a very different weather pattern. The fog had disappeared overnight and had been replaced by a strong wind that was blowing in from the east and causing a heavy swell.

The swell caused the *King Orry* to roll heavily and life became unpleasant for the members of the crew who had still not regained their sea legs. At just after 07.00, the crew were called to action stations when three unidentified aircraft flew overhead.

Fortunately for the airmen, the aircraft were identified as being friendly before the *King Orry's* gunners commenced firing anti-aircraft shells in their direction. No sooner had this threat receded when another situation presented itself.

At just after 08.00, one of the lookouts reported a steamer, the *Leonardo* making her way towards a restricted zone, apparently unaware that she was doing anything wrong. The *King Orry* hoisted a signal ordering her to stop but the Captain of the *Leonardo* either did not see the signal flags or chose to ignore them.

Having failed at the first attempt to stop the offending vessel, the *King Orry's* Captain ordered a blank 4" shell to be fired to bring the attention of the offending steamer's Captain to the fact that he had been ordered to stop. Almost unbelievably, the *Leonardo* remained on course towards the restricted zone.

The guard ships were required to maintain a full head of steam at all times and be ready to move at a few minutes notice. The Captain therefore gave the order to weigh anchor and give chase. Despite the weather conditions, the *King Orry* soon began to overhaul the *Leonardo* and two more shells were fired, although this time with live ammunition and two huge waterspouts shot up immediately in front of the offending steamer's bow.

The latter tactic proved successful and the *Leonardo* slowed down and finally hove to. Her Captain was informed that he was about to enter a restricted zone and that as a result of his actions, his vessel would be impounded until she could be inspected by contraband control officers.

By the time that the *Leonardo* incident had been dealt with it was nearing midday and the *King Orry* did not return to the anchorage that she had occupied during the previous night, but moved towards Ramsgate and anchored a few hundred yards from the breakwater.

After the crew had eaten lunch, she weighed anchor again and moved down towards Deal where she was due to meet the Admiralty drifter, the *Lord St Vincent*. During this rendezvous, she collected Lieutenant Commander Chamberlain who had been appointed to the armed boarding vessel for temporary duty before the *King Orry* returned to her anchorage in the North Downs.

As dusk approached the *King Orry's* crew looked forward to a peaceful night in their bunks and hammocks. Unfortunately, at 21.20, when most of the crew thought that their wish of a peaceful night had been granted, the alarm bells sounded and they had to rush to their action stations.

A signal had been received informing all ships in the area that unidentified aircraft were approaching from the east. As the gun crews reported that they were closed up, searchlight beams began to scan the sky from the direction of the coastline and gunfire could be heard from somewhere in the darkness, although it was impossible to establish whether it was directed at the reported unidentified aircraft.

The crew was eventually fallen out just before midnight. Although aircraft had been heard overhead, they had not be visible from the *King Orry* and for a second time that day her gun crews had been denied the chance of an anti-aircraft shoot. Just as the crew had returned to their various mess decks, a large explosion was heard and a vivid flash was seen towards

*Able Seaman Ray Hughes mans one of the **King Orry's** Lewis machine guns as he prepares to defend the ship against attacks from German aircraft. Unfortunately, he appears to have forgotten to attach the magazine! (David Handscombe collection)*

the south. The cause of the explosion was not known, but it was probable that a mine had found an unsuspecting victim.

Shortly after 07.00 the following morning, a mine was spotted on the starboard beam at a distance of about a mile. The anchor was immediately raised and the *King Orry* moved cautiously towards the lethal weapon. With the thought of the large explosion and flash only a few hours previously still in their minds, nobody wanted this mine to claim the *King Orry* as a victim.

Having been issued with rifles, a group of seaman were mustered on the Boat Deck and as the *King Orry* drew abreast of the object, they opened fire. The bullets began to hit their target and cause little spouts of water to jump up all around it. Everyone braced themselves for the explosion but rather than explode, the mine suddenly sank below the surface and disappeared,

Following this incident, the *King Orry* returned to her anchorage and remained there for the remainder of the day.

The *King Orry's* involvement in the events of the previous two days would be repeated in similar circumstances for the next couple of months. Although she would not be involved in any confrontation with enemy warships, her crew would see much evidence of enemy action. Large amounts of wreckage drifted past on the afternoon of 12th February, while on the following day her gun crews would respond to numerous reports of enemy aircraft approaching. On each occasion the aircraft remained distant and her guns remained silent.

Following a week acting as the North Downs guard ship, the *King Orry* was relieved by the *Lormont* early on the morning of 14th February.

Once the handover had been completed, she moved to Dover, entering the harbour at just before 09.00. She was met by the tug *Simba*, which, after securing a rope to the *King Orry's* bow, moved her alongside the tanker *War Sepoy*. Once secure, the water barge *Aqua* was also brought alongside to replenish her tanks with fresh water.

Having taken on board 120 tons of fuel oil and refilled her water tanks, the *King Orry* left Dover Harbour via the eastern exit at just before midday.

Once clear of the harbour, she turned northwards and steamed up to Deal where she arrived at 12.30 and anchored off the beach. The motor launch *Fervant* came alongside during the afternoon and delivered mail, fresh bread and meat. The ship remained at anchor until the morning of 16th February, when at 07.00 she proceeded to relieve the *Lormont* as the North Downs guard ship.

Over the next few days, she lay at anchor near the North Goodwin buoy, occasionally weighing anchor to intercept shipping that was heading towards restricted waters.

At 07.30 on 18th February another floating mine was spotted near to the North Goodwin buoy and the *King Orry* remained at anchor as it drifted past, although she quickly summoned a minesweeper from Ramsgate. This arrived about an hour later and duly dealt with the lethal weapon. The minesweeper then moved away from the *King Orry's* position shortly afterwards and dealt with two other mines, their demise being signalled by loud explosions to the north east later in the morning.

During the afternoon one of the crew became unwell and the Captain asked for a medical officer to be brought out. The motor launch *Fervant* eventually arrived with Dr Palmer, the Admiralty Surgeon and agent from Ramsgate before the patient, Petty Officer Peckham, was taken ashore to hospital shortly afterwards.

Heavy gunfire was heard to the south of the *King Orry's* position throughout the morning of 20th February but, as thick fog moved in during the early afternoon, the sounds of gunfire ceased. The fog finally cleared as dusk approached and at 07.30 the following morning the *Lormont* arrived to relieve the *King Orry* as guard ship.

Just as when she had been relieved by the *Lormont* on 14th February, the *King Orry* sailed to Dover to take on fuel oil and water from the tanker *War Sepoy* and the water barge *Aqua*.

The *King Orry* arrived at Dover at 10.30 and having filled her oil and water tanks left the harbour by the eastern exit at just after 13.00. However, on this occasion she was ordered to relieve the armed boarding vessel *Goodwin* as the South Downs guard ship.

The *Goodwin* was relieved at 14.30 after which the *King Orry* dropped her anchor near the southern end of the Goodwin Sands in a position approximately one mile from the Kent coast and two and a quarter miles north-west of the South-West Goodwin buoy. Shortly after anchoring, the Admiralty drifter *Lord Collingwood* came alongside and delivered mail.

At this time, none of the *King Orry's* crew had any inclination that this small drifter would play a very significant part in their lives in the not too distant future. The *King Orry* remained at her anchorage until the morning of 26th February when she was relieved by the auxiliary vessel, *Holdfast*. The *King Orry's* spell as South Downs guard ship has been uneventful, although gunfire and large explosions could be heard to the south of her position throughout this period.

*Bracing themselves against the bitter cold, members of the **King Orry's** crew assemble for snow clearing duties during the winter of 1939. (David Handscombe collection)*

The *King Orry* then weighed anchor at 08.30 and proceeded along the Kent coast, stopping off at Deal for a couple of hours before finally dropping anchor outside the breakwater at Ramsgate.

During the afternoon, the tug *Guardsman* came out and delivered mail while the launch *Fervant* again brought out Dr Palmer. He had come to collect a sick member of the crew, Steward Davis, who needed to be hospitalised ashore.

AT ANCHOR OFF RAMSGATE

As dusk approached, the *King Orry* moved further inshore and dropped anchor just off the breakwater. As the crew had finished their work for the day, it was announced that leave would be given to the non-duty watch that evening, which would be the first leave that they had been given since the *King Orry* had left the West India Dock on 7th February.

A launch came alongside at just after 18.00 and took members of the off-duty crew ashore. The liberty men were allowed to remain ashore until the following morning but for those who wished to return on board that night, a launch was provided at 23.00.

Joe Jones and Jimmy McCallum were not amongst those allowed ashore. Unfortunately, the liberty men who had returned to the *King Orry* at 23.00 were not given the luxury of climbing into their bunks and hammocks to sleep off their run ashore as, shortly after they had returned, unidentified aircraft flew over the harbour and the ship was called to action stations. However, the air raid warning was short lived and the crew was stood down as the aircraft flew off into the night without attempting to attack either the town or the ships in the harbour.

The *King Orry* remained at anchor throughout the following day although a launch came alongside at 08.30 and brought back the few liberty men who had remained ashore all night. Most of them now realised that Ramsgate during February was not the best place to remain ashore as after the pubs had closed there was little to do, and those of them that had not been lucky enough to find somewhere to sleep had huddled together in the railway station waiting room.

Leave was again granted at midday and this time Joe Jones and Jimmy McCallum were lucky enough to get ashore. As the *King Orry* did not have any suitable boat with which to take them, a local launch was hired and it was from this that Joe took a photograph of the *King Orry* as she lay off the breakwater. This has proved to be the only picture discovered to date, that depicts the *King Orry* in her Second World War configuration. The picture is now water stained and the reason for this will

*The King Orry at anchor off Ramsgate on 27th February 1940. This is the only known photograph of the **King Orry** that shows her during the Second World War. (Joe Jones)*

be come apparent when the final stages of the *King Orry's* story unfolds.

The 28th February found the *King Orry* at anchor again off Ramsgate throughout the day but on this occasion no shore leave was given as the crew were all employed repainting the Promenade Deck.

At 08.30 on 29th February, the *King Orry* weighed anchor and proceeded to Dover where she was scheduled to take on oil from the *War Sepoy*. During the refuelling period fresh water would also be taken on board from the *Aqua*. This was completed by midday and shortly afterwards, the *King Orry* sailed from Dover Harbour. After her few days stand-down from duty she was due to rendezvous with the armed boarding vessel *Lormont* off the Goodwin Fork buoy and relieve her as the South Downs guard ship.

February and March 1940 were bitterly cold months with frequent blizzards blowing in from the east making life very unpleasant for those members of the *King Orry's* crew who were required to work on the Upper Deck. Joe Jones recalls that on one occasion when he was messenger on the bridge, a blizzard had reduced visibility to no more than a few feet in front of the bridge windows.

As the lookouts on both bridge wings could see little more than those fortunate enough to be in the wheelhouse, the Captain ordered that they should be brought inside to prevent them from catching hypothermia. When the snow was not making life in exposed positions unpleasant, strong easterly gales whipped up the sea causing the *King Orry* to pitch and roll heavily as she laboured about her duties.

The crew of the *King Orry* came from all walks of life, some were former merchant seamen but the majority came from non-nautical, civilian backgrounds. For example Joe Jones and Ray Hughes had both been steel workers at John Summers Steel Works at Shotton, although Joe had spent a couple of years at sea as a fisherman when he had left school.

Their friend Jimmy McCallum had been a tailor. The only prior connection that many of the crew had with the sea was that they had joined the Royal Naval Volunteer Reserve a few months before the war started and had spent a couple of hours a week, and the occasional weekend, on board a drill ship, albeit in most cases a concrete one. Jimmy recalls that when the crew discovered he had been a tailor before the war, his skills were soon utilised.

The uniforms that the reservists had been issued with came direct from the naval stores and were not made to measure like those issued to the peace time members of the Royal Navy. Their bell-bottom trousers lacked the traditional bell-shaped flare and their jackets were only a loose fit. Jimmy McCallum was kept busy altering both jackets (or jumpers as the Royal Navy call them) and trousers, reshaping them so that their wearers looked like the traditional Jack Tar when they went ashore.

The *King Orry's* Captain, Commander Elliott, had joined the ship as a Lieutenant Commander and was promoted to Commander shortly after the *King Orry* had commissioned. The Captain wanted the extra gold stripe sewing onto his jacket and the gold braid attaching to the peak of his cap. His steward had informed him that Jimmy had been a tailor and the young Scotsman was soon tasked to alter his commanding officer's uniform. It took about an hour to attach the extra gold stripe to the sleeves and the braid to the cap. However, before the jacket and cap were returned to their owner, one of the seamen asked if he could borrow them in order that he could have his photograph taken wearing them alongside the emergency steering wheel on the Poop Deck. As this would only take a few minutes, Jimmy agreed.

Unfortunately for Jimmy, a few more members of the crew decided that they also wanted their photographs taken wearing the Captain's uniform and before long a queue had started to build up. As the sailors poised for their photograph, their laughter attracted the Master's attention and needless to say, when he peered down at the sailors, he was not amused and Jimmy was summoned to his cabin.

However, he did not receive the reprimand he had anticipated but instead the Captain thanked him for his work and offered him a ten shilling note. Jimmy must have looked surprised, for the Captain apologised and took it back, giving him a pound note instead.

CHARACTERS

Ships will always have characters that stand out from the other members of the crew and the *King Orry* was no exception.

Able Seaman Alfie Haynes and a seaman who was known as Hestor filled these positions. Alfie Haynes was in the same watch as Jimmy McCallum and was noted as being an exceptionally good poker player. The members of his watch would often cover his duties for him and allow him to slip away to the stokers' mess deck which had a well organised, if somewhat illegal, card school.

Before going down to the mess, he would collect a couple of shillings from each member of the watch. Jimmy McCallum recalls that nine times out of ten Alfie Haynes would return from the game triumphant and repay everybody with a profit.

On another occasion Alfie failed to turn up for the muster at the end of his watch and some time later he appeared in the seamen's mess deck having stained his skin dark brown with cocoa and wearing a turban and a sarong, both made from towels. He then proceeded to play a tin whistle and everybody watched with amusement as an imitation snake, also made from towels began to rise from a wicker basket that he had placed in the middle of the mess. The snake was attached to sail-maker's yarn that had been hooked over a deck head pipe and was tied to one of Alfie's arms. As he moved his arms up and down, the snake acted accordingly. It was light-hearted entertainment such as this that helped to pass away the boredom during the periods when the *King Orry* was acting as guard ship.

The other character on the seamen's mess deck was the seaman called Hestor who would strut around the ship carrying a bugle. One night while the ship was in the West India Dock, he disappeared and despite a thorough search of the ship he was not found. On the following night he was heard playing his bugle somewhere on board and another search of the ship was commenced. He was eventually found with a beaming smile on his face, huddled up in a sleeping bag in one of the lockers beneath a set of bunks.

He was promptly arrested and, still with a smile on his face, was taken ashore under escort and handed over to the police to await the arrival of the naval patrol. His escort was a young nineteen-year-old seaman and once they were ashore Hestor had suggested that they both went for a farewell drink as it was obvious that he was destined for a period of imprisonment in the naval detention quarters.

One drink led to another, then another, and before the evening was over, both prisoner and escort were drunk. The landlord had to send for the military police as both sailors refused to leave the premises. By the time that they arrived, the seaman acting as Hestor's escort had decided that he was not going to hand his prisoner over to the army and this culminated in a fight with the military police. Eventually the sailors were overpowered and both were handed over to the civilian police to await the arrival of the naval patrol. The young nineteen-year-old sailor was eventually returned to the *King Orry* to await the wrath of the Captain but Hestor was never seen on board again.

PHONEY WAR ENDS

Despite appalling weather conditions, the *King Orry* continued with her patrol duties throughout March and April, although the weather did start to improve as April drew to a close.

On 23rd March, the *King Orry* had a record score when she destroyed five floating mines within an hour, using only rifle fire. One was rather close to the ship and she was given a violent shaking when it exploded.

While the ship lay at anchor at Ramsgate on 29th March, Joe Jones celebrated his 19th birthday. The occasion was enhanced later in the day when the mail arrived on board and Joe received a birthday cake from home. This he duly shared with his messmates.

While on Patrol, unless a attack was imminent, the *King Orry's* crew only closed up at action stations for a short period just before and just after dawn and dusk. This routine was standard practice throughout the Royal Navy as the half-light at dawn and dusk were considered to be the ideal time to sneak up upon an unsuspecting enemy.

During action stations, Joe Jones was employed as part of the six man crew that manned the 12 pdr anti-aircraft gun located on the after end of the Promenade Deck, as were his friends Jimmy McCallum and Ray Hughes. The other members of the gun crew were Petty Officer "Bogey" Knight (in charge), George Pellett, and Sam Jones. Joe Jones states that members of

the 12 pdr gun crew were often exchanged with those of the 4" gun for trainingto ensure that each gun crew could fire another crew's gun, should the need arise.

The crew of the 12 pdr worked well as a team and were all good friends. However, Joe Jones recalls that he changed his opinion of one member of the gun crew following an incident which occurred while the *King Orry* was at anchor off Dover.

Joe had gone to the bathroom for a wash and found that one of the cooks was also there. Joe and this particular cook were good friends and they chatted away while they both washed themselves. The cook finished washing before Joe and left the bathroom but as he departed one of the other seamen from the 12 pdr gun crew came into the bathroom.

This particular seaman was a bit of a practical joker and rejoiced when he saw that the cook had left his false teeth on the shelf above the sink. Before Joe could do anything to stop him, he picked up the teeth and threw them out through the open port hole. Joe was appalled, but the other seaman thought that it was a great joke and walked out of the bathroom chuckling to himself. The cook never did find out what happened to his missing teeth and Joe never forgave the seaman for his cruel joke.

During March and April 1940, while the *King Orry* continued with her patrol duties off the Kent coast, the period known as the phoney war came to an abrupt end when Germany suddenly escalated her aggression towards the allied powers in Europe.

On the morning of 9th April, a peaceful Norway awoke to the sounds of battle as German troops, warships and aircraft began to attack its principal towns. The unprepared Norwegians fell back under the onslaught and Britain committed her armed forces to support her besieged ally on the following day.

Meanwhile, back in the English Channel, the tempo had also heated up. At dusk on 21st April, as the *King Orry* was being relieved by the *Lormont* as the North Downs guard ship, both ships came under attack from German aircraft and both returned fire, the *King Orry* engaging the aircraft with her 12 pdr gun and two Lewis light machine guns.

Neither ship scored any hits on the enemy but their concentrated fire forced the aircraft to fly off out of range. This brief action now over, the *King Orry* departed and left the *Lormont* to begin her patrol. Shortly afterwards, as the *King Orry* made her way to Dover to take on fuel and supplies, a German seaplane arrived on the scene and flew menacingly around the armed boarding vessel for a couple of minutes. The *King Orry's* gunners opened fire, forcing the seaplane to keep its distance.

*Members of the **King Orry's** 12 pdr gun crew prepare to carry out gunnery drill during April 1940. (David Handscombe collection)*

Suddenly the plane swooped down and over flew the Manx ship, its machine guns clattering and forcing members of the *King Orry's* crew in exposed positions to dive for cover. As the plane flew overhead a large cylindrical object attached to a parachute fell from the aircraft and splashed into the sea some 200 yards astern.

The seaplane then flew off, apparently unscathed, despite the anti-aircraft fire that the *King Orry's* guns had put up. It was assumed that the object dropped by the seaplane was a magnetic mine and the *King Orry's* captain sensibly kept his ship clear of the area. The parachute was floating on the surface but whether it was still attached to the mine could not be established from the distance that the *King Orry's* crew were observing it.

A hasty signal was sent to the naval headquarters at Ramsgate informing them of the incident. The reply to this signal ordered the *King Orry* to remain in the vicinity overnight and to warn other ships to keep clear of the area before a minesweeper could be sent out at first light to deal with the mine.

At just after 07.30 the next morning, a trawler that had been converted into a minesweeper arrived and relieved the *King Orry* from her lonely vigil, allowing her to continue to Dover. What became of the mine is not recorded but Jimmy McCallum recalls that the two

attacks on the *King Orry* that evening were the first that had actually targeted the armed boarding vessel since she had joined the Dover Patrol.

Although the crew of the 12 pdr gun were disappointed that they had not shot down any of the German aircraft, they were elated that they had at last fired their guns in anger at an enemy that was seeking to destroy their ship. As they sat in their mess deck that evening, they boasted that they had saved the *King Orry* and that the Luftwuffe had run away from the menacing guns of the little Isle of Man steamer.

German aircraft were now frequently seen flying over the Goodwin Sands and the Downs and the *King Orry's* gunners were called to action stations on numerous occasions over the next few weeks.

While she was patrolling to the north of the Goodwin Sands on 3rd May, a Dutch motor coaster known as a schuit came into view. These vessels were motorised seagoing barges and were a development of the towed barges so familiar on European rivers.

The vessel was identified as the *Pascholl* and she had already had a couple of altercations with the *King Orry*.

Her skipper was always in too much of a hurry to wait for the Channel convoys and attempted to make his own way through the restricted areas. The *Pascholl* was ordered to stop an order which her captain duly ignored. As this particular type of ship had a flat bottom and only drew few feet of water, the *Pascholl's* skipper was obviously well aware of the advantage that he had over the *King Orry* with her much deeper draught. As the coaster increased speed, she suddenly made a ninety-degree alteration to her course and headed straight for the Goodwin Sands, which were now hidden under the high tide.

The *King Orry* increased her speed to 19 knots in an attempt to head her off and to demonstrate that she meant business the forward 4" gun put a couple of shells across her bow. Unfortunately for the *King Orry* all her attempts to stop the Dutch coaster were to no avail and she was soon skimming across the Goodwin Sands and made good her escape. By the time that it would have taken the *King Orry* to steam around the sands and continue the chase, the *Pascholl* would have long since disappeared over the horizon. As on previous occasions, the *King Orry* was forced to abandon the chase.

While the *King Orry* busied herself with chasing ships such as the *Pascholl*, events on the other side of the English Channel were about to deteriorate as the Germans took another aggressive step.

DETERIORATING SITUATION

In a move similar to that which it had taken during summer 1914, Germany attacked Belgium on the morning of 10th May 1940.

German paratroops and glider-borne troops were dropped in proximity to the heavily defended Fort Eben-Emael which was located near the town of Liege on the Albert Canal, near to Belgium's border with Germany.

The Belgian troops were caught by surprise and despite a bitter resistance, the fort capitulated towards noon on the following day. German troops and armoured vehicles now poured into Belgium. At the same time as they were attacking Fort Eben-Emael, their paratroops were being dropped around the Dutch towns of Dordrecht, Rotterdam, Delft and The Hague. Although the Dutch Government had been prepared for an attack and had put her armed forces on full alert on 9th May, like their Belgian neighbours they were no match for the Blitzkrieg tactics of the army and luftwuffe.

Although the Germans were concentrating their efforts into attacking Belgium and Holland, they did not reduce their attacks on shipping in the Channel.

The *King Orry* again came under attack from aircraft on 14th May when a bomber swooped out of the clouds and dropped three bombs. Fortunately they all missed and exploded harmlessly in the sea less than two hundred yards away. She was due to secure alongside the tanker *War Sepoy* in Dover on the afternoon of 15th May but German aircraft had mined the approaches to the harbour and the port was now closed to shipping until minesweeping operations were carried out.

As the *King Orry* still had sufficient fuel for a couple of days she returned to her patrol duties, her Captain assuming that he would be allowed into Dover Harbour on the following day. Unfortunately, it took longer than had been anticipated to clear the mines and the Captain was informed that he would not be able to enter the port until the afternoon of 18th May.

By the afternoon of 17th May, the *King Orry* had nearly emptied her fuel tanks and by the following morning the situation was critical. As the *King Orry* slowly made her way towards Dover, the inevitable occurred. The oil fired blowers which heated her boilers went out and the *King Orry* slowed to a halt. Embarrassingly she had to summon the assistance of a tug and was ordered to return to sea as soon as she had refuelled to take over as the South Downs guard ship.

The rapidly deteriorating situation across the English Channel dictated that the Royal Navy needed to be ready to respond to any situation at short notice and this meant keeping all available warships at an immediate state of readiness for action.

On 15th May, while the *King Orry* was being turned away from Dover Harbour, the first of the disasters that would herald a domination of Europe by Germany occurred when Holland capitulated. Germany now concentrated its aggression towards Belgium and France and the beleaguered British Expeditionary Force (BEF) that had crossed the English Channel to support its allies the previous autumn.

Belgium collapsed on 28th May and the eventual fall of France was now a foregone conclusion. Even before Belgium had capitulated the British Government had decided that Britain must be able to stand alone and continue the fight against Germany. Secret plans to evacuate large numbers of troops from France and Belgium had already been drawn up.

On 26th May, two days before Belgium capitulated, Lord Gort, the Commander of the BEF had received instructions from Anthony Eden, the Secretary of State for War, advising him that he might wish to fight his way back to the French coast where all beaches east of Gravelines would be available to evacuate troops.

On the same day, Vice Admiral Ramsey received orders at his headquarters in Dover Castle to initiate the evacuation plan. The plan was to be codenamed Operation Dynamo and the events of the next few days would go down in the annals of British maritime history.

*Members of the **King Orry's** crew gather around her emergency steering wheel during May 1940. The crazing on this photograph is as a result of the negative being immersed in sea water during the loss of the ship on 30th May. (David Handscombe collection)*

King Orry

Operation Dynamo

The *King Orry* had been taken off regular duties as early as 22nd May and ordered to remain at anchor in the Small Downs and await further instructions.

Although the crew knew that Germany had invaded France, Belgium and Holland, they were unaware of the crushing defeat that the allies were facing as the German army and air force relentlessly attacked their positions.

Rumours began to spread around the ship that they were about to embark on some important mission, but nobody had any idea that this would involve rescuing thousands of soldiers from the beaches of Dunkirk.

Apart from cleaning up the ship and being at a moment's notice to close up at their action stations, the crew of the *King Orry* did not have a lot to do as she swung around her anchor waiting for her sailing orders to be issued.

To help pass the time, a few members of the crew decided to put lines over the side and attempt to catch some fish. As they were using scraps of food from the galley as bait, it was not surprising that they only caught a few dog fish which were not considered edible and were subsequently cut up for bait.

While the crew entertained themselves with their fishing escapades, the Captain and First Lieutenant were being summoned ashore to meetings at both Dover and Ramsgate. They returned back on board after one of these meetings with two tins of fish bait which they had acquired ashore. The tins were duly given to the fisherman and they were encouraged to catch as many fish as possible. No doubt the Captain had been given details of the number of passengers that the *King Orry* may have to carry once she commenced her new duties and he wanted to ensure that sufficient food was on board.

No sooner had the new fish bait been dropped, than the intrepid fisherman began to haul in some of the most edible fish that they had ever seen. The news soon spread around the ship and before long everyone who could be spared from his duty was casting a make shift fishing line over the side. The ship must have been anchored above a shoal as the decks were soon covered with fish of every variety. In the galley, the cooks were kept busy selecting the best before putting them into the cool room to await future use.

SAILING ORDERS

The long awaited sailing orders arrived at 09.00 on the morning of 26th May. The *King Orry* had been detailed to join the fleet that was being despatched to Dunkirk to commence the evacuation of the army before it was forced to surrender to the Germans.

Shortly after receiving her orders, the *King Orry* weighed anchor and moved to Dover to collect stores and to allow her Captain to attend a final briefing before departing for France. During the afternoon an Admiralty trawler came alongside and delivered piles of life jackets and a huge amount of fresh bread. Even though the *King Orry* had now been given her final orders, only the officers had been given the full details of their mission and the crew would have to wait until she was under way before they found out what was in store for them.

In order that the Germans should not be given any advance warning of the arrival of the rescue ships, the journey to Dunkirk would be made under the cover of darkness and to this end the *King Orry* and her consorts were ordered to sail from Dover at dusk.

At just after 21.30, the *King Orry* weighed anchor and began her passage to Dunkirk and the unknown while another former Isle of Man steamer, the *Mona's Isle*, had sailed from Dover some thirty minutes earlier.

The *King Orry* sailed with her crew closed up at their action stations and her gun crews pointed their weapons skywards as they waited for the inevitable onslaught from the German air force.

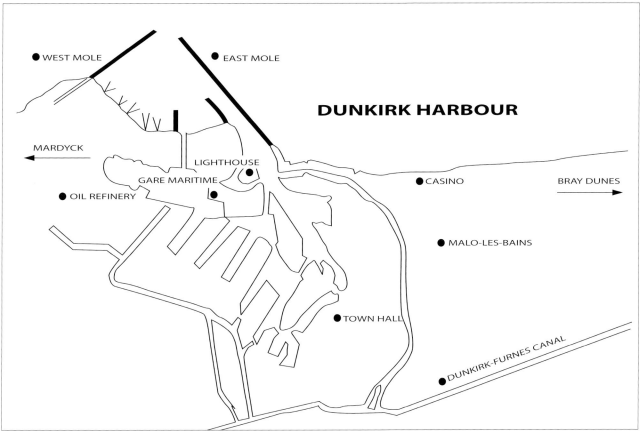

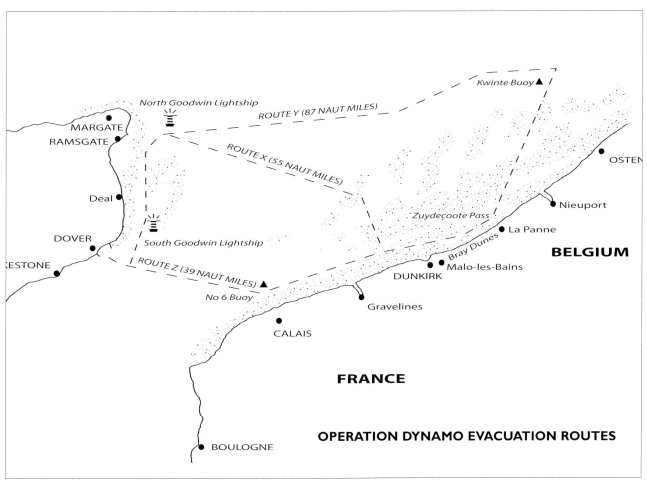

OPERATION DYNAMO EVACUATION ROUTES

No sooner had she got under way than the steamer ran into a fog bank and the visibility dropped to a few feet beyond the bow. The Captain decided to drop anchor and wait for it to clear rather than risk a collision with one of the other numerous vessels that were now dashing to and fro across the Straits of Dover.

By midnight the fog had cleared sufficiently for the *King Orry* to get under way again. Her course from Dover to Dunkirk was to take her across the Channel towards Calais and when she approached the port, she would turn eastwards at Buoy 6 and then steam parallel to the French coast towards Dunkirk. This route had been codenamed Route Z and was a total distance of some 39 miles.

Although patchy fog banks persisted, the passage over to Dunkirk was uneventful. As the *King Orry* neared the French coast a dull red glow could be seen in the vicinity of Calais indicating that the town was ablaze.

The crew had been finally briefed on the *King Orry's* mission during the passage from Dover and now, at just before 04.00 as they approached Dunkirk, the full horror of the battle for France confronted them.

Dunkirk had just had an air raid and large areas of the port and town were ablaze and thick black clouds of oily smoke billowed up into the sky from burning oil tanks.

As she slowly steamed into the harbour, the wreckage of war was all around. Jimmy McCallum recalls that the harbour entrance was very narrow and the *King Orry* had to creep past a burning ship that had been sunk alongside the breakwater just inside the entrance.

The *King Orry's* Captain, Commander Elliott, quickly decided that due to the narrowness of the harbour entrance it would be easier and safer for the *King Orry* to leave the port bow first, bearing in mind that she may have to make a hasty exit. To this end, he gingerly swung the ship before slowly taking her astern her down into the inner harbour towards a wooden jetty.

Turning the *King Orry* around in the tight confines of the harbour was fairly easy as her twin propellers made her very manoeuvrable, especially when going astern. Jimmy McCallum goes on to recall that as the *King Orry* moved alongside the jetty, it became obvious that it was rather rickety and was not strong enough the hold her weight. To emphasise this fact, a French official was seen running down the jetty towards the ship calling out and frantically waving his arms, beckoning that the *King Orry* must move away.

Noting that the *Mona's Isle* was berthed alongside a nearby stone quay, Commander Elliott took his ship away from the wooden jetty and berthed her astern of the other Manx steamer. The adjacent quay was littered with piles of rifles, equipment and abandoned army lorries which were being rendered unserviceable by soldiers.

Joe Jones was one of the first members of the crew to proceed ashore as he assisted with securing the berthing ropes to the bollards on the quay. He recalls thinking that this was the first time that he had ever set foot on foreign soil, however he was soon returned to reality as nearby explosions shocked him out of his momentary lapse of concentration.

As soon as the *King Orry* was secured and a gangway put in place, large columns of troops began to approach her. Despite all of the activity and confusion in the port area, the troops remained calm and waited for their turn to board the ship. As they streamed on board they were each given a piece of fried fish and a chunk of bread - the cooks had been busy with the supply of fish that had been caught a couple of days previously.

Ray Hughes recalls that it reminded him of the passage from the Bible when Jesus fed the 5,000 with loaves and fish. Jimmy McCallum mentions that he had never before seen anybody as grateful as these soldiers after they had been being given hot food. Looking cumbersome in the life jackets that they had been issued as they boarded, the soldiers were crowded into every nook and cranny. Ray Hughes was issuing the life jackets and remembers telling the recipients to hold them down by the front if they had to abandon ship as failure to do this could result in breaking their necks as they jumped into the water.

By 08.00, the *King Orry* had embarked 1,131 soldiers and the Captain had decided that it was now time for his ship to make her escape. Daylight had heralded the arrival of the Luftwuffe and their aircraft had swooped down on the ships and columns of troops, dropping bombs and firing machine guns at anything that moved.

The *King Orry* edged away from her berth at 08.03 and steamed out of the harbour. Her return route to England was to be a reversal of that she had used on her outward journey a few hours earlier.

UNDER ATTACK

Unknown to the *King Orry's* Captain, the Germans had occupied Calais and now in broad daylight any ship that steamed along the French coast presented herself as an ideal target. The *King Orry's* gun crews strained their eyes into the sky as they searched for aircraft but as they approached Calais, huge columns of water suddenly shot up all around the vessel, the only warning of their arrival being high-pitched whistles a few moments before.

The gun crews searched for the attacking aircraft and suddenly realised that they were under fire from German shore batteries. It did not take long for the German gunners to get the *King Orry's* range, and shells soon slammed into the armed boarding vessel causing casualties amongst her crew and the embarked soldiers.

One shell landed adjacent to the 12 pdr gun and showered the gun's crew with shrapnel. Joe Jones and Alfie Haynes were blown over by the blast but escaped injury.

Unfortunately, the remainder of the gun's crew had not been so lucky. Jimmy McCallum was nearest to the shell burst, was hit by its blast and knocked off his feet. Such was the force of the explosion that his sea boots were blown off, as was one of his trouser legs. He remembers that he landed near the after 4" gun and that he was in intense pain as a result of sustaining multiple shrapnel wounds in both legs.

Ray Hughes had been blown into the scupper, loosing his steel helmet in the process. At first he thought that he was uninjured but as he attempted to stand up, his left arm gave way and it was only then that he noticed that blood was pouring from above his elbow and that he now lay in a pool of blood. Petty Officer (Bogey) Knight was lying close by; his arms had also been ripped open by shrapnel. The fourth member of the gun's crew to be injured was Ged Pellett who had shrapnel wounds in his lower back and buttocks. The uninjured members of the gun crew pulled their wounded comrades under cover and Joe Jones states that there were pools of blood all over the after end of the Promenade Deck and that he feared for the life of his friend Jimmy McCallum who appeared to be badly injured.

The Captain immediately ordered a zig-zag course and turned the ship away from the coast. Although shells continued to fall around her, she received no further hits and was soon out of range. Although the *King Orry* was now out of range of the shore-based guns, the Luftwuffe had no problems and continued with the onslaught that the shore batteries had started.

Steaming at high speed on a zig-zag course, the *King Orry* raced across the English Channel throwing up a barrage of anti-aircraft fire. Finally, as the White Cliffs of Dover loomed up ahead, the German planes flew off to find another target nearer the French coast.

An initial assessment of the damage revealed nothing that would affect the *King Orry's* seaworthiness and she continued at over 19 knots towards safety. She arrived off Dover at 11.00 but had to wait her turn to get alongside the quay to commence unloading her human cargo.

A convoy of ambulances awaited as she secured to the quay and, once the gangways were put in place, a team of medical staff came on board to help the *King Orry's* crew take the wounded soldiers and sailors ashore. The wounded members of the 12 pdr gun crew were carried ashore by their shipmates. All wounded were taken to a hospital in the nearby town of Deal. The troops were kept on board the *King Orry* until the wounded had been landed but once this had been completed, the army officials ashore gave orders for the troops to disembark.

Apart from the four members of the 12 pdr gun crew who had been injured, there were many casualties amongst the embarked troops. A shell had exploded near a group of soldiers from the Royal Army Service Corps who were sheltering on the Poop Deck and five were killed and a further twenty wounded.

Once the troops had left the *King Orry*, a team of naval artificers came on board to assess the damage that she had sustained during her dash home from Dunkirk.

The degaussing loop had been ripped away from around the stern and had been severed in several places along the port side. The port side superstructure and after ends of the Promenade and Poop Decks were also peppered with shrapnel holes but luckily none of these were below the water line. The shells that had exploded on board the *King Orry* had fortunately not caused any serious damage.

It would take 24 hours to repair the damage to the degaussing loop and insert wooden plugs into the larger holes in the ship's side. The damage to the superstructure, Promenade and Poop Decks was not repaired as it was considered that it would not affect the *King Orry* putting back to sea and could be repaired at a later date.

The *Mona's Isle* had also returned to Dover having followed the same route as the *King Orry*. She too had fallen victim to the German shore batteries and had received several direct hits before she managed to get out of range. Like the *King Orry*, once she was out of the range of the shore batteries, the aircraft of the Luftwuffe had taken over, raking her decks with machine gun fire. She sustained 23 killed and 60 wounded before the entered the sanctuary of Dover Harbour.

Although Dover did not share the same degree of devastation that the *King Orry's* crew had witnessed at Dunkirk, the scene within the harbour was one of utter confusion.

Ships were berthing alongside each other as there was insufficient room to secure a berth on the quays, while ashore thousands of soldiers milled about as they waited for transport to move them to mustering points further inland. Dotted around the harbour buildings were numerous field kitchens that were being run by both the army and the civilian voluntary services that were providing hot tea and soup to the weary troops as they waited to be moved out.

INTO HELL A SECOND TIME

The essential repairs to the *King Orry's* structure and degaussing gear were complete by midday on 29th May.

No sooner had this news been relayed to the naval headquarters at Dover Castle than she received orders to proceed back to Dunkirk. The *King Orry* left Dover and set course for the French port at about 12.30 although on this occasion she would cross the English Channel by a longer route.

Owing to the German occupation of Calais, Gravelines and the surrounding coastline, the route by which the *King Orry* had steamed to Dunkirk on the morning of 27th May was now considered to be too dangerous and the entrenched German artillery was targeting the rescue ships as if they were on a fairground shooting gallery.

There were two other routes by which the ships could reach Dunkirk which had also been given a code name and were known as Route X and Route Y.

The shorter of these two alternative routes was Route X, which had a distance of 55 miles, whereas Route Y had a distance of some 87 miles. The more obvious of the two remaining routes to take was the 55 mile Route X. This would take the ships up through the Downs and out to the North Goodwin Lightship before turning southwards and heading across the English Channel towards the Ruytingen Bank, which lay off the French coast. After passing through the Ruytingen Bank, they would steam eastwards towards Dunkirk.

However, Route X was full of dangerous shoals and known to be heavily mined. The remaining choice, Route Y was by far the safest, even though it was the longest. As with Route X, the ships would pass northwards through the Downs and then out to the North Goodwin Lightship before turning eastwards and heading towards the Kwinte Buoy, which lay a few miles off Ostend in Belgium. On reaching the Kwinte Buoy, they would then take a dogleg turn to the south-west and steam parallel to the Kwinte Bank before passing through the narrow Zuydecoote Pass and into Dunkirk Harbour.Being conscious of the fact that the safety of the rescue ships must be paramount, Admiral Ramsey ordered all ships to use Route Y until minesweepers could sweep a clear channel through the shorter Route X.

Sadly, the *King Orry's* log books for this period did not survive but it can be assumed that she headed towards Dunkirk on the longer Route Y. This assumption can be supported by the fact that it took her over five and a half hours to reach the French port, arriving off the harbour entrance at just before 18.00 on 29th May.

The trip had not been without its hazards as the *King Orry* was moving at high speed and a sharp lookout had to be kept as the Luftwuffe was determined to stop the ships reaching their destination, and drifting mines were frequently seen in the slight sea swell.

Needless to say, the gun crews were closed up and everybody searched the sky as they waited for the inevitable arrival of German bombers. Replacements had joined the 12 pdr gun crew to take the place of the wounded sailors that had been landed at Dover, but little did they know that they were about to fight for their lives.

As the *King Orry* approached the French coast, palls of smoke could be seen rising in the proximity of Dunkirk. Black puffs of smoke could be seen bursting all over the sky as the ships put up a barrage of anti-aircraft fire in an attempt to fight off the merciless onslaught of bombs and machine gun fire from German aircraft.

Suddenly, it was the *King Orry's* turn to enter the fight for survival. Before anybody had time to shout a warning, a bomber appeared from nowhere and swooped down on the *King Orry*.

Joe Jones recalls that he could actually see the faces of the aircrew as their aircraft flew over the ship at masthead height. Half a dozen bombs dropped from its underside and landed in the sea all around the armed boarding vessel.

Huge mountains of water erupted into the air as they exploded, followed by a deluge as the water crashed back down onto the *King Orry's* decks. Shrapnel whizzed around the 12 pdr gun crew but miraculously nobody was injured.

As the water drained off the *King Orry's* decks, she emerged from the onslaught unscathed and raced on towards the harbour entrance. The gun crews worked frantically as they fed their guns with shells and added to the massive barrage of fire that shot skywards from the besieged warships.

The *King Orry* slowed down as she approached the harbour entrance as wreckage was floating everywhere and here and there could be seen the khaki uniforms of dead soldiers as their bodies floated in the oily slime that covered the surface of the sea.

The whole town of Dunkirk and its harbour installations seemed to be on fire making the *King Orry's* crew cough as they breathed in the toxic fumes from the oil tanks that burned nearby.

Without warning, the Luftwuffe again picked out the *King Orry* as a target. Stuka dive-bombers screamed towards the ship and released their deadly cargo through the hail of gunfire that the armed boarding vessel and her consorts were putting up. As the bombs exploded harmlessly all around the *King Orry*, her 12 pdr gun crew ducked down behind their gun and sought cover from the razor-sharp shrapnel that ripped into the superstructure and decks.

Suddenly one of the gun's crew lost his nerve and before anybody could stop him, he ran along the Promenade Deck and disappeared. Joe Jones states that this incident effectively stopped the 12 pdr gun from firing as the sailor who had deserted his post was responsible for inserting the fusing key into the shells, which armed them and enabled the gun to fire. Without this key the shells were useless and the 12 pdr gun fell silent. As there was no longer any point for the gun's crew to remain in an exposed position around their gun, the gun captain ordered them to run for cover.

THE FINAL ONSLAUGHT

The *King Orry* steamed through the harbour entrance between the ends of two long breakwaters which extended seawards and which was barely wide enough for a large ship to pass through. These breakwaters, or moles to use their correct name, extended out from the east and the west of the port, with the eastern mole being the longer at some 1,400 yards in length.

The moles, and in particular the eastern mole were not substantial stone structures and had never been designed as a berthing facility for large ships. It was constructed of concrete piling with a wooden walkway attached to the top. However, the importance of the eastern mole as a temporary berth for the numerous vessels that swarmed into Dunkirk Harbour had been realised the day before when it had been noticed that the Luftwaffe were concentrating their attacks on the inner harbour, leaving the mole unmolested.

Unfortunately, this reprieve did not last for long as the German pilots noticed that vessels were now using the mole instead of entering the inferno of the inner harbour. The *King Orry* had been ordered to berth on the inside of the eastern mole ahead of the sunken ships that now surrounded its seaward end.

Unknown to any of the *King Orry's* crew, the ship that was sunk on the outside of the mole was one of the Isle of Man Steam Packet's two newest vessels, the *Fenella*. Two bombs had hit her earlier in the afternoon: one had penetrated her Promenade Deck while the other had exploded between her side and the structure of the mole. Large chunks of concrete had been blasted through her hull plating below the waterline and her Engine Room had quickly flooded and she sank before the water ingress could be brought under control.

To approach her berth on the inside of the mole, the *King Orry* had to make a tight turn to port once she was inside the harbour. She had just commenced this manoeuvre when she came under attack again. A couple of Stuka dive bombers had singled her out as a target and swooped down towards her, the high-pitched scream from their wing-tip sirens filling the air.

Having run for cover from the 12 pdr gun, Joe Jones was about halfway down the Promenade Deck on the port side when the scream of the Stukas alerted him to the imminent danger. As he heard the whistling of their bombs when were released from beneath the aircraft wings, his instincts made him crouch down and seek cover alongside the bulkhead to one of the officers' cabins.

The *King Orry* suddenly bucked up into the air as at least two bombs exploded in the water alongside her stern. As she again settled back onto an even keel, she was rocked to port as more bombs exploded abeam of the bridge on the starboard side.

A split second after the first set of bombs had exploded, Joe Jones was struck on the buttocks by a heavy object which knocked him over and left him lying face down on the deck. His first thought was that he had been seriously injured but he soon realised that he was not in any great pain, his arms and legs still worked and there was no sign of any blood. Although his buttocks ached, he dragged himself to his knees and looked around to see what had struck him. To his surprise, he found that he had been struck by the heavy mahogany door of the cabin by which he had crouched. This had been blown open by the shock wave created by the blast from the bombs and the door was now swinging harmlessly to and fro with the motion of the ship. Having gathered his thoughts, he clambered to his feet and looked out over the ship's side to see what was happening.

The *King Orry's* slow turn to port after she had entered the harbour had saved her from a direct hit by the bombs. Although she had narrowly missed damage that would have probably sent her to the bottom of the harbour, she had not escaped unscathed.

The bombs that had exploded around her stern had caused considerable damage to her steering gear and wrecked her Poop Deck. The steering motors had been rocked from their mountings and the rudder was now jammed to port.

Shrapnel from the bombs that had landed along the starboard side had ripped through the bridge structure and smashed the steering wheel, binnacle and engine room telegraphs beyond repair.

Miraculously, although nobody had been killed or seriously injured, numerous holes had been punched below the water line, both around the stern and along the starboard side and were now letting water flood into the Engine Room, Boiler Room and stern compartments at an alarming rate.

With her steering gear out of action and the engine room telegraphs on the bridge damaged beyond repair, the Captain was neither able to stop the *King Orry* swinging to port nor inform the Chief Engineer to put the engines astern and stop her making headway.

Without steerage, the *King Orry* slowly moved ahead and continued her swing and before anybody could take avoiding action, she struck the east mole with a resounding crash.

As her bow dug deep into the structure, concrete piling collapsed and a section of the wooden walkway disintegrated leaving a gaping hole.

As Joe Jones leaned out over the port side, he had realised that the *King Orry* was not under control and had braced himself for the collision as he saw the mole looming up ahead. He recalls that there was a line of soldiers on top of the wooden walkway and as the *King Orry* crashed, some of them fell into the sea. Many were still wearing their heavy webbing equipment and were drowned before they could free themselves from its weight.

FATAL DAMAGE

Within seconds of the bombs exploding around the *King Orry*, the Engine Room staff had become acutely aware of the damage that she had sustained. As water poured in through the numerous holes in her starboard side, they quickly started the bilge pumps in an attempt to control the water level.

The damage to the steering gear and jammed rudder had been detected by the Chief Engineer who attempted to inform the bridge but soon realised that the telephone line was dead and that the telegraphs were not recording. Unable to advise the Captain of the situation, he made the decision to put the engines astern to prevent the *King Orry* from careering ahead out of control. Unfortunately this decision came too

*Her decks awash, the sunken **Fenella** laying against the seaward end of the East Mole on the afternoon of 29th May 1940. (Ships of Mann)*

late. With her screws racing astern, there was insufficient time to stop her headway before she buried her bow into the mole. Following the impact, Chief Engineer Stanley Cowley gave the order to stop the engines and after confirming that the pumps were coping with the ingress of water and that the fires below the boilers were still alight, he made his way to the bridge to give a situation report to the Captain.

Having arrived, he surveyed the damage around him and was amazed to find that it now looked more like a pepper pot rather than the former nerve centre of the ship with shrapnel holes punched through every bulkhead.

A few members of the crew who had either been on the bridge or in its immediate proximity had minor cuts caused by fragments of glass from the smashed windows or small splinters of wood from the bulkheads. He briefed the Captain about the condition of the Engine Room, Boiler Room and steering gear and then the two of them discussed the immediate priorities that they now faced with regard to keeping the *King Orry* afloat and putting her under way again.

Even with her rudder jammed slightly to port, it would be possible to steer the vessel by using her propellers and by frequently putting the starboard screw astern, it was hoped to counteract her constant swing to port. However, while discussing the possibilities of steering the *King Orry*, both the Captain and Chief Engineer noticed that she was starting to develop a slight list to starboard.

After the *King Orry* had collided with the mole and the Chief Engineer had stopped her engines, she had drifted clear of the collision site and had been pushed alongside the mole by the tide. The crew had quickly thrown lines to the many helping hands who still stood there and the *King Orry* was soon secured alongside.

Many of the crew, including Joe Jones, also began to notice that the *King Orry* was developing a list to starboard while the Chief Engineer hurried back down to the Engine Room to reassess the damage.

A Royal Navy Commander then clambered over the *King Orry's* bulwark and asked to be taken to the Captain. He was quickly taken up to the Boat Deck and introduced to Commander Elliot. Having witnessed the *King Orry's* dramatic arrival, the Commander was keen to establish whether the vessel was still in a seaworthy condition.

With two ships already sunk alongside the mole (the Isle of Man steamer *Fenella* and the armed trawler *Calvi*), the last thing he wanted was for the *King Orry* to founder at her berth and add to the congestion that was already causing problems for ships trying to get alongside.

While he was talking to the Captain, the Chief Engineer and his team were working frantically down in the bowels of the ship. Damage control teams were busy attempting to plug the holes that were letting water into the *King Orry's* Engine and Boiler Rooms, The Second Engineer, Sub Lt (E) Laurie Quince, and a team were trying to repair the damaged steering gear but unfortunately the repairs that were required were beyond the capability of the ship's staff and needed dockyard support.

However, they did manage to decrease the angle at which the rudder pointed and moved it back into a more central position, but the Commander informed the Captain that unless his vessel could be made sufficiently seaworthy to allow her to continue with her trooping duties, she was to be moved away from the berth and if necessary beached in shallow water outside the harbour.

Although as a beached vessel she would be of no more use to the evacuation, she could at least use her guns to help defend the ships that were still entering and leaving the port. Having finished his discussion with the Captain, the Commander left the *King Orry* as dusk approached. While the engineers were being kept busy down below, the remainder of the *King Orry's* crew was not left idle.

THE FINAL HOURS

The gun crews of the 12 pdr gun and after 4" gun were ordered to clear away the wreckage that lay around their gun mountings and then to man the guns and be prepared to provide anti-aircraft fire should the *King Orry*, or the eastern mole come under attack again.

Fortunately as dusk had now turned into darkness, the onslaught from the German air force had dwindled and the gun crews could relax a little.

The sailor who had run away with the vital key that fused the shells for the 12 pdr gun had been found and returned to his post. However, Joe Jones recalls that every member of the gun's crew watched him, in case he decided to abscond again. He also recalls that he looked up at the Boat Deck and was alarmed to see that most of the lifeboats had been reduced to scrap wood by the shrapnel that had rained down on the *King Orry* during her bombing ordeal and subconsciously checked that his lifebelt was still in place around his chest.

While the gunners cleared away the wreckage from the after end of the Promenade Deck, a group of seaman were being employed clearing away the wreckage from inside the bridge. With the engine room telegraphs and telephone line to the Engine Room destroyed, a portable damage-control telephone line was run between the bridge and the engineers' control position to allow the Captain to talk to the Chief directly.

The engineers and damage-control teams worked like trojans to repair the *King Orry* and make her seaworthy enough to resume her duties but by midnight it was apparent that they were only just keeping ahead of the ingress of water and that if the pumps failed, she would soon sink.

The naval Commander who had boarded the *King Orry* and spoken to the Captain a few hours earlier had returned on board at about 23.00. He discussed the *King Orry's* immediate future with the Captain and Chief Engineer and was informed that the steering motors were beyond local repair and that as the emergency steering wheels on the Poop Deck had been destroyed by the blast from the bombs that had exploded alongside the stern, the only way to steer the *King Orry* would be by using her propellers. The Chief Engineer went on to inform him that the pumps were only just holding their own and that any drop in steam pressure and subsequent drop in performance from the pumps may herald the vessel's demise.

The decision was made to continue with the repairs for another hour but by midnight when the tide was at its highest, if the situation was still the same, the *King*

The East Mole at Dunkirk viewed from the bridge of a destroyer during Operation Dynamo. Its fragile structure and the improvised gangways that the troops had to use are clearly shown. (Imperial War Museum)

Orry would have to leave the berth and proceed out of the harbour. She would then be beached in shallow water to prevent her becoming a hazard to other shipping using the main channel.

The official records state the *King Orry* went astern from the mole at just after 00.30 on the morning of 30th May and experienced difficulty in manoeuvring out of the harbour and pointing her bow seawards.

At about 02.00 she suddenly took on a violent list to starboard and foundered before she could reach shallow water.

The motor yacht *Bystander* was astern of the *King Orry* when she sank and her crew immediately began to rescue the survivors from the stricken vessel, pulling 32 of them from the sea before she left the scene. Three trawlers, the *Lord Grey*, *Lord Collingwood*, the *Clythness* and a motor launch from HMS *Excellent* (the Royal Navy gunnery school at Portsmouth) arrived shortly afterwards and assisted with the rescue. Although the *King Orry* rolled over onto her starboard side as she sank, daylight revealed her sitting on the bottom in an upright position with her funnel and masts protruding above the surface.

The most likely explanation for this is that she settled on a sand bank and was pushed upright by the motion of the tide.

JOE JONES' STORY

Able Seaman Joe Jones now takes up the story and recalls his experiences on board the *King Orry* during her final couple of hours.

The order to close up at harbour stations was given at just after midnight and Joe was released from the 12 pdr gun crew in order that he could proceed to the forecastle where he would form part of the forward berthing party.

Once the berthing ropes had been released and hauled back on board, the *King Orry* attempted to move astern away from the mole but without the use of her rudder and with a strong tide pushing her back against the mole, this manoeuvre proved to be more difficult than had been envisaged.

After a couple of attempts, the *King Orry* finally managed it at about 00.30 when the Captain decided to take the ship out of the harbour stern first and then turn the *King Orry* around once she was in clear water.

Joe recalls that the bombing had now stopped but the whole of the town and harbour installations appeared to be on fire. The surface of the sea was covered in oil and littered with wreckage of all types and the occasional khaki or navy blue-clad body bobbed up and down in the slight swell.

After about an hour of manoeuvring both ahead and astern, the *King Orry* finally cleared the harbour and moved stern first into the open sea but, as her bow began to swing seawards, the list to starboard suddenly began to increase.

In the meantime, Joe had been released from the forecastle party and had wandered down towards the galley where he had heard that the chefs had made jugs of steaming tea and plates of sandwiches for distribution to the crew and he intended to collect the ration for the sailors who still manned the 12 pdr gun on the Promenade Deck.

As he made his way to the galley, he passed by the NAAFI canteen and was surprised to see that the canteen manager was giving away the stock. Having enquired what was happening, he was informed that as it was obvious that the ship was going to sink, why should the stock go to the bottom of the sea as well? Joe was therefore advised to get a bag and fill it with whatever he wanted.

As most sailors do not have to be told twice to take something that is being given away, Joe found a bag and duly filled it with cigarettes, chocolates and sweets and having secured his unexpected gift, he continued on his way to the galley.

It was at this moment that the *King Orry* gave her sudden lurch to starboard and impressed upon Joe Jones that perhaps the canteen manager was correct about her sinking. Forgetting all about the tea and sandwiches in the galley, Joe quickly made his way up to the Boat Deck.

At the same time, the engineers in the Engine Room and Boiler Room were being confronted by a sudden deluge of water pouring in from all directions and the Chief Engineer soon realised that this new influx was going to be too much for the pumps to cope with. The increase was probably due to the many shrapnel holes that had been punched in the *King Orry's* side just above the waterline. While the ship was stationary at the mole they poised no threat but with her now moving through the water and rolling in the slight swell, the holes were now constantly being submerged.

Chief Engineer Cowley informed the Captain that he was no longer able to guarantee keeping a full head of steam as the rising water was in danger of putting the boiler fires out and there was also a danger of the boilers exploding if they became immersed in the cold

sea water. The Captain asked him to keep going as long as he could but not to put the lives of his men at risk if it was obvious that the battle against the rising water could not be won. The Captain then informed the First Lieutenant that it was probable that the *King Orry* would not stay afloat for much longer and that the plan to beach her in shallow water might have to be abandoned.

Meanwhile Joe Jones arrived on the Boat Deck. Although he cannot now remember why he chose to go there, at least he would not be caught below decks if the *King Orry* decided to take a sudden plunge. He checked that his lifebelt was still secure and then huddled into his duffle coat to keep warm, even though it was a fairly mild night.

As his eyes became accustomed to the dark, he looked around the Boat Deck and noticed that it was littered with the remnants of battle. The lifeboats hung in their davits, either smashed completely or peppered with shrapnel holes while shattered life rafts sat in their cradles and items of personal clothing and equipment lay everywhere. He then looked forward towards the bridge and, although he was aware that the ship was no longer being steered from there, he knew that the Captain would not be far from its shattered remains. Looking aft, he could see that the 12 pdr gun was not manned and wondered whether the remainder of the crew had decided like himself that it was time to think about survival if the ship sank.

The Boat Deck was cast in an eerie shadow of flickering shapes caused by the reflection of the flames in the water from the fires ashore. The whole horizon was a mass of flames and explosions as the Germans continued to shell the town and port facilities. Joe could see the eastern mole silhouetted against the flames and estimated that the *King Orry* was still in the main channel and just to the north of the port. Although he could not see them, he knew that the roads and beaches were still filled with the tired survivors of the BEF and their French and Belgian allies all hoping for ships like the *King Orry* to come to their rescue.

Suddenly there was a roar of steam as the funnel safety valves vented and, at the same moment the vibration caused by the engines ceased. Down below in the Engine Room the *King Orry's* former Steam Packet Chief Engineer, Stanley Cowley had lost the battle as the water had risen to a dangerous level and he had ordered the boiler fires to be put out rather than risk an explosion as the sea water flooded into the furnaces. He ordered the Engine Room and Boiler Room crews, which included the other four Manxman on board, to get out onto the Upper Deck and prepare to abandon ship. One of these, Reggie Scarffe, decided that he wanted to retrieve some of his belongings from his cabin so he went and casually packed his suitcase as if he was going on leave.

Up on the Boat Deck, Joe Jones noticed that the *King Orry* was now beginning to take on a alarming list to starboard and so he grabbed hold of a Lewis machine gun mounting to prevent himself from losing his balance and sliding down the sloping deck. As he hung onto the gun deciding what to do next, he remembered that this was the same gun that his friend Ray Hughes had been photographed with a few months earlier. Ray was now safely ashore in hospital and Joe wished that he was also on dry land.

He did not remember hearing any order to abandon ship but it was obvious to him that the *King Orry* was about to roll over and that it was now time to go. He took off his duffle coat and adjusted his life belt, ensuring that it was fully inflated as he was a poor swimmer. Dressed only in his uniform jumper and bell-bottom trousers, he clambered up the sloping Boat Deck to the port side, having remembered being told not to abandon ship by the side that she was listing, in case she rolled over on top of you while you were in the water.

With difficulty, he climbed over the guard rail and looked down towards the water. It was only then that he realised that immediately below him was the large opening to the Promenade Deck and if he let go of the rail he would fall into it rather than slide down the ship's side.

He therefore slid sideways along the guard rail until he was over one of the deck stanchions that supported the Boat Deck and then gently lowered himself over the cavernous hole which led into the Promenade Deck. Once clear of the opening, he let go and hoped for the best.

Joe recalls that he fell down the ship's side, rather than slid down and hit the wooden belting before toppling head first into the sea.

Even though it was the end of May, the water seemed freezing and he caught his breath and took a mouthful of water as he plunged below the surface. It was then that he discovered that the sea was covered in fuel oil and as he spluttered back to the surface gasping for air, he involuntarily swallowed some of the pungent slime.

His life belt quickly returned him to the fresh air, but not before his head was covered in the sticky substance and his mouth, nose and eyes began to burn as the oil penetrated them. Fearing that the *King Orry's* boilers may explode at any moment or even worse that he may be sucked down as she sank, Joe made frantic

efforts to swim away from her hull. As he was not a good swimmer, he wasted a lot of energy in his floundering attempts and inevitably swallowed more of the oily slime, his clothes soon became impregnated, which restricted his movements and added to his problems.

While he was struggling in the water, he became aware of an ear-piercing screech of grinding metal accompanied by heavy crashes, the hiss of escaping steam and a gurgling sound: then silence. He knew that the *King Orry* had gone but he did not turn round to look.

Apart from the sound of distant gunfire, the only sound that could be heard were the cries of men like himself, desperately trying to stay alive in the cold water.

One of the *King Orry's* officers, a Royal Naval Reserve Lieutenant who was known to be a strong swimmer, swam past and Joe called out for assistance but was disheartened when his pleas were ignored. After what seemed to be an eternity, he heard splashing in the water and it was with great relief when he realised that it was coming towards him. As he stared into the darkness through his oil-stained and smarting eyes, he saw a dark shape moving through the water and then noticed that it was being pushed by two swimmers. He called out for help and was answered by a voice that he recognised. "Hold on mate, we'll have you soon". The dark object turned out to be one of the *King Orry's* large wooden seat-type life rafts which were stowed on the Upper Deck and in happier times had been used as seats by the passengers. It was being pushed by two Royal Fleet Reservists, one of whom was a leading telegraphist named Nugent and the other a seaman called Smith.

*The Promenade Deck of the **Manxman** (2) (1955) showing wooden deck seats which were identical to the type that Able Seaman Joe Jones clung to after the **King Orry** sank. (David Handscombe collection)*

They both pushed Joe onto the top of the raft as by this time he was too exhausted to swim or climb onto it on his own. Once out of the water the effects of the cold began to take hold and he started to shiver uncontrollably and began to loose control of his actions.

As he lay there he recalled stories about German aircraft machine-gunning survivors in the water and hoped that on this particular night the German pilots could not see in the dark. A short while later, a small boat passed by their raft, frantically being rowed out to sea by its two occupants. One of the two reservists called out for assistance but the reply came in a tongue that Joe could not understand and he thought that they might be Frenchman trying to escape from the German occupation of their homeland.

After what appeared to be a lifetime, but was probably only and hour or two, their life raft was suddenly illuminated by a shaded searchlight and the thumping sound of a steam reciprocating engine became audible. The next thing that Joe remembers is that a ship's side suddenly loomed alongside the raft and he was grabbed by strong hands and pulled on board the vessel, which turned out to be the trawler *Lord Collingwood*.

Joe was cold and stiff and initially could not help himself, so two crew members from the trawler stripped off all of his oil-sodden clothing and wiped as much of the remaining oil from his body as they could before wrapping him in a dry blanket and giving him a mug of hot tea. This warmed Joe from the inside but the oil that he had swallowed earlier reacted with it and he thought that he was going to be sick, although this nausea soon passed.

As he began to recover from his ordeal and started to realise just how lucky he was to be alive, he noticed that the trawler's decks were covered with what appeared to be dozens of seamen and soldiers all looking tired and exhausted. Apart from his two comrades from the life raft, he failed to recognise any other members of the *King Orry's* crew and began to fear that they were the only survivors.

Fortunately, he later heard that nearly all of the crew had been rescued by other vessels (presumably the *Bystander*, *Lord Grey* and the *Clythness*). The trawler moved slowly through the dark oily water, occasionally illuminating swimmers with her searchlight before hauling them on board. Dawn was now approaching and it was beginning to become possible to see without the aid of the searchlight in the dim light,

Joe did not believe what he saw next and rubbed his eyes to make sure that they weren't playing tricks on him. Sure enough, the trawler's light had illuminated two men who appeared to be walking on the surface of the sea. As the vessel drew towards them, their saintly images gave way to that of two men dressed in naval duffle coats and Joe immediately recognised them as Commander Elliott, the *King Orry's* Captain and the chief boatswain's mate.

The trawler's small boat picked them up and once they were aboard he noticed that apart from their feet, they were bone dry. Joe found it difficult to comprehend that they were not wet but it was soon explained. As the *King Orry* began to sink they had both climbed to her highest point, the roof of the shattered bridge. Although the *King Orry* now rested on the bottom outside Dunkirk, her bridge roof was only just below the surface.

As the trawler withdrew from the wreck site, she swept the area with her searchlight and it was very eerie to see the funnel and foremast of the *King Orry* protruding above the water. Joe once again thought about how many of his shipmates were still alive.

Daylight was now approaching and as the trawler already had dozens of exhausted survivors from both the navy and the army on board, her Skipper decided to seek the relative safety of the open sea.

It was some years later that Joe Jones discovered that the young Royal Naval Reserve Skipper of the trawler was to rise to greater things, his name was Geoffrey Marr and in later life he rose to be the Captain of the liner *Queen Elizabeth* and Commodore of the famous Cunard Line.

As the trawler headed away from the coast, the old V and W Class destroyer *Vivacious* approached and offered to unload the survivors. The offer was accepted and the men quickly transferred to the decks of the warship. As soon as the last man had clambered on board, the *Vivacious* sped away from the French coast and made for Dover and the safety of British soil.

Although the survivors' ordeal was over, the now empty trawler returned to the beaches to continue her rescue work.

As if to remind them that the battle for France was not yet over, the *Vivacious* was attacked by German aircraft and bombed as she charged homewards across the English Channel, an all too familiar experience for the *King Orry's* survivors. Luckily, due to expert ship handling and aggressive anti-aircraft fire from the destroyer's crew, she managed to avoid the bombs and fought off her attackers, suffering no damage or casualties.

While on board, Joe met another survivor from the *King Orry*, his friend from Connah's Quay, Able Seaman Sam Jones. To his surprise, Sam handed him a water- logged leather wallet and when he opened it he

The Manx steamer **Tynwald** *passes the sunken remains of the* **King Orry** *as she leaves the harbour at Dunkirk with another boat load of exhausted British soldiers on 30th May 1940. (Imperial War Museum)*

found that it was his own. Sam had found it floating in the water and believing that Joe must have drowned, was going to give it to his family when he returned to Connah's Quay.

The wallet contained the negatives of some photographs that had been taken on board the *King Orry*, although they became stuck together when they dried out, they were successfully separated and cleaned by the Photographic Department at HMS *Heron*, the Royal Naval Air Station at Yeovilton in Somerset during 1995. Prints were made and although they show signs of water staining, they have been included in this book.

Shortly after 11.00, the *Vivacious* tied up alongside the train ferry berth in Dover Harbour and quickly unloaded her human cargo. The Royal Navy survivors were all taken to Ramsgate where they were given food and dry clothing to replace the blankets and remnants of uniform that some were still wearing.

Towards the end of the afternoon they were given orders to report to Portsmouth and were put on a train that would take them on the first part of their journey, which was to be via London. A pleasant surprise awaited them when they arrived at the capital, as they were taken to the Union Jack Club, which was just outside Waterloo station, and told that they would sleep there overnight.

Few of them had any energy left to consider exploring the club to see if any of the bars were open and the dormitory that they had been allocated soon rattled to the noise of the snoring of exhausted sailors. They were awakened fairly early next morning, given breakfast and then escorted over the road to the railway station where they boarded a special troop train for Portsmouth, which reached its destination at 11.30.

They were met by a Petty Officer who directed them to a lorry which took them on the short journey to the Royal Naval barracks, known as HMS *Victory*.

Following the issue of the bare essentials of uniform and having his personal details recorded by the drafting officer, Joe Jones was informed that he had been granted 14 days survivors' leave and was given a railway warrant and put on another lorry which took him back to the railway station. He caught the 17.40 train from Portsmouth which got him up to London in time to catch the 21.20 train from Euston to Chester.

By the time that this train arrived at Chester, having stopped at what must have been every station on route, it was 03.00 and Joe was not sure how he was going to get from Chester to his home town in North Wales. He asked the solitary porter on the platform if he knew how he could get to Connah's Quay and to his surprise, the porter ushered him to a man who was about to depart by car to the very town. Once he had explained his predicament and recent experiences, he was relieved and very grateful when he was offered a lift.

Three hours later and only 48 hours after jumping for his life from the listing decks of the *King Orry*, he was walking up the road to his house.

CHAPTER ELEVEN

Aftermath

While Able Seaman Joe Jones was relaxing at his home in Connah's Quay, another member of the *King Orry's* crew was relating his adventure at Dunkirk to his wife in the Isle of Man.

After being given the order to evacuate the Engine Room, 4th Engineer Reggie Scarffe decided to go to his cabin and pack his suitcase. Although the *King Orry* was already listing to starboard, he must have decided that she was not about to take her final plunge and that he had time to gather his possessions.

Having packed his suitcase and put on his overcoat, he went out onto the Shelter Deck and must have looked more like a holidaymaker rather than somebody who was probably going to have to swim for his life.

He walked down towards the shattered remains of the Poop Deck and spotted a large motor launch stopped in the water, about 25 yards from the *King Orry's* stern. Having called out to the launch, which was possibly the launch from HMS *Excellent*, it came alongside and took Reggie off.

In later life he recalled to his grandson, Bernard, who was only 7 years old when the *King Orry* was sunk, that he must have been the only survivor to have left the ship who did not even get his feet wet.

As with Joe Jones' family, the first news that Reggie Scarffe's relatives received about the loss of the *King Orry* was when he walked into his house in Laxey on the Isle of Man, a few days later. Reggie Scarffe was 62 years old when the *King Orry* was sunk. His grandson Bernard seems to think that he never went back to sea again but spent the remainder of the war helping his wife Winnie run the small grocery shop that was located in the front of their house.

THE LOST

Sadly, not everybody on board the *King Orry* was as lucky as Able Seaman Joe Jones or 4th Engineer Reggie Scarffe and four members of the crew lost their lives when the ship sank.

Leading Seaman Charles Frederick KEMP P/J27483

Charles (Charlie) Kemp was a Royal Fleet Reservist who had been recalled for active service at the commencement of hostilities in September 1939. He was a married man who came from London.

Jimmy McCallum recalls that he was a popular member of the ship's company and that he had been introduced to his wife when she visited the *King Orry* while the ship was undergoing repairs in the West India Dock.

Charles Kemp was employed on board the *King Orry* as a quartermaster, but had the secondary duty of being the leading hand of the seamen's mess deck As such, he was the only member of the seamen division to lose his life. The records held by the Commonwealth War Graves Commission give no details of his grave and it can therefore be assumed that his body was never recovered, or if it was, that it remained unidentified.

Leading Seaman Kemp's name is recorded on panel 92 of the Portsmouth Royal Navy Memorial, which is located on Southsea Common, near Portsmouth in Hampshire.

Junior Engineer Frank Charles CLARKE

Frank Clarke was 25 years old at the time of his death and is recorded by the Commonwealth War Graves Commission as being Naval Auxiliary Personnel (Merchant Navy). He has no known grave, but is recorded on panel 15, Column 1 of the Liverpool naval memorial. This memorial is situated at the Pier Head in Liverpool and commemorates the members of the Merchant Navy who lost their lives while serving with the Royal Navy during the Second World War.

Fireman William FOX - 916205

William Fox was the oldest member of the *King Orry's* crew to loose his life, being 53 years of age. He is also recorded by the Commonwealth War Graves

The Merchant Navy War Memorial on the Pier Head at Liverpool commemorates the merchant seamen who lost their lives while serving with the Royal Navy during the Second World War. (David Handscombe collection)

Commission as being a member of the Naval Auxiliary (Merchant Navy). He has no known grave and is recorded on Panel 15, Column 1 of the Liverpool naval memorial.

Assistant Cook Edmund George HUNT - 826427

Edmund Hunt was 47 years of age at the time of his death and was a South African by birth, having been brought up in Epping Garden, Cape Province. He was yet another member of the Naval Auxiliary (Merchant Navy). He has no known grave and is recorded on Panel 15, Column 1 of the Liverpool naval memorial.

None of the survivors who were contacted during the research for this book could give any details of the circumstances that resulted in the deaths of the four members of the *King Orry's* crew. It should be noted that members of the Naval Auxiliary (Merchant Navy) were those personnel from the Merchant Navy who agreed to serve with the Royal Navy under the T124 scheme. They retained Merchant Navy rates of pay and conditions of service, but were subject to the Naval Discipline Act.

On completion of his survivor's leave, Able Seaman Joe Jones was drafted to HMS *Peregrine*, the Royal Naval Air Station at Ford, near Arundel in Sussex. After being attached to 829 Naval Air Squadron, he went on to serve onboard the aircraft carriers *Formidable* and *Illustrious*.

In 1943 he volunteered for minesweepers and spent the remainder of the war on this type of vessel, operating mostly from Newhaven. He was finally demobbed from the Royal Navy in October 1945.

The names of the former merchant seamen who lost their lives when the **King Orry** *was sunk on 30th May 1940. (David Handscombe collection)*

After his marriage to Lucy, he settled down in Alsagers Bank near Stoke-on-Trent and spent the remainder of his working life in the motor trade. At the time of writing, Joe and his wife still live in Alsagers Bank.

Ray Hughes and Jimmy McCallum both recovered from their injuries and returned to duty. Jimmy went on to serve in both the Middle East and Far East on board the destroyer *Jervis* and the escort aircraft carrier *Ravager*.

Both Ray and Jimmy were demobbed at the end of the war and returned to their hometowns of Connah's Quay and Paisley. Jimmy recalled that the shrapnel wound in his leg gave him pain for the rest of his life. Sadly, both Jimmy and Ray died before they could see their memoirs recorded in this book.

After Operation Dynamo had drawn to a close, the exploits of numerous officers and men were rewarded.

The *King Orry's* Captain, Commander J Elliott RNR was one of these and he was subsequently awarded the Distinguished Service Order (DSO) for his outstanding leadership qualities which were tested to the extreme during Operation Dynamo.

It will be recalled that prior to the *King Orry's* participation in Operation Dynamo, she had chased the Dutch schuit *Pascholl* on more than one occasion as she evaded the naval patrol by skidding over the Goodwin Sands. After the fall of Holland, the *Pascholl* managed

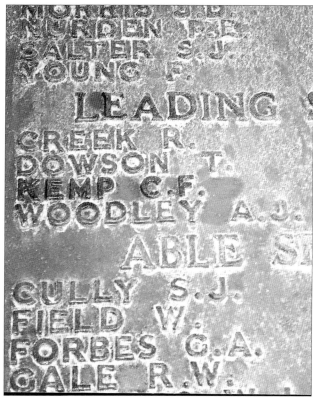

Leading Seaman Charles Kemp's name is recorded on the Southsea Royal Naval Memorial in Hampshire. (David Handscombe collection)

to escape back across the English Channel and when Operation Dynamo commenced she was lying at Poole.

Like many similar vessels, the Royal Navy immediately commandeered her. Despite her previous confrontation with the Dover Patrol, her Dutch flag was replaced by the White Ensign and with a mixed crew under the command of a Royal Navy officer, she took part in Operation Dynamo and is accredited with rescuing some 695 troops.

THE STEAM PACKET'S ROLE

Although the *King Orry* had been sunk and her survivors had returned to England on board various vessels, the battle to rescue the remnants of the BEF and elements of the French Army from Dunkirk continued until the afternoon of 4th June.

By the afternoon of 4th June, the rearguard of the BEF and French army had been forced back onto the beaches by the German army, Vice Admiral Ramsey therefore decided that it was no longer a viable proposition to attempt to rescue any more troops from Dunkirk and called Operation Dynamo to a halt.

Between 4th June and 25th June when the French armistice came into force, the evacuation of troops continued from the French ports that had not yet been occupied by the Germans. The German army and air force continued their onslaught against the rescue ships

The Royal Navy War Memorial on Southsea Common records the names of those men from the Portsmouth Division who died during both world wars. (David Handscombe collection)

at Dunkirk until the last vessel disappeared over the horizon, leaving the soldiers who had not been lucky enough to escape to face uncertain futures as prisoners of war.

A total of 338,226 soldiers had been plucked from the beaches of Dunkirk during Operation Dynamo and the Isle of Man Steam Packet had been at the forefront throughout. Apart from the *King Orry*, seven other Steam Packet ships took part in the operation: the *Lady of Mann, Mona's Queen, Ben-my-Chree, Fenella, Tynwald, Manxman* and the *Mona's Isle*. Between them they were responsible for rescuing 20,871 troops which is broken down as follows:

King Orry	1,139
Lady of Mann	2,906
Mona's Queen	1,312
Ben-my-Chree	3,845

Fenella (Over 600 troops were initially embarked at Dunkirk, but left the ship after she was bombed and sunk alongside the eastern mole)

Tynwald	6,880
Manxman	2,298
Mona's Isle	2,630

The Steam Packet can proudly claim that they carried more soldiers on board their ships, albeit some ships were in Royal Navy Service, than any other company that had vessels at Dunkirk.

THE *MONA'S QUEEN*

Apart from the *King Orry*, two other Steam Packet ships were sunk during Operation Dynamo and a third was badly damaged. Unfortunately, the two other vessels that were lost were also two of the Company's newest ships.

The first ship to be sunk was the *Mona's Queen*, which had been built by Cammell Laird in 1934.

After being requisitioned at the commencement of hostilities in September 1939, she had been employed as a troop transport, retaining her merchant navy status and the bulk of her Steam Packet crew.

She had made her first visit to Dunkirk on 26th May when she had taken 1,312 troops back to Dover although this was not her first trip to France as she had evacuated some 2,000 troops from Boulogne on 23rd May.

On the evening of the 28th May while the *Mona's Queen* was still at Dover, Captain A Holkham had taken over command of the vessel from Captain Duggan. Captain Holkham had been the last peace time Master of the *King Orry*, while Captain Radcliffe

Duggan had been her Chief Officer during 1928/29 and 1932/33.

The *Mona's Queen* sailed from Dover early on the morning of 29th May with a cargo of canned fresh water. She had a trouble free crossing and approached Dunkirk at just after 05.30. When about a mile and a half from the harbour entrance, the ship was rocked by a violent explosion when she detonated a magnetic mine. It exploded directly underneath her keel and had broken her back. The ship crumpled amidships and within two minutes had rolled over and sunk.

Twenty four members of her crew, mostly from the Engine Room and Boiler Room lost their lives and seventeen of them were from the Isle of Man. Fortunately, the destroyer *Vanquisher* was close by and she rescued 32 members of her crew, many of whom were badly injured. Captain Holkham was amongst those saved.

Amazingly, there had been sufficient time for two of the *Mona's Queen's* lifeboats to be launched and these contained about half of those rescued. Sadly one of those, Purser Roy Gallagher, died shortly after being pulled on board the destroyer. His escape from the *Mona's Queen* had been miraculous as he had managed to squeeze through a port hole as the ship capsized.

THE *FENELLA*

The second vessel to be lost was the *Fenella* - the twin sister of the *Tynwald* and had only joined the Steam Packet fleet in 1937.

Like the *Mona's Queen*, the *Fenella* had been requisitioned as a troop transport in September 1939 and under the Command of Captain Walter Cubbon, she also retained the bulk of her Steam Packet crew. Owing to a fuel shortage, she crossed over the Channel to Dunkirk at reduced speed on the morning of 29th May, arriving off the harbour at about 13.00.

Captain Cubbon eased her alongside the outside of the mole and as soon as her berthing ropes were secure, troops began to clamber on board. At about 15.30, after some 600 troops had embarked, the eastern mole became the target for the Luftwuffe and bombs rained down on the ships that were berthed there.

The mole must have presented a target that was too good to miss as with the *Fenella*, the Dover - Calais cross-Channel steamer *Canterbury*, the Thames excursion paddle steamer *Crested Eagle*, the destroyers *Grenade* and *Jaguar* and a cluster of fishing boats were all secured alongside.

The *Fenella* received a direct hit from a bomb on her Promenade Deck while a second exploded on the mole and blasted large chunks of concrete through her hull below the water line. A third bomb exploded in the water between the mole and the ship's side and wrecked her Engine Room. As water poured in through the many holes that now punctured her hull, it was soon obvious that she was going to founder.

As the troops and her crew scurried ashore, the *Fenella* settled on the sea bottom in an upright position with her forecastle, Shelter Deck and Poop Deck awash. All of the crew survived although one of them, Junior Steward Tom Helsby sustained severe burns and was eventually taken prisoner by the Germans.

He received expert treatment at a German Field Hospital and became the only member of a Steam Packet crew to become a prisoner of war. In a peacetime environment, the *Fenella* would have been salvaged and probably put back into service but despite rumours that the Germans had done this, she was eventually broken up where she lay.

THE *BEN-MY-CHREE*

Having already made two previous trips to Dunkirk, the *Ben-my-Chree* was severely damaged on 3rd June. She had sailed from Folkestone the previous evening and was approaching Dunkirk at about 02.30 when she was involved in a collision with an unknown vessel that had altered course right across her bow. The *Ben-my-Chree* sustained extensive damage to her starboard side as well as damaging her bow and rudder.

At first it was thought that the mystery vessel involved in the collision was the excursion steamer *Royal Daffodil* but it was later established that the she had collided with a vessel called the *Holland*, which was waiting to be sunk as a blockship. The *Holland* never reached her planned destination as she sank shortly after her confrontation with the *Ben-my-Chree*. The ship took no further part in Operation Dynamo and returned to Dover, she proceeded to Birkenhead a few days later to undergo repairs.

Various other Steam Packet vessels sustained damage from bombs and shells during Operation Dynamo, especially the *Mona's Isle*. Fortunately they all survived the onslaught and continued with their duties until stood down on 4th June. It was reckoned that one in every fourteen soldiers who were evacuated from Dunkirk was on board an Isle of Man Steam Packet vessel.

THE MANX ENGINEERS

Chief Engineer Stanley COWLEY

Stanley Cowley remained at sea for the remainder of the war and served on board various Steam Packet vessels.

In 1946, his efforts to keep the *King Orry* afloat after she had been damaged at Dunkirk were recognised by the Directors of the Steam Packet when he was given the honour of being the first Chief Engineer on board the new *King Orry*.

After serving on board the *King Orry* for a couple of years, he was appointed to the *Lady of Mann* as Chief Engineer. At this period of time, the *Lady of Mann* was the flagship of the Steam Packet fleet and she carried the Commodore as her Master. To be appointed Chief Engineer on the Company's flagship was yet another sign that Stanley Cowley was held in high esteem. He remained on board the *Lady of Mann* until he became of pensionable age, when he retired from the Steam Packet and life at sea.

Second Engineer Lawrence "Laurie" QUINE

"Laurie" Quine also returned to the Company after the war and initially served as Second Engineer on board the *Mona's Isle*. After serving on board various other Steam Packet vessels he eventually became the Chief Engineer of the cargo vessel *Conister*. He remained on board *Conister* until he retired.

Third Engineer H G "Griff" HUGHES

"Griff" Hughes continued with the Steam Packet until he retired in 1958, due to ill health. He is remembered as being a very conscientious and reliable engineer and served on board many of the company's ships, including the *Rushen Castle, Mona's Isle, Lady of Mann, Snaefell, Peveril* and the *King Orry (1946)* as 3rd Engineer.

Fourth Engineer "Reggie" SCARFFE

Little is known about "Reggie" Scarffe after he returned to the Isle of Man following the loss of the *King Orry*. As already mentioned, he was 62 years of age when the *King Orry* was sunk and his grandson Bernard seems to recall that he never returned to sea and assisted his wife in the running of their small shop.

There is no record of what became of Donkeyman George Campbell and Greaser Arthur Corlett.

THE WRECK OF THE *KING ORRY*

The wreck of the *King Orry* remains on the sea bed off Dunkirk to this day. Records held by the United Kingdom Hydrographic Office at Taunton show that she lies at a depth of 13.2 meters in position latitude 51 deg 03' 983 north - longitude 002 deg 20' 750 east, which puts her wreck at just over half a mile in an approximate NNW direction from the end of the east mole. Originally her two masts and funnel protruded above the surface but today no evidence of the ship can be seen above water.

There are no records available that suggest the Germans may have attempted to salvage the *King Orry* during the war although it is very probable that their divers examined the wreck and searched compartments such as the bridge, chart room and wireless office for secret Admiralty code books.

In 1946, the *King Orry's* remains were marked with two buoys, a green conical buoy with a square topmark to the south west and a green conical buoy with a triangular topmark to the north west of the wreck.

During 1947, the buoy to the north west of the wreck was replaced by a black conical buoy with a flashing light and triangular topmark. Over the years various types of buoy marked the wreck site and during November 1957 an experimental whistle was fitted to one although this was removed within a few weeks.

The French carried out salvage operations on the wreck during the early part of 1965. These lasted for 4 months and resulted in the remains of the *King Orry* being dismantled by both explosives and cutting up. This event was recorded in the Isle of Man newspaper "The Mona's Herald" and the article mentions that one of the buoys had a nameplate with the inscription *King Orry* painted on it.

In October 1996, the wreck is recorded as being only 1 metre above the seabed in 13.5 meters of water. The salvage operations carried out during 1965 obviously reduced the remains of the *King Orry* to little more than a pile a twisted steel plating and ribs.

The other wreck that remains off the beaches of Dunkirk is that of the *Mona's Queen*. She lies in position latitude 51 deg 04' 100 north - longitude 002 deg 23' 303 east and poses a much more serious threat to shipping than the *King Orry*, as the uppermost section of her wreckage is only 3 meters below the surface at low tide.

During August 1989 a French diver examined the wreck and positively identified it as the *Mona's Queen*, stating that she was lying in a NNE/SSW direction and broken into three pieces.

RETROSPECT

The sad loss of the *King Orry* in May 1940 marked the end of 27 years of illustrious service to both the Isle of Man Steam Packet Company and the Royal Navy. One of her claims to fame is that she is the only vessel that was built for the Steam Packet that served under the White Ensign as one of His Majesty's Ships during both World Wars.

It is true that other Steam Packet ships did see war service during both World Wars, for example the *Viking* and *Manxman*, but neither of these two vessels and indeed any of the other ships involved were commissioned into the Royal Navy as warships in both conflicts. In the case of the *Manxman*, she was not even owned by the Isle of Man Steam Packet during the First World War.

The Isle of Man Steam Packet Company did not forget the heroic deeds of the *King Orry* and her crew. When peace returned to the world in 1945, the Directors of the Company placed orders with Cammell Laird at Birkenhead to replace the ageing steamers that were nearing the end of their useful life and the vessels that had been lost during the war.

The first of these new ships entered service in April 1946 carried the proud name *King Orry*, a second vessel joined the fleet later in the same year, and she carried another heroic name, the *Mona's Queen*.

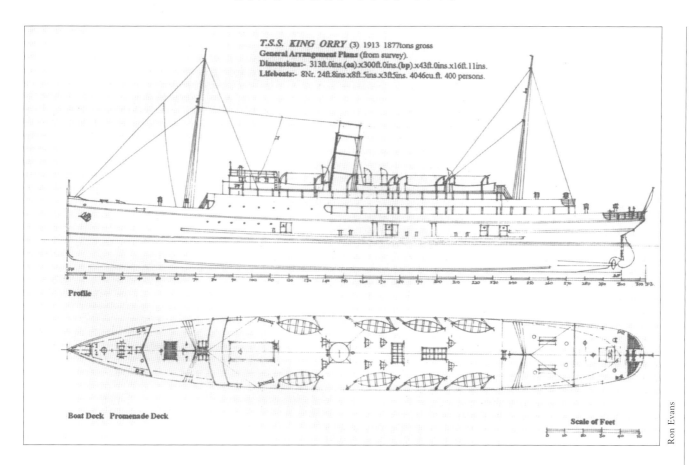

T.S.S. *KING ORRY* (3) 1913 1877tons gross
General Arrangement Plans (from survey).
Dimensions:- 313ft.0ins.(oa.)x300ft.0ins.(bp.)x43ft.0ins.x16ft.11ins.
Lifeboats:- 8Nr. 24ft.8ins.x8ft.5ins.x3ft5ins. 4046cu.ft. 400 persons.

Profile

Boat Deck Promenade Deck

Scale of Feet

Ron Evans

*The **King Orry** dressed overall for her maiden voyage on 8th July 1913. (David Handscome collection)*

*The **King Orry** in the River Mersey during her preliminary sea trials on 7th June 1913. (Wirral Museum Service/Cammel Laird Archive)*

Acknowledgements

During my research into the history of the *King Orry*, many people have given me valuable assistance and in some cases have gone out of their way to help:

Charlie Cooil & Peter Babb – Fleet Engineers Department – I.O.M.S.P.Co
Marjorie & Paul Redshaw – Widow & Son of Chief Petty Officer Crispen Redshaw - *HMS King Orry* - WW1
Yvonne Creswell - Manx National Heritage
Maritime and Coastguard Agency – Archive Department
Public record Office – Kew
Research and Wrecks Department – UK Hydrographic Office –Taunton
National Maritime Archive – University of Newfoundland
Olga Comloquoy "The Young Olga" – Shetland Islands
John Cooil – Steward – *King Orry* – 1938 –1939
Stanley Gale – Fireman – *King Orry* – 1938 –1939
Joe Jones – Able Seaman RNR – *HMS King Orry* – 1939 –1940
Ray Hughes – Ordinary Seaman – *HMS King Orry* – 1939 – 1940
Jimmy McCallum – Ordinary Seaman – RNVR – *HMS King Orry* – 1939 – 1940
Bernard Scarffe – Grandson of *HMS King Orry* Engineer – 1939 –1940
Ernie Ruffler – Cammell Laird Archivist
Captain Jack Ronan – Former Master I.O.M.S.P.Co
Captain Harry Kinley – Former Master – I.O.M.S.P.Co
Cecil Mitchell – Silverdale – Isle of Man
Ray Pugh – Steam Packet enthusiast – Southport
Edward Paget Tomlinson – Easton, Wells, Somerset
Guildhall Library – London
Commonwealth War Graves Commission
The Royal Navy Museum – Portsmouth
Naval Historical Branch – Ministry of Defence (Navy)
W S Hewinson – Author – *This Great Harbour – Scapa Flow*
National Maritime Museum – Greenwich
Captain B G McShane – Mersey Docks and Harbour Company
The Port of London Authority
Harry Crawley – Former Engineer – I.O.M.S.P. Co
Stromness Museum – Orkney
Dick Clague
Timothy Cowsill
Richard Stafford

The following people or organisations were kind enough to allow me to use photographs of the *King Orry* from their collections

Paul Eastwood – Williamson Art Gallery – Birkenhead
John Shepherd – Former Purser – I.O.M.S.P.Co
Richard Danielson – Onchan – Isle of Man
Peter Stewart – Ship enthusiast
Imperial War Museum